CHRISTIAN LIVES GIVEN TO THE STUDY OF ISLAM

Christian Lives Given to the Study of Islam

Edited by

CHRISTIAN W. TROLL, S.J., AND C. T. R. HEWER

FORDHAM UNIVERSITY PRESS

New York   2012

Library of Congress Cataloging-in-Publication Data
Christian lives given to the study of Islam / edited by
Christian W. Troll, S.J., and C. T. R. Hewer.
p. cm.
ISBN 978-0-8232-4319-8 (cloth : alk. paper)
1. Christianity and other religions—Islam.
2. Islam—Relations—Christianity. 3. Islam—Study
and teaching. 4. Middle East specialists—Biography.
I. Troll, Christian W., 1937– II. Hewer, C. T. R., 1952–
BP172.C41955 2012
261.2'70922—dc23
2012023009

Printed in the United States of America
14 13 12   5 4 3 2 1
First edition

Over the centuries, many Christians, too many to mention, have trodden this path before us. This work is dedicated to them all. In the modern period, amongst many others, we mention the following:

Jean-Mohamed Abd-el-Jalil

Georges Anawati

Roger Arnaldez

Serge de Laugier de Beaureceuil

David Brown

Robert A. Bütler

Arnulf Camps

Robert Caspar

Victor Courtois

Norman Daniel

André Demeerseman

Redmond Fitzmaurice

Louis Gardet

Peter Gowing

Jacques Jomier

David Kerr

Henry Martyn

Louis Massignon

Youakim Moubarac

Paul-Mehmet Mulla-Zadé

Constance Padwick

Geoffrey Parrinder

Joachim Rosario

Wilfred Cantwell Smith

Marston Speight

Benvenido (Benny) Tudtud

Afif Usayran

William Montgomery Watt

CONTENTS

Grace Builds on Nature

A Lenten Journey

Journeying toward God

"From the brook by the path": Formation and
Transformation in Meeting Muslims

Intelligence, Humility, and Confidence:
An Agenda for Christian Engagement with Islam

So What Have We Learned?

CHRISTIAN LIVES GIVEN TO THE STUDY OF ISLAM

Introduction

Christian W. Troll and C. T. R. Hewer

"Do to others as you would have them do to you" (Lk. 6:31). Seek to understand others as you would have them seek to understand you. Teach about others as you would have them teach about you. This might be seen as the underlying principle of the articles in this collection. This book represents a half-century: the half-century that saw the biggest change in Christian attitudes to Islam in history, the half-century between the youngest and the oldest of our contributors, and the half-century of their lives that many of these writers have committed as Christian students of Islam and as servants in the cause of Christian–Muslim relations.

This new epoch was ushered in by the Second Vatican Council (also known as Vatican II), developments under the auspices of the World Council of Churches and the shifts that took place in Christian ideas of mission. It coincided with the decades after the European powers' withdrawal from colonialism and the significant increase in settled Muslim communities across Europe and North America. The majority of those who have contributed to this book are now seventy or older, hence the reason why we felt the need to get their experiences on record before they die. When a new generation sees the need, they will have a mine of information, approaches, and reflections upon which to draw.

Our contributors come from across the range of Western Christianity; they represent fifteen nationalities and constitute a significant part of an imaginary Who's Who of Christian study and engagement with Islam and Muslims during this period. They write from various perspectives and with diverse experiences, which all add to the rich tapestry of the subject. No single volume could ever do justice to everyone who is worthy of inclusion; their number and names are known best to God, who rewards all as he knows best. We wish to place on record our thanks to Mesdames Penelope Johnstone, Angela Verdier, Anna-Regula Sharp, and Dr. Damian Howard for their assistance in translating and revising the six articles that were originally written in French.

The Tents of Kedar

Kenneth Cragg

They are pitched in the Book of Common Prayer version of Psalm 120, "Woe is me that I am constrained to dwell with Mesech and to have my habitation among the tents of Kedar." That opening "woe" will have to have a sense, not of unhappiness or regret but, quite the contrary, of something strenuous and taxing. Mesech seems to have been a region bordering the Black Sea. Kedar, far to the south, is the region of Arabia Petraea, whither Paul sought a soul retreat after his conversion on the Damascus road.

But if these "tents of Kedar" are to serve here for a story biographical they certainly fit the kind of nomadism which fell to me—in formal terms—between 1956 and 1974—as Canon (Residentiary?) in Jerusalem and as bishop in the Anglican Jurisdiction centered there—a period which was "interluded" by duties in Canterbury and a sojourn in Cambridge. The nomadism could be symbolized by the names of churches—St. John's, Casablanca; St. George's, Tunis; Christ the King, Tripoli; All Saints' Cathedral, Cairo; St. George's, Baghdad; St. Peter's, Basra; St. Paul's, Kuwait; and emerging chaplaincies down the Gulf to Muscat. Between 1939 and 1947, however, I had a settled ministry at All Saints' Church in Beirut.

3

Why, however, was I this nomad at all? At Jesus College, Oxford, I had been a member of the Oxford Inter-Collegiate Christian Union (OICCU) from 1931 to 1934, and one of its emphases was a readiness to serve outside the United Kingdom. Accordingly, after my three-year curacy in Tranmere, Birkenhead, in the Diocese of Chester, I went by a sort of strange "constraint" to duties in Lebanon. I had been awarded the Ellerton Theological Essay Prize at Oxford in 1937 with an essay titled "The Place of Authority in Religious Belief," writing which helped me to resolve some of my own problems. With part of the prize money, I purchased the two volumes of Wright's famous *Arabic Grammar*, as well as other books that might help toward "orientation." Meanwhile in those three years in Tranmere, I had learned something about pastoral discipline in the "care of souls."

Once in Beirut, it developed into a dual ecclesiastical/educational situation. There was the chaplaincy of All Saints' Church but also, from 1942, a post at the American University of Beirut (AUB) which, founded in 1866, was the only large English language institution of higher education in the Middle East. My recruitment there to the Department of Philosophy had been necessary for the opening of a hostel for Palestinian youths coming to the university from the three schools run by the diocese. The hostel was a project dear to the heart of Bishop George Francis Graham-Brown, who was bishop from 1932 until his tragic death in a car accident at an unguarded level-crossing (road and rail) *en route* home after inaugurating the hostel in September 1942. Just like Henry Hill from my parish in Tranmere he has remained my beloved "father-in-God" to this day.

We named the hostel St. Justin's House. Though he was always known in history as "Justin Martyr," we canonized him since "martyr house" would have been incongruous. Justin was a second-century Palestinian and a scholar who kept his philosopher's role on becoming a Christian. It seemed the authentic "patronage" for the task we had in mind, sustaining and enriching an intellectual faith in the mazes of the living world.

It was in my modest share in the Department of Philosophy of the AUB that I came to know Dr. Charles Malik, then head of the department until his departure to Washington in 1945 as Lebanon's ambassador, when I succeeded him as head of the department. Later he became president of the UNO General Assembly and a major force, with Eleanor Roosevelt, in the drafting of the Declaration of Human Rights.

It was, in part, the impact of his personality and his lectures in the AUB that deepened my sense of the contemporary issues in the mind of Islam and of the capacity of its leadership to undertake them. For philosophy poses to religion and theology the salient issues of authority and of metaphysics: What can we know and by what means of knowing? How to behave whether in society or politics?—the ultimate perplexities of epistemology and ethics.

Earlier, by my school nurture and family heritage, my concern for Islam had been evangelical and, as such, it has so continued. For the Christian Gospel has that which ever deserves to be told, for it is found nowhere else in the wide universe of faiths. It is that which rings so powerfully in the music of Handel: "Worthy is the Lamb that was slain" and "Surely, surely, He has borne our griefs and carried our sorrows,"—"the Word made flesh," the Gospel of a love that comes and suffers, that tells eternity in a babe in a manger and the Infinite in a man on a cross. As long as we are in the world and God is thus, the human scene must be made to echo with this "sound going out," as the prophet said, "unto all lands." For it can never be a private thing, a mystical secrecy, a doctrinal privilege. It requires to be told in all the earth.

Yet, precisely because Christian faith has this utterly distinctive dimension and character, it is the more urgent that it should *negotiate* its meaning for and into what doubts, scouts, misreads, or disowns it. The term *negotiate* here does not refer to checks, treaties, or bargains. It derives from the Latin *neg otium*, "saying no to sloth, leisure or repose." Hence the usage "dialogue" and hence also its being companion to witness. The two are not inconsistent with each other, given that each is understood aright. "Go ye into all the world and discuss the Gospel" was not the great commission. Nor does Islam exist to be debated. Both are categorical and, as Kant would say, "categorical imperatives." Yet they are not served as such if their voice is only strident or aggressive, demanding a hearing that has no listening. What is forever distinctive concerning, in Paul's phrase, "God in Christ" needs, as he said elsewhere, to "let patience have her perfect work." Hurdling is not mere running: it has obstacles to clear and *clear* is the verb for much that needs making so between us.

There is not only the distinctive "thing in trust" that requires this *neg otium*. There is also a deep psychic reason. People "aggressed" are likely to be aggressive in reply. To sense attack is to muster retaliation. The answer that turns away wrath is the one that has readily heard the question.

I remember when I was fifteen being in an audience addressed by Dr. Samuel Zwemer. It was perhaps my earliest alerting to Islam. He had been, during the first two decades of the last century, a missionary in the Arabian/Persian Gulf region, from the American Reformed Church. I think it was the appeal of its remoteness in those years before oil exploitation that drew both his faith and the enthusiasm of his heart. Before 1928, he had published *The Disintegration of Islam*, in which he studied what he saw, *inter alia*, as the meaning of the secularization of Turkey under Kemal Atatürk, at which time all Islamic education was proscribed, Arabic-lettered Turkish language Latinized and mosque worship ended so that the Pillars of Islam could only be had in clandestine ways. The Middle East then had French and British mandates in position and the dominance they allowed, so that Islam in its geographical cradle seemed to be at a discount, with Britain in India part of the same equation. All in all, if one was so minded, it was possible to think of Islam almost in terminal decline. In fact the reverse would soon be the growing truth with the amazing benison of oil and the rapid rise to prominence of what became the Arab Emirates on the international map.

I well recall a voyage down the Gulf in January 1957 from Bahrain to Muscat. There was a stop at Abu Dhabi and, half an hour or so later, at Dubai. I asked the ship's purser, "Why two halts such a short time apart?" He said it was a matter of prestige. The ship could not halt at one and not at the other. In neither was anything discernable on shore except a desert haze. Either place now is a haunt for wealth and elegance and Dubai has the highest and proudest skyscrapers in the world and builds afar into its desert sands. Change is the relentless reality here but what heightens it is the sheer pace it has. Here is a world where grandfathers dived for pearls from *dhows* in Kuwait or lazed on benches in the torrid sun and lived with camel tracks not with highways. One can now be in a traffic jam at rush hour and be on the edge of the desert, as I remember well.

There is so much more beyond what may be physically narrated in the sphere of change. There is the fascination of transculture, the conundrums of daily living, and the authority of old standards in new times, with the tensions these create between the generations. Given radio and television and the onset of a digital age there are no immunities behind which the traditional can hide, no writ for religious faith except its own resilience or if writ there remain—a survival power rooted in lethargy rather than a liable mind.

Is it not here that the Islamic mind encounters, with the West, the issue of the *secular*? That term is often used in contrast to what is *religious*. Yet inescapably we are all secular by virtue of being alive at all, namely immersed in a world of things, of values, choices, and ideas where we have no option but to act, decide, and belong. In that sense there is no being other than *secular*. The word, however, is ambiguous and may mean avowedly nonreligious, whether agnostic, atheist, or merely indifferent. When meant in that way, the term demands our religious resistance, a positive will to consecration of all sense experience as, in Christian terms, sacramental. Islam does not use that word, but the theme within it is explicit in the Qur'an's recurrent term *ayah* (pl. *ayat*), seeing nature as a realm of *signs*. These register in the double sense that they arrest the intelligence and thus make feasible the sciences and their technology, so that we humans exercise a *khilafa*, or dominion over the external world. Those same *signs*, however, in equipping us for *rôles entrepreneurial* also alert us to reverence and thanksgiving. What bestows control has also to evoke gratitude. Hence the Qur'an's radical contrast between *shukr* and *kufr*. *Kufr* is that *denial*, or willful concealment of significance as resident in the natural order and perceptible to sense experience. It is the *unbelief* which refuses the recognition of God as the creator and sustainer of creation and so of our human status, at once lofty and lowly, as its masters and its subjects. This reality of our creaturehood is a perennial source of wonder and glad surprise to the sign-attentive people, while it is lost upon the indifferent or discounted by the trivialist. Outright secularity will say, "we are on our own," "there is no-one there," life, the earth, the universe have no divine source, no explanation outside themselves.

It is plain that this is a conclusion that, if we wish, we can reach about our situation. The option for unbelief, even for nihilism, is there and ours to take. "There is no compulsion in religion," as the Qur'an has it. Allah and his claim *can* be ignored, so that—in this sense, not essentially—God is on and by our sufferance. He can be "let not be" by a negligence, a disavowal, on our part.

This, in our very creaturehood, is the real necessity of prophethood, sent to us for "guidance" since the privilege we enjoy entails so great a risk on the part of the Creator, a risk of which we are the crux. There would be neither point nor meaning in "messengers" to a human not entrusted, to a world of puppets who were not masters of themselves. Prophethood is thus the supreme attestation of creaturehood so that the theme of Allah is *textual* towards us, i.e. as "scripturising our situation" for our obedience is central to both Christian and Muslim faith, however radically different our concept and reception of sacred writ may be. Thus the shape of Scriptures becomes a major issue between us and a strenuous theme for dialogue.

All this is captured for us in the resounding question in Sura 7:172, "Am I not your Lord?" It is addressed to the entire humanity across all space and time and it is in the negative, as if, by implication, there is a withholding of the recognition due. Negative questions are looking for the answer, Yes! Here, then, is Omnipotence seeking, asking, desiring acceptance on our part. What must this mean for our conception of almightiness in Allah?

The same point is made by the hundred or so times when we have in the Qur'an the particles *la'allakum, la'allahum* with verbs like "come to your (their) wits," "understand," "be thankful," and "perhaps you (they) will consider." So the human relation responsively to God hinges on consent, on intelligence and love, as these spring from the realization of our earth-residence, our human vocation.

This is the great inter-theme between our two monotheisms, as of Judaism also, with the unique Judaic dimension of a "chosen-ness" which is theirs alone, whereas—in all creaturehood—there are only chosen *peoples*, in the plural, via the God-willed diversity of the races on earth.

I have a lively recollection of reflecting on this common theme with an audience of students at the University of Benghazi. There was also a similar topic in the Great Mosque in Addis Ababa, where I was invited by a graduate of the AUB, who was a lawyer in the Ethiopian capital and who heard of my being there visiting St. Matthew's (Anglican) Church and also having sessions in the Theological School of the Ethiopian Church. It was after I had become a bishop, so they told me, "This is the first time that any Christian 'ecclesiastic' has spoken here and lectured to us in Arabic." Later, as was our custom, I made a courtesy call on the Acting Patriarch, Theophilus, of the Ethiopian Church. I told him eagerly of my visit to the mosque, thinking he might venture there too. To my disappointment, he merely commented, "Muslims? They have no theology." I remember how, in Benghazi, some of the older *ulama* wanted the discourse to stop, but the students urged that it continue.

The unity between us via this great divine/human theme is manifest enough. We must pursue it in all its authenticity, neither as patronizing each other nor as being condescending or tactical but simply because it is true. Also as an agreed theme, it is the source of how we differ. For, paradox though it may seem, it is only out of agreeing that we differ. There is no *whether* about this human situation being an entrustment and a risk. It is about *how* we measure up to its claim and meaning. Broadly the Islamic dictum runs: "To know is to do." Ignorance, *jahiliyyah*, is the problem. Hence *huda*, revelation, is the answer. Humans are amenable to law: They can respond to "thou shalt" and heed "thou shalt not." The New Testament knows that we can know and not do. We have a defiant ability, a recalcitrance that flouts what it quite well understands. It is this perversity which needs redemption. The world is not righted by good advice but a love that suffers, that *bears* and thus only *bears away* the wrong and can thus forgive. For Christian faith this redemptiveness characterizes the very nature of God as told in "the throne of God and of the Lamb."

The sovereignty that is enthroned in heaven is this unison of power and love, where there is no duality, where *and* does not add but identify. For to transcend is to suffer and in that suffering to transcend. This is the ultimate theological issue between the Qur'an and the New Testament, the mosque and the church.

The theme inherent in it of human perversity is solved in Islam in one of two shapes—the one, as we have seen, being laws and guidance to which amenability answers (unless Allah decrees otherwise, as in the final judgment), the other is and was the power of the political regime, the arm of the state. During the *Sira* or career of the Prophet, human perversity, the capacity to say "no!" to Allah, was evident enough in the resistance of the Quraish to his message. They had their vested interest in pagan pilgrimage and its trade, their tradition of plural worships, which Muhammad was seen as disrupting. So for thirteen long years they opposed and vilified him. Often he was told during that time *ma 'alaika illa al-balagh*, "your sole liability is what the message tells." The preached word was the whole vocation. It was an onerous situation borne with fortitude as the Qur'an itself commended. "God was all the witness he needed."

However, and at length, after the death of Khadija, his wife, and his protecting uncle, Abu Talib, the decision was made to emigrate from Mecca to Yathrib, soon to be renamed Medina, in response to an invitation made by some of its people, the *Ansar*. The Qur'an has no explicit command on this Hijra, which begins the dating in 622 of the Islamic calendar, but it is held to have been divinely willed and prospered. Muhammad's band of believers, the *Muhajirun*, settled with the help of the *Ansar* and the faith of the *balagh* in Mecca became the regime of the *umma* in Medina. It was a watershed indeed. In Medina began the consolidation of the tribes before and after Muhammad's death in 632 and the swift entrance of the faith into the Near East and the whole Mediterranean scene in Western Europe. Thus Islam—which had been, in origin, a verbal, word-borne, creedal message—became a powered entity, belligerent and expansionist.

The question must follow around this resolution of Islam's meaning, its transformation into a structure of rule and force. Was the Hijra either necessary or appropriate? Might the Quraish have been persuadable over time? There is evidence around the "Satanic verses" that they were ready to acknowledge Muhammad's Allah as "supreme among many." They might have moved on to "He is God alone." Faithfully he did not compromise in allowing their intermediate position; but was Hijra the right way to uphold his loyalty to the divine Oneness?

It is possible to argue that the Hijra was right then, in the circumstances of seventh-century Mecca. The evidence is there after Muhammad's death of how feud-minded Meccans were. The question now is whether what the Hijra meant in powered terms is valid in the twenty-first century, where it is urgent that religions should not sanction, nor connive with, the enmities that divide the world.

There can be no doubting the absolute priority of Mecca. However we evaluate the Hijra now, it was ever and only for the sake of the Meccan message. It was never some act of violent brigandage for its own sake. Rather its warrant lay in its being on behalf of the preached word, the single *balagh*. Reckoning with this defining priority of the Meccan Islam in today's scene and time must argue the nonviolent destiny of Muslim loyalty. For a coexistent Islam is a vital prerequisite for the peace of nations, whereas the suiciding, destructive shape some Muslims now give to their Islam is a dire prescript for its tragic jeopardy. Those who eliminate themselves in acts of terrorism are saying that their faith is no longer worth living for, no longer a creed or calling they must live to tell. They have died in its denial. They offend against the basic precept both of the Talmud and the Qur'an that, "he who kills a single soul is as if he had killed all mankind, and he who saves a single soul as if he had saved all humanity." "Those who corrupt in the earth and shed blood" —i.e. deliberate, intentional killers— are outside these provisions. So there is this terrible paradox about suiciding terrorists that what would be their own salvation is defied by their own deeds. The body cannot be the vehicle of the bomb without defying the Creator who gave it life, as if self-exempting itself from his creation, taking dying out of his all-ruling hands.

Is not an Islam, coexisting with human diversity, the clear logic of the great Talmudic/Qur'anic principle? Might it not then consider away the agelong Islamic distinction between a *Dar al-Islam* and a *Dar al-Harb*, the contrasted realms of Islam and non-Islam?

Its "them and us" mindset disowns the universal human. Moreover, the incidence of faith and unfaith, of belief and disbelief cannot be delineated in geographical terms. The so-called *Dars* inter-act and inter-penetrate amid the tensions of society because, while the world is one, its perplexities are legion. The need for religious inter-existence, whether pro or con each other in varying measures, is paramount in the here and now. This must argue the abiding priority of Mecca in the world's reckoning with Islam and of Islam's with the world.

By the *Dar al-Harb* concept, Muslims in minority situations, whether in continental Europe, the Americas and Canada or in postpartition India, must be inherently subversive, since what doctrine requires is that they migrate from it into Muslim rule, or work for its overthrow. That is, *de facto*, an impossible concept and, therefore, coexistence is the reality. Pakistan was created because a territorial Islamic identity could be nationally discerned and created. Thus Pakistan ensued as a Medina version of Islam but new "pakistans" cannot be contrived across the sundry Muslim populations that are not already nations, as Saudi Arabia, Egypt, Malaysia, Iran, the Emirates and so on. In these the different acid test will be their "allowance" of non-Muslim elements within themselves. Thus there is that about the contemporary scene which makes *de facto* coexistence mandatory. Theory then, whatever theological/political thought may do with it, becomes tributary to fact.

However, the "Islam" the world needs Islam to be for the sanity, security, and satisfaction of all, must be defined and achieved from within Islamic principles by Muslim minds. The appeal is not for some secularization by imitation of the West but for an Islam that returns to its prime definition in its original Mecca. This will not or need not be a disowning of the historic Hijra of 622, whence its ongoing years will still be dated. Rather it means a mental Hijra into the contemporary order, a dispersing that abides, an abiding that disperses. On this necessity it is well that interfaith encounter concentrates.

So, personally, I have stayed keenly interested in serving, however the outsider may, this direction of hope, by drawing out its case from the Qur'an and thus, as some Muslims have been urging, a sidelining of Hadith or Tradition and a new emphasis on the role of *ijma* or consensus. These have strong bearing on both the concept and the content of Shari'a law, into which a fresh dimension of human sympathy has to come, given the inclusivity of our single creaturehood. Brutality, whether "legal" or merely savage, can never be under divine warrant if Allah be *al-Rahman al-Rahim*. "*Ma nahnu bi masbuqin*," says the Qur'an, "We are never overtaken" (outpaced, left behind, outdated). God is ever "contemporary," his writ is not museumised, always abreast of what Shakespeare called "cormorant [or all-devouring] time." With that assurance the past need not dismay the present, nor the present despair of the future. In *Mosque Sermons* (published in January 2008) I tried to argue that case, while celebrating seventy years of Christian "diaconate," with reflections on ordination in "The Order of the Wounded Hands."

One aspect of all the foregoing has been how to work to have Islam "pacify" itself or discover the paradox of forbearance and a turning of "the other cheek." It seemed to me that Joseph/Yusuf, a revered figure common to us both, with the Genesis 39–45 narrative and Sura 12 having so much in common, could be the exemplar of such a nonretaliatory, irenic, positively suffering figure—one that we all shared and might each emulate. Hence in 2008 the publication of *The Iron in the Soul*—of a Joseph fettered in iron in prison, a Yusuf "steeled" by adversity to reach near Pharaonic mastery.

The *where-abouts* of dialogue are in the *here-abouts* of the heart, long dwelling in "the tents of Kedar."

Following a Path of Dialogue
Maurice Borrmans

It was in November 1945 that I discovered North Africa. At age twenty, I was there to complete my spiritual and theological formation at Maison-Carrée (Algeria) and at Thibar (Tunisia). I had decided to join the Missionaries of Africa (White Fathers) to fulfill an ideal first glimpsed thanks to the Christian Scouts and Catholic Students movements during my adolescence and secondary studies. I had been strongly attracted by the North African projects of Cardinal Lavigerie, Archbishop of Algiers, by the remarkable witness of Fr. de Foucauld, the hermit of Tamanrasset, and the writings of Ernest Psichari, grandson of Renan. Had not Psichari redis-covered a fully Christian faith during his military service in Mauretania? His two books, *Les voix qui crient dans le désert* (*Voices Crying in the Desert*) and *L'appel du centurion* (*The Call of the Centurion*), in particular had left an impression on me. Later, I was to discover Louis Massignon and many others who had found again their childhood faith thanks to the "challenge of Islam." Was there some strange mystery of providence in this?

After being ordained a priest on February 1, 1949, I took an introduc-tory course in Arabic for two years at the Institut des Belles Lettres Arabes (IBLA) in Tunis, and then pursued advanced studies at the University of

Algiers (Licence ès Lettres). This allowed me to deepen my knowledge of North African history and civilization, in which I found both Arab and Berber influences in their Islamic tradition during the course of a thousand years, and in the contemporary setting in which Europeans were noticeably present, in Tunisia and Algeria as well as in Morocco. Starting in October 1954, I was called to teach in the same IBLA which had educated me, while I was also engaged in various ministries and services among Christians and Muslims in Tunisia. In those days there was practical and uncomplicated cooperation, Christians and Muslims mutually respected each other's religious convictions. These were years of reflection and meditation upon "the meaning" of the ways in which Christians and Muslims both agreed and differed.

At Maison-Carrée, my first initiation into the Arabic language had been given by Fr. Joseph Sallam, born an Egyptian Muslim, who had become a Christian and a priest, a missionary in Uganda and the first member of IBLA. His life story, too, attracted me, as later I was to be fascinated by the life stories of Fr. Jean-Mohamed Abd-el-Jalil, a Moroccan, of Mgr. Paul-Mehmet Mulla-Zadé, a Turk, and Fr. 'Afîf 'Usayrân, a Lebanese. Already at Maison-Carrée, Fr. Henri Marchal had shown me "the great qualities of the Muslim soul" and taught me that many could be saved without baptism, belonging to "the soul of the Church," thanks to their sincere adherence to the demands of their conscience. All this was to be confirmed by the Second Vatican Council's decrees from 1962 to 1965. In fact, its "Declaration on the Relations of the Church with Non-Christian Religions" (*Nostra Aetate*) and paragraph 16 of its "Constitution on the Church" (*Lumen Gentium*) give a perfect summary of what IBLA was trying to impart to its students at that time.

In 1964 my work in Tunisia came to an end with the move of our institute of study and teaching to Rome, where it soon took the title of Pontificio Istituto di Studi Arabi e d'Islamistica (Pontifical Institute for Arabic and Islamic Studies; PISAI). Pope Paul VI had very recently founded in Rome a Secretariat for Non-Christians, with which our team of teachers was soon collaborating, in all relevant areas, as permanent consultants. From then on PISAI accepted students from all over the world, preparing them for a degree in Arabic and Islamic studies, in both French and English. In this way it wished to be at the service of the universal Church, preparing for it "participants in dialogue," in the same spirit as the council. Professional specialization then led me to complete the teaching of Arabic language, to present the modern evolution of Muslim law, and to initiate reflection on the history of the relations between Christians and Muslims during the course of history. Then, in February 1971, I defended my doctorate at the Sorbonne in Paris, with a thesis on *Statut Personnel et Famille au Maghreb de 1940 à nos jours* (*Personal Status and Family Law in North Africa from 1940 to the Present Day*), in which I analyzed the evolution of family law before, during, and after the coming of Independence.

It is thus within the setting of PISAI that I was able to develop co-operation of an editorial nature with Muslim professors who came to teach there. After serving as the editor of the educational documents *Etudes Arabes* (*Arabic Studies*) from 1962 onwards (classical and modern Arabic texts, with an annotated French translation), I was led in 1975 to found the Institute's annual trilingual journal (French, English, Arabic) *Islamochristiana*, of which I was the editor until 2004.

At about the same time the Secretariat for Non-Christians entrusted me with producing a second edition, enlarged and updated, of its book *Orientations pour un dialogue entre chrétiens et musulmans* (*Guidelines for a Dialogue Between Christians and Muslims*). This project was completed in 1981, and was translated into Dutch, German, Italian, Turkish, Arabic, and English. Subsequently, in 1982, I collaborated with Prof. Mohamed Arkoun to publish our reflections on *Islam, religion et société* (*Islam, Religion and Society*), published also in Italian, and the French translation of Prof. Mohamed Aziz Lahbabi's philosophical novels, *Morsure sur fer* (*Biting on Iron*, 1979). Other works followed: *Tendances et courants de l'Islam arabe contemporain* (*Tendencies and Currents of Contemporary Arabic Islam*: Egypt and North Africa) in collaboration with Fr. Georges C. Anawati (1982); *Islam e Cristianesimo: le vie del dialogo* (*Islam and Christianity: The Ways of Dialogue*, 1993); *Dialogue islamo-chrétien à temps et contretemps* (*Islamic-Christian Dialogue, Whether or Not at a Good Time*, 2002). Two books are currently in French and Italian: *Jésus et les Musulmans d'aujourd'hui* (*Jesus and the Muslims of Today*, 1996, rev. ed. 2005) and *Prophètes du dialogue islamo-chrétien: L. Massignon, J.-Md Abd-el-Jalil, L. Gardet, G. C. Anawati* (*Prophets of Muslim-Christian Dialogue: L. Massignon, J.-Md Abd-el-Jalil, L. Gardet, G. C. Anawati*, 2009).

As a collaborator of the Roman Secretariat, which became the Pontifical Council for Interreligious Dialogue (PCID), I was also called on to take part in a good number of Muslim–Christian meetings of official dialogue. After the first meeting in Tripoli, Libya, in February 1976, other meetings were held in Tunis, Amman, Beirut, Athens, Rome, Istanbul, Dakar, Algiers, Paris, Rabat, and Brussels—so many opportunities for sharing and reflecting on common topics with Muslim university staff, and for forging friendly relations enabling a better mutual understanding. On these occasions I was often led to present the Christian faith and to speak about Jesus Christ in a language that my listeners could understand. From this emerged a practice for such encounters of dialogue and an evangelical spirit of sharing, which enriched both my knowledge of Islam and the specific nature of my own Christian faith. In Rome it also came about that I had to respond to certain requests from the Vatican: It was a joy for me, in 1985, to have been able to participate in the drafting of John Paul II's address to the young Muslims of Casablanca (August 19). And what can one say of visits to Rome and Assisi with Muslim professors who wished to discover, on the spot, what the Catholic faith was then and is today!

Clearly all this was possible only through a spirituality of contemplation on "the mystery of the nations" and of intercession for "those who are near and far away" at the same time. Very close to the Little Brothers and Little Sisters of Jesus, and much influenced by those who were my teachers, Louis Gardet, Jean-Mohamed Abd-el-Jalil, and Georges C. Anawati, as well as Fr. André Demeerseman, for many years director of IBLA in Tunis, I was obliged to integrate both an intellectual and scientific dimension, and at the same time one ascetic and mystical. The discipline of study and research, and their successive discoveries, then encouraged me to make my own the insights of Louis Massignon and the generous nature of his *badaliya*, a spirituality of compassion and substitution. Better to explore the workings of grace in the world of Muslim mysticism and of its most genuine witnesses (for L. Massignon, al-Husayn ibn Mansur al-Hallaj was their model *par excellence*), I discovered that there have been within Islam "righteous" and even "saints" of the Muslim way. How could one not welcome them, in the name of Abraham, into the common tent where the three guests of Mamre can reveal themselves in a shared way? For L. Massignon, in a sort of mystical ordeal, both permanent and generalized, between sincere and generous believers, following on from what did not come about in reality neither at Medina between Muhammad and the Christians of Najran nor at Damietta between Francis of Assisi and the Muslim sultan of Egypt, it is a case of living a spiritual emulation. This would allow the hidden presence of Jesus, son of Mary, to grow in an autonomous way in the consciousness of all those who already know him, to some degree, from afar or from close to, so as to be finally builders of a "calm peace between Muslims and Christians" as the seventh Beatitude would wish.

It is indeed within this perspective that PISAI in Rome understood its work, and it is in this spirit that many of its former students have committed themselves in so many countries throughout the world, to a brave and generous dialogue between Christians and Muslims, even if it should come to bearing witness by the gift of a death offered for all. Six of those, who were my students, died a sudden untimely death in Algeria through their fidelity to Jesus Christ and solidarity with the people of Algeria—Christian Chessel, Jean Chevillard, Charles Deckers, Alain Dieulangard, Odette Prevost, Christian de Chergé—and another met a similar end in Trebizond in Turkey, Andrea Santoro. On the Christian side, there have been many men and women who have wished to live this spirituality of sharing and sacrifice.

The Journées Romaines, an event held every two years from 1956 to 1999 in Rome that brought together about a hundred Christians of all denominations, were for them the opportunity for a fraternal reflection, to give a theological backing to the implications of this spirituality, and give an evangelical renewal to its realizations. I had the honor of leading these sessions four times, from 1969 to 1975. Their aim was always to live "a witness offered and a word shared" with the Muslims whom God the Father entrusts to us as long-term neighbors or companions on the way. All this demands of these Christians a constant discipline of studious meditation, a personal gift of daily contemplation, and an evangelical capacity of wonder at another's religious values.

For my part, knowing that Muslims are sensitive to the Gospel values but dispute the genuineness of our gospels, I have always thought that Christians are to be "a living gospel," a fifth gospel, or as St. Paul says, "a letter of Christ, written not with ink but with the spirit of the living God, not on tables of stone, but on tables of flesh, on our hearts" (1 Cor. 3:3). This means that, through our whole being, and in silence, we may reveal to them the Father and the Son through the mystery of our lives hidden in God and offered to Him as a unique and definitive free gift, then to let them discover the ever-present welcome and the unlimited obedience of the Son who made himself close to all and the servant of the most humble, and finally cause them to glimpse that the will of God consists of building up his "Kingdom of justice and peace" among us, by asking him to help us in this effort through the gift of his Spirit. It is within this perspective that the Christian can then, humbly and with prudence, work upon structures and attitudes through dialogue, whether cultural or explicitly religious. And it is still within this perspective that he or she can with discretion accompany the personal journeys of Muslims who wish to turn to the values of the Kingdom of God, then to God-the-Father of this same Kingdom, then to Jesus Christ who is its presence and promise, and finally to the Church which is its starting point and its sacrament.

Even though I "retired" in 2004, I still live this spirituality and share it with many others. This is why I thought it useful to go on writing in this vein.

In collaboration with Prof. Hmida Ennaifer of Tunis, I wrote a book titled *Mustaqbal al-hiwar al-islami al-masihi (The Future of the Muslim–Christian Dialogue)*, published in Damascus/Beirut in 2005. In Italy, a popular booklet with a big print run, *ABC per capire i Musulmani (ABC for Understanding Muslims*, 2007) should help Christians to understand Muslims. To make one of my teachers better known, I wrote, in French and Italian, *Jean-Mohamed Abd-el-Jalil, témoin du Coran et de l'Evangile (Jean-Mohamed Abd-el-Jalil, Witness to Qur'an and Gospel*, 2004); I also published a useful collection of correspondence: *Massignon—Abd-el-Jalil, parrain et filleul, Correspondance, 1926–1962 (Massignon—Abd-el-Jalil, Godfather and Godson, Correspondence, 1926–1962*, 2007) and *Deux frères en conversion, du Coran à Jésus, Correspondance entre Mulla-Zadé et Abd-el-Jalil, 1927–1957 (Two Brothers in Conversion, from Qur'an to Jesus: Correspondence between Mulla-Zadé and Abd-el-Jalil, 1927–1957*, 2009). In January 2010 the Editions du Cerf published my *Louis Gardet, philosophe chrétien des cultures et homme de dialogue islamo-chrétien (Louis Gardet, Christian Philosopher of Cultures and Man of Muslim-Christian Dialogue)*, and in January 2011, *Louis Massignon, Badaliya, au nom de l'autre, 1947–1962 (Louis Massignon, Badaliya, In the Name of the Other, 1947–1962)* with all the texts of *The Badaliya of Massignon*, presentation and notes by myself. The collective memory of the Christian communities should thus be informed of what the pioneers of Muslim-Christian dialogue have done during the twentieth century. It is for this reason that other projects are in hand. The dream remains of writing one day some *fioretti* of this same dialogue, which would illustrate the small miracles of "daily living together" among Christians, Jews, Muslims, and people of goodwill, wherever God has willed that they should meet and have respect for one another.

The historical developments of the Muslim world in its threefold interpretation—since there are an Islam of Law, an Islam of Wisdom, and an Islam of Mysticism—and the ubiquity of today's Islamic institutions, strengthened by oil income, certainly present a spiritual challenge to contemporary Christians who must here "give an account of the hope that is in them." Without having to devise a theology properly so-called of Muslims' religious experiences, they are called upon to distinguish clearly between the cultural, juridical, economic and political aspects of an institutional Islam and the spiritual and devotional aspects of an "Islam of confident submission to God." The texts of the Second Vatican Council can enlighten them in that area. But the question remains: where does this "Islam" fit into the history of salvation? It has enabled millions of men and women to gain access to the mystery of the transcendence of the living

God in serving him through prayer, almsgiving, and fasting, thus fulfilling the desires of their naturally religious consciousness. But it has also forbidden them entry into this same mystery, rejecting all communication or communion between the Creator and his creature, and denying to Jesus Christ his role of mediator and redeemer at the same time. Louis Massignon spoke, paradoxically, of "a natural religion revived by a prophetic revelation," terms rather ambiguous. In fact, as the Muslim theologians say, it is a matter of a "rational natural religion," which makes use in its own way of a large part of the biblical heritage, while reinterpreting it by its own method. Thence comes the feeling Christians experience: The Muslims are at once both very close to them and very distant.

This is why, in all my writings, I have invited both sides to "necessary human co-operation." Even if their scriptural and theological justifications are different and sometimes hostile, Christians and Muslims know that they must take part, together with all people of good will, in "bringing the world to fulfillment" for the glory of God. And this happens through the "service of all people" who enjoy the same dignity and are all the more to be respected when they are weak and humiliated. As has been the focus in numerous dialogue meetings over more than forty years, the "management of human civilization" demands of all that they join in promoting the dignity of marriage and the mission of the family, the flourishing of arts and culture while respecting specific identities, economic and social equilibrium in the name of the common good, the harmony of political communities in the name of an international order which should guarantee peace and justice while totally respecting freedom of all kinds. In doing so, believers know well that they are then imitating, each in their own way, those "most beautiful names" of God which are equally models and challenges.

But these same believers would not be able to rest content with this service to their fellow human beings. Muslims and Christians, each in their own personal way, live a unique spiritual experience. This is why they have to question themselves on their "possible religious convergences" in the name of an "open spirituality." My books and articles have always aimed to remind them of this. They have many things to say regarding "the mystery of God": without setting the Most Great God of the one in opposition to the God of Love of the other, they do know well that a certain "exchange of divine attributes" is possible. The "gift of the Word," the "role of the Prophets," and the "presence of the Communities" are for them existentially very significant ways to realize a worship "in spirit and in truth." Concerning the "secrets of prayer," these belong to both, and find in the Psalms their best expression, handed on through little books of prayers on

both sides, in accordance with the great diversity of their paths of spirituality. These, moreover, always consider that the mystics and the saints are
their favored witnesses and challenging models with the aim of reaching
the fullness of "the perfect man" or of the "righteous among the righteous." On the path of a spiritual dialogue between Christians and Muslims,
there are plenty of milestones that can assist an "emulation in good works,"
such as are recommended by both religious traditions.

It is in this double perspective that I have always seen my friendships
with many Muslims, and written my articles addressed to my fellow
Christians. It is obvious that both groups are present in my daily prayer,
and especially in the Eucharist where Jesus Christ gathers together all his
brothers and sisters in humankind. Following L. Massignon's example,
I try to make them my guests in taking up the "threefold prayer of Abraham"
in the setting of the triple daily Angelus of Catholic tradition: Here the
great mystery of the Incarnation of the Word is thus a constant subject of
meditation through humble intercession on behalf of Sodom and its inhabitants in the morning, of Ishmael and the Muslims at mid-day, and of Isaac
and the Jews in the evening. L. Massignon spoke of doing so "in this mission of intercession, where we unceasingly ask God for the reconciliation
of these well-loved souls, for whom we wish to substitute ourselves
fî l-badaliya, in paying their ransom in their place and at our cost." Without
going that far, it is not forbidden to think that an increase of prayer, fasting,
and almsgiving by Christians might in the end obtain "that a greater
number should belong to the soul of the Church, should live and die in the
state of grace."

For my part, I have learnt from Jean-Mohamed Abd-el-Jalil, from Paul-
Mehmet Mulla-Zadé, and from 'Afîf 'Usayrân that their faith in Jesus
Christ, which made them "sons of the Father," in reality, through the
power of the Spirit, was no more than going beyond and fulfilling what
their "childhood Islam" had already given them. So, considering that the
Qur'an of the Muslims constitutes for them a spiritual sustenance on their
religious journey, I can only hope that they may draw from there the best
of what will bring them close to that Jesus, Son of Mary, of whom they
know that he is somehow related to the "word of God" and that he can, as
he has said, obtain a "table laid which can be a feast for all" (Q. 5:114).
My triple daily Angelus likewise includes what the Qur'an tells us of Mary
"chosen, purified, and chosen among all the women of the world"
(Q. 3:42), to whom "the good news was given of a Word coming from
God," whose name is "the Messiah, Jesus, son of Mary" (Q. 3:45).
Mysterious presence of the virgin mother and of her son, outstanding

prophet performing miracles never surpassed, who wishes upon himself "peace" on the day of his birth, of his death, and of his resurrection (Q. 19:33). How could one not see there a kind of "preparation for the Gospel" which the Spirit alone is able to bring to completion? Such is indeed the questioning that pursues me, as it also faces many of my brothers and sisters in Jesus Christ. This is why they have no hesitation in themselves using this prayer, which has for long been my own:

Lord Jesus,
make us enough like to them,
that our prayer and theirs can become one in Thine,
that our almsgiving and theirs can express only Thine,
that our death and theirs can find meaning in Thine.
Make us resemble Thee enough
that in our face, they may discover Thine,
that in our words, they may understand Thine,
that in our actions they may recognize Thine,
and that in our lives as Thy children they may learn Thy condition of Son,
in waiting for the Hour
when, recognizing at last that they are sons with Thee and with us,
the Manifestation of the Father will be complete and definitive
in the unity of the Spirit.
Amen.

This chapter was originally written in French, translated into English by Dr. Penelope Johnstone, and second-read by Anna-Regula Sharp.

God-Consciousness

Sigvard von Sicard

There is One God; and there is none other but He.

(Mk. 12:32)

la ilah illa huwa (There is no god except Him).

(Q. 11:14)

inna lilahi wa inna ilayhi raji'una (Verily to God we belong and verily to Him we return).

(Q. 2:156)

You shall not bear false witness against your neighbor.

(Ex. 20:16; Dt. 5:20)

Therefore all things whatsoever you would that men should do to you, do you even so to them: for this is the law and the prophets.

(Matt. 7:12; Luke 6:31)

Having grown up in Africa, I had been influenced by the African setting where you imbibed respect for the view, opinions, and ways of others. Likewise my father's dedication to the study of the traditions of the Shona and the Lemba deepened my appreciation of the African heritage.[1] During my studies at the University of Rhodes in South Africa, I had had an opportunity to study social anthropology under Monica Hunter-Wilson which widened my horizons further.[2]

When I enrolled in the Faculty of Theology at the University of Uppsala one of the requirements was a course in Comparative Religion. For me African Traditional Religion would have been a natural choice. Unfortunately this was not on the syllabus at the time. Religion of Israel was part of "Old Testament" studies and the Zoroastrian, Hindu, and Buddhist traditions seemed irrelevant in relation to my background, so why not Islam. I was aware that this tradition existed in parts of Africa but I was unaware of its history or Semitic origins. The lecturer was Helmer Ringgren, who was well versed in all the religious traditions but with a special penchant for biblical and Islamic studies.[3] Reading around the subject one encountered much of the medieval polemic repeated *ad nauseam* to this day, but one book turned out to be quite different and stood out more than any other, that of Tor Andrae, *Muhammad, the Man and His Faith*.[4]

Most sources presented Muhammad as a greedy, premeditating, calculating, sly and dishonest character. John of Damascus (c. 700–c. 753) described Muhammad as a "forerunner of the Antichrist" and Islam as "the deceptive superstition of the Ishmaelites."[5] Emperor Manuel Paleologus (d. 1425) challenged his Persian interlocutor to "show me just what Muhammad brought that was new, and there you will find things only evil and inhuman, such as his command to spread by the sword the faith he preached."[6] The same attitude is reflected in more recent literature such as the statement, "If there is one thing that is certain about him, his character, his personality, it is that he was essentially a pathological case."

1. H. von Sicard, *Ngoma lungundu, eine afrikanische Bundelade*. Studia Ethnographica Upsaliensia, vol. 5 (Uppsala; Almqvist and Wiksell, 1952); *Ngano dze Cikaranga/Karanga Märchen*. Studia Ethnographica Upsaliensia vol. 23 (Uppsala: Almqvist and Wiksell, 1965).

2. M. Wilson, *Reaction to conquest* (Oxford: Oxford University Press, 1936); M. Wilson, *Ritual of kinship among the Nyakyusa* (Oxford: Oxford University Press, 1956).

3. H. Ringgren, *Studies in Arabian Fatalism* (Wiesbaden: Harrasowitz, 1955); *The faith of the psalmists* (London: SCM Press, 1963).

4. Tor Andrae, *Muhammad, the Man and His Faith* (London: George Allen & Unwin Ltd., 1936, repr. 1956), French translation 1984; *Mystikens psykologi: besatthet och inspiration* (Uppsala: Sveriges Kristliga Studenrörelse, 1926).

5. D. J. Sahas, *John of Damascus on Islam* (Leiden: E. J. Brill, 1972), 133.

6. A. T. Khoury, *Sources Chrétiennes*, vol. 115 (1966), 142f.

". . . Muhammad with his vivid imagination and morbid fancy."[7] Such statements from the past could be multiplied a hundredfold. It is tempting to think that such attitudes existed only then. Alas, they persist to this day.

Tor Andrae on the other hand—dealing with the life of Muhammad on the basis of the psychology of inspiration, based on his work *The Psychology of Mysticism*—argued that the message Muhammad proclaimed clearly did not come from himself or from his own ideas and opinions.[8]

These insights, whether one agrees with them or not, seemed to point to the epigraph of this essay. They became the basis for my involvement in the study of Islam and Muslims. At every turn I would seek to look into what Islam and Muslims represented in the light of the Qur'anic dictum: "For each We have appointed a divine law and a traced-out way. Had God willed He could have made you one community. But that He may try you by what He has given you (He has made you as you are). So vie with one another in good works. Unto God you will return, and He will then inform you of that wherein you differ" (Q. 5:48).

Church History and Systematic Theology were a great help in understanding the reason for Muhammad's apostolate. The Christological controversies, the fissiparous tendency of the body of Christ and the absorption and secularization of the Church into the Roman imperial structures made it clear that the Church needed a challenge in order to be true to its calling. The Qur'anic message was and continues to be a clarion call to the Church to return to its original God-centered message to the development of a great God-consciousness as in the prayer, "Today O Lord, keep my eyes on You, my mind seeking You and my heart filled with You."

It was not until some years later that I had the opportunity to delve into the teachings of the Qur'an and Islam under the guidance of Kenneth Cragg. As documented elsewhere, his first students were the guinea pigs for his work on *The Call of the Minaret*.[9] These studies gave me a deeper insight into Islam. Later I studied Arabic and the Qur'an at the American University in Cairo with two *shuyukh*, Shaykh Ahmad and Shaykh Naguib

7. D. B. Macdonald, *Aspects of Islam* (New York: The Macmillan Co., 1911), 60, 63 *et passim*.

8. T. Andrae, *Mystikens Psykologi* (Uppsala: Sveriges Kristliga Studentrörelses Förlag, 1926); *Mohammed, Sein Leben und Sein Glaube* (Göttingen: Vandenhöck & Ruprecht, 1932); English Translation: *Mohammed. The Man and His Faith* (London: G. Allen & Unwin Ltd., 1956), 47ff.

9. K. Cragg, *The Call of the Minaret* (New York: Oxford University Press, 1956). "On being a guinea pig" in *A Faithful Presence*, ed. D. Thomas and C. Amos (London: Melisende, 2003), 71–77.

Effendi Ali from al-Azhar. Under their guidance I had the opportunity to memorize passages and discern the meaning of these passages and so to enter into the psyche of what this holy book meant to a Muslim. At the same time I had the opportunity to delve deeper into Islam under Edwin Calverley who had previously taught at the Kennedy School of Mission.[10] This led me to the discovery of the approach I had been looking for. It was first highlighted in the work of F. A. Klein in his book *The Religion of Islam*.[11] Its careful and exclusive use of Arabic and Islamic sources was a model that seemed appropriate. You allowed the Muslims to speak for themselves. You allowed the Qur'an to be its own interpreter, i.e. interpreting the Qur'an by the Qur'an.

But the experience was not just an intellectual and spiritual one. Living with a number of Muslim students from various countries in the Middle East while studying at Cairo and Ain Shams universities helped me in a practical way to open up the different ways the Qur'an and Islam impacted on their everyday life. As a student of Islam it was easy to relate to one's fellow students as there were many opportunities to ask perfectly natural questions for clarification about their understanding of the application of the teachings of the Qur'an and the Hadith in constantly occurring situations they were facing. This revealed an educational methodology which forced them to dig deep into their own faith for answers while requiring me to face and reconsider my own. As Muslims and Christians we carry a heavy baggage of tradition that we accept without question. Adherents of both traditions need to be "ready always to give an answer to every man that asks you a reason for the hope that is in you with meekness and fear" (1 Peter 3:15).

It was also in Cairo that I discovered the spiritual depth of a Muslim. Being in the presence of Shaykh Ahmad one felt a kind of saintliness. He exuded faith. Already at the beginning of my pilgrimage, I had been struck by the insistence on five daily prayers and had thought to myself that even as a theological student, I certainly did not observe or have that commitment. Here in Cairo I experienced it. I have since experienced it with a number of Muslims. There was the occasion of *salat al-maghrib* in a mosque in Durban where in the stillness of the evening the presence of God was tangible as my hosts prayed and I meditated and communed with "the Lord

10. E. E. Calverley, *Worship in Islam* (Madras: Christian Literature Society of India, 1925).

11. F. A. Klein, *The Religion of Islam* (London: Kegan Paul, Trench, Trubner & Co. Ltd., 1906).

of the worlds." As the Psalmist says, "The Lord is nigh unto all them that call upon Him, to all that call upon Him in truth" (Ps. 145:18).

Then there were the years of fellowship and cooperation with Sayyid Akhtar Rizvi (1927–2002) of the Ithna Ashari Community in Arusha and later as he built up the Bilal Mission in Dar-es-Salaam. Here was once again a person deeply God-conscious with whom it was possible to share common spiritual experiences and insights.

Is this not what lies behind Jesus's words, "If you only greet your brothers and sisters, what more are you doing than others? Do not even the gentiles do the same?" (Matt 5:47). The challenge is clearly to reach out in love and friendship in the way God himself is continuously doing. One may not be able to be as perfect as he is, but one can strive towards that goal.

Perhaps the deepest expression of this spirituality is to be found in the prayer of Rabi'a al-Adawiyya (717–801): "O my Lord, if I worship You from fear of hell, burn me in hell, and if I worship You in hope of paradise, exclude me from it, but if I worship You for Your own sake, then withhold not from me Your eternal beauty."[12]

Or in the words of a Muslim colleague, who pointed out that every time the tongue moves to touch the roof of the mouth it is in the position to form the name: Allah.

Studying the Islamic tradition and Muslims, and the Christian tradition and Christians, makes clear the truth of E. W. Hoch's statement, that:

> There is so much good in the worst of us,
> And so much bad in the best of us,
> That it hardly becomes any of us
> To talk about the rest of us.[13]

Perhaps it would also be appropriate to adapt the words from the ABBA song "I have a dream" and say, "I believe in angels, something good in everyone I meet."

The conviction of this God-consciousness and attitude was manifested among Christians and Muslims in villages and towns in East Africa where adherents of the two traditions were members of the same family, lived together, worked together, and shared in each other's joys and sorrows.

12. Quoted by M. Smith, *Studies in Early Mysticism in the Near and Middle East* (London: Sheldon Press, 1931), 234.

13. Quoted in *Everyman's Dictionary of Quotations and Proverbs*, compiled by D. C. Browning (London: J. M. Dent & Sons Ltd., 1952), 146, item 1919.

These occasions bore witness to the African concept of a common human-ity that manifests itself in so many ways. This commonality was under-pinned by the use of a common language, Swahili. Christian and Muslim scriptures used the same Swahili words and expressions such as *adabu* (*adab*): good manner, *adhabu* (*adhab*): punishment, *ahadi* (*ahd*): promise, *ibada* (*ibada*): worship, *neema* (*ni'mah*): grace, *rehema* (*ramah*): mercy, *utabibu* (*tatbib*): medical doctor.[14] This made for a much easier and natural com-munication and understanding between them.

These experiences and lessons led to an ever-greater consciousness of the similarity and common heritage Muslims and Christians have above all in their respective scriptures, etymologically and linguistically, and by implication, spiritually. Many of the central theological terms in these scriptures, coming from common Semitic roots and their Greek equiva-lents bear witness to this—*raham-rahmah-eleos* (mercy), *aman-iman-pistis* (faith), *kapara-ghafara-didonai* (forgiveness), *shahaha-ibadah-latreia* (worship), *shalom-salam-eirene* (peace).

If one considers the potential of this "commonality" one can only hope that instead of stressing dogmatic interpretations of these and other terms developed over the centuries in varying contexts one might call to mind the words of Jesus, "I have come not to condemn the world but to save it" (John 3:17).

Anyone who has had the privilege of exploring the deeper spiritual meaning will be convinced that it is in sharing our experiences of God at work in our lives that we can draw more closely to him and to each other.

Herein, however, lies a danger. Observing some attempts at relating to Islam and Muslims it is deeply disturbing to come across what can only be described as artificial and insidious, one might even describe them as Machiavellian attempts to read Christian meanings into Qur'anic terms and expressions or alternatively reading Islamic meanings into biblical terms. What is sorely needed is for the Christian and the Muslim to share the deeper meaning of his or her own text while intently listening to the other.

The concept of *ikhlas* (sincerity) in the Qur'an is stressed constantly, particularly in relation to God. The same applies in the Bible. Thus a pure comparison of terms and their interpretation is inadequate. It is in the implementation in daily life that their meaning is shared. One cannot

---

14. I. Bosha, *Taathira za kiarabu katika kiswahili pamoja na kamusi thulathiya* (Dar es Salaam: Dar es Salaam University Press, 1993); F. Johnson, *A standard Swahili-English dictionary* (London: Oxford University Press, 1951).

consider prayer unless prayer is an integral part of the lives of those who share their experiences in prayer. The same would apply to any other aspect of the faith; developing relations in the search for God demands mutuality. Sincerity then is not commitment to some doctrine or dogma but to the living God that Muslims and Christians worship and adore. Sincerity calls for a willingness to detect reverence in unexpected places and situations.

Experience has shown that dialogue can go on indefinitely without leading to any meaningful engagement. In that context it may be well to remember the words of Jesus: "Every idle word that men shall speak, they shall give account thereof in the day of judgment, for by your words you shall be justified and by your words you shall be condemned" (Matt. 12:36–37).

Often deeper insights start in very mundane situations and matters, in sharing in needs, projects, or situations common to Muslims and Christians in any given situation. This process has come to be termed *diapraxis*.[15] In those situations the question "Why are you involved in this?" crops up. Here it is appropriate to recall the exhortation, "Be ready always to give an answer to every man that asks you a reason for the hope that is in you with meekness and fear" (1 Pet. 3:15).

The spirit of *diapraxis* is summed up in the technical term *maslaha al-amma* (public welfare or the common good). It is in this that Christians and Muslims can unite because their respective scriptures call them to make efforts for the welfare of all. "Now we exhort you, brethren, warn them that are unruly, comfort the feebleminded, support the weak, be patient towards all people. See that none render evil for evil unto anyone; but ever follow that which is good, both among yourselves and to all people" (1 Thess. 5:14–15).

Diapraxis offers a context within which one can raise deeper issues of faith naturally. It offers an alternative to the traditional dialogue situation where *apologia* and *polemikos* take turns. In *diapraxis*, Christians and Muslims are faced with a common task concerning their common wellbeing; it is in theological language, "an incarnational situation," in that situation common humanity lends itself to a search for a meaningful expression for the "hope"

15. The term *diapraxis* was first proposed by Lissi Rasmussen in "From Diapraxis to Dialogue. Christian-Muslim Relations" in *Dialogue in Action. Essays in Honour of Johannes Aagaard*, ed. Lars Thunberg, Moti Lala Pandit, and Carl Vilhelm Fogh-Hansen (New Delhi: Prajna Publications, 1988), 277–93 and subsequently developed in her book, *Diapraxis of dialog mellem kristne og muslime* (Aarhus: Aarhus Universitetsforlag, 1997). See also S. von Sicard, "Diapraxis or Dialogue and Beyond" in *Dialogue and Beyond: Christians and Muslims together on the Way*, ed. S. von Sicard and I. Wulfhorst (Geneva: Lutheran World Federation, 2003), 131–53.

that is inherent in one's faith. Raising questions of faith in such a situation offers each person an opportunity to reflect and respond to someone with whom a relationship has been established. At the same time both the question and the answer provide an opportunity for the person who raises the question to look at and reconsider aspects of the question in relation to his or her own faith.

Relations between Muslims and Christians have been bedeviled by the concepts of *conversion* and *reversion*. The biblical concept of *metanoia* has been misappropriated into meaning becoming an adherent of a particular group. The biblical expression, however, implies an "about turn," a turning back to God. Both Christians and Muslims worship God, not some system or doctrine. Their worship may take different forms but in the end their aim is to worship God and all that it entails in every Christian's and Muslim's daily life.

> You must worship God and be among the thankful. (Q. 39:66)[16]
>
> Religion that is pure and undefiled before God and the Father is this, to visit the fatherless and widows in their affliction. (James 1:27)
>
> Worship God . . . (showing) kindness to parents and to the near of kin, and orphans, and the needy, and the neighbor who is a kinsman and the neighbor who is not a kinsman, and the fellow traveler and the wayfarer. (Q. 4:36)

Diapraxis, however, as intimated by the above quote from 1 Peter 3:15, does not end in simple explanations, but offers an opportunity to those involved in "the trivial round and common task" to share more profoundly in the deeper meaning their respective faith has for them. It is in such sharing that one discovers the common spiritual source of the faith in God. This will be expressed in different linguistic, ethnic, and theological terms, which will challenge inherited concepts, but will open up a deeper understanding and new insights in the richness of God's all-embracing and all-pervasive *hesed* (loving kindness, grace, favor, benevolence).

Some of this richness, but also a warning, is expressed in the hymn by F. W. Faber (1814–1863):

> There's wideness in God's mercy
> Like the wideness of the sea;
> There's a kindness in his justice

16. Q. 107 is a summary of what worship requires expressed in the negative of those who do not worship God in their daily lives.

Which is more than liberty
For the love of God is broader
Than the measure of man's mind;
And the heart of the Eternal
Is most wonderfully kind.
But we make His love too narrow
By false limits of our own;
And we magnify His strictness
With a zeal He will not own.
If our love were but more simple
We should take Him at His word;
And our lives would be illumined
By the presence of our Lord.

Called from My Mother's Womb

Lucie Pruvost

As I look back over what has been a long life, I can say it is the encounter with Muslim believers that has been the constant thread running through my whole existence, from the day of my birth, right up until today, especially in my work as a Missionary Sister of Africa (MSOLA, commonly called the White Sisters). All this makes me think that I must have been called to it even from my mother's womb. As the Constitutions of our institute foresee, "Faithful to its origins, the Congregation pays particular attention to Muslim believers."[1] This was indeed an essential element of the missionary plan of the founder, Archbishop (later Cardinal) Lavigerie of Algiers, who wrote in 1881: "I do not know a single missionary who has abandoned the Arab mission, and, for my part, I shall carry on with it until I die."[2]

I was born in Algeria some eighty years ago on a farm in the countryside. For various reasons, my father, though his studies had prepared him

1. Constitutions of the Missionary Sisters of Africa (MSOLA), No. 18.
2. Letter to members of the Council of the White Fathers, June 1881, *Enseignements du Cardinal sur la vie religieuse et l'apostolat africain* [*The Cardinal's*

for other activities, found himself running a modest farm. It was situated in the southern foothills of the Djurdjura—at the edge of the Great Kabylie and of the Arab land that stretches towards the High Plateaux before reaching the Saharan Atlas and then the Sahara itself—an almost desert region where the vicissitudes of history led the Berber populations, Jewish and Muslim alike, to take refuge from the Arab invasions of the eighth and twelfth centuries. With the family settled on the farm, we lived at close quarters with the farm workers employed to cultivate the land. So I grew up side-by-side with their children, especially with a girl of my own age with whom I used to play. What is more, we learned early on to speak not only our own but also each other's mother tongue: French, for her, and the Arabic spoken in the region, for me. It was a rural form of Arabic, sometimes mixed with borrowings from the Berber language that was also used in the region.

Things might have stayed like that but being so close allowed me to observe the cycle of the whole Muslim liturgical year, which these people, so hard-working and deeply rooted in faith, used to follow. This is how I began to discover the Muslim religion, by watching the performance of certain rituals that mark daily life, and to make out the pillars of faith, which were expressed quite simply and without any hint of aggression. All this helped me to discover a very practical kind of Islam and, later on, through comparison, to deepen my own Christian faith.

The first thing to strike you on arriving in a region or an area where most of the inhabitants are Muslim is how openly they practice at least two of the five pillars of the religion, the ritual prayer (*salat*) and the fast during the month of Ramadan (*sawm*). From my earliest years, I was able to see my playmate's grandmother, originally from a family of settled Arab nomads, perform her prayers at the various hours of the day. No need for a *muezzin* to call her, or even of a clock. She reckoned her time by the sun or by instinct if the sky was cloudy. We could watch her preparing carefully a set place for prayer, either on the beaten earth floor of her little house or outdoors, depending on the season. There she laid a small carpet of woven jute, specially kept for this purpose, and made her ablutions with a little water or with a stone made smooth by use; then, facing the east and focusing her attention, she began her prayer. This was an introduction to something, the significance of which I would learn later: the need for various ritual cleansings, of the body first with the ablutions, then of the space,

---

teachings on the religious life and the African apostolate] MSOLA mother house, St. Charles de Kouba (Algeria), 253.

then arranging the place and facing towards Mecca. My friend's grand-mother had taught us not to cross the space just in front of her. Ever since, I have remembered never to cross the space just in front of a person in prayer, even up until today. I was still too young to understand the meaning of the various postures laid down and of the content of the prayer, or to know that the alternation of Qur'anic verses with prayers took place according to a set order. One invocation was repeated often, *Allahu akbar*, and I was well able to understand its significance.

I discovered later that this grandmother had been initiated into prayer by another woman who came frequently to visit her; a member of the Rahmaniyya (a Sufi order, a branch of the Khalwatiyya, widespread in Algeria), which had established itself in this region close to Kabylie. It was also much later that my Islamic studies helped me to grasp the exact con-tent and significance of *salat* for a Muslim believer. In my family, though Christian, prayer was not a daily practice although I had been sent to cat-echism classes almost from the time I started school. It was thanks to this woman, and with that mystical instinct children have, that I sensed that something really important was taking place. In fact, this would prove to be an introduction to a vital relationship with God, the meaning of which I would subsequently understand more fully. I continued my initiation as I went along with the help of other key events of the Muslim year, like the month of Ramadan, which everyone observed faithfully. There was also the great Feast of Sacrifice, which they called the Feast of Sheep. On this occasion even the poorest families around us did not hesitate to take on long months of debt in order to buy a sheep to ritually slaughter, of which we always received a portion.

This early experience was not jeopardized by my schooling, which took place wholly within the state education system. In Algeria, then a French colony, it was French law, especially concerning compulsory education, which applied to every citizen, whether French by birth or by naturaliza-tion. Any indigenous man could become French on fulfilling the required conditions, which included a certain level of education, and this status he passed on to his descendants. For children whose parents were not French but "subjects of personal status," there was no compulsory schooling. They could, however, receive instruction, always in French, in a different section of the village school, with curricula adapted to their situation. Moreover, because of the French laws of separation between Church and State,[3] there was no question of introducing any sort of religious education into the

---

3. French law of December 9, 1905.

state schools or arranging a special timetable for children who were enrolled for catechism. The Thursday "free-day," replaced later by Wednesday, had been fixed, however, to compensate for this lack. Christian children could then attend catechism, while Muslim children were introduced to Islam—in the family, in the mosque, or in the *zawya* schools.

In my nominally Christian family, although regular religious practice was not observed, we nevertheless kept certain aspects of the Catholic faith, including baptism, marriage, First Communion, and Christian burial, all underpinned by a moral code inspired by Christianity and in particular a respect for other people's religion. My parents moreover had close ties of friendship to the Muslim family of a legal interpreter from the Lesser Kabylie. Yet the fact that there were Muslim pupils among my classmates added nothing special to our schooling. For example, the calendar of school holidays was the same as that in mainland France. It respected the big Christian celebrations: Christmas, Ascension, and the Mondays of Easter and Pentecost, but it took no account of Muslim feast days. My schooling continued in the same fashion in one of the girls' secondary schools of Algiers where Christians of different denominations, Jews and some Muslims were educated side-by-side. It so happened, in the upper classes, that I had some good opportunities of sharing with a Muslim fellow pupil. It remains the case that it was thanks to all these factors that I acquired a practical knowledge of Islam as it was lived in Algeria.

It was later that I was introduced to a more formal knowledge of Islam and to an explicit interreligious dialogue. Around 1955, having come to live in Algiers, I started to visit a library run by the White Sisters where young women, both Christian and Muslim, used to meet. The sisters would organize activities to encourage Muslim and Christian readers to talk to one another. A certain number of them had been educated either in the state system or in Catholic schools which, towards the end of the 1940s and at least in Algiers, had begun to accept some Muslim pupils, mainly from the immediate surroundings. The sisters had set up an interreligious group in which we were able to share our religious beliefs in a genuine atmosphere of respect. We thus set about learning how to carry out an increasingly well-organized interreligious dialogue in which each person could speak freely about her faith and begin to discover the reasons behind the belief of the other. These exchanges helped me greatly in my later journey. It was the start of an "in-service training" which I would later follow up in tasks that would be assigned to me at the end of my religious formation.

My first posting in 1962 was well suited to my desire to work in a Muslim environment, preferably in North Africa. This was in Tunis, the capital of

Tunisia, which had been independent since 1956. In this country I discovered a completely new atmosphere. The protectorate France had applied to Tunisia had not had the "deculturating" effect that colonization had produced in Algeria, an effect that had made Algeria into an extension of France, which claimed officially that it reached from Dunkirk to Tamanrasset. Moving from rural surroundings to a city, I got to know a country which had kept its Arab-Islamic cultural heritage almost intact, whilst at the same time, it had acquired a sound experience of the French language thanks to the bilingual education practiced by various of the country's secondary schools; the university still operating entirely in French. I thus had everything to learn, starting with Tunisian Arabic, more formal than the language of my childhood. In around 1954, the MSOLA had opened a language study center, intended in the first place for MSOLA members themselves, then gradually opening up to other women religious sent to Arabic-speaking countries, and later to any non-Arabic-speaking foreigner. The study center also offered courses in Islamic studies given by MSOLA sisters and the Missionaries of Africa (White Fathers), who were teachers at the Centre for Arabic and Islamic studies that moved to Rome in 1964, becoming the Pontifical Institute of Arabic and Islamic Studies (PISAI). This center had been opened during the 1930s by Frs. Henri Marchal and André Demeerseman, for whom a Christian–Muslim encounter based upon sound knowledge was of the greatest importance. The MSOLA and the other students were the first to benefit from it. The study center also contained a library intended for Tunisian pupils from nearby secondary schools, which allowed the MSOLA students to put their language skills into practice. Whilst taking care of the library, I had the pleasure of learning Tunisian Arabic, then of being introduced to literary and modern Arabic as well as Islamic studies. This was how I started to systematize the knowledge of Islam that I had picked up as a child and which had been consolidated during a summer session at PISAI.

In 1968, my superiors suggested that I should follow a university course; for me, this was a new starting point, helping me to serve Muslim–Christian dialogue better. I was therefore enrolled at the Faculty of Law in Tunis for a degree in private law, which finally led to the submission of a thesis for a state doctorate. Among the subjects taught there, knowledge of both Tunisian and French law used to cross over each other. This made us familiar with the two systems between which we could then make comparisons. Through the research it entailed, it was in connection with my vocation to Muslim–Christian encounter that I chose the topic for my thesis, "The Establishment of Filiation in Tunisian law." This choice opened the way for me to study Islamic personal law. Subsequently, it was out of intellectual interest and for the needs of my teaching work that, teaching myself, I went into *fiqh*, a discipline that is a key requirement for understanding Muslim culture and civilization. As I had never had the opportunity to study the Shi'a or Kharijite branches of Islam, my research was limited to the study of the Sunni branch and its various schools which, up until today, I still feel keenly to be inadequate.

This training allowed me to become a member of the permanent staff at the research and study center for the diocese of Algiers from 1981 to 2004. Founded in 1971 by Mgr. Duval, this center offers to anyone interested the opportunity to learn the languages spoken in Algeria and in Muslim–Christian encounter. It also contains a library that, for both Algerian researchers and foreigners, is a mine of information in Arabic and French on the history of Algeria and its institutions. Between 1981 and 1992, I was especially entrusted with teaching in Islamic studies, which was then scattered across all the religious communities in Algeria.[4] It was then that, for the requirements of my teaching, well resourced by the documentation gathered on site and supported by the director at the time, Fr. Pierre Claverie,[5] I started research in Islamic studies at university level. This research was above all concerned with the position of women in Islam. It was important for me to start from primary sources, preferably in Arabic, without, however, neglecting good translations into European languages. My two primary sources were thus the Qur'an, where I selected the legal and normative verses which, all told, are relatively few,[6] and the Sunna as reported by the classic collections of Hadith.[7] I could then elucidate the meaning through the Qur'an commentaries made available to me.[8] For over twenty years (1981–2002) as a visiting lecturer, I also provided PISAI

4. See L. Pruvost and L.A. Ammour, *Algérie Terre de rencontres (Algeria, Land of Encounters)* (Paris: Karthala, 2009).

5. Pierre Claverie OP (1938–96), Bishop of Oran (1981–96), assassinated on August 1, 1996, on account of his commitment to Muslim–Christian encounter.

6. Verses with normative judicial content represent 3 to 5 percent of the 6,234 verses of the Qur'an. They occur mainly in the suras of the Medinan period (622–32).

7. See, for example, al-Bukhari, Muslim, Ibn Maja, Abu Dawud, al-Tirmidhi, Ahmad ibn Hanbal (all in the 3rd/9th century), al-Nisai (4/10th cent.)

8. Some "classical" commentaries: Abu Ja'far Muhammad ibn Jarir al-Tabari (3rd/9th century); Fakhr al-Din al-Razi, *Mafatih al-ghayb* (6/12th century), al-Qurtubi, *al-Jami li-ahkam al-qur'an* (7/13th century); contemporary: Muhammad 'Abduh and Rashid Rida, *Tafsir al-qur'an al-hakim.* Cf. Ennaifer H'mida, *Les commentaires coraniques contemporains—analyse de leur methodologie* (bilingual Arab-French), trans.

with introductory courses on *fiqh* and its practical application in the personal statutes of several Muslim countries of the Hanafi or Maliki tradition, in particular Morocco, Algeria, and Tunisia.

This teaching gave me the tools I needed to make friends and swap ideas with a number of Algerian lecturers. We assembled a small multidisciplinary team covering history, sociology, anthropology, and law, directing our research and our writings towards the position of women in Algeria and the Arab-Muslim world. Beyond the friendship that brought us together and the opening gained by this work in collaboration with women from a Muslim culture, this led to me publishing a book about the position of women in society, the family, and public law. Published in Algeria, it seems to have been well received in French-speaking circles.[9] Not wanting to get caught up in a highly political debate, I had three goals: to offer as decent a university education as possible to French-speaking Algerians who had no solid Islamic training; to help Christians acquire a better knowledge of Islam so as to enable them to meet those who are different, something I knew personally to be fruitful; and to put my knowledge at the service of women and, if possible, the development of their legal position. All this enabled me to take part in several colloquia organized locally by various official Algerian authorities, sometimes as a speaker.

These years of living and working in Muslim countries could not fail to put their mark on my own Christian faith, to the point where some Muslim friends acknowledged, always with great respect, that they were astonished to observe that I had not become a Muslim. I always replied by affirming unambiguously my faith in a God at once triune and singular. Theologians will no doubt judge my argument to be simplistic: God being the Father, expresses himself through an incarnate Word, to which he remains united by the Spirit of Holiness; all the while realizing full well that my explanation still had no real meaning for the person listening. I learnt, however, to beware of any show of what could be understood as obvious "Christolatry," a form of polytheism or associationism for which Christians were blamed by some Muslims, whose faith was not fully educated. During my studies in Tunis, however, I did meet a Muslim student—an imam, no less—in his local mosque. He was well versed in his faith and opposed to a government that he upbraided for its secularism, but he did not show the same openness.

Michel Guillaud (Rome: Pisai, 1998). (Coll. "Studi arabo-islamici del Pisai" no. 10, *Etudes arabes*, no. 93).

9. L. Pruvost, *Femmes d'Algérie. Société, famille et citoyenneté* (Algeria: Casbah Editions, 2002).

In his eyes, I, as a Christian, was condemned to everlasting fire (*al-nar*), or hell, as he told me one day. It is worth remembering that, for Islam, God is not "Father" but "Creator." The Word of God (*Kalimat-Ullah*) could not be Son since it is "created," a status shared with the Spirit of Holiness (*Ruh al-quddus*). The Qur'an and Muslims following it, do nonetheless express their deep respect for Jesus, recognized as Messiah who, according to the Qur'an, clearly denies having claimed to put himself on the level of the one God.[10]

The strict monotheism professed by the Prophet of Islam explains his horror at all polytheism or "associationism" (*shirk, mushrik*), a horror probably inspired by the Christian deviations and heresies he came across during his travels with the caravans, or the sight of the pre-Islamic pilgrimage in Mecca with its Ka'ba and its many idols. Yet I have met several Muslims who started out with the Qur'anic Jesus, only to move gradually towards the Christ of the Gospel, who fully answered their interior searching; the Qur'anic texts having left them dissatisfied, with their denial of the incarnation, redemption through the cross, and the mediating role of Christ. My many meetings with Muslims, along with the personal formation that resulted from them, led me to an ever more pronounced adoration of the Trinity, an ineffable mystery, as the unanimous tradition of the Church defines it, which enfolds and shapes our whole life.

My experience is far from unique. It is true of all those pastors and members of the churches of North Africa, who have lived many years in Muslim lands and have there reflected upon an appropriate pastoral theology.[11] The challenge of daily interreligious encounter has been for them the driving force behind an invigorating meditation on the person of Jesus; the question which Jesus himself put to his disciples, "Who do you say that I am?" The Jewish–Christian encounter presents a similar challenge.[12] The person and nature of Christ are a stumbling block for many, even for certain Christians, as witnessed by the history of various heresies and of the great Christological Councils. This quest has been

10. Qur'an 3: 45, 59; 19: 34-5; 88–92.

11. On the Muslim–Christian encounter and the challenge it presents in theological terms, see, for example, CERNA, Conference of the Bishops of the North African region, "Le sens de nos rencontres," *Documentation catholique*, no. 1175 (1979); H. Teissier, *Eglise en Islam—Méditations sur l'existence chrétienne en Algérie* (Centurion, 1984); P. Claverie, *Lettres et messages d'Algérie* (Karthala, 1996).

12. On the Jewish–Christian encounter and the challenge it presents to Christology, see G. Bernheim and P. Barbarin, *Le rabbin et le cardinal—Un dialogue judéo-chrétien d'aujourd'hui* (Editions Stock, 2008), 169–88.

expressed well by Fr. Christian de Chergé, prior of the Trappist monastery of Tibhirine in Algeria.[13] It is clearly put in his will, distributed after his death worldwide and even in Algeria as *Urbi et Orbi*. This text sums up his vision of Muslim–Christian encounter and the impact it had on his life:

> It is too easy for such people to dismiss, in good conscience, this religion as something hateful by associating it with violent extremists. For me, Algeria and Islam are quite different from the commonly held opinion. They are body and soul. I have said enough, I believe, about all the good things I have received here, finding so often the meaning of the Gospels, running like some gold thread through my life, and which began first at my mother's knee, my very first church, here in Algeria, where I learned respect for the Muslims.
>
> Obviously, my death will justify the opinion of all those who dismissed me as naïve or idealistic. . . . But such people should know my death will satisfy my most burning curiosity. At last, I will be able—if God pleases—to see the children of Islam as He sees them, illuminated in the glory of Christ, sharing in the gift of his passion and of the Spirit, whose secret joy will always be to bring forth our common humanity amidst our differences.[14]

Another question arises for every Christian concerning the place of Islam in God's design and in the economy of salvation. Why did God permit the birth and rapid development of this monotheistic religion, which appeared some seven centuries after what Christians call the "close of revelation," knowing that each of these three monotheisms presents itself as a way of salvation,[15] a status that Islam claims also for the Qur'an named the "seal of prophecy"? Knowing also that "God wills that all men should be saved and come to the knowledge of the truth. For God is one, as also is the mediator between God and humankind, Christ Jesus, himself a man, who gave himself up as ransom for all" (1 Tim. 2:4-6a). For neither Judaism nor Islam admits the divinity of Jesus or *a fortiori* his role as mediator. The question can then become problematic, for example, regarding the well-known saying "outside the Church there is no salvation," a phrase that was actually applied to any Christian who had in any way denied his

---

13. Christian de Chergé, *L'invincible Espérance* [*Unconquerable Hope*], Texts collected and presented by B. Chenu (Bayard Editions/Centurion, 1996).

14. See C. Salenson, *Christian de Chergé—Une théologie de l'espérance* (Bayard, 2009), 107–28.

15. In 2007, Christianity represented around 33 percent of the world population, Islam 20 percent, Judaism 0.2 percent.

belonging to the Catholic faith or, more strictly, to Christianity. Therein lies a paradox that can be understood only through a renewed and wider vision of Christ.[16]

With the declaration *Nostra Aetate*, the Second Vatican Council opens wide the door to a new way of living the encounter with the religions of the world.[17] The passage about Islam is the fruit of the long experience of missionaries, notably White Fathers, who have been living in majority Muslim countries like those of North Africa. It is in Algeria, in the Kabylie Mountains, that these young missionaries, having left everything to proclaim the Gospel and wishing to found an indigenous church, began to instruct and baptize the orphans who they received into their institutions. The practice met, of course, with fierce resistance from the Muslim brotherhoods active in the region. Aware of the problem, Mgr. Lavigerie, then Archbishop of Algiers, as early as 1873 forbad "until further notice, Jesuit fathers as much as missionaries, to speak of religion to the Kabyles except for dogma which they accept. For the time being, we shall limit ourselves to caring for the sick and providing education for children."[18] After Lavigerie's death in 1892, this instruction seems to have become a dead letter, which aroused again the opposition of the Muslim brotherhoods. The missionaries were thus required to rediscover Lavigerie's insights. Under the leadership of Frs. Marchal and Milinault,[19] they recognized the need to change their apostolic methods. The plan took shape and, in 1937, was put in place following a conference of the superiors of Kabylie, which marked a decisive turning point for the apostolate in Algeria and Tunisia.[20] It would no longer be a matter of imposing their own vision of things, but

16. See C. Salenson, *Christian de Chergé—Une théologie de l'espérance* (Bayard, 2009), 108 ff.

17. The Declaration *Nostra Aetate*, on the non-Christian religions, October 28, 1965, para. 3. See Robert Caspar, "La religion musulmane," in *Les relations de l'Eglise avec les religions non chrétiennes*, (Editions du Cerf, Coll. Unam Sanctam no. 61, 1966), 201–36.

18. Monsignor C. Lavigerie (1825–92), Archbishop of Algiers (1866–92), founder in 1868 of the Missionaries of Africa (MAfr or White Fathers) and in 1869 of the Missionary Sisters of Africa (MSOLA or White Sisters). See *Lettre de Lavigerie au supérieur des Jésuites*, Lavigerie Archives D 9/31 (MAfr Generalate, Rome). Cf. François Renault, *Le Cardinal Lavigerie*, Fayard, 1992.

19. Fr. Henri Marchal, member of the General Council of the MAfr from 1912 to 1947 and Fr. Milinault, provincial superior.

20. See Marie Lorin (MSOLA), *Après 'L'Histoire des Origines de la Congrégation 1910–74'*, stenciled document, 148 pages plus annexes, MSOLA Archives (2000), 57–58.

rather of making the effort to enter into the other's tradition with sympathy and understanding.

Sixty years later, *Nostra Aetate* places itself in the same line urging "Christians and Muslims to forget the past and to work sincerely for mutual understanding and to preserve as well as to promote together for the benefit of all mankind social justice and moral welfare, as well as peace and freedom." "To promote together": this is exactly what has been set in motion, both in practice, and by the repeated appeals of the Popes. In their encyclicals, they call for shared action on behalf of the poor, the development of peoples, and respect for the dignity of the human person, "the indestructible image of the Creator God, an identical image in each one of us" as Pope John Paul II put it. More specifically: "To those who, like us, believe in a just and merciful God, the Muslims, I make . . . this appeal, which is also extended to all the disciples of the great world religions."[21] This call was amply confirmed by the "Message to the People of God" of the Second Special Assembly for Africa of the Synod of Bishops, which calls for "combining our spiritual resources." "Starting from the many values shared between them, Muslims and Christians can work together to bring about the rule of peace and reconciliation in our countries. . . . Dialogue and collaboration will take place in a context of mutual respect."[22]

Such is indeed the general perspective that should support Christian students of Islam in their commitment to the service of the encounter between Christians and Muslims. They are called upon to give themselves a sound intellectual foundation to strive always for a better understanding, as if from within, of the peoples to whom they will be sent. This presupposes a particularly strict discipline regarding the natural wish Christians have to bring them the Good News of salvation. This wish is sure to be satisfied once they have understood that an authentic dialogue with others who are different has itself a fully evangelical dimension. For surely the Lord Jesus acted in the same way with many of the people that he met, in particular with the Roman centurion and the Samaritan woman, who perhaps for the first time in her life, felt listened to and heard as she sought out a new life.

This chapter was originally written in French,
translated into English by Dr. Penelope Johnstone,
and second-read by Dr. Damian Howard.

21. See the Encyclical *Sollicitudo rei socialis* (1987), para. 47.

22. Second Special Assembly for Africa of the Bishops' Synod, Rome, October 2009. "Message to the People of God," part vii, para. 40 and 41.

A Life between Church and Islam

Seeking True Discernment

Jan Slomp

The following essay is the result of an effort to describe how I have become a missionary, a Christian student of Islam, and a dialogue partner for Muslim friends and counterparts. My tale contains personal, ecumenical, apologetic, cultural, political, and theological dimensions. Not every dimension gets equal emphasis. I will not repeat what I have written elsewhere or if need be only briefly in order to avoid incoherence. It is not a story only about me, because being a Christian implies being part of the Church, as a worldwide community, with a history and a future, a household of faith with many mansions. In this household I played only a minor part. Moreover in my contacts with Muslims I did not present myself as a "reformed" Christian but as simply a Christian linked ecumenically with many others and rooted in the same apostolic faith that was formulated by the ecumenical councils of the ancient church. I have worked hard on these ecumenical connections as will be evident below. In my travels in the borderlands of two world religions, I have always been accompanied, encouraged and helped by many fellow travelers. Some of them have become friends for life. They come to life in the pages of this travelogue.

Since March 1964 when our family arrived in Pakistan, I have continually traveled in my mind and in reality between church and mosque. I have traveled in as many Muslim countries as possible. This traveling has become more than second nature to me; it is a lifelong commitment. My presence in Pakistan was not an aimless or random event. It was motivated by a vocation and based on a conviction; it was the result of our choice between other options. I use the plural because my wife was always involved in such choices. The final decision was guided by our understanding of the biblical message and became gradually focused on one overriding purpose: improving relations between Christians and Muslims. This purpose remained the same after our return to Europe in 1977. It has often been tested by political events. For about the last thirty years, my guiding motto has been the prayer of the apostle Paul (Phil. 1:9–10), for the increase of abundant love (*agape*), insight (*epignosis*), and sensitivity (*aisthesis*) and ending with for me the most important line: *so that you may be able to discern what is best* (NIV). I have come to realize that in dialogue (speaking only for myself) I have to love my Muslim friend including, as far as possible, his religion, which is part of him, as I love my fellow Christian and the Church, despite our shortcomings. I have to be sensitive to the feelings on both sides, Christian and Muslim, and I have to try to discern between essentials and nonessentials; *ta diapheronta* in the Greek text of Phil. 1:10. That means never take things for granted, mistrust your own prejudices, do not follow the madding crowd, take the time for research, study the history of a problem, deepen your knowledge, ask critical questions, seek a new positive angle of approach, disclose Islamophobia and so on. A year before we left for Pakistan a friend sent me a brochure with the title *On loving Islam*. The author was an American, Jim Gittings, treasurer of the Presbyterian Mission in Lahore. I never met him, but his brochure changed my view of Islam. I received it at the right moment. It brought into focus what I had learned from Johan Bavinck and Kenneth Cragg (see below). Years have gone in the preparation of this itinerary. But before I continue my tale, I should sound a warning. The great danger to which all autobiographical accounts are exposed is self-centeredness, resulting sometimes in boasting. Echoing the apostle, Isaac Watts wrote the well-known hymn: "Forbid it Lord that I should boast." The Dutch scholar of religion Hendrik Kraemer (1888–1965) during the celebration of his seventieth birthday, which I attended, applied to himself the words of Jesus: "We are unworthy servants, we have only done what was our duty" (Lk. 17:10 RSV). What should I, a much lesser servant than Kraemer, state in self-defense? In retrospect I feel that I have been, by the grace of God, a very privileged person. I was born into a loving family, I am happily married, I have a family, and I often met the right people and was thus more than once advised to take what turned out to be the right decisions. But my missionary itinerary of so far forty-five years in *dar al-islam* was preceded by a long period of meaningful preparation. In a way every period in a person's life is always an anticipation of what follows.

Childhood during the War and Occupation

In the manse of the village of Heemse, in the municipality of Hardenberg, near the German border, where I was born on December 7, 1932, I did not learn right away that in the late thirties my parents had faced disappointment because they could not accept a call to serve in the Dutch West Indies. My mother had not passed the medical tests; but this event would have far-reaching consequences, to which I will return. Foreign missions were a familiar subject at home. Stories about aunt P. ten Kate, a younger sister of my mother, who was a medical missionary in the Dutch East Indies, impressed me. As a boy I was even more fascinated by what I learned about Albert Schweitzer. But happy dreams about foreign lands were soon eclipsed by the dark, but for me also exciting, war years. For me as a boy, resistance against the Nazi occupation seemed the obvious and normal thing to do. I witnessed how my parents rescued Jews and helped people to hide who had refused to work in German factories or serve in the *Wehrmacht*. Gradually I began to realize that I did not live in an average family. At that time, I was sternly told to maintain total secrecy concerning everything I saw and heard. When the *Gestapo* came to arrest my father and he escaped, when years later he was caught but rescued from the Cupola Prison in Arnhem and, in order to avoid reprisals, we all went into hiding in different places and under different names until the end of the war, it started to dawn on me that my war experience was special. It would leave an indelible impact on my future life. Only after the war did I find out that my father had been instrumental, thanks to the initiative of Mrs. Helena Kuipers-Rietberg, in founding the largest resistance organization against the Nazi occupation the Netherlands have known. Mrs. Kuipers died in the concentration camp of Ravensbrück. My father survived. My father's coworkers came from all walks of life. Most of them were Christians, Protestant and Catholic, and some were Humanists. The organization counted more than fifteen thousand workers, seventeen hundred of whom did not survive. Among my father's best "war friends" were two Catholic priests. My mother would later declare: "It was after all providential that my health was not good enough for hot climates." They both had a strong sense of divine guidance. My father and other leaders of his organization declined royal recognition, to the disappointment of Queen Wilhelmina, and declared, with his surviving friends, "We have only done what was our duty." My war experience made me allergic to ideologies, whether political or religious. I always have remained alert to find the right relation between religion and politics. We also had learned to look beyond the narrow enclosures of our own Reformed Churches. My father was extremely annoyed by the internal bickering during the war within our churches about dogmatic questions, which resulted in a schism. The church itself became a war casualty! His letter of protest to the synod was to no avail. Though my freedom-loving father was a strong, sometimes dominating, personality, he encouraged and helped both my sister and me to make our own choices in life, even if he disagreed with us. But I could not escape from the fact that many people kept seeing in me the son of the well-known "war veteran." Years later this resulted not only in larger audiences for my sermons and lectures, but also in higher expectations. I have tried to live up to them. Since about 1995, because most of the surviving resistance workers had passed away or for reasons of age and health had stopped telling their stories, I have been increasingly involved in programs and activities meant to keep memories of World War II alive.

Education and Early Ministry

Other things went into making me a missionary. In September 1945 I was sent to Rotterdam, then a city with a devastated center as a result of the Nazi bombardment in May 1940, where a brother of my mother was associate rector of the Christian Latin school, called *gymnasium* in Dutch. When in 1946 my parents moved to Hoorn, my school, until 1951, was the municipal gymnasium of Alkmaar with a Jewish Rector, Dr. J. Hemelrijk. He had survived several concentration camps and had maintained his human dignity. He was a fine humanist who taught us not only to translate but also to understand Plato. I became a Christian Platonist in my own way and thus thought of myself in the company of St. Augustine. In this secular school I learned to defend my faith.

During that period, discussions in school about Dutch colonial policies in Indonesia were exacerbated by the fact that my father happened to be an army chaplain on Java until 1949, when the former colony became independent.

In September 1951, I became a student of theology at the Calvinist Free University in Amsterdam. Until the last moment I had hesitated between theology and history. This fascination for the past would later become useful, when I dealt with the history of Christian–Muslim relations by studying in more detail the thought of Anselm of Canterbury, Martin Luther, and John Calvin in relation to Islam and Muslims. My studies since 1974, on the so-called Gospel of Barnabas, have been characterized by an historical approach (see below). Initially I devoted too much time to student activities. In my Oratorical Society Lysias, founded in 1932, I also made friends from other faculties. But for spiritual growth the Student Christian Movement (SCM) was of great importance. As a member of the local and national board of the SCM, I attended conferences in England and Germany and of the World Student Christian Federation (Geneva). In the SCM board, I met Iny Mobach, later to become my wife. In 1956 the SCM asked me to chair the Student Committee for Foreign Missions, founded in 1928. We had the names of seven thousand Christian students in our database. This database was used to start the Dutch program: Laymen and Laywomen Abroad (Dienst Over Grenzen). The Netherlands Missionary Council in Amsterdam provided free office space. We organized well-attended conferences and edited our own study bulletin. The motto of William Carey: "Expect great things from God and attempt great things for God" happened to be a strong motivator. We could not foresee that during following decades missionary enthusiasm among students would gradually decline due to the increasing secular spirit of the age and because white missionaries were less welcome. In 1958 I obtained, as the first student of the Reformed Churches in the Netherlands, a scholarship for the seventh semester of the Graduate School of Ecumenical Studies of the World Council of Churches (WCC) in Château de Bossey, not far from Geneva. Our subject was the Roman Catholic World. Students came from all continents except Australia and from twelve confessions. Of particular importance to me were the new dimensions opened by two of our teachers. First the Greek Orthodox Dr. N. Nissiotis, under whose guidance I wrote a paper on the French edition of Vladimir Lossky's, *The Mystical Theology of the Eastern Church*. The other was my countryman Prof. Johannes Willebrands, later the cardinal in charge of the Pontifical Council for Christian Unity. His ecumenical views, which he shared with us in some long conversations, would become influential during the Second Vatican Council. One spin-off of Bossey was a network of friendships that were maintained during reunions, the last in 2007. During my stay in Bossey, I followed a course on Islam in the University of Geneva. When I returned from Bossey I was invited to join a pressure group in our churches that advocated membership of the WCC through writing in various theological and ecclesiastical publications. I had to stop these activities when we left for Pakistan in 1964. Our churches joined the WCC in 1971. Ecumenical training in Bossey turned out to be very helpful in Pakistan and later in the Council of European Churches (CEC) and Council of Catholic Episcopal Conferences (CCEE) (see below). While in Bossey during the week of prayer for Christian unity in January 1959, I paid my first visit to the Community of Sisters of Grandchamp near Neuchâtel, a monastic, ecumenical community within the reformed tradition. One of the Dutch sisters happened to be a close friend of my fiancée. In the long run this visit resulted in lifelong commitment of both of us as a *foyer de l'unité*. Grandchamp has added a depth dimension to my life. During long periods of exposure to Islamic ways of thinking and living, I need as a counterbalance regular immersion in Christian life and practice, prayer and meditation, worship and Bible study. Bible study, not in a scholarly way going to the Hebrew and Greek sources as for preparing a sermon, but Bible study as *lectio divina*. Monasteries have always been places of spiritual restoration. I am thankful for the fact that the churches of the reformation have rediscovered their importance in times of secularism and mass communication.

Before I continue I should tell how my interest in Islamic studies got started. In 1953 the lectures of Prof. Johan Bavinck on Islamic mysticism kindled my interest. He himself was a sort of Christian mystic. During that same period I followed a course in the Mission Seminary in Baarn, where Dr. F. L. Bakker, a pupil of the famous Christiaan Snouck Hurgronje, taught Islamic theology. These two men did not suggest that I should specialize in Islamic studies, but they certainly motivated me. Moreover they never spoke about Muslims and Islam in a negative or derogatory way. So when I returned from Bossey in 1959 I continued my studies of missiology, Islam and Arabic at the Free University in Amsterdam. In June 1960 I wrote a paper about Kenneth Cragg's *The Call of the Minaret* (1956). This paper resulted in a correspondence with the author and a friendship, which has lasted until the present day. What I owe to Kenneth Cragg I have described elsewhere; in two words, very much! In April that same year my fiancée and I and three other couples started studying Urdu with Dr. K. de Vreese, a specialist in Indian languages. In 1960 these three couples left for Pakistan; we had to wait until early 1964. Three efforts to find a proper task for us had failed. In the meantime, I was ordained to serve the local reformed congregation of Zijldijk a village in the most northern corner of the Netherlands. Initially it felt like an exile but it turned out to be a good place to learn discipleship and ministry.

Missionary Service in Pakistan

Little did we realize in March 1964 when we journeyed on the Italian liner Victoria of the Lloyd Triestino Line from Genoa to Karachi that with the closure of the Suez Canal in 1967 the colonial era had definitely come to an end. Traveling by air between independent countries was to be the future. We joined the mission of the Associate Reformed Presbyterian Church (ARP) in Montgomery; the ARP had its home base in the American South. During our first four years with the ARP Mission, we had difficulty accepting that mission and church were still two different entities. To our surprise the final say in matters of policy belonged to the foreign mission. For us Dutch missionaries, who were originally trained for Indonesia, this felt like a setback. Moreover mission was perceived by the ARP as active evangelism aiming at conversion through rural campaigns, distribution of literature and medical care of Muslim patients, combined with Christian prayers for healing. Muslim opposition to such activities gradually changed ideas and practices. For me as a district missionary, my primary task consisted of training evangelists and pastors, promotion of adult literacy and providing facilities for an agricultural project. In 1966 the colonial name Montgomery was changed into Sahiwal with a big celebration. What I most appreciated was that the ARP made me their delegate to the Study Committee of the West Pakistan Christian Council (WPCC) in Lahore. This committee had published a course on *The Practical Approach to Muslims* and had employed a convert from the Ahmadiyya Movement to provide training in Muslim evangelism. But gradually a different attitude started to prevail and new ideas came in from abroad. Several members of the committee had read *The Call of the Minaret* by Kenneth Cragg. Our Roman Catholic member from Switzerland, Dr. Robert A. Bütler, S.J., introduced the declaration of the Second Vatican Council, *Nostra Aetate*, dated October 28, 1965, with the by now famous line: "Upon the Muslims too, the Church looks with esteem." The WCC started promoting the idea of study centers meant to deepen the understanding of the majority religious culture. But unfortunately the Henry Martyn Institute of Islamic Studies (founded in 1930; now in Hyderabad), which had been based for several years in Lahore, concentrated its work on the Indian side of the border. It could no longer provide the assistance needed in Pakistan. After the war between India and

Pakistan during the summer of 1965, border crossings became impossible. In the autumn of 1965, the Study Committee appointed a subcommittee to prepare a study center in Pakistan and made me its secretary. We wrote letters asking for advice to the twenty already existing centers worldwide, both Catholic and Protestant: nineteen replied! During the summer of 1967, the center was opened in Rawalpindi. A board was organized. The WPCC appointed me its first moderator. Our first full-time staff member, Dr. B. L. Haines, recently returned from Harvard, was appointed secretary. The well-known Pakistani educationalist and poet Dr. M. A. Q. Daskawie became the first Director. During the spring of 1968, Dr. F. S. Khairullah became chairman of the board. His first activity was appointing me as a staff member, just before we went on our first furlough. During that furlough my professor of Arabic and Islam, Dr. D. S. Attema asked me whether I had made any progress with my plans to write a thesis about how Ibn Taimiyya (1263–1328) dealt with the Christian doctrine about the Holy Trinity in his *Al-Jawab al-Sahih*. I told him that I had collected material and read some books but had not yet started writing. My priority had been to improve my Urdu, which left little time and energy to continue reading Arabic. So I stopped working on Ibn Taimiyya. Years later I was happy to learn that Thomas F. Michel, S.J., who in the meantime has become a good friend, had published a beautiful book on Ibn Taimiyya, *A Muslim Theologian's Response to Christianity*, in 1984. His advisor in Chicago had been Fazlur Rahman, who as Director of the Islamic Research Institute in Islamabad had visited us in the Christian Study Centre (CSC) several times. Since 1999 I have returned to writing about the Holy Trinity, which constitutes the heart of the Creed. This series in the Christian Weekly (*Christelijk Weekblad*) is meant to encourage ministers who have to preach on Trinity Sunday.

CHRISTIAN APOLOGETICS IN PAKISTAN

In January 1969 we moved from Sahiwal to Rawalpindi, by now the twin city of Islamabad. During this time, the Protestant seminary in Gujranwala invited me to teach Islam and Catholicism. Members of staff at the CSC were invited to speak at conventions and to give courses and lectures all over the country. A major effort was publishing the quarterly *Al-Mushir/ The Counsellor* in Urdu and English. The center promoted understanding through the publication of books and brochures and other activities. Muslim and Christian scholars from inside Pakistan and from abroad started visiting the center. In 1971 Dr. Daskawie, the Reverend Alexander John Malik (now Bishop of Lahore), and I attended a consultation of study centers convened by the WCC in Hong Kong. On the way home I visited Indonesia. Despite several joint efforts with Muslim friends we did not succeed in establishing a good structure for encounter and dialogue. Our best meetings with Muslim scholars were occasioned by visitors from abroad, among them Jacques Jomier, Georges Anawati, Kenneth Cragg, Daud Rahbar, Charles Adams, Noel King, and after our departure Hans Küng. Several visits of Prof. Annemarie Schimmel also provided platforms for encounter, although more on cultural rather than interreligious subjects. In 1973 I was asked to respond to a series of articles in *The Pakistan Times* defending the so-called Gospel of Barnabas. Dr. Daskawie, the Reverend Alexander Malik, and I saw the chief editor but he allowed us only a brief reply. My Pakistani colleague Prof. Yusuf Jalil wrote a brochure against it in Urdu. I decided to see Maulana Mawdudi on September 26, 1976, in Lahore when I discovered that he had written a long preface in the Urdu translation of this so-called gospel; all to no avail. When *Encounter* in Rome and the *Bulletin* of the Secretariat for Non-Christians (the present Council for Interreligious Dialogue) published my articles on this subject there was no escape anymore from apologetics. As a result I decided to research the ideology of Mawdudi. In a lecture in Holy Trinity Church in Murree on August 14, 1975, I called his Islamism a Trojan horse in Pakistani society. From then on I began to collect Mawdudi's publications. Years later I would write a number of articles about his thought. In 1975 another priority, besides the international debate on the Gospel of Barnabas, interfered with my academic plans and ambitions. The Christian Study Centre had embarked on two joint projects with the Roman Catholic Church. Under the supervision of the United Bible Societies, we were working on a new translation of the New Testament, meant to become *Today's Urdu Version*. One team was working in India with Dr. Samuel V. Bhajjan in Hyderabad. Dr. Daskawie was working in the Pakistani team together with Dr. John Joseph of Christ the King Seminary in Karachi (later he became Bishop of Faizalabad). I was invited to be consultant for Greek. At the same time we were working on an *English–Urdu Dictionary of Christian Terminology*. Dr. John Joseph chaired this committee. Most of the preparatory work had been done by Fr. Liberius Pieterse OFM and the Scottish Presbyterian, Dr. Willy Young, Bishop of Sialkot. Fr. Liberius was going to prepare it for the printer but had to postpone this for several reasons. The day before his sudden death at Rome airport, he had told his provincial in Karachi: "If I do not return alive from Rome, you should ask Jan Slomp to finish the job." I could only accept his legacy. But it meant I could not at the same time work on Mawdudi's ideology. In 1994, the year of my retirement, the reformed Theological University in Kampen granted me a doctorate *honoris causa*. My father had studied at this institution and would have deserved this honor more than I did.

European Challenges

In June 1976 at the initiative of Prof. Dr. D. C. Mulder, the moderator of the Mission Board under which we served in Pakistan, the synod of the Reformed Churches appointed me to start an Islam desk for the formation of church members in their encounters with Muslim migrants from Turkey, Morocco, and other countries. I started on July 1, 1977. In Pakistan I had worked with the intention of helping an indigenous Christian minority to find its place in an Islamic state. In my new task, I was dealing with a growing Muslim minority of foreign origin. The first debate in our church was about aims and objectives of this new desk. Some members of the board for evangelism under which this new Islam service desk was working expected that I should train colleagues and church members how to evangelize Muslims. Dr. Anton Wessels, Dr. D. Bakker, and I prepared a discussion paper in which we formulated the ABCD of the new task of our churches: the A of acceptance of this new minority, the B of "Begrip" or understanding Muslims and their religion, the C of cooperation in society, and the D of dialogue, just as with the Jews, the followers of the oldest Abrahamic monotheist religion. This new view had to be defended during several meetings of the national synod and was finally confirmed in a pastoral letter addressed to all the local churches (1991). This letter was translated into English, German, French, and Indonesian. Dialogue in this view implies mutual witness resulting in the possibility of change of religion either way, but its aim is not conversion. The final result is to be left to God's guidance. I should add that I am not surprised when some Muslims invite me to join their faith, saying: "You should know after so many years how perfect Islam is." On the other hand Muslims often are surprised or even irritated when Christians urge them to accept Christ as their savior. My advice is to leave it to God's Spirit. It is clear that for myself, I see no Christian reasons to become a Muslim. However discussions become very subtle and personal while counseling young couples, comprising a Muslim and a Christian partner, helping them to make decisions with discernment.

My new assignment in the Netherlands immediately took on international dimensions. In July 1977 the Church of Sweden invited me for an Islam conference. In February 1978 I represented my church during an

Islam consultation of the Conference of European Churches. When the president of the conference, David Brown, the Anglican Bishop of Guilford, fell ill, I was asked to write the final statement and to defend it during the last session. Shortly afterwards the General Secretary of the CEC, Dr. G. G. Williams, invited me to become the first secretary of a new Consultative Committee on Islam in Europe. Bishop David Brown became the new moderator. When David Brown died suddenly in 1983, the German pastor and scholar Michael Mildenberger succeeded him. During our consultation in March 1984 in St. Pölten, the conference adopted a statement concerning a conditional limited recognition of the prophet-hood of Muhammad. Because I was often invited to defend that decision, I felt urged to write about this subject resulting in several publications about the Prophet Muhammad. During my moderatorship of the Islam in Europe Committee of the CEC and the CCEE (1987–94) we developed ideas to improve theological training of pastoral workers in the light of the Christian-Muslim encounters in Europe. The report was published in several languages including Dutch, Italian, and Russian. In 2009 the new CEC and CCEE Committee for Christian–Muslim Relations in Europe prepared an update of this report edited by Andrew Wingate. I was asked to write the paragraph on the Netherlands. Since my retirement in 1994 I have to some extent been involved in the political, social, and cultural debates about Islam in the Netherlands, with more time to write and publish. Since 1996 I have been on the International Advisory Board of the Journal of Muslim Minority Affairs and in 2001 was awarded the International Muhammad Nafi Tschelebi Media Award of the Zentralinstitut Islamarchiv Deutschland in recognition of my services. Since 2003 one of my concerns has been peace between Israel and Palestine, a subject that also negatively affects Christian–Muslim relations. I was invited to moderate a secular committee founded by a Jewish lady in Amsterdam. Our foundation is devoted to support Israeli peace movements and human rights groups. We publish a quarterly, organize debates, and join protest meetings. The subject deeply divides my denomination, the Protestant Church in the Netherlands, as if the statehood of Israel were a new dogma. The conflict shows how a political ideology, in this case Zionism, can create religious tensions, from which there is so far no escape.

A Philosophical-Theologian's Journey

David B. Burrell

Jung reminds us how the story of our lives will always be the story of our times as well. As a Catholic, I was reared ecumenically by an English Catholic mother and a Scottish Presbyterian father, baptized an Anglican by his mother in Montana. So my life would be tracked by ecclesial realities in a different key from many American Catholics, yet arriving in Rome to study theology at twenty-three (1956). I would realize how Protestant my sensibilities were. I had been fortified at the University of Notre Dame by a rich "great books" education in the Western classics, and by the intercultural witness and instruction of a Holy Cross mentor who had studied theology in France in the thirties. So when the Second Vatican Council commenced in 1962, it would not only be a welcome breath of fresh air, but also provide an opening for which I had been prepared. By that time I was a vowed member of the Congregation of Holy Cross.

Serendipitously, I found a family in Holy Cross, intended by its nineteenth-century founder, Basil Moreau, to be a microcosm of a church: male and female, lay and clerical. I came to suspect that he had masked the radical nature of this prospect even from himself by the pious image of the Holy Family: priests as Jesus, sisters as Mary, and brothers as Joseph.

Rome did not permit a canonical mix of men and women, but as the church itself became sensitized to the need always to present a male and female face, our familial structure came to fulfillment in fact, especially in Asia, Africa, and South America. A semester teaching in Bangladesh in 1975 confirmed my attraction to Holy Cross, as I discovered how well men and women can cooperate in doing God's work, which I also experience now in the East African context.

This vignette accentuates some key realities of my life and times in the Catholic Church. Noting how the original vision of Basil Moreau was for a time eclipsed—only to emerge in the culture fostered by the renewal of Vatican II—indicates how a person's lifetime can be intimately intertwined with history in the making. The educational dimensions of my life colluded to thrust me into an interfaith world, as professional and religious realities elicited a personal response. Those same realities have also converged to bring me to Africa, where the dire consequences of a Western-directed globalization forcibly accentuate other socio-political realities, much as a decade in the Holy Land presaged American misadventures in Iraq.

So the original gift from my religious congregation of theological study in Rome, followed twenty years later by a semester in Bangladesh, set a pattern of reflective distance from American origins. These gifts would lead me to an ongoing critical assessment of our country's presence around the world. For liberation theology established once and for all the relevance of Christian faith to socio-political realities, as those realities affect our understanding and pursuit of faith. We were reminded how our lives make the most eloquent statements, as proponents of the theology of liberation, like Oscar Romero and the Salvadorian Jesuits, have given ultimate witness to their grasp of truth, as did Martin Luther King and Mohandas Gandhi during this same epoch. Once my early studies in Rome made me realize the inherent connection between "Catholic" and "Italian," my fate was sealed; despite northern European origins I became a Mediterranean person. Though readily at home in Western Europe, my heart was soon fixed in the Mediterranean basin, as a preternatural draw to that region would effectively determine ten years' presence in the Holy Land. My life had become fascinated with difference: different languages and practices, different skin hues and dress, different ways of approaching and understanding reality. That arc moved from the Asian subcontinent to Iran, from Arab to Turk, from Spanish to Mestizo, from Chinese to central Asian, from all of these to African. Yet among peoples whom we call African, there are countless differences, for the very name is a European construction of the nineteenth century, as the Treaty of Berlin (1884) identified a continent to exploit, not a culture to respect, for the continent embraces countless cultures.

The interfaith journey begins in earnest in 1980, after completing a decade as Chair of Theology at the University of Notre Dame, where we had succeeded in incorporating a Judaica position into our faculty by reconfiguring Hebrew Scriptures, New Testament, and early church under the rubric, Judaism and Christianity in Antiquity. (Ironically, if ours had been a Religious Studies faculty, we could easily have engaged someone to teach rabbinics without altering anything. As it was, four astute colleagues— Joe Blenkinsopp, Stan Hauerwas, Robert Wilken, and John Howard Yoder—helped me welcome a Jewish colleague into the heart of our faculty of theology.) I have always been grateful for that entrée into comparative theology, in a crucial step beyond easy "supersession" to recognize that one cannot become a Christian without first allowing oneself to be a Jew. Yet to go on to struggle with the relation between these two covenants (Paul van Buren), or these two phases of a single covenant (Thomas Aquinas), is to recognize that we will never quite "get it right"; indeed, it often seems like a divine joke. I could not be a follower of Jesus if I did not recognize, as his initial followers did, that he brought the Hebrew Scriptures to an unprecedented focus. Yet I have come to suspect that articulating that focus resists human ingenuity.

Fresh from that experience of collegiality, and imbued with the realization that Christianity could never be what it is without an intrinsic link to Jews and to Judaism, I still felt something missing. Guided by an American philosopher, Charles Sander Peirce, who invariably introduces triadic relations to overcome the dualism inherent in bipolar relationships, I had a premonition that Jewish–Christian relations, like any bipolar relationship, could easily become stuck. So at the outset of a trans-European backpacking trek to Jerusalem during the summer of 1980, in an effort to slough off nine years of administration, I made a visit to David Kerr at the Centre for the Study of Islam and Christian–Muslim Relations at Selly Oak Colleges in Birmingham. My destination was the Tantur Ecumenical Institute, where I had been deputed to serve for the year as its rector, with the mandate to find my successor and the promise of a sabbatical as the incentive. Founded in 1967 by the then-president of Notre Dame, Theodore Hesburgh CSC, at the behest of Pope Paul VI, Tantur's brief was inter-Christian ecumenism, Orthodox–Catholic–Protestant (including Anglican), yet it was located between two societies—Israeli and Palestinian—in which Jews or Muslims predominated. That geographical fact was to shape the rest of my life, and would gradually open fresh perspectives for the Institute itself.

A group of us had already been introduced to the world of Abrahamic faiths at Tantur itself in 1975, through Marie Goldstein RSHM, an American sister, whom the Lilly Endowment assisted to gather a group of Jews, Christians, and Muslims for a summer in the Holy Land, to learn their respective faiths from each other. Few had the foresight at that time to include Muslims in such exchanges, so we have ever been grateful for that opportunity, as lasting friendships grew out of shared experience in the Holy Land. Moving directly from Jerusalem to serve our Holy Cross religious community in Bangladesh introduced me to Islam in the Asian subcontinent, an experience that made me want to learn yet more about this multidimensional faith. So the prospect of an entire year in Tantur drew me to ask advice across Europe regarding ways to undertake the study of Arabic so as to expand Jewish–Christian exchange to include the logical third, Islam, to enter a new world of "Abrahamic faiths."

Two years in Jerusalem would act like an intellectual and emotional crucible. I needed to come to know as much about Islam as I had about Judaism, to enrich the attraction of the semester in Bangladesh by intellectual inquiry into Islam. That opportunity would present itself before long, as the culturally Jewish milieu of west Jerusalem drew me to the figure of Moses Maimonides, who had been on the periphery of my consciousness since completing a study of the philosophical theology of Thomas Aquinas in 1979, *Aquinas: God and Action*. Culminating my European *hegira* (migratory journey) by ferry from Piraeus to Haifa, I entered an *ulpan*, an Israeli institution for linguistic assimilation, hoping to gain a working knowledge of Hebrew as a stepping-stone to Arabic. I have always been grateful for that tactic, as mixing with Persian Jews emigrating to Israel in the wake of the Iranian Revolution offered me a rich sense of the mosaic of Jewish culture, normally eclipsed in Israel by dominating European (or Ashkenazi) Jews, and in Jerusalem by their black-coated ultra-orthodox counterparts. The presence of Sephardic (or Arab) Jews in the *ulpan* would contrast with their virtual absence among Israeli intellectuals whom I would later encounter in Hebrew University. The pecking order of this fledgling Israeli society, as it began to emerge, betrayed a fatal flaw in the Zionist dream, whose bizarre result has turned out to resemble "a bit of Holland" in the Middle East.

Fortunate to identify within a few months my successor as rector at Tantur—a distinguished English Catholic academic and spiritual activist, Donald Nicholl—I was free to relish the inherent advantages of this ecumenical institute located on a hill between Jerusalem and Bethlehem, a thirty-five acre walled-in oasis at a checkpoint, poised between the worlds of Israel and Palestine, so sandwiched between Jewish and Muslim majorities. I came to love the place itself, in part because its prescient location meant one dared not overlook either population or cultural group, and because its largely Palestinian staff evidenced a quality of hospitality and dignified longsuffering which would teach me how to jettison my native American optimism for something more theologically tenable: an enduring hope. Over nearly forty years of existence, countless scholars have discovered what Oscar Cullman, one of its founding lights, found: *Heilsgeographie* (salvation geography) is every bit as instructive as *Heilsgeschichte* (salvation history).

My role as rector also introduced me into the ecumenical atmosphere of Jerusalem. In the wake of his encounter with the Ecumenical Patriarch, Athenagoras, on the Mount of Olives, Pope Paul VI had invited my confrère, Theodore Hesburgh, to help him respond to the urging of the Protestant observers at Vatican II by founding an ecumenical institute in Jerusalem "where we had all once been one!" Yet as Vatican Secretary of State, Montini certainly realized that Christians are nowhere more divided than they are in Jerusalem, so the witness of Tantur would have to be a gradual one, and often exhausting for its rector! For me, the posturing of ecclesiastics in Jerusalem, often without substantive communities to serve, offered an x-ray vision of a major pitfall of progress in ecumenism which Karl Marx could have predicted: property! On the other hand, I found the immensely rich panoply of interfaith exchange both fascinating and intellectually challenging. Moreover, the ensuing year of study would reveal how the subject of my recent study, Thomas Aquinas, had found critical inspiration from both Jewish and Muslim thinkers for sustaining his project of showing how sacred doctrine could be a proper mode of knowing. Yet generations of western students of his thought had in fact failed to follow his citation trail to notice the role these Jewish and Muslim thinkers played in his work. So I came to appreciate the critical role of culture in scholarship, as the Mediterranean perspective of Jerusalem, and later of Cairo, supplemented European studies to open me to discover how his *Summa Theologiae*, the acknowledged syntheses of Christian theology, was an intercultural, interfaith achievement.

As a philosophical theologian sinking roots in the exchange among Jews, Christians, and Muslims in a medieval period formative for all three religious traditions, the prospect for comparative theology loomed inescapably, as a path of fresh discovery that is inherently dialogic, not as an

extra but as already constitutive of inquiry in each of our Abrahamic traditions. The medieval precedents I discovered: Avicenna, Maimonides (and
later, al-Ghazali), with Aquinas, revealed how our traditions had long been
engaged in significant exchange, however indirect, and carried out when
the climate for interfaith relations was far less propitious than it has become
after the challenge of the Second Vatican Council, of *Nostra Aetate*, to all
Christian churches, prompted intellectual inquiry in the west to move
beyond an Orientalist cast.

It would take a few more years to show that, in the supportive Dominican
milieus of Isaiah House in Jerusalem (1980–81), with the inspiring presence of Marcel Dubois OP (d. 2007), and of *L'institut Dominicain d'etudes
Orientales* in Cairo, with its commanding presence, Georges Anawati OP
(d. 1994). These mentors introduced me to the inescapably philosophical
dimensions of interfaith work, Dubois with Jews and Anawati with Muslims,
as comparative work will always involve entering into different traditions
in such a way as to see how one can fertilize the other. Yet as the summer
at Tantur in 1975 had shown us all, only persons can engage in dialogue,
holding out the hope of moving forward "one friendship at a time," as my
late Notre Dame colleague, Michael Signer, exemplified so well. In my
own case, the twin Dominican venues in Jerusalem and Cairo encouraged
me to enter a world of medieval exchange in philosophical theology, out-
lining the shape of our task today. The results have been presented in two
books, *Knowing the Unknowable God* (1986) and *Freedom and Creation in
Three Traditions* (1993), supplemented by translations of three major works
of the "Islamic Augustine," al-Ghazali. But such historico-systematic inqui-
ries can only prepare us for the drama of twenty-first-century Christianity
to be enacted on the ecumenical world stage, especially in the Holy Land
where myopic forces adamantly resist the fruitful exchange needed for
peaceful coexistence.

This rich and transforming journey has brought me to the point of
paying homage to these mentors, with the milieus which they inspired and
which sustained them, by forging a narrative *Towards a Jewish–Christian–
Muslim Theology* (2011) across the centuries. Not that I will attempt to
document the actual exchange between these traditions, for I am not a
historian, and there has been really very little. But rather, I hope to show
how each of these traditions has been constrained, in Lonergan's terms, to
track the inevitable questions that their respective revelations induce, so as
to struggle with intractable issues. It is often by commiserating with each
other, as we try to avoid nonsense in speaking of the divinity who calls us

in specific ways, that we come to appreciate our common task as it executes diverse trajectories.

In anticipation, I'll explore three such intractable issues that have become neuralgic in Christian–Muslim dialogue, beginning with that of *trinity*, to illustrate how interfaith exchange can now offer an apt vehicle for developing doctrine. Christian–Muslim disputations regularly opposed Muslim insistence on the unicity of God to a Christian Trinitarian presentation. Yet every student of the history of Christian thought knows that it took nearly five centuries of Christological controversies, plus another century of conceptual elaboration, to hone a "doctrine of trinity," precisely because of the *shema*: "Hear, O Israel, God our God is one" (Deut. 6:6). So if Muslim teaching showcasing divine unity, *tawhid*, has been developed polemically over against the "threeness" of the one God, Christians need to recall how long it took to articulate "threeness" in God without prejudice to God's unity, so how easily *trinity* can be misunderstood. Moreover, Islamic thought soon came to see how, as God's Word, the Qur'an must be coeternal with God, lest God be mute! So once we emphasize the Johannine expression of "word" rather than the synoptic usage of "son" in dialogue with Muslims, we will at once be able to converse with them less polemically, and also realize how thoroughly our baptismal formula refines the ordinary notion of *son*. So rather than diminishing the presentation of our faith, we will have come to a more refined understanding of what we have long been affirming. The fact remains that our faith is indeed "Trinitarian" while theirs is not, yet the process of dialogue will have brought us to a better articulation of our respective understandings of *trinity* and of *unity* in God, rooted in Christian adherence to the *shema*.

The next example comes as a corollary to the intradivine relations, called (in common parlance) "persons," though certainly not the distinct individuals we normally identify as persons. It focuses on the mediating role of Jesus in effecting our relationship to God. Muslims insist that while the Prophet delivers the Qur'an, which presents us with the very Word of God, our response to God's very Word affects an immediate relationship with God. Given the gift of the Qur'an, there is no need for a "mediator," nor should one think of Muhammad as one. On the other hand, Christian scripture and theology speaks in countless ways of Jesus Christ as "mediator between God and human beings." Now the ordinary use of *between* makes it sound as though Jesus operates in a space between the creator and creatures, yet that would be an Arian view, explicitly repudiated in the early councils. So that Jesus's mediation must operate *theandrically* in orthodox

Christian belief; that is, as something intrinsic to his divine-human constitution, carefully elaborated in early councils from Nicaea to Chalcedon.
In other words, in effecting an immediate relation to God as Father, Jesus
does not mediate as a "go-between." So the very feature of mediation
which Muslims deny to the Prophet, presuming that to be Jesus's manner
of mediating, represents a distortion of Christian thought, though one in
fact sometimes proposed by Christians as well. One thinks of sixteenth-
century debates between Protestants and Catholics, where the polemical
edge doubtless distorted a more classical meaning of *mediation*. For
Catholics had elaborated a sense of *mediator* to include ecclesial structures
and personages, so that ordained persons *mediate* the saving power of God
to the faithful. But just as Jesus could not be construed, thanks to the *shema*,
as a "being alongside God" (the meaning Muslims attach to *shirk*: something, either created or uncreated, on a par with the creator), so Christians
falsify their own faith if they conceive of Jesus's mediation (or, *a fortiori*,
that of the Church) as situated *between* the creator and creatures. As the
Word who is God, Jesus's mediation effects that immediate relation to God
as Father which Christians enact in their recurrent prayer: "Our Father."

A final example explores the polemical stance both Jews and Muslims
take with regard to Christian teaching regarding "original sin." Yet applying Aquinas's hermeneutical cautions here, we find that diverse Christian
lexicons offer widely divergent versions of "original sin," so that one is
never sure which one of them is at issue. The meanings Christians attach
to this teaching range from a characteristically Catholic view, captured in
Chesterton's insistence that "original sin is the only empirically verified
Christian doctrine" ("Murphy's Law" in the moral order), to the most stark
contention that its effects render our intellectual and voluntary faculties
utterly dysfunctional. Now all of these views require that Adam's transgres-
sion somehow affects and infects us all by a path which remains obscure, so
all focus on the universal human need for redemption exemplified in and
effected by Jesus's death on a cross. If this remains a sticking point for
Muslims, an adequate way of articulating "the atonement" continues
to elude Christian theology, which deems Anselm's account deficient on
several counts, but has yet to find a satisfactory formulation.

Yet we can all recognize that rational creatures are incapable of achieving their inbuilt goal of union with God, requiring some action on the
creator's part to make that possible. Now a closer look at the Muslim
view of human beings' capacity for "drawing near to" God shows less difference between us than first appeared. Islamic thought readily applies to
the entire world the situation in the Hejaz before the Prophet's preaching

the Qur'an: bereft of divine revelation, human beings are bound to wonder aimlessly, seeking to fulfill their own desires and inevitably engaging in deadly combat, as we see every day! On this view, the Torah or the *Injil* (gospel, i.e. New Testament) serves the purpose for Jews or Christians that the Qur'an does for Muslims, since human beings left to themselves would never make it. So while Christianity focuses on the death and resurrection of Jesus, Muslims locate the redemptive act *par excellence* in the unmerited and serendipitous "coming down" of the Qur'an from God through the Prophet. Human beings are invited to respond to this gift, while their ever-lasting destiny depends on the quality of that response. So this dynamic reinforces the fundamental analogy between Jesus and the Qur'an: as Christians believe Jesus to be the Word of God made human, Muslims believe the Qur'an to be the word of God made book. Each of these examples can show us how comparative inquiry will inevitably highlight dimensions of our own theological task, by accentuating items in our own traditions, which need clarification and development.

Moving beyond examples to the grammar proper of theology, we can note the "play" of theological inquiry, rooted as it must be in practice, to display Aquinas's contention that our language, at best, will "imperfectly signify" divinity (ST 1.13.3). And if theological expression will ever be inadequate, theological inquiry will always be comparative, seeking the least misleading modes of expression. Yet that requires refinement of judgment, gained by weighing different expressions relative to each other, as we try better to articulate what Augustine called "the rule of faith." And if there can be no adequate expression, we shall always be weighing candidates relative to each other. So as we learn to accept diverse ways of arriving at conclusions, we will also find that we can employ the skills learned in one tradition to follow reasoning in another. Traditions, in other words, are often found to be *relative to* one another in ways that can prove mutually fruitful rather than isolating. The traditions which prove to be so will be those that avail themselves of human reason in their development, as the patterns of stress and strain in their evolution will display their capacity for exploiting the resources of reason. (On this point, Pope Benedict was "spot on," as the thirty-eight Muslim scholars noted, for Muslim as well as Christian traditions!) In short, fears about "relativ*ism*" give way to the human fact that all inquiry takes place within a tradition. So as medieval ways of resolving apparent conflicts between faith and reason turned on critical hermeneutics with regard to texts, complemented with critical assessment of the reasoning one is employing, so interfaith comparative inquiry will require skills of reading one set of texts in relation to another.

So where have we come? To an interim conclusion, using the skills we have developed to subvert the perfectly normal desire of each religious group to show it is superior to all comers. For characteristic efforts to do so will invariably involve presenting the other in ways that can at best be contested for fairness, and at worst display brutal colonization. A final charitable look at the Vatican statement *Dominus Iesus* (2000)—"On the unicity and salvific universality of Jesus Christ and the Church"—can suggest a way of putting things less contentiously than that document did. For while purporting to proclaim abiding Christian truth, article two of the document effectively derails that intent. After expressing the elements of Christian faith in the words of the Nicene Creed in article one, the authors go on to claim, with disarming self-assurance, that "in the course of the centuries, the Church has proclaimed and witnessed with fidelity to the Gospel of Jesus." But proclamation inherently involves witness, since *truth* can hardly be proclaimed merely verbally. If an effective combination of proclamation and witness had indeed been the case, past centuries would have been radically different and our own century surely unrecognizable. Yet a contestable assertion can fault an entire document, as this claim to have witnessed faithfully throughout the centuries, so contrary to the historical record, can only make its proclamations sound arrogant and monopolistic. For intellectual humility is as intimately related to ethical humility as proclamation is to witness, as Americans experienced in watching an Amish community forgive the murderer of their children, and Palestinians and Israelis can observe in the mediation of the Christian Peacemaker team in Hebron. Witness must cost, if it is to be more than authoritative pronouncement. And an effective preparation for authentic witness can be found in that purification of mind and heart aptly prepared in the crucible of listening to those who profess a faith other than our own. If the "village atheist" served over the centuries to awaken believers from their dogmatic slumber, today it is "other-believers" who challenge each of us to a more mature and articulate rendition of our respective traditions.

A Pilgrimage amongst the Treasures
of Islamic Traditions

Arij Roest Crollius

It began with Arabic studies. It was intended by my superiors that I should prepare myself to succeed Fr. J. Houben, S.J., as professor of Islamic studies at the University of Nijmegen. I had always felt an attraction to Asian cultures, Taoism, Hinduism, and Buddhism, but of Islam I had no more than a vague idea. As a Jesuit one obeys.

First I spent three years in Lebanon: at the language school in Bikfaya, at St. Joseph's University in Beirut, and also teaching English at a Jesuit High School. For reasons that may or may not be relevant here, the students with whom I made friends were mostly Muslims. I still have, among the few books I carry around, a small edition of the Qur'an, with a dedication on the first page: "To my friend Fr. Arij, from Ahmed."

Then three years in Egypt with studies at Cairo University. The Faculty of Arts offered an enormously rich array of courses. Among other topics, I chose History of Islamic Philosophy, Methods of Sociological Research, Philosophy of Culture, *Juwaniyya* (a form of existentialism), and *Tasawwuf* (study of the Sufi paths). This last course on Islamic mysticism left a deep impression. The *shaykh* who taught us was blind and quoted all texts

by heart. But his heart was not filled with texts only. He radiated a deep
sense of personal sanctity.

Fellow students became interested in my way of life. A group of friends
established itself, with the vision to invent a Jesuit-like society for Muslims.
We still had to select an appropriate name and were already writing our rules.
On the three pillars of our brotherhood we agreed: *shahada* (witness by words
and our style of life), *khidma* (service), and *jihad* (an effort to strive against our
laziness and egoism). Two friends remain very present to me until today:
Hamdi, who took me to his home, where his father blessed our friendship.
We also visited together various *dhikr* sessions during the nights of Ramadan.
The other was Ruslan, from Indonesia. We were often together to cook
Indonesian dishes or discuss all manner of topics between heaven and earth.

Before leaving for Lebanon in 1958, I had been preparing myself for
future work in the then Soviet Union. The superior general had asked
young Jesuits to present themselves for this work. It was judged that I was
too young to start special studies, but I could begin with Russian and thus
acquired a fair knowledge of that language. When in the Near East,
I became aware of the Muslim peoples of Soviet Central Asia. In 1966
I met in London and Paris some of the great specialists in the study of this
region and returned with the plan to begin studying Turkish and Kazakh,
just in my free time naturally. But also theology had still to be studied, with
a view to ordination to the priesthood. In 1964 I was sent to Rome for
theology and was also requested to look out for ways to prepare myself for
service in Central Asia. Little did I foresee that my residence would not
change for the next forty years, until 2005 when I moved to the Côte
d'Ivoire. (In fact I was only in Rome for twenty years, the rest of the time
I was traveling for research, teaching, and meetings.)

In Rome and far beyond, I discovered three main ways of contact with
Islam and Muslims. First, institutionalized Christian–Muslim dialogue.
Second, the teaching of various aspects of Islamic history and culture, with
the necessary research. Third, an inner journey toward the deepest sense of
Islam, further than rules, rites, and dogmatic definitions. A few words then
on each of these ways.

Institutionalized Dialogue

In Rome, in 1965, after the Second Vatican Council, a Vatican Secretariat
for Non-Christian Religions was established. In due time, I was appointed
consulter to this Vatican body but even before that Cardinal Marella, the

president of this Secretariat, regularly called me for meetings and discussions, including with representatives of other religions. A style developed for these dialogue meetings, documented by various publications of the Secretariat. The development of this style for dialogue was perhaps the most important fruit of these initial stages. The scope of these meetings was simply mutual understanding with a view to a more harmonious coexistence and perhaps even collaboration. Yet there were also those participants who thought that they had to convince their interlocutors of their own convictions. When governments or religious bodies were involved, things did not always go smoothly.

There was a more open and free mode of exchange in meetings organized by academic institutions. This type of colloquium belongs to a genuine tradition of universities and other institutes of higher learning and has not begun only in the second half of the twentieth century. However one can assume that after the 1939–45 war, a greater need was felt for encounters between representatives of different cultures, and that the rapid development in the means of transport and communication has contributed enormously to facilitate a real globalization of the typical international character of universities.

In addition to the many meetings in Rome, I have traveled around the globe to spend time in dialogue with Muslims, either by myself, with a mission from higher authorities, or with a group formed in Rome. Thus I spent time in Iran and Indonesia, Libya and Cairo, and Istanbul and Cordoba, to mention just a few. What have I learned from all this? First, I came to know human beings and their ways of behaving. With some, one immediately felt the bonds of friendship, with others, one had to wonder about the diversity of people and to exercise patience. Moreover these meetings were often an occasion of learning new aspects of the Islamic creed and culture, which helped me also in my academic activities. Finally, I also had the sense of having contributed, in a minimal way, to the progress of mutual understanding between different peoples. It would be ungracious to mention in this context the moments of unpleasantness and ennui. These little things have only enhanced the sense of joy and gratitude in having lived these adventures of dialogue.

Research and Teaching

While completing my doctoral thesis in fundamental theology at the Gregorian University, the decision had not yet been made about where

I would teach. The superior general, Fr. Pedro Arrupe, intervened in an unexpected way and called me to be his secretary for the missions (a kind of director of the interreligious and intercultural apostolate of the Jesuits) and also to be his special councilor in all that had to do with Islam. In order that I might keep up-to-date on what is happening around the world, he suggested that I be out of Rome for at least six months each year. The visits to Jesuit confrères in various countries gave me the opportunity to see Islam through their eyes and to meet with Muslims who otherwise I would never have seen. Here and there I could also encourage superiors to set Jesuits free for Islamic studies and facilitate the formation of groups of Jesuits with a special interest in Islam (like JAMI in India).

Even though I was not always present in Rome, I was invited to teach introductory courses there on Islamic history and culture: first at the Gregorian University and then also at the IBLA (the current PISAI) of the White Fathers, which had recently arrived in Rome from Tunis. In 1974 I was appointed professor at the Gregorian University with a teaching program that can best be called interreligious and intercultural studies. Islam held a central place in this project. We established agreements on the exchange of professors, amongst others with Ankara University. I went there several times for lectures and conferences. During a number of years, I also taught an intensive course at the University of Innsbruck. Interest in Islam was great there, partly because of the increase in the immigration of Turkish and other Muslims in the 1970s. A few years later, I began to deliver a regular course on the program of the Theological Faculty of Zagreb. During long summer recesses from the Gregorian University, I taught in various institutes of theology in India and was also a regular guest professor at the Sophia University in Tokyo. The latter appointment gave me the precious opportunity to spend time in Buddhist monasteries. I also visited many other places in Africa, Asia, the Americas and Europe, either for a few days' meeting or for a single lecture. The deepening of my knowledge of and training in Hinduism, Buddhism, and Kebatinan (in Indonesia) owes much to this mission of facilitating interreligious and intercultural encounter, especially with Muslim people.

Following the wishes of my superiors, two new centers of interest were added to, or rather, became intertwined with, my basic concern and activity: inculturation and Jewish studies. During the 32nd General Congregation of the Society of Jesus (1974–75), I was requested to fulfill the role of secretary to a commission that had to prepare a decree on the intercultural apostolate. There I proposed, instead of *acculturation* or *culture contact*, to employ the term *enculturation* or *inculturation*, so as to express better the growth of a Christian community in the culture of its people. In endless conversations and notes, I had to explain this term and became known, even at the Vatican, as "the father of inculturation." Courses, articles, and conferences were added to my habitual themes of academic activity, and the inculturation approach gave a new slant to my interest in Islam. My research became more geared towards the rich variety of cultures that composes the Islamic community and also to an effort to identify and understand the various forms of social and political behavior within this community, particularly in its relations with those who do not belong to the *umma*. The tension between fundamentalism and modernization became a key to appreciate the difficulties experienced in many Islamic societies and movements to accommodate to a pluralist form of society.

In the midst of all these activities, I was surprised by a new request from my superiors: to begin a center for Jewish studies at the Gregorian University. The fact that I had not undertaken formal studies in Jewish culture and religion did not seem to be a problem and Jewish friends even saw this as an advantage, because in this way I would not have any preferences among the various forms of Jewish life and doctrines. Ignorance thus helped me to start this center; after a few years called "The Cardinal Bea Centre for Jewish Studies." From the beginning it has been a project of international collaboration. Jewish and non-Jewish benefactors have assisted in rendering possible the various activities of the Cardinal Bea Centre and in teaching and publication there has been, from the beginning, a lively collaboration between specialists from the two religious communities. We were able to sign a formal agreement between the Gregorian University and the Hebrew University of Jerusalem for an exchange of professors, researchers, and students.

In the context of this essay, it is worth mentioning that a deepening of knowledge and understanding of Judaism contributed to a better appreciation of the Qur'anic idea of the heavenly religions: Judaism, Christianity, and Islam. However, given my predilection for clear thinking and an abhorrence of confused ideas, I have been able to steer clear from ventures of "trialogue." The new task with which I was entrusted, without being relieved of previous ones, has also opened up for me a new circuit of meetings and lectures; first of all in Rome, naturally, but also in Jerusalem, Germany, the United States, Argentina, and other countries. The invitations came from Jewish or Christian communities or institutes of learning. The topics mostly concerned the changes in Judeo–Christian relations, especially from the Catholic side. Since I had undertaken research on analogous themes in connection with Islam, these lectures could be enriched by earlier experiences. For the last several years I have been teaching theology and comparative religion at the The Jesuit Institute of Theology (ITCJ) in Abidjan, Côte d'Ivoire. This has helped me to deepen my knowledge of various types of Islam in Africa.

Thus my contact with Islam has greatly widened the scope of my experience and activity. I have been able to admire the great esteem with which divine and human *logos* are held, not only in the Qur'an and its commentaries but also in other branches of Islamic learning. A rich tradition of the rational approach enlightened by faith can be found in various treatises of Sufi authors.

The Inner Journey

In research and teaching, I have always made an effort to privilege the common, "orthodox" type of Islam, the Islam of the Qur'an and the Hadith, of the five pillars and the four schools of law and of the history that is in great part shared by Muslims, Christians and others. Somehow I considered Sufism as too unproblematic an approach: an aspect of Islam that is easily sympathetic to Christians and with which we have many elements in common. Yet already during studies at Cairo University, I was brought into contact with the *Nazm al-Suluk* (The Song of the [mystical] Progress) of Ibn al-Farid.

IBN AL-FARID (1182–1235)

The *Nazm al-Suluk* is a long poem, comprising 760 verses all ending with the letter "t" and because of this it is also called *al-Ta'iyyat al-kubra*. A particularity of this song is that the divine Beloved is represented as a female being, a language I had already encountered in Heinrich Seuse's (1300–66) booklet on the Eternal Wisdom. Because of a certain poignancy in the expressions of love on the part of the mystic, the saintly, blind *shaykh*, who explained this song to us at Cairo University, now and then had to call students to order when they expressed their amazement at these religious expressions by giggles and titters. What I remember especially from his lectures, is the "consolation beyond consolation and desolation." He sounded as though repeating certain passages of *The Imitation of Christ* in stressing that those who are seeking consolation are similar to those who work for money and that love is far from their hearts. Love consists in going beyond the difference between consolation and desolation, and desiring the Beloved for herself alone. But even then, the Beloved can freely deny her presence. As to presence and absence, he said, there is still something beyond that pair of opposites. I no longer have the notes of these lectures but the teaching has remained present to me for well over forty years.

Ahmed Ghazali (d. 1126)

Another witness for me to the inner experience of love has been Ahmed Ghazali, brother of the better-known Shaykh Abu Hamid al-Ghazali. He has written in Persian a brief treatise titled "Thoughts on Love." In this treatise I found what I can best describe as a metaphysics of love. It certainly has illuminated my perception of human life and history, and gave me also new insights into an approach to the divine mystery along the path of the *logos*, the inner force of which is love. Several memories are linked for me with this booklet. Once I was in Tehran, invited by the Iranian Ministry of Foreign Affairs, to give a series of lectures on "Diplomacy in a Pluralist World" at the School for Diplomatic Service. (The Iranian Ambassador to the Holy See knew that I was the spiritual moderator at the Vatican School for Diplomacy.) In my free hours, I often had conversations with a specialist on Ahmed Ghazali, conversations in which words and silence were intermingled. Another memory is the request from a Vatican prelate, who wanted to read something new on love. I gave him a translation of the "Thoughts on Love." It was returned to me a few months later, after the prelate had died, with all the signs of having been read and reread.

Dara Shikoh (1615–59)

Dara Shikoh has become guide and companion for me on the path of interreligious dialogue. He was the eldest son of Shah Jahan and would normally have succeeded his father on the Mughal throne of the empire. The orthodox Muslims in the realm found in one of his brothers, Aurangzeb, a protagonist in the fight for the purity of law and dogma. Dara was declared an apostate and subsequently killed in prison by a band of assassins.

During his relatively brief life, he had several important encounters with masters of other religions, such as Hindus and Sikhs, and it may be surmised that in his youth in Lahore, he had known Jesuits at the court. It may even be that he followed the example of his great-grandfather Akbar, who invited Muslim, Hindu, Sikh, and Jesuit representatives to discuss matters of faith in a hall especially built for this in Fatehpur Sikri, his new capital, which he never inhabited, near Agra in North India. Dara Shikoh translated about fifty Upanishads into Persian, and this translation, once further translated into Latin, became the first source of knowledge of Hindu scriptures in Europe. His most famous work is *Majma' al-Bahrayn* (The Mingling of the Two Oceans; an allusion to a Qur'anic expression) which is one of the earliest works of comparative religion in world literature. In this writing, he attempts to express in Muslim terminology in Persian the road of the Hindu spiritual experience: two "Oceans" of religious doctrine. The list of his other writings is impressive. I do not enter into the doctrines discussed there. Dara Shikoh is mentioned here because he has encouraged me to proceed on the path of interreligious and intercultural dialogue. I have learned three key things from him. First, the importance of the study of languages in order to understand the meaning of the convictions of people of other religions and cultures. In his work of translating Hindu texts, Dara Shikoh shows a keen knowledge of the meaning of Sanskrit terms. In this he has been a pioneer. Second, his interpretation of continuous prayer on the rhythm of the breath is, to say the least, quite original. The brief third chapter of the *Majma'* may be seen as a commentary on the use of AUM in Hindu meditation. It can still be helpful today. It has strengthened my conviction that learning from one another's practice is more important in dialogue than discussion and research. Third, as a final note to these encounters and also an open-ended conclusion of this brief essay, I learned about the heart and mind of Dara Shikoh. In attempting to find an answer to the question "Can Dara still be considered a Muslim?" I discovered a deep, inner kinship with him. So often, followers of other religions have asked me to join their way of practice and belief. My answer is beyond yes and no. I recognize myself in some of the statues of Henry Moore, as I have admired them on a rainy day in the Hakone Sculpture Garden in Japan, while the wind blew through the wide openings in the breast and belly of the inclining figures. These statues possess a solid identity, yet are unthinkable without the Spirit that powerfully passes on and of whom no one knows whence it comes and where it goes. I am convinced that the deeper one enters into one's own spiritual and religious experience, the more one discovers the storm of the Spirit that is at its origin. It is a bewildering storm of love and generation in which God becomes so close to man and man to God, that man can be born anew to that fullness of being in which Love is the very *raison d'être*, the deepest *logos*.

Seeking a Theological Encounter

Etienne Renaud

Devoting my life to the encounter with Islam was not an early vocation. In fact my first contacts with Islam go back to my military service in Algeria, where, like all young French men at the time, I was posted during the Algerian war. I was appointed as officer for "Algerian affairs," as a member of the corps known as the Blue Kepis. Their task was to administer the villages in war-affected zones, a task that the civilian administration was unable to undertake. This first contact with North Africa encouraged me to acquire the first rudiments of the Algerian dialect. I have since retained a genuine liking for the different dialects of the countries that I have had occasion to visit. At the end of my military service, after a short spell in the seminary of the Paris diocese, I entered the congregation of the White Fathers (Missionaries of Africa). When the time for the final vows arrived, we were asked in what sort of mission we would like to serve. I said at the time that I would not be averse to going to a Muslim country. Thus after my ordination, I was appointed to Tunisia, and this took me quite naturally to the Pontifical Institute for Arabic and Islamic Studies (PISAI), which was entrusted to the White Fathers and had recently been set up in Rome. I should say that PISAI played an essential part in my commitment to the

encounter with Islam. The teaching there was very thorough. It was based
on the Arabic language, generally viewed as the "highway" into the Islamic
world. Under the direction of Fr. Maurice Borrmans I thus engaged in an
intensive study of the Arabic language, based on the logic of the Arab
grammarians. Although my previous training was more scientific and
mathematical, I became genuinely attached to this Semitic language and its
own specific way of thinking. I have never regretted this investment in the
Arabic language, which I consider essential: it seems to me crucial to any
real knowledge and understanding of Islam.

Islamology was taught by very able teachers. In particular, I can recall
Robert Caspar, whose teaching had a strong influence on me, strongly
influenced himself by Massignon and Louis Gardet. He taught Muslim
theology and Sufism. What I appreciated particularly was the fact that he
presented Islam in a manner with which a Muslim could identify. A few
Muslim teachers completed the team, mostly from Tunisia. I must admit
that at the time I devoted myself wholesale to this study. I consider that the
Institute helped me to take Islam seriously: in particular the excellent
library enabled us to measure the literary, theological and spiritual heritage
of thirteen centuries of Muslim tradition.

The normal period at the PISAI lasts three years, but I was allowed to
leave for a third year in Damascus in Syria, using a grant I had obtained
from the French government. This year in Damascus was extremely valuable for me. I attended lectures (without sitting exams) in the faculty of
letters and also in the Muslim law faculty (*shari'a wa usul al-din*). My contacts with the university were rather particular, my main lessons in Arabic
being dispensed in individual tuition.

During my stay in Damascus I visited a large part of the Middle East:
Jordan, Iraq, Bahrain, and, of course, Lebanon where I went frequently.
I got an enormous amount from this year in Syria. Damascus at the time
was still very "provincial," with few outsiders allowed in; this was in 1969,
only two years after the Six Day War. I got into the habit of regularly meeting an Imam in a mosque, who, with great kindness, commented on the
Qur'an for me. I really appreciated the freedom of contact in Syria at the
time, and the freedom to enter a mosque, since Syria follows the more
liberal Hanafi rite. And I naturally had very friendly contacts with the Arab
Christians, despite all their divisions, which I feel do not always serve the
Christian message.

At the end of 1969, I found myself in Tunisia at the Institut des Belles
Lettres Arabes (IBLA) which had long been present on the cultural scene
in Tunis. On the strength of my scientific and technical training (I was

indeed what is known as a late vocation, following qualification from the Ecole Polytechnique[1] in Paris), I worked for three years in the electricity company in Tunis, STEG, in the computing department. Islam as such did not surface often in conversations with my fellow engineers, but I made numerous interesting encounters and developed excellent contacts. I did, however, have the feeling that Islam in the Maghrib, compared to the Islam I had encountered in Damascus, was a little narrower, distant from the sources of the Arab world and Islam. I sometimes felt that my colleagues had difficulty constructing a synthesis between a Western scientific training as engineers and a Muslim subconscious that received little intellectual nourishment.

In 1972 I was called on to accompany a community of nursing nuns to establish a foundation in Yemen, in the capital Sana'a. The Yemeni experience, which lasted eight years, was the turning point for me in entering deeper into the world of Islam. During these eight years I had the good fortune to be housed by a very ordinary little Yemeni family, and I view this opportunity of a lifetime to have contact on a daily basis with a family in the developing world as a great privilege. The Islam I experienced there was tranquil, and not particularly narrow; I was able to have a share in all the family events—births, circumcisions, marriages, deaths, and even my landlord's departure for the Hajj and the festivities that surrounded his return. As earlier in Tunisia, I was working with the electricity company, where I was in charge of issues relating to training, and where I gradually came to establish a training center in collaboration with the French government cooperation services. Through the company staff, I had numerous and varied contacts. I am particularly grateful to an accountant in the company who was a member of a large family of Sayyids who initiated me in Zaydi Islam, a form of Islam found only in North Yemen.[2] This exploration of Zaydi Islam was very rewarding; it is a branch of Islam that is considered to be Shi'ite, although it in fact has little in common with other Shi'as, and at the time it was very little known. Yemeni Zaydi Islam is very different from the puritan Wahhabi Islam of its large neighbor.

Obviously there was a dose of exoticism in the pleasure I derived from living in Yemen, a country that had remained closed to Western influences. But I felt that the Yemenis were at ease with themselves and the world.

1. This famous *grande école* produces what are known as *ingénieurs* in France, and the diploma constitutes one of the highest possible qualifications in the scientific and technical fields in France (translator's note).

2. The Sayyids are descendants of the Prophet.

Since they had never been colonized (except briefly by the Turks) there had been no quarrel with the Christians, with whom they were only acquainted through the Qur'an. This was not true in North Africa, where the colonial presence had left deep and lasting wounds in people's hearts. In Tunisia, people were still talking to me about the Carthage Eucharistic Conference in 1930 where the young people from the schools had processed dressed as Crusaders.

In 1980 I was appointed to PISAI. It is an understatement to say that I was sorry to leave Yemen, its mountains, its day-to-day routine, and all the friendships I had built up there. But I did gain the advantage of a return to intellectual discipline, a good library, and the practice of in-depth study. I, of course, found myself teaching Arabic and various Islamic sciences. I developed a degree of specialization on the Hadith, although overall I have remained a generalist. In fact I had not previously had any specific training beyond the basic PISAI curriculum.

I was also in charge of the journal entitled *Etudes Arabes* which produced a certain number of Arabic-French features on important themes: the Muslim Brothers, Wahhabism, the *ba'th*, the application of the Shari'a, *tawhid*, and so on. This required good collaboration on the part of the teaching staff. PISAI was largely conditioned by its Maghrib origins, and there was some foot-dragging at making the effort to turn over to the use of English (not to mention Italian!) and to take account of Islam worldwide.

During my first stay in the Institute, I had been fascinated by the novelty of what I was learning. I admit, with the passage of time, that I was probably too taken up with the novelty to really develop a critical view. In the course of this second period, I discovered a certain number of limitations in this religion that had interested me so much. I noted the pseudo-scientific nature of certain Islamic disciplines, such as the transmission of the Hadith or the history of the composition of the Qur'an.

At the time we were already witnessing the rise of Islamic fundamentalism. The result was that in the various events, whether seminars, conferences or merely in private conversations, we were always coming to the social or even political aspects of Islam, while what I really wanted was to concentrate on Islam as a religion, and I could indeed say as a faith. This tension has never left me, whether in my own encounters or in wider conferences. Roughly speaking, I could say that starting from a faith, I found myself encountering a religion, and even encountering a whole social system. I will return later to this difficulty and this imbalance that has always troubled me.

From 1986 to 1992, I was chosen to be the general superior of the White Fathers' congregation. As a result, for the next six years, I took up my pilgrim's staff to travel to the majority of African countries and a certain number of others in Europe and the New World. In this period, I had relatively little contact with Islam. In fact I must admit that this break was welcome. To be honest I was suffering from a sort of overdose of Islam.

After this period, which brought me much, both in human and in spiritual terms, I returned to Tunisia for two years as the head of IBLA. As soon as I arrived, I had occasion to appreciate the faithful friendship of relations I had established in the course of my first stay there, where, twenty years on, I could take up the conversation where it had been left off. I came to hold the conviction that a large part of Muslim–Christian dialogue is played out through friendly relationships and the time commitment that is entailed. It takes time for fruit to appear. I also noted, among the students in the institute, a new interest in Christianity, and a need to go beyond preestablished frameworks. In this work lay the possibility for new, promising exchanges on the Trinity, the Second Vatican Council, the social doctrine of the Church and other such issues.

But then, in 1994, I was called back to Rome to take over the direction of PISAI. Apart from the unavoidable administrative tasks, I was nevertheless able to explore other domains, and in particular I developed an interest in Shi'a Islam. In the course of this period I recruited a Libyan teacher for two years. His name was Aref Nayed, he had a doctorate in philosophy and in-depth knowledge of Islam, in particular the Sufi component. I remember and value our exchanges over these two years.

In 2000, relieved of my duties in PISAI, I set out for the island of Pemba, one of the two islands in the Zanzibar archipelago (I had no idea beforehand that Zanzibar was not a single island). There I discovered another brand of Islam. The island of Pemba was rather like a vast monastery: As people had nothing to do all day (there was very little economic activity), they flocked to prayer, and everyone observed Ramadan. It was relatively difficult for me to find my place in this new landscape. There was also the frustration of the language: I had to learn Swahili within a few months, not such an easy task when your hair is graying. Fortunately a third of the vocabulary in Swahili is Arabic, which helped me to progress, but this enterprise was short-lived.

The experience came to an end in the middle of 2001 when I was called to the Sudan to head a small institute that carried the picturesque acronym of CLIK (Catholic Language Institute of Khartoum). There I returned to the teaching of Arabic in two forms: in the mornings I taught literary

Arabic to Sudanese from the south, where they had been trained in English, which created certain problems for them in Khartoum where everyone spoke Arabic. In the afternoons, in contrast, the task was to teach the rudiments of Sudanese dialect to volunteers, such as those from Médecins sans Frontières, or Action Contre la Faim, many of whom were then headed to Darfur. I also had the job of organizing several series of lectures, mainly on Islam as it is lived in the Sudan.

Sudan is a country that grows on you. The brotherhoods were prominent and afforded numerous contacts. I really had the feeling that interreligious encounter was easier than in North Africa, where I had spent considerable time in the past. The personality of Mahmud Mohamed Taha fascinated me: this elderly sage, known as the Sudanese Ghandi, was executed in 1985 at the age of seventy-seven by President Numeiri, because he had taken up an open stance against the application of the Shari'a. I had the opportunity to experience the living memory of him among his family and disciples.

Finally, after a period of two more years at PISAI as director of studies, I settled in Marseille a few months ago. Our community is in the northern quarters of the city. I am first of all trying to reestablish real contact with grassroots Islam and I have deliberately refrained from any teaching activity for a time. To reform this contact, I am developing two types of activity: First, I am a public letter-writer in a post office in a quarter where a large part of the population is Muslim (Maghrib and Comoros); secondly, I have engaged in literacy coaching with women from the Maghrib in a social center in our quarter.

Following this largely autobiographical overview, I would like to return to certain aspects of my relationship with Islam. I will start with the official dialogue with Islam.

I must admit to being somewhat disenchanted with large conferences. First of all I feel there is an imbalance among participants: on the Christian side we have specialists not only in their own religion, but also in Islamic studies. On the Muslim side those we encounter are most frequently university scholars who are generally serious in their commitment to Islam and are well informed about it, but they have only limited knowledge of Christianity, to which they have devoted little intellectual effort. Dialogue under these circumstances naturally is restricted to generalities. In addition, direct theological discourse fairly soon reaches a dead end, since the Qur'an, considered to be the direct Word of God, explicitly denies the three main Christian mysteries: the Trinity, the Incarnation, and the Redemption. Furthermore, as I have already mentioned, there is the risk of deviation towards political issues. This all generates a degree of frustration with these large events. In these encounters with Muslim partners, I would like each side to feel able to believe in the sincerity of the spiritual purpose of the other: all too often there are certain misunderstandings and certain political presuppositions.

This is the reason why I much prefer individual encounters. This can be likened to the fourth form of dialogue in the now classic typology of Muslim-Christian dialogue, i.e. the dialogue of life, dialogue of common action, encounters among specialists, and sharing of religious experience. It is indeed this last aspect that attracts me most. Occasions are in fact few, but when they do occur they make up for numerous frustrations. In individual encounters, two people are not one facing the other, but side-by-side before God, disarmed before his mystery, instead of each being shut up in the citadel of his own religious system. It is on these occasions that we can share the best of ourselves. In such moments I feel no desire to convert, only to enter into deep communion. I am convinced that the real encounter with Islam occurs among people who are genuinely seeking God. One of my most ardent desires is that Islam will find a way to reconcile itself with its immensely rich spiritual tradition.

It is clear that my prolonged contact with Islam has had an impact on my Christian faith: I quite naturally felt called upon to go deeper into what fundamentally constitute our differences, that is to say above all the mystery of the Holy Trinity. I prefer to talk about Trinitarian monotheism, and I do indeed appreciate the habit that Oriental Christians have of making the sign of the cross and saying "In the name of the Father, the Son, and the Holy Spirit, the one and only God, Amen." My exploration of Trinitarian monotheism is of course deepened by the meditation on—or, more precisely, the contemplation of—the expression "God is Love"; this name is not included in the ninety-nine names of God in Islam, beautiful though they are. The God of Love cannot be static or monolithic; he appears to me as a flow of life in which I am invited to take part. My prayer consists in opening myself up to this flow of life.

To sum up the way in which I view the essential difference between Islam and Christianity in a short statement: "In Islam God gives to us, in Christianity God gives himself to us." This is to me the ultimate basis of our differences. The mystery of the Incarnation is obviously the direct consequence of the fact that God, being love, gives himself to us and thus comes to meet us. I also needed to go deeper into the mystery of the Redemption: in contrast to Islam which presents itself as a religion of success (this is found even in the call to prayer), the issue in Christianity is to integrate failure, suffering, and the cross. To some extent, it seems to me that Shi'a Islam, on account of its history, lends itself better to this than Sunni Islam.

However, the fact that I have lived in Muslim countries has encouraged me to adopt a contemplative attitude—to consider, as the Second Vatican Council suggested, that Islam is part of God's plan for humanity. The issue on both sides is to adopt God's own patience, a "geological" patience as Fr. Monchanin used to say.

Nevertheless, after all this, I do not think that I am likely to convert to Islam. Naturally, Muslims have often said to me "since you know the Qur'an so well, why don't you convert?" In many instances I think this invitation is superficial and not well thought out. In others, it arises from a genuine concern to have me share in what my interlocutor holds most dear, and in this case I appreciate the attitude. In general I respond by saying, "I am in my mother's religion." This response often has the happy effect of leading to a consideration of the conditioning each one of us has received through the circumstances of our place of birth, social environment, and influences encountered.

Nevertheless, I am still fascinated by certain practical aspects of Islam. Its great coherency calls me back to my own fidelity. I can see in it a sense of adoration and an acute sense of community (while in fact Muslims talk of it less than we do); there is also the respect for the Word of God, manifest in particular by the way in which they treat the Qur'an; and there is the practice of hospitality, inviting me to develop a sense of the other, according to Massignon's well-known saying: "The truth can be found only by practicing hospitality."

I also greatly admire certain practical aspects of Islam. I think Muhammad showed genuine religious genius in planning the believer's day by way of the five prayers, his week by the Friday Prayer, his year by the remarkable practice of Ramadan, and his lifetime with the pilgrimage. I sometimes envy this practicality. I like to share in the Ramadan *iftars*; I like to hear the accounts of pilgrims returning from the Hajj. And I sometime surmise that Muhammad was in fact more practical than Jesus. Imagine for one moment what would have resulted if Muhammad had said, "Ramadan is for man, and not man for Ramadan." I think Ramadan would no longer exist, and it is indeed what has happened to a large extent to the Christian Lent. Christ called us to freedom, he gave us freedom, and I am very grateful for it. But I am sad to see that man has not really succeeded in living fully this invitation to freedom.

This has led me to develop a sort of theory: I am deeply convinced that Christianity is far better equipped than Islam for those who wish to commit themselves deeply, i.e. the elite (in Arabic *al-khass*). However for "ordinary mortals" (*al-'amm*) Islam with its practical realism sometimes seems to me to be better suited. People unfortunately need to be told what they should do, and Islam certainly does tell them. Jesus confronted us with our freedom, but what do we do with it? Nevertheless, I, of course, still believe, like St. Paul, that "Christ is the end of the law so that there may be righteousness for everyone who believes" (Rom. 10:4 NRSV).

This contrast between the elite and the common people brings me to another thought: I can see that my judgment about Islam contains a degree of ambiguity. On the one hand I can see the development of Islam, the widespread practice, and the increasingly visible demographic growth in France. In this connection, I have in my mind the picture of a scene encountered during a trip to India: the Friday Prayer in the grand mosque of Delhi, or again in Hyderabad, where you see 20,000 men performing the gestures of prayer all together; viewing this scene I experienced a feeling of enormous strength, which is also a source of inertia; and I was thinking to myself, where are the new thinkers of Islam? On the other hand, I hear the concerns of numerous Muslim intellectuals. It is enough to quote the titles of a certain number of recent books: *Le livre du musulman désemparé pour entrer dans le troisième millénaire* (*The Book of the Muslim at a Loss How to Enter the Third Millennium*); *L'islamisme contre l'islam* (*Islamism versus Islam*); *La crise de la culture islamique* (*The Crisis in Islamic Culture*); *Le malaise arabe* (*The Arab Malaise*). In the 1980s the Tunisian author H'mida Enneifer founded an extremely interesting journal, *15/21*, which signified that Islam was entering the fifteenth century while Christianity was entering the twenty-first century.

So who can decide whether this is development or crisis?

I have of course lived too long in direct contact with Muslims ever to confuse the tranquil Islam of the "silent majority" with the sometimes violent extremism that fills the headlines. But I do find myself thinking that this tranquil Islam, which claims to be a religion of peace, is too timid in setting itself apart from extremist Islam, and because of this it carries a good measure of responsibility. To cut out the canker from the fruit requires more positive action. I am convinced that Islamic fundamentalism ultimately is the enemy of Islam.

The twentieth century was very much the century of ecumenism. I am convinced that the twenty-first century will be the century of interreligious relations. And I think that the theology of non-Christian religions, like the theology of religious pluralism, is still in its cradle. I subscribe to what Hans Küng says: "There will be no peace in the world without peace among the religions." And I subscribe even more wholeheartedly to the words of Abraham Lincoln, the sixteenth president of the United States: "Let us not rush to say that God is on our side, let us pray to be on God's side."

This chapter was originally written in French,
translated into English by Angela Verdier,
and second-read by Anna-Regula Sharp.

Engaging in Christian–Muslim Relations

A Personal Journey

Michael L. Fitzgerald

I have already written about the origins of my involvement in relations with Muslims,[1] but in a word I could say that I owe everything to the missionary society to which I belong, the Missionaries of Africa (White Fathers). It is true, though, that when as a boy I left home to start training for the missionary priesthood, I was not thinking about the Islamic world. The attention of the White Fathers in the United Kingdom was focused on Black Africa. The imagination of the young minor seminarians was nourished by stories about Ghana and Nigeria, Tanzania (Tanganyika as it was then called), and Uganda. It was in the senior seminary, during the second year of philosophy, that one of the staff members talked about his time in Tunisia and aroused my interest. I volunteered to continue my

---

1. Cf. *Dieu rêve d'unité. Les catholiques et les religions: les leçons du dialogue. Entretiens avec Annie Laurent* (Paris: Bayard, 2005), 5–15; "My Pilgrimage in Mission" in *International Bulletin of Missionary Research* 30, no. 2 (April 2006): 88–91; Michael L. Fitzgerald and John Borelli, *Interfaith Dialogue. A Catholic View* (London and New York: SPCK/Orbis Books, 2006), 1–12.

studies in North Africa and was eventually sent to Carthage, Tunisia, where the White Fathers had an international theology seminary.

The 1957 General Chapter of the White Fathers decided to give a specific direction to each of the four theological centers. For Carthage this meant, quite naturally, a greater focus on relations with Muslims. The program was enriched with a course on Islamic studies. What would have been more useful would have been a reflection on the different fields of theology—fundamental, dogmatic, moral, and sacramental—from the point of view of dialogue with Muslims. Unfortunately the staff members lacked the training to provide this. However, a small dose of classical Arabic was introduced, two hours per week, with teachers such as Fr. Maurice Borrmans and Fr. Jean Quéméneur initiating us and at the same time demonstrating their enthusiasm for this language, which is a key to understanding Islam. We also benefited by talks from Fr. André Demeerseman, one of the founders of l'Institut des Belles Lettres Arabes, a center for cultural contacts with Tunisian society. I also remember a visit from Fr. Serge de Beaureceuil, a French Dominican who spent many years of his life in Afghanistan. He, too, gave witness to the mission of "presence" so characteristic of the religious men and women living in majority Muslim countries.

Some of my fellow students set themselves to learn the Tunisian dialect. I had missed out on this, as I had been told to improve my French, but I did accompany them, from time to time on days off, on visits to the surrounding villages. They would engage in conversation with anyone they met, share food, and try to put in a good word based on the Gospel. We were, after all, budding missionaries.

One other thing I learned, not from theology classes but from conversation with a fellow student: the importance of relating to Jesus as a person. Before that my religion had been very cerebral. This more experiential approach has proved most valuable in sustaining me throughout the years of mission through dialogue.

Although I volunteered for mission among Muslims, with Nigeria as my first choice, I was sent to Rome after ordination to the priesthood for further studies in theology. Thinking that I was destined for formation work in seminaries, I tended to leave aside Arabic and the Islamic world. To my surprise, at the end of this period, I was asked to join the staff of the Pontifical Institute of Arabic Studies (IPEA) which had just been transferred from Tunis to Rome. The superior general asked me to reflect well since this would determine the rest of my life, but I could hardly refuse. It did mean, however, further training in Arabic, which I was allowed to undertake in London, at the School of Oriental and African Studies (SOAS).

What struck me at SOAS was the respect that staff members—Jews, Christians, and Muslims—showed to a young priest. There was, in fact, a strictly academic atmosphere, with a rather reserved attitude to religion, giving no space to proselytizing or polemic. From time to time, not often enough really, I went to Regent's Park mosque to get help with Arabic from the resident imam. I remember one day when the imam came to a meeting in the junior common room at SOAS and suddenly said: "Now Father Michael will explain the Trinity in five minutes." I demurred, thinking then, as I still do, that the right atmosphere has to be created if we wish to talk about the deepest mysteries of our faith.

On my return to the IPEA in Rome, I started to help initiate the first-year students into the rudiments of Arabic. At the same time I followed the classes on the Qur'an given by Fr. Robert Caspar, as also a seminar on *tafsir* lead by him. His approach was philological but at the same time religious. We were lead to appreciate the message of the Qur'an as it developed historically, as also the Muslims' understanding of their own Holy Book. Caspar also taught courses on Islamic theology and mysticism and produced textbooks for these, which were to prove immensely useful to me later. In his writings, he displayed a sympathetic attitude towards Islam, while at the same time a readiness to engage in a Christian evaluation of this religion. He later crystallized his reflections in his useful book *Pour un regard Chrétien sur l'Islam.*[2] It is, I think, important to seize the dynamics of this approach. He was not looking at the Qur'an or *kalam* through Christian glasses, but trying to expound the religious realities of Islam as objectively as possible, and only then seeing how they challenge Christians.

After one year, I was again on the move, this time to the Department of Religious Studies and Philosophy at the University of Makerere, Uganda. My official post was as lecturer in Christian and Islamic theology. In fact, I was never asked to take courses on Christianity, and for at least half the time I spent in Makerere I was the only lecturer in Islamic studies. When I arrived, I was welcomed by my Muslim colleague, Said Hamdun, a Kenyan from the coast. He was friendly with Christians and was often asked to give talks on Islam in seminaries and theological colleges. I learned that he had been in favor of having a Christian colleague sharing with him the burden of Islamic studies I must admit that I was expecting him to

2. Robert Caspar, *Pour un regard chrétien sur l'Islam* (Paris: Centurion, 1990), 206-7.

reserve to himself the more sensitive courses on the Qur'an and the beliefs of Muslims, leaving me with the historical development of the religion. In fact he left me free to choose which courses I liked. This openness and confidence I found most encouraging. Unfortunately Said was to leave for Nairobi a few months later.

It was, nevertheless, with some trepidation that I applied myself to the task of lecturing on Islam. First-year students in religious studies all had to take the course Introduction to Islam, so there were both Christians and Muslims present in class. Second- and third-year students, however, who had chosen Islam as their special subject, were all Muslims. How would they react to a Catholic priest as their lecturer? From the outset, I made it clear that my task was not to teach them, but to help them to study and learn. They did not need to accept what I said, but they had to present good arguments for holding a different position.

In some ways I was lucky, for the majority of the Muslim students were Ismailis, followers of the Aga Khan. They knew very little about Sunni Islam, which I had studied, and so they could learn from me. At the same time, in conversations outside of classes, I learned much from them about their own tradition. I never hid the fact that I was a Catholic priest, and it was known that I was part of the community that worshiped in the Catholic chapel. It seems to me that this rootedness in my own religion, combined with a respectful attitude towards Islam, helped towards acceptance. In an evaluation at the end of the first year, I asked the students if they had been satisfied. Most replied yes, though one girl added that she would have preferred to have had a Muslim lecturer. This raises a much debated point: Can a religion be taught by a person not of that religion? In a meeting organized by the World Council of Churches, some Nigerian Muslims were holding forth strongly that the teaching of Islam in universities should be reserved to Muslims. I was told that the Muslim cochair of the meeting, who happened to be a former student of mine from Makerere and who was at that time Ugandan ambassador to Saudi Arabia, intervened in the debate saying that this proposition was ridiculous. He pointed to his own experience. He had studied under a Catholic Father who had encouraged him to specialize in Islamic studies and when he had to leave the University of Nairobi on becoming ambassador, he had seen to it that his post was taken over by a Christian lady. The best solution, probably, is for a joint venture where Muslims and Christians (or people of other religions) work together as a team.

After two years in Makerere, I was called back to Rome, yet there was no hurry, since the academic year in Uganda finished in April and the new academic year in Rome did not begin until October. I was able to journey slowly, spending time in Ethiopia, Sudan and Egypt. In Cairo, I was a guest of the Institut Dominicain d'Etudes Orientales. There I met Fr. George Anawati and Fr. Jacques Jomier, both pioneers of Christian–Muslim dialogue. I was probably too timid to draw from them information and insights, but the friendship formed was to stand me in good stead in future years.

In Rome the institute to which I returned was undergoing a transformation. Much work had been undertaken by Fr. Joseph Gelot, the Director, to insert it into the network of higher educational establishments run by the Catholic Church in Rome. New statutes had been prepared, and authorization had been obtained for granting degrees, first the licentiate and then later the doctorate. The institute eventually adopted a new name in Italian, Pontificio Istituto di Studi Arabi e d'Islamistica (PISAI), by which it is now known. Horizons had also broadened. In Tunisia the teaching institute at Manouba had been training people mainly for North Africa and to a lesser extent for sub-Saharan Africa. The transfer to Rome had made it imperative to think of other areas of the Islamic world, particularly Asia, but also to take into account the encounter with Muslims in Europe. This entailed launching a program for English-speaking students, and also providing some introductory courses of Arabic and Islamic studies in Italian. The teaching through French continued of course, and for a couple of years I found myself standing in for Fr. Caspar who had opted to stay in Tunisia. Fortunately his course notes provided solid food for a fledgling lecturer. If I consider my own attempts at a Christian evaluation of Islam, I would say that I was influenced by Karl Rahner. It was not so much his theory about "anonymous Christians," but rather an essay in the collection *Qaestiones Disputatae* on the continuing role of prophets and prophecy in the Church.[3]

I think that what sustained all these activities of PISAI, undertaken by a small staff, was a sense of service to the wider Church. Pope Paul VI had wanted to have this institute for the study of Islam in Rome, and had arranged to have it housed in a prestigious building, Sant'Apollinare. The least we could do in return was to give our best. This included being of service to other Catholic institutes in Rome, through teaching (for several years I taught at the Pontificia Università Urbaniana, the missionary university) or through publications. I remember hesitating when an article

---

3. Karl Rahner, *Visions and Prophecies*, Qaestiones Disputatae 10 (London: Burns and Oates, 1963; org., *Visionen und Prophezeiungen* [Herder, 1963]).

had been solicited for the journal published by the Congregation for
Catholic Education. It was Fr. Gelot who encouraged me to share some of
the little knowledge I had accumulated.[4] This was, in fact, the first of many
articles on different aspects of Christian–Muslim relations.

The spirit of service was perhaps the key to accepting the role of director of PISAI to which my superiors decided to appoint me at the beginning
of the academic year 1972. I was the youngest member of the team, and the
least experienced, but the task entrusted to me was essentially one of coordination. I continued what my predecessor had started, in particular the
invitations to visiting professors, both Muslims and non-Muslims. The
program of these visits usually included a talk given for a larger public,
since we wished to allow the moderate voices of our Muslim friends to
reach a wider public. Whenever this was acceptable, we offered the visiting
lecturers the possibility of being guests of the community. Hospitality
has often been emphasized, by Massignon and others, as an important
component of dialogue.

IPEA/PISAI had its own publication, *Etudes Arabes*, directed at former
students in order to encourage them to keep up their study of Arabic. Each
issue consisted of a selection of Arabic texts translated into French, plus
some other pedagogical material. At first merely cyclostyled, it later developed into a printed publication. Some of the translations were reproduced
in another cyclostyled publication run by the White Fathers in France,
Comprendre, and later *Se Comprendre*. PISAI undertook to provide an
English-language equivalent. *Encounter: Documents for Muslim–Christian
Understanding*, which has been published since 1974. Then it was decided
to launch a scientific review on Christian–Muslim dialogue, and thus was
born in 1975 the journal *Islamochristiana*. All this would not have been
possible without the commitment and enthusiasm of Robert Caspar and
Maurice Borrmans, and the contribution of the whole staff of PISAI.

As if he does not have already enough to do, there seems to be a tradition of confiding other tasks to the director of PISAI. He is traditionally
appointed to be a consultor (i.e. an advisor) of the Pontifical Council for
Interreligious Dialogue (formerly the Secretariat for Non-Christians).
This brought me into contact with Cardinal Pignedoli, who was a great
example of dialogue through friendship, and Monsignor Rossano, who was
the theological force behind the cardinal. Mgr. Rossano was a biblical
scholar by training, and not a specialist in any particular world religion.
This perhaps gave him a certain freedom when engaging in dialogue. It has

4. "The Islamic approach to God" in *Seminarium* no 2 (1972): 328–39.

become my conviction that our partners in dialogue, while happy to find in us a sympathetic approach to their religion, do not really want to listen to us talking about their religion, but rather about our own. Dialogue is hindered if we are not able to articulate our Christianity in a way that is understandable for our partners.

Even before becoming a consultor I had been asked to represent the Secretariat for Non-Christians at an international Christian–Muslim dialogue meeting, organized by the World Council of Churches (WCC) in Broumana, Lebanon, in 1972. I remember having been disappointed by this meeting, mainly because too many subjects were tackled and nothing studied in depth. Yet I learned later that follow-up meetings in Accra, Ghana, and in Hong Kong, had allowed the experience to be shared with a larger number of people. This showed me that international meetings can serve a useful purpose if the participants, on their return to their own countries, are willing to share what they have learnt. Broumana was also important as an ecumenical initiative, and the ecumenical dimension of the work of dialogue has from this time been important for me.

Another task given to the director of PISAI was to be the organizing secretary of the Journées Romaines, an international gathering of Christians engaged in Christian–Muslim relations held every two years.[5] These meetings allowed for a sharing of information, experience and concerns, facilitated by such prominent actors in dialogue as Mgr. Henri Teissier, former Archbishop of Algiers, and Fr. Samir Khalil, S.J., the well-known Jesuit scholar of Egyptian origin. The Journées Romaines were not exercises in dialogue, but rather an opportunity for Christians to reflect on their relations with Muslims. This intrareligious dialogue or time of evaluation, though fastidious for some, is necessary for the development of a balanced approach to Christian–Muslim dialogue. Such gatherings were also of great encouragement to those who often felt marginalized in their attempts to reach out to their Muslim brothers and sisters, sometimes in very difficult circumstances.

At one time during this period, I was invited to be a resource person in a seminar on Christian–Muslim relations that the Oblates of Mary Immaculate were organizing for some of their members in different countries of Asia. The seminar was to last a week and to be held in Singapore. Since PISAI was now reaching out to Asia as well, I requested the staff to allow me a month's leave of absence for a study tour. They in fact gave me

5. Cf. Maurice Borrmans, "Les 'Journées Romaines' et le dialogue islamo-chrétien" in *Islamochristiana* 30 (2004) : 111–22.

two months, which allowed me to visit the Philippines, Indonesia, India, and Pakistan.

In the Philippines I particularly wanted to visit the diocese of Iligan, in Mindanao, because the bishop, Mgr. Bienvenido (Benny) Tudtud was at that time taking a sabbatical at PISAI. When Bishop Tudtud returned to the Philippines he received permission to relinquish the part of his diocese that had a majority of Christians, and to set up the new prelature of St. Mary's in Marawi, a predominantly Muslim city and region. He initiated a new way of mission, in dialogue through presence, calling for volunteers who would share his vision.

During this short time in the Philippines, I was entrusted with a mission on the part of the superiors of the Missionaries of Africa. Our Society had been invited to the diocese of Marbel, in South Cotobato, in order to initiate the clergy into Christian–Muslim dialogue. It was suggested that a commitment of three or four years would be sufficient. I was asked to assess the project. My conclusion, after having visited several mission posts and having spoken with the bishop and others, was that a time span closer to thirty years would be necessary in order to accomplish the task properly. Since the purpose was to build relations between Christians and Muslims, those engaged in the project would need to be able to talk with both groups. They would therefore need to learn Visayan, the language of the majority of the Christians who were immigrants to Mindanao from the Central Islands of the Philippines, and also Maguindanaon, the language of most Muslims in this area, as well as perhaps other languages. This could surely not be done in a short time. How could my confrères initiate others into a dialogue if they were not able to enter into dialogue themselves? As a result of this fact-finding mission, the White Fathers did not accept the invitation to Marbel. This, perhaps, was disappointing for those who were counting on us, but my conviction then, as it still is now, is that dialogue is a slow process and that it is useless to try to look for quick results. The Gospel parables of the Kingdom, the seed sown, the leaven in the dough, inculcate in us this confident patience.

During this same trip, I visited the Henry Martyn Institute in Hyderabad, India, where Andreas D'Souza, a former student of PISAI, was working. Andreas arranged for me to give a public lecture at an Islamic university on the topic: "A Christian's Appreciation of Islamic Mysticism." I remember that after the talk some objections were raised. "You have referred to the Qur'an, but never in Arabic. Do you know Arabic?" I was asked. I apologized, but said that for reasons of time I had preferred to give the English version of the passages referred to. The second question was more fundamental: "You have spoken with enthusiasm of Sufism, so why are you not a Muslim?" In answer, I had to give my own witness to the plus values that I find in Christianity and in particular in a personal relationship with Jesus Christ. We always have to be ready to give an account of the hope that is within us.

The Singapore seminar gave rise to a further invitation to the Philippines the next year, to take part in a weeklong assembly of the Vicariate of Jolo, in Sulu. All the priests, religious men and women, and consecrated lay people were being brought together to reflect on the mission of the Vicariate in this area of which 97 percent of the population was Muslim. There were two resource persons: a Jesuit from the East Asian Pastoral Institute in Manila for the theological grounding of the reflection, and myself for the Islamic context. The facilitator, Terry Waite (who later became famous after being kidnapped in the Lebanon), insisted that the resource persons should give only one input each but should be ready to add comments as necessary all through the proceedings. This was fine by me, for the less work the better, but my Jesuit colleague was irate. He was a busy man; he had given up a number of engagements to be present; he had much more to contribute. Terry Waite, however, remained adamant— only one formal talk, the rest of the reflection would be based on the shared experience of the participants. One result of this method was that the participants discovered that they knew very little about Islam and requested that a series of lectures be given to them the following year, which was done. Responding to felt needs was, I am sure, a much more effective method than bombarding them with information to which they would not have been receptive.

After finishing two three-year mandates as director of PISAI it was time to hand over the position and leave my successor, Fr. André Ferré, space to maneuver. I asked to be sent to an Arabic-speaking country and was appointed to Sudan, to Halfa Jadida, a small town in the archdiocese of Khartoum, situated near the Ethiopian border about 370 miles by road from the capital. There our White Father community was engaged in both proclamation and dialogue. We looked after the small Christian community, made up mainly of Southern Sudanese, and went out to propose the Christian faith to those who had not yet committed themselves to a world religion. At the same time we made efforts to relate to the majority Muslim community, running a center for adult education and through other contacts. In both aspects of our apostolate we met with opposition. The Christians resented the time we gave to Muslims, thinking that all our attention should be devoted to them. For their part, our Muslim friends felt that we were wasting our time with these poor black southerners who, in their opinion, were good for nothing. Needless to say, this opposition only confirmed us in our dual approach. We had to show that the Church could not become a club catering only for its own, but must be open and at the service of the whole of society, and at the same time we felt that we were only following the Gospel of Jesus Christ in reaching out to those who were poor and despised.

I used to go from time to time to listen to a sheikh who, in a nearby quarter, ran a *halqa*, a study circle where he expounded the Qur'an and other Islamic texts. I admired the man. He lived simply and I saw that he would go out to visit people in their homes. He radiated goodness. When I was about to leave Sudan for good, I went to the *halqa* and told him I was going. At the end of the session he prayed for me, that I might see the light at last and embrace Islam. This did not annoy me. He had never made any attempts to convert me to Islam but I found it natural that he should wish to share with me that which he held most precious, namely his faith. To my mind, this incident throws light on a distinction that needs to be made between the *desire* that someone adopt my religion, and the *proposition* of this religion or the *invitation* to adhere to it. The first is universal, applying to all, whereas the second is specific and is dependent on circumstances and the inspiration of the Holy Spirit.

After two years in the Sudan, I was expecting to return to PISAI, but I was elected for a six-year term as a member of the General Council of the Missionaries of Africa. I was again based in Rome but there was much travelling to different countries, in Africa and elsewhere. Part of my brief was to foster interest in the apostolate of Christian-Muslim encounter. This has always been a distinctive element in the work of the White Fathers but it was only a part of our work, and a small part at that. There were many times when promoting contact with Muslims seemed to be an uphill battle. Sustaining this effort was the vision of our founder, Cardinal Lavigerie (1825–92), who did not encourage the baptism of individual Muslims, without first attempting to change the whole of society (he was archbishop of Algiers). The cardinal's intuitions were developed by Henri Marchal (1875–1957), whose writings my confrère and friend Jean-Marie Gaudeul studied and rendered accessible.[6]

When this period of service came to an end, the expectation was again to rejoin PISAI, and I did in fact become a member of the community

6. Jean-Marie Gaudeul, *Encounters and Clashes. Islam and Christianity in History*, I A Survey (Rome: Pontificio Istituto di Studi Arabi e d'Islamistica, 2000), 314–20.

once more. However, early in 1987, I was appointed secretary of the Secretariat for Non-Christians (to be renamed the following year Pontifical Council for Interreligious Dialogue [PCID]). For over fifteen years, I worked closely with the then president of the council, Cardinal Francis Arinze, and drew strength from his deep faith, his readiness to listen, his willingness to engage with people of all religions, his sense of humor, and his capacity firmly to uphold a Christian position without giving offence. I joined the council just after the major event of the Assisi World Day of Prayer for Peace, an initiative of Pope John Paul II. I often used to say that, in the field of interreligious dialogue, Pope John Paul was way out ahead of us, and we were running to catch up with him. We always received great encouragement from him.

Working in PCID entailed an enlargement of scale. It was no longer only a question of relations with Muslims, but now with people of all religions. This, in fact, turned out to be an advantage, since it put Christian–Muslim relations into a broader context. Christian–Muslim dialogue continued, of course, and indeed increased as more Muslim partners sought to have relations with the Vatican. These dialogues were in most cases of an official nature that brought with it certain limitations: It could not be expected that the Holy See, or our partners representing various Muslim institutions, would come out with daringly new positions. The value of the meetings was perhaps more of a symbolic nature, showing that Christian and Muslim religious leaders *could* meet, and thus encouraging further encounters at the local level.

There were also trilateral and multilateral meetings. Since PCID was not responsible for relations with Jews (this was the task of the Commission for Relations with Jews which came under the Pontifical Council for Promoting Christian Unity), the trilateral dialogues were a response to initiatives of the World Council of Churches. Let it be mentioned here in passing that cooperation with the dialogue office of the WCC has been strong from the beginning and a number of joint projects have been carried out over the years. Personally, I found these ecumenical contacts very stimulating.

PCID was doing nothing exceptional but only fulfilling its brief in organizing occasional multilateral meetings. There was, for instance, one on marriage and the family, where the different religious traditions were represented by couples. There was another meeting on resources for peace that was a sharing on the Holy Books of the different religions. The most spectacular meeting, and perhaps the most successful, was the Interreligious Assembly held in the Vatican in preparation for the new Millennium.

It brought together over two hundred people from around twenty religious traditions who spent most of their time discussing together in small groups. Cardinal Arinze decided against a draft statement and insisted that the groups should provide the material for the final declaration and message. This was done, almost miraculously, and the message was solemnly read out, in the presence of Pope John Paul II during a ceremony in St. Peter's Square, which ended after nightfall in a sea of candles.

During these years the PCID, together with the Congregation for Evangelisation, brought out the document *Dialogue and Proclamation*,[7] a balanced and realistic statement. It is nevertheless a previous document, *Dialogue and Mission*[8] that has provided me with greater inspiration. In this document interreligious dialogue is placed firmly within the overall mission of the Church, together with the simple presence of the believing community, prayer and worship, service to humankind, and announcing the good news of the Gospel in preaching and teaching (paragraph 13). Dialogue is thus not a marginal activity of the Church, but an essential task, and one for which there may be special vocations. The document also has a Trinitarian thrust to it, insisting on God the Father's "pervasive love unlimited by space and time" (paragraph 22), the unity of the Son of God made man with every single member of the human race (paragraph 23), and the action of the Holy Spirit in the depths of people's consciences leading them towards the truth. "The Spirit both anticipates and accompanies the path of the Church," and so it is the Church's task to discern the Spirit's presence and to follow the Spirit's lead "as a humble and discreet collaborator" (paragraph 24). What will the result be? That is in fact God's affair, not ours. But the goal of dialogue is conversion, not to be understood in the sense of a change of religious allegiance, but in the biblical sense of "the humble and penitent return of the heart to God in the desire to commit one's life more generously to Him" (paragraph 37). This is a fruit that concerns both our partners in dialogue and ourselves, a fruit worth aiming at, and worth waiting for.

---

7. "Dialogue and Proclamation. Reflections and Orientations on Interreligious Dialogue and the Proclamation of the Gospel of Jesus Christ (1991)," in *Interreligious Dialogue. The Official Teaching of the Catholic Church from the Second Vatican Council to John Paul II (1963-2005)*, ed. Francesco Gioia (Boston: Pauline Books & Media, 2006), 1156–89.

8. Secretariat for Non-Christians, "The Attitude of the Church toward the Followers of Other Religions. Reflections and Orientations on Dialogue and Mission (1984)," in Gioia, 1116–29.

In February of 2006, I was appointed by Pope Benedict XVI to be his representative in Cairo. Interreligious dialogue was to be pursued in a new context. My mind goes back to Bishop Benny Tudtud (mentioned above). At whatever time of day you would meet him—morning, afternoon or evening—Benny would always say "good morning." This was not a mistake in English, which he spoke perfectly. It seemed to me that he was implying that every encounter is a new beginning. We have to receive from the Lord, from the Spirit, new energy to begin again. May it always be so.

All Over the World, the Spirit Is Moving

Jean-Marie Gaudeul

For as long as I can remember, I have lived and moved in an atmosphere of faith. Both my parents came from a traditional Roman Catholic milieu and had gone through an experience of conversion to deeper, personal faith in Christ. I received from them a real thirst for a personal relationship with him, from which I knew with certainty, at the age of six or seven, that he was calling me to be a missionary in Africa, a "White Father." By inclination, I would rather have chosen to become a medical doctor following my father's footsteps. I cannot say that I was particularly keen on religious practices but the "call" was always there.

This is how at seventeen, I joined the seminary of the Missionaries of Africa and went through their training, which at the time took seven years—in France, North Africa, the Netherlands, and England. Halfway through these studies, I was called up for my military service. This was during the Algerian war of independence. With all the young Frenchmen of my generation, I was sent to Algeria. At my request, I did not serve in a fighting unit but in a body of officers whose mission was to bridge the gap between French administration and the population. This was my first encounter with Muslims. Although the situation, dominated as it was by guerrilla warfare, was not conducive to establishing personal friendships, my religious training allowed me to see believers in the Algerians that I met. Their faith—different though it was from my own—meant that they lived on a level that was familiar to me and this led to brief episodes during which we simply met as praying people next to one another.

Nevertheless, the general climate of violence in which we lived— murders, repression, arrests, tortures, and executions—generated in many of us a state of moral and physical tension so that I was happy to escape at the end of those twenty-eight months of service, to resume my theological training in London. I was ordained to the priesthood three years later.

Tanzania

Having learnt the language (this is always the first task of the members of our missionary society), I was sent to Mwanza, a town situated on the southern shores of Lake Victoria, for parish work at the cathedral. My first interest did not lie in the direction of dialogue with the Muslims, even though they formed more than 45 percent of the town's population. My attention was rather drawn to the division between the various Christian communities who worked in the area. I was the youngest and the least of all the priests working there but they let me get in touch with all the churches, one by one, offering to organize regular and friendly contacts. In general, I was well received and within a few months, we priests and pastors met to talk about doctrinal and pastoral matters.

Mwanza was a meeting point of people of various national and religious origins: there were Africans, Indians, Europeans, Hindus, Sikhs, and Sunni, Shi'a, and Ibadi Muslims. Quite naturally, I began to visit non-Christian religious leaders as well as Christian parishioners. This did not develop any further because I was asked by my superiors to go to Rome. They asked if I would be interested in learning Arabic over a period of three years and specializing in the study of Islam. Indeed I would! Especially since the aim was to come back to Tanzania and try to combine parish work and inter-religious dialogue.

Islamic Studies and First Contacts

My stay in Rome marked a turning point in my life on several counts. At the Pontifical Institute for Arabic and Islamic Studies (PISAI), my first task was to learn Arabic. Knowing that I was supposed to go back to Tanzania where the language spoken was Swahili and not to go to the Arab world, my aim was to learn the language of the Qur'an and of the main sources of Islam. In view of the sort of encounters I had already experienced, I memorized passages from the Qur'an, Hadith, and spiritual texts which could draw the conversation to the level of spiritual exchanges. I sensed that Christians and Muslims were sharply at odds on matters of doctrine but could meet fruitfully on the subject of spirituality: attitudes of faith, prayer, trust in God, patience, and so on.

At that time, the Catholic Church was attempting to put into practice the orientations of the Second Vatican Council. That, combined with all the turmoil of the world crisis of values, did shake the old institutional and traditional ways; many left the priesthood or their religious orders. One could not but experience anxiety at the wisdom of one's past commitments to mission work.

It is in that context that I was hit by an event that changed my outlook and my life completely. Up until then, my response to God had been largely a matter of will power. At the end of 1971, I was led to discover the grace of yielding to the Holy Spirit, receiving from him direction and energy, peace and joy. I finished my studies and went back to Tanzania trusting in the Holy Spirit to guide me in my ministry to Christians and in my encounters with Muslims.

I was sent to two towns successively: Tabora and Singida. These were not big cities. The parishes in which I served were of a size that allowed sufficient time to know the parishioners and to become acquainted with Muslim leaders.

I went about it without preconceived pastoral plans. I prayed and trusted God to lead me to the people he wanted me to meet. And that he did. One encounter led to another, and a time came when the imams of that city found it indispensable that I share in their festivals as a friend and honored guest. These developments did not prevent parish work, preaching, counseling, and contact with other Christian churches. What sustained me was the daily discovery that I could draw from my spiritual experience to help Muslim friends as well as Christian brethren in their difficulties when they happened to share them with me, provided that I kept listening to God's guidance minute by minute.

From time to time, I was asked to go to the major seminary to teach a course on Islam to the students. A Lutheran training center asked for a course, then a session for Catholic priests. Over these three years, I had been feeling increasingly tired and suddenly I was struck down, sent to hospital, rushed to Nairobi by the flying doctor and then to a hospital in Paris. My days in Africa were over.

Teaching in Rome

As I was slowly recovering, I was asked to go back to PISAI in Rome and join the staff. My knowledge of Arabic, as I mentioned above, was not sufficient, in my eyes, to enable me to teach that language. My job was to teach Islamic studies to English-speaking students.

I was still trying to regain my strength but I accepted. It was hard work. I had to spend hours and hours of feverish preparation to offer to the students the level of teaching that they were entitled to expect from an institute of that kind. Giving a general initiation course meant delving into history, theology, law and more. Shortage of personnel led to me teaching other special subjects: Islam in Africa, Shi'a Islam, modern trends, and even the history of Christian–Muslim controversies. Fortunately, I found some balance in my life attending prayer groups and counseling a number of people.

If I had few occasions to get in touch with real flesh and blood Muslims— there were guest lecturers every now and again—these days of research immersed me in the ocean of Muslim thought. The situation in which I found myself, giving presentations that made sense to the students, required intense reflection on the material offered by the library. Little by little, events, books, and authors sorted themselves out into some sort of order; on many subjects, the picture was coming into focus.

Of course, even then, my most precious conviction was that however clever my ideas and courses, the reality far exceeded—and perhaps contradicted—what I thought I understood. In my seven years at PISAI, I never lost a sense of being unequal to the job that I had been asked to do.

Living in Rome and teaching in English meant that the students came from all over the world: Indians, Pakistanis, Filipinos, Malaysians, and Indonesians met with Africans, Americans, Australians, and Europeans. These students were sent by their churches to be trained in things Islamic before returning to their home countries. They all brought to the Institute some experience of Christian–Muslim encounter in their homeland. Frequently they spoke of situations of violence and oppression and I was often touched by their courage and determination to transform resentment into love. Living a sheltered life as I was, made me feel humble in the light of their example. One student of mine told me that my course had influenced him to go and work with Muslims! He was killed a few months later.

It was at that time that I began to be invited by the White Fathers' novitiate to give an introductory course on Islam to the novices. A novitiate is not a study center; the emphasis is not on learning. The essential is to reflect prayerfully on one's life to discern whether one is called to belong to this missionary society with its particular tradition and experience. It just happened that I have always felt a great attraction to the life of our founder, Cardinal Lavigerie (1825–92). This may be due to the fact that we came from the same region. As a result, over the years, I had tried to see how the mission work done by my confrères and I fitted with the orientations given by the founder. All sorts of discussions were taking place in the Church and in our Society on the content and the relevance of these orientations after the Second Vatican Council. People argued and pulled in opposite directions. I needed to see clearly what was what if I wanted to make sense to the novices.

I asked and got permission to spend hours in our archives to study as closely as possible what had been the experience of White Fathers in Muslim regions of Africa. How did they try to live out their vocation? Did the founder's directions help them? That research helped me considerably: In the texts as well as in the facts, a certain approach had been found focusing on the Kingdom of God. Our priority, in Muslim circles as well as in other contexts, should be to speak of the Kingdom as Jesus did in his sermons. He did not call people to become Christians; he called them to respond to God's call as little children. From there the Spirit of God would lead them wherever he wanted.

These orientations were followed for a time but they were often overlaid with the desire to work for the Church as an institution. The spread of violent conflicts in Muslim countries then reduced the witnesses to silence; hence the lack of clarity in the minds of those who had come on the scene later.

I felt greatly encouraged and confirmed in my ministry. Writing later on the history of Christian–Muslim discussions (*Encounters and Clashes* [Rome: PISAI, 2000]), I found it necessary to summarize my findings on the subject in a few pages in the last chapter.

By 1982 all these activities brought about a state of fatigue such as to make it necessary to ask for a change. I asked to leave PISAI. I returned to Tanzania but after three months in Dar-es-Salaam, it became evident that I could not stand the climate. I was given a year of "rest" in our General House in Rome. In fact, it had been agreed that I would use that time to write one of my courses as a book which ended up being a doctoral dissertation: *Encounters and Clashes—A Historical Survey of Christian–Muslim Relations*. Once more, my health had broken down and since I could not envisage a return to Africa, I was appointed to France.

A Roaming Ministry

At first, I prepared an edition of the correspondence between a Muslim and a Christian of the ninth century for PISAI. Soon however, another idea took hold of me: For a number of years, I had tried to understand what the Muslims said of their faith and practices. Were the Christians active in telling the Muslims something of their own good news? And if they were, were their Christian words adapted to the Muslim minds in their search for truth?

With these questions in mind, I began searching everywhere for books, booklets, leaflets, tapes and other media devised by various groups to offer "a Christian word to Muslims." This brought me into contact with a great variety of groups, mostly from evangelical churches, who felt called to mission work among Muslims and spent their lives answering that call as best they could.

Their zeal and dedication were a source of inspiration to me. These people did not deserve the contempt in which many members of traditional churches held them. Of course, that contempt was often returned and these churches were accused of being tepid and lacking courage. Standing in between, I felt a bit lonely in my attempt to be fair to both sides.

What could I use from the best of all the material I had found? I could have tried to pick and choose from a theological or pastoral standpoint but I felt that it would be wrong to impose my own criteria, however sound, to judge what could be useful or profitable. I decided that it was preferable to see what was useful and profitable in actual fact. What were the ideas and arguments that Muslims appreciated and thought relevant to them? What were the ideas and arguments that were used by the Spirit of God to touch people and draw them to God's love manifested in Christ?

This is how I began to collect the testimonies of Muslims who had been touched by the Christian message and had come to faith in Christ. These stories were intensely personal and, of course, extremely complex as are all deep changes. After a few years, I thought I could discern some patterns in these itineraries and tentatively wrote a book about them: *Appelés par le*

Christ (Cerf, 1991), later published in English as: *Called from Islam to Christ* (Monarch Books, 1999).

Another ministry began at that time. The Catholic Faculty of Lyons, then the Catholic Institute of Paris asked me to give a few courses to their students. It became a steady commitment and for years I commuted between Lyons and Paris to give courses on modern trends in Islam, Christian–Muslim dialogue, Islam in France, and Islam in Africa. The French Catholic daily newspaper, *La Croix*, asked me to comment regularly on the news that involved Islam in France or in the world. Finally, the office of the French Bishops for Relations with Muslims (SRI) asked me to join their national council, which met several times a year, in an advisory capacity.

These commitments drew me away from my books and plunged me into the turmoil of our present world. The rise of radical Islamic groups and their violent manifestations were arousing the fear and distrust of many Christians and I tried to point to the possibility of a spiritual encounter that went deeper than the clash of cultures and civilizations. At the same time, that call to a deepening faith had to acknowledge the grounds for anxiety, the need of discernment and prudence, and the distortions that violent militants brought into the spirituality of Islam.

I have always been gifted with a facility to teach and to preach. This may explain why I began to receive invitations to give sessions on Islam or to preach spiritual retreats in many parts of the world: I found myself spending weeks and even months in countries such as Sierra Leone, Ghana, Mali, Ireland, Canada, Bangladesh, Australia, the Philippines, Morocco, Algeria, or Tunisia. The list is not complete but I thank the Lord for the opportunity to help all the people in those lands who worked to bring about a world built on God's plan of love for humankind. I was coming as a temporary guest or preacher, but those people who listened to my words with all their hearts and minds, were offering, at the risk of their lives sometimes, service and defenseless love to others, Muslims or Christians. I felt so small!

For some that love cost them everything and they were killed. Quite frequently, I thank God for the privilege of having known Bishop Tudtud in the Philippines; the four White Fathers killed in Tizi-Ouzou in 1994; Christian de Chergé, my friend for forty years, killed with his monks in Algeria; Bishop Claverie, killed in Oran in 1996 and so many others. The way in which they accepted to risk everything out of love is a constant source of strength and a very humbling reminder that I am far from their dedication. To realize that their sacrifice has been recognized and celebrated in many Muslim circles is a tremendous source of comfort and strength.

Officialdom

In 2000 I was asked to direct the SRI. This office of the French Bishops' Conference was founded in 1974 as part of the support services of the Church in France. I had been on its national advisory council for the previous fifteen years and was familiar with its mission. A year before, I had been appointed to the Vatican commission for dialogue with Muslims, which is part of the Pontifical Council for Interreligious Dialogue (PCID).

With these two appointments, I found myself working for the official administration of the Church. It meant working on the sidelines, since mine was a very minor position. On the one hand it meant a lot of speaking commitments and even more contacts. Ideally, the SRI must be in touch with the main representatives of the Muslim community in France. I tried to maintain those links and make them as friendly as possible. On the other hand, that function meant lots of meetings with Church circles, movements, and groups. Here again, I could feel the tensions and fears brought about by the "sudden" appearance of a new religion in France where the Catholic Church had long been in a dominant position. The temptation one could feel is that of stiffening against the new "dangers": secularism and Islam.

More than ever, it was necessary to show that a Christian does not draw his or her sense of identity from his or her opposition to the "other" but from a deeper listening to the voice within which calls each one of us by name. At the end of these six years at the SRI, I am not sure that being an "official voice" makes it easier to draw attention to that call within. However, I marveled at the response given by a number of Christian–Muslim couples when they were shown that they could share in spiritual matters even though discussion was so difficult at the doctrinal level. To help them find their way, we published a leaflet on praying together (*Vivre ensemble . . . et prier?* [SRI, Paris]).

From time to time, these functions brought invitations to official events of dialogue, in Rome, Libya, or Qatar. These events were interesting and allowed friendly contacts with officials on both sides. At the same time, one could not but wish there had been time for more informal dialogue.

And Now?

All those activities are over. I am well over the age limit for teaching: my notes and my books gather dust on the shelves. I am still producing a little publication called *Se Comprendre*. It is time to surrender all those years of work to the Lord. Let him use what he wants from all the words spoken or written and all the smiles and handshakes. He has let me see that some of those writings have been used here and there, even in other churches, to help prepare Christians to meet Muslims. Praise Him!

My greatest joy at this time is to remember Jesus's words: "Raised from the earth, I will draw all men to myself" (John 12:32). In many ways, visible or invisible, he is doing just that. His Spirit is drawing all men and women—Christians, Muslims or others—to listen to the call of selfless love. If God is love (1 John 4:8), his fatherly love can have no other aim than that of drawing all human beings to himself and hugging them in a fatherly embrace. Praise Him!

Synchronized Spiritualities

Paul Jackson

A feature of life at Marist College Ashgrove, in Brisbane, Australia, was an annual retreat. In the final year, this was done in a Carmelite monastery. Apart from talks by the priest conducting the retreat, a generous supply of pamphlets on various religious topics was made available to read. The writings of an American Jesuit priest, Daniel A. Lord, struck a chord within me. He was writing for teenagers. What he wrote came across to me as being "deep and meaningful." A desire to write something "deep and meaningful" was kindled within me and eventually led to a desire to become a Jesuit, like Fr. Lord, and write something that was helpful for others. A request to enter the Society of Jesus was made and, on January 18, 1956, an invitation to join the Jesuit Novitiate in Melbourne was received.

In late 1960 the Australian Provincial selected me to go with Peter Jones to the mission of the Australian Jesuits in Hazaribag, India. This came as a surprise, as thoughts about going to our Hazaribag mission had never occurred to me. Now, obviously, it was what God wanted, so that was the end of the matter. Tom Keogh joined Peter Jones and me and we set sail from Melbourne on December 27, 1960, and reached Mumbai on January 18, 1961.

We were assigned to St. Xavier's English Medium School, Hazaribag, which had about 450 boys in the hostel as well as day scholars. In December 1963 a couple of us young Jesuits took boys in a reserved carriage by train to Calcutta. Their parents would be waiting to receive them at the railway station. I was going through a difficult period at the time. Being a missionary, for me, meant sharing Jesus Christ with people. After all, I was a member of the Society of Jesus. Jesus was the focus of my life. The problem was that, apart from the Catholic boys who joined us for daily mass, the policy of the school was that we were not to talk to the boys about Jesus. They studied the story of his life in seventh class and that was their total exposure to Jesus.

Something happened in St. Xavier's College, Calcutta, to change my whole line of thinking. Fr. Putz, a famous Jesuit theologian and expert at the Second Vatican Council (1962–65) had just returned from the 1963 session. He gave a talk to the members of the community. He spoke about the vision of Pope John XXIII: "After the Council of Trent, the Church was like a fortress on a hilltop defending itself. That is not my idea of the Church. We must open all our doors and windows and reach out to all groups of people."

His words struck a chord within me. "Yes, that is what the Church should be like!" Walking on the college terrace, I surveyed Calcutta by night, which lay spread out below me. I began to reflect on the Pope's desire that the Church should reach out to all groups of people. It was clear that, in our Hazaribag mission, we were reaching out to the tribal people, the Adivasis, the "original inhabitants" of our region. The next group was that of upper caste Hindus. Most of the boys at St. Xavier's School belonged to this group. Then there were the low caste Hindus, known as Harijans in those days, but now referred to as Dalits, a word denoting oppressed people. Fr. Len Forster was trying to do something for some of these people. Was there any other group? The answer to this was simple—the Muslims! Was anyone trying to do anything for the Muslims? The simple answer was "no." Was anyone likely to do anything? Well, you would have to learn Urdu to do so, and no one was studying Urdu or was likely to do so. The whole focus of our attention was on learning Hindi. Faced with this situation, and still without having had a chance to study Hindi, I made a resolution: "Let me try to do something!" I had no idea what this "something" might be, except that it would involve learning Urdu after I had studied Hindi. From that night onwards my life had a specific direction— doing something for the Muslims of Hazaribag—without having any clear idea what this ultimately would be.

Back in St. Xavier's, Hazaribag, I took up reading about Islam in the limited time available to me. Even more importantly, I began to interact more consciously with the handful of Muslim boys in the hostel. One fine young lad was Zubair Ahmad. Without any conscious action plan on my part, this original way of acting actually became the pattern of my life. It would be devoted to serious study, combined with meeting and befriending Muslims. This symbiotic pattern of study leading to friendships, and of friendships encouraging and sustaining me over long years of study, has proved most enriching.

From mid-1964 until mid-1965, the opportunity to learn Hindi took me to Manresa House, Ranchi. Unfortunately, I fell sick with hepatitis and this interfered with my studies. In January 1965 my sister Norma came to do voluntary nursing in the Holy Family Hospital, Mandar, not far from Ranchi. Her presence was a great consolation. During this period, I kept up my interest in learning about Muslims and their religion by reading the entire collection of *Notes on Islam*. This collection was the work of Fr. Victor Courtois of Calcutta. The series came to an end with his death in 1960. Fr. Courtois could not hide his love for Muslims even if he had wanted to. It shone through the pages of his *Notes on Islam*. He was also a very learned man, as the series amply reveals, and had many Muslim friends, as I subsequently discovered.

From mid-1965 until March 1969, the study of theology was the task entrusted to me. St. Mary's Theologate was situated in Kurseong, in the Himalayan foothills. It was on the road to the well-known hill resort of Darjeeling. When I had fully entered into the rhythm of study, I undertook a project that brought me into contact with the Muslims of Kurseong Town. I volunteered to teach the children in the small school attached to the mosque. I proposed to teach the small children spoken English by the direct method. This meant using no words other than English. There are courses available that are designed along these lines. The basic principle was to begin with simple sentences, getting the children to recite their newfound English in unison. Each unit had to build carefully on the previous one. Charts were needed. These simple classes took a great deal of preparation, otherwise disaster would strike. My keenest student was the children's teacher. When the class was over, he would give me a lesson in Urdu and I then went to another teacher for a second lesson in Urdu. This was the routine for two afternoons each week for quite some time. Again the "study and personal contact" pattern naturally fell into place.

There then followed some years of teaching and working in schools, so that it was only in mid-1972, at thirty-five years of age, that I was finally allowed to explore possible courses of study. I lined up three universities: Aligarh Muslim University, Delhi University, and Lucknow University. I was keen to study Urdu. My first destination was Aligarh, where I promptly had a severe attack of asthma and was forced to go to Delhi where I was admitted to the Holy Family Hospital. My asthma disappeared as it had been an allergic reaction, but Bob Slattery suggested a visit to the Salesians at Don Bosco Technical School to see about accommodation and then to inquire about studying at Jamia Millia Islamia. Both of these institutions were within walking distance of the hospital and of each other.

The Salesians said I would be welcome but the final decision was in the hands of their provincial superior in Calcutta. The next visit was to Jamia Millia Islamia, where I met Prof. Mujeeb, the vice chancellor. When I explained that I was interested in studying Urdu, he realized the practical difficulties involved and suggested I study Medieval Indian History. On the basis of my philosophical studies, I could be accepted onto the two-year master's course. This is what I agreed to do. Unfortunately Mujeeb Sahib had a stroke and never formally taught me. I used to visit him regularly, however, and was amazed at how he retaught himself English and Urdu. His patient yet persistent application was a far more valuable lesson than anything taught in a lecture hall. He was graciousness personified.

While the history lectures kept me busy, I had not forgotten my desire to learn more Urdu. During my second year I was able to study for a diploma in Urdu from Delhi University. This involved setting out by motorcycle at 7:30 A.M. for the 8 A.M. class three days a week, and then leaving immediately after the class finished at 9:30 A.M. in order to attend the history lectures at Jamia Millia Islamia. It was a demanding schedule but very fruitful. I did well in both subjects.

During this period an International Seminar was held on Baba Farid, a famous early Chishti Sufi who lies buried in Pakpattan, Pakistan. I was invited to attend. It had an unexpected result. Not only were Muslim scholars present but also Hindu, Christian, and even Sikh scholars. My insight was a simple one: "The Sufis bring people together!" That was when I determined to study the life and teaching of a Sufi. I did not want to study any Sufis around Delhi, as there were plenty of scholars in Delhi and Aligarh to do that. Who the Sufi would be was yet to be determined.

The serious study of a Sufi of the Indian subcontinent was not possible without a knowledge of Persian because the vast number of Sufi writings were in that language. I wanted to learn Persian where it was spoken and asked if I could study it either in Afghanistan or in Iran. The choice was left to me.

As the plane taxied towards the Kabul air terminal, I realized that I would not be studying in Afghanistan. After a few days in Kabul, I caught a bus to Herat and then crossed over into Iran and went to Mashhad. There I discovered a course on colloquial Persian, being given to American Peace Corps volunteers. I tried to gain admission to the course but failed. The director gave me a copy of their textbook as a consolation prize. I then caught a bus to Teheran.

When I finally found the Dominican Residence in Teheran, I was in for a rude shock. I had written to them before leaving India and told them about my plans. I discovered they had sent a letter telling me not to come! This was because of some unfortunate incident that had occurred in the past. They welcomed me, however, and, having come to know me, made a suggestion. The Catholic chaplain in Shiraz wanted to do a yearlong course at the Tavistock Institute in England. Would I agree to take his place during this period? Arrangements were made and I became a student of Persian during the day and a priest involved in pastoral visitation in the evening. Most of the Catholics were Americans working for Westinghouse, which was setting up an electronics industry for the Shah of Iran.

My first step, with the help of the Peace Corps textbook and a young Christian lady who gave tuition in Persian, was to learn the spoken version of the language in order to be able to converse with ordinary Iranians. This part of my studies went well and I became quite fluent. Then I began auditing classes on written, classical Persian at the University. This was a mistake, in the sense that I looked only at pre-fourteenth-century Persian. It was somewhat akin to going to Chaucer and such authors in order to study English. I should have simply immersed myself in ordinary Persian. It should be pointed out, however, that fourteenth-century classical Persian is quite close to modern formal written Persian.

When I went to Iran, I knew that I wanted to work on a Sufi but still had not found a suitable one. An aerogramme from England arrived one day, handwritten by my friend Christian Troll, who was working on a doctoral thesis in London. He had met Simon Digby in Oxford; a man well-known for his knowledge of Indian history. He suggested two names. The first was Gesu Daraz of Gulbarga. "That's in South India," I thought, "but I want to work on a Sufi from North India!" Then I read the second name: Sharafuddin Maneri of Bihar Sharif! My astonished reaction to this was to marvel that Bihar had a famous Sufi. I had never even heard his name mentioned. I checked out some information about him, such as the large number of works written either by him or about him, and the fact that these writings were all in Persian. Here was my Sufi right on my doorstep, so to speak. I had passed through Bihar Sharif several times and knew where it was. It was on the main road to Patna.

I returned to India in January 1976 and went to Hazaribag before beginning Tertianship, the final spiritual program of my Jesuit training. It was conducted at St. Stanislaus College, near Hazaribag. There was a new superior for the Hazaribag Region, Fr. Bernard Donnelly, but he was in Rome for a program. He had informed me that we would discuss my future on his return. Unofficially some Jesuits in Hazaribag said that I would be staying at St. Xavier's School, teaching history at St. Columba's College and doing my doctorate. I knew there was no way I could do a doctorate in Hazaribag. In realistic terms, the choice was simple. I could either stay in Hazaribag and teach or go to Patna to make use of my Persian and study the life and teaching of Sharafuddin Maneri. The whole point of learning Persian was for the sake of this study. I would be able to meet my new superior only after the completion of a thirty-day retreat, an early component of the Tertianship.

The whole point of the thirty-day retreat was to be able to turn to God in total, loving submission to his will and thus be enabled "to find him in all things." Even before the retreat began, I fell sick. It was a combination of an allergic reaction to something in the air at Sitagarha, where the college was situated, combined with a real dilemma as to what God wanted me to do: teach history in Hazaribag or go to Patna and do a doctoral study of Sharafuddin Maneri's life and teaching. I wanted to run away before the retreat began. I could use my sickness as an excuse. The real reason, however, was my apprehension that I might be asked to give up all ideas of a doctoral study of Maneri and devote my life to teaching history at the local college. The struggle was that I knew I would do what my superior told me to do, as this would be clearly God's will for me, but it might go totally against all that I aspired to do.

One evening I stood in my room, clinging to a piece of furniture and shaking uncontrollably. I thought it was a satanic onslaught. I was severely tempted to run away. I thought of Jesus in the Garden of Gethsemane and had a faint idea of what he must have gone through. I decided to stay.

I was plagued by asthma and chronic bronchial infections, which no amount of antibiotics could control. I would rise in the middle of the night because of the need to clear some of the congestion in my chest. I took the forced opportunity to spend an hour doing a night meditation.

After the retreat, my superior called to see me. I shared my dilemma with him. He said that he would put my case to the consult, as it is called. The regional superior or provincial had four consulters. They are supposed to meet once a month. After the consult, Fr. Bernard Donnelly kindly came to inform me that the consulters needed more information. One thought I was "backing into" the whole thing. One consulter had already left and I had a meeting with the superior and the other three. The meeting went on for about three hours. I had to face all sorts of questions. At the end, however, everyone agreed that this was clearly the course I should take, namely to go for a doctoral study of Maneri and then follow wherever this led me. This was my mandate from the Society of Jesus in March 1976 and it still holds good until today.

As I sat in the bus from Hazaribag to Patna on the last Sunday of June 1976, two questions troubled me. The first was simply whether I could do an in-depth study of the life and teaching of Sharafuddin Maneri from the original Persian source material. My doubt turned to alarm when I tried to read the Persian of Maneri's *Hundred Letters.* I had hoped to go through this work, which contained Maneri's basic teaching about the spiritual path to God, in order to pick out his main teaching. This was clearly impossible. This left me the option of trying to translate the whole work, then go through it and pick out the main teaching. As this would supply the material for half my thesis, it was the approach that was followed. It would have proved impossible for me if I had not received unstinted assistance from my guide, the late Prof. Syed Hasan Askari. We would sit side by side at the table reserved for manuscripts in the Khuda Bakhsh Oriental Public Library. Whenever I had a problem, I would simply turn to him. Sometimes I could not read a particular word. From the context he could easily tell me what the word was. Anyone who had dealt with old manuscripts knows it is sometimes difficult to distinguish letters. It was thanks to Askari Sahib that my first apprehension was laid to rest.

The second question that was troubling me during my bus ride to Patna concerned what course of action I should take if, as a result of my own personal study of the original Persian texts, I doubted that Maneri was in fact a great saint who undoubtedly deserved his reputation of being Bihar's greatest Sufi. As I laboriously struggled to translate Maneri's *Maktubat-i Sadi* (The Hundred Letters), it did not take me long to realize that he was all that people said he was. I was astonished at what I was reading, a whole exposition of the Sufi path in the form of a hundred letters written from 1346 to 1347.

This judgment was not based on knowledge of Persian alone, as my Muslim friends clearly understood. Maneri's letters to Qazi Shamsuddin were actually addressed to anyone who seriously wished to submit totally to God—the meaning of being a Muslim—in quest of an ever-deepening union with him. Although there were struggles, falls, and shortcomings in my attempt to be a faithful Jesuit, a member of the Society of Jesus, founded by St. Ignatius Loyola in the sixteenth century, nevertheless my whole life was an attempt to give myself wholly to God and do what he wanted me to do. I had a vow of poverty; I could not own things, only make use of what was needed for my life and work. I had a vow of chastity; forgoing the natural fulfilling roles of husband and father of a family. I had a vow of obedience; to go where I was sent and do the work entrusted to me. I even had a vow to go anywhere the Pope wanted to send me.

From what has been shared, it is clear that obedience was the most challenging vow—not my will, but yours be done! I had had no desire to go to India but was sent there. I have shared various struggles, culminating in the experience of my time just before, during, and after the thirty-day retreat. Obedience clearly includes dialogue but the superior has the final say. Our founder, St. Ignatius Loyola, was crystal clear that he wanted obedience to be the hallmark of a Jesuit. Shakespeare wrote a play called *The Taming of the Shrew*. You might say that obedience is the means of bringing the human ego to heel, to tame it thoroughly.

My friends realized that I not only brought some knowledge of Persian to the task of translation, no matter how limited, but also a lived experience of what Maneri was attempting to inculcate in his readers. Time and again I was confronted with a real challenge to understand something Maneri was saying until an insight, based on my own experience, shed instant light on what he wanted to convey. Nowadays, we have synchronized swimming events in the Olympic Games and elsewhere. It seemed to me that Maneri and I had what might be termed "synchronized spiritualities."

Translating *The Hundred Letters* took a year longer than I had anticipated. When the translation was complete and I was getting ready to harvest Maneri's teaching for the second half of my thesis, Askari Sahib said simply: "Publish it!" I demurred, pleading that I would have to revise it. "I'll help you," was all that he said. By this time Askari Sahib was not merely my guide but my second father as well. I had no option other than to carry out his wish.

When the work was ready to be sent for publication, I sent a copy to Ravi Dayal at Oxford University Press, Delhi. I also sent a copy, through a friend, to the United States. I was unaware that I should have sent only one copy at a time.

After a while I was overjoyed to receive a positive answer from Ravi Dayal. He said that Oxford University Press would print 1,000 copies of the book. I wrote to him, expressing my gratitude. Then an offer came

from the Paulist Press in New York. They offered to publish my book in
their series, "The Classics of Western Spirituality." Sixty volumes were
projected, of which twelve would be devoted to Muslim spirituality; they
offered to print my book in this category. The letter had a very glossy
folder along with it. The series seemed most impressive indeed. I learned
that Annemarie Schimmel, Fazlur Rahman, and Bruce Lawrence had all
recommended the publication of my translation. Clearly more than a thousand copies would be involved, as many libraries would have a standing
order for all the books in this prestigious series. I even received a phone
call from Bruce Lawrence saying he was ready to do the on-the-spot editing if the book was published in the series. This was clearly a better offer,
having the twin advantages of being published in the United States and in
a prestigious series. I wrote to the Paulist Press and explained my problem,
for I had accepted Ravi Dayal's offer. There had not been any formal agreement signed but I had made a commitment. I said I would be going to
Delhi to meet Mr. Dayal and gave the address in Delhi where I would be
staying.

I was under great tension, with name and fame on one side and fidelity
to my word on the other. I had a touch of indigestion in the train after
breakfast and had to lie down for a while. Later I came to know that I had
suffered a mild heart attack because of the tension. At lunch I was handed
a letter from Paulist Press. The one important point that I remember was
the statement that they proposed a print run of 10,000 copies.

The following morning I went to see Ravi Dayal. I showed him the
original letter from Paulist Press and the glossy folder about the series.
He was not impressed. Then I handed him the letter I had received the
previous day. When he read that the proposal was to print 10,000 copies,
he simply said: "I cannot stand in the way of a proposal to print 10,000
copies!" I heaved a sigh of relief. The first copies of the book reached me
in the first week of March 1980, a day or two before my proposed departure from Patna en route to Australia on March 7.

After completing and defending my thesis about the life and teaching of
Sharafuddin Maneri, I had requested some time in an Arabic-speaking
country so that I could learn Arabic in a natural setting. My superior
thought this might be dangerous. I was to study Arabic at the Australian
National University in Canberra, while teaching Persian to first-year students and lecturing on Sufism. The students of Persian were few in number
but extraordinary in their linguistic ability. The classes were a delight.
The lectures on Sufism did not receive such an enthusiastic response.
Arabic proved difficult for me. It was hard slogging with nowhere near the

hoped-for progress. Then, on November 27, 1980, I suffered a massive
coronary infarct, which put my life in the balance. My left anterior coronary artery was completely blocked. Calvary Hospital in Canberra, to
which my sister Mary drove me, could offer no more than medication
under the supervision of an expert cardiologist, Dr. Frank Long. I survived
but with a permanently blocked artery and a damaged heart. That put an
end to my Arabic studies!

My return to India in early 1981 provided an opportunity to reflect on
where I should live and work. Because of the appreciative reception of my
translation of Maneri's *Hundred Letters* and the expert editing of Bruce
Lawrence, it was decided that I should return to Patna and translate more
of Maneri's writings. This decision was reinforced by the welcome the
translation received in Muslim quarters. The American volume was expensive and so an inexpensive paperback edition was duly printed in Mumbai
at an affordable price. Muslims in Patna and in other parts of Bihar were
happy that their saint had become widely known because of the English
translation.

This does not mean that there were no difficulties. One emerged when,
after preparing my thesis for publication, it was published as *The Way of a
Sufi: Sharafuddin Maneri*. The thesis was based on manuscript evidence.
This was because it was strictly speaking a thesis in history. The traditional
dates for Maneri's birth and death are 1263 and 1380 respectively. The
Wafat Nama, an account of Maneri's final hours, clearly gave the evening of
January 2, 1381, as the time and date of his death. As it was his faithful Zain
Badr Arabi who wrote this account, its accuracy could not be questioned.
As a result of studying a number of Maneri's reminiscences, especially of
his time in Sonargaon, and setting them against the widely accepted general history of the period, the evidence pointed to his birth as having
occurred around 1290, not 1263. This upset some devotees who had
accepted the traditional chronology. The difficulty is not with the sequence
of Maneri's travels but with the dates assigned to them in the early part of
his life. The latter part of his life, once he had attained fame, is accurately
recorded. There was also a problem involving the identity of the mother of
Zakiuddin, Maneri's son, born while he was in Sonargaon.

Because of my heart condition and other commitments, the translation
work has proceeded slowly over the years. A great deal of time has been
devoted to various commitments to the Islamic Studies Association (ISA).
This is a Catholic organization, which was founded in Agra in March
1979. It is meant to promote understanding between Christians and
Muslims.

For some twenty-five years, I have conducted introductory courses on Islam in various seminaries and houses of formation for religious sisters. The most fruitful of these has been an "Exposure to Islam" program conducted for the first-year students of theology at our small regional theologate in Khaspur, near Patna. I would visit various towns in Bihar and meet people in *madrasas* and Sufi centers. I would rely on the assistance of one of our schools to make contact with middle-class Muslims, and evening schools, social centers, and dispensaries to make contact with poorer Muslims. I would get permission from the people I met to send two students of theology to learn about Islam directly from Muslims. After briefing the students and giving them written instructions, I would send them in pairs to the towns I myself had visited. Usually they stayed with the local Catholic priest but some managed to stay in *madrasas* and others with Muslim families. They would leave on a Monday morning and return on Wednesday of the following week. This would be followed by three days of sharing and reflection on their experience. If some points needed further elaboration, this task would fall to me. Each student then had to write a paper on his experience and his reflections on it. Many of these have been published in *Salaam*, ISA's quarterly magazine. The program has proved to be very fruitful for the students. It gave them experience-based knowledge of Muslims, which helped them become more objective in assessing reports of communal disturbances, for example.

There were also opportunities to attend various conferences and seminars. These were enriching experiences. Mention also has to be made of the joy of many friendships with various Muslims over the years. For many years I regularly visited Phulwari Sharif, about six miles from my residence. This was on a Friday when the Khuda Bakhsh Library was closed. Instead of staring at Persian manuscripts, I took the opportunity to meet and chat with ordinary Muslims in Phulwari Sharif. It has a long history of Sufism, as the many tombs of Sufis, beginning with one dated 1385, clearly indicate. In 1921 the Imarat-i Shari'a was set up in Phulwari Sharif. It is devoted to Muslim law, as its name indicates. The Imarat runs quite a number of courses but the best-known one is for higher studies in Islamic law. This is for talented young men who aspire to be Qadis (judges) or Muftis (persons qualified to give a *fatwa*, an authentic opinion on some point of Islamic law). Seats are limited and students come from different parts of India. The late Qazi Mujahidul Islam Qasmi, a famous scholar of Islamic law, set up the program.

One principle that has guided me over the years is that of transparency. As far as possible, my words and actions should flow from what is in my heart. This involves the "cultivation" of the heart, so to speak, so that wholesome thoughts and actions can spring up like flowers.

It is hard to know what the future holds because of a series of heart attacks on my return to India on June 27, 2009. The taxi from the airport had no sooner reached St. Xavier's School, Delhi, than the first attack occurred. Three times I had to undergo defibrillation, then angiography, then triple bypass surgery, again defibrillation the very day after the bypass surgery, and finally the insertion of an implantable cardioverter defibrillator.

One thing is clear, however, and this is a felt invitation to become an ever more caring person. My precarious health certainly limits the action that can be undertaken as the fruit of a caring attitude but such an attitude in itself can "bring comfort to hearts"—to use one of Maneri's favorite expressions.

On Being a Servant of Reconciliation

Christian W. Troll

My commitment to pursue a deeper understanding of Muslims and Islam, their culture and religion, developed gradually during the years 1957 to 1961 when I was studying Christian theology at the universities of Bonn and Tübingen. From 1959 I worked under the guidance of the church historian Hubert Jedin on an extended paper entitled "The China Missions in the Middle Ages." One day by chance I came across the essay "The Need for Islamic Studies" by the Dutch Jesuit J. J. Houben, then professor of Islamology at Nijmegen (Holland) and Beirut (Lebanon). The following statement, made in the context of discussing the importance of a renewal of religious thought in contemporary Islam, impressed me:

> Not only the missionaries working in Muslim countries but every Catholic throughout the world must realize that the fate of hundreds of millions of Muslims hangs in the balance and that in order to help them to solve the difficulties along religious lines, a deeper knowledge of their mentality and of Islam in general as a religion and as a polity is certainly one of the most pressing needs for the Catholics of our times. (Ibid., 191)

Soon after reading Houben's essay I managed to meet him in person. He stressed that a proper study of Arabic and of Islam was quite demanding. Hence I should think twice before embarking on this road. I persisted. The following morning Houben entrusted me with a letter addressed to my archbishop, Josef Cardinal Frings of Cologne, in which he proposed that I should be allowed special studies in Arabic and Islam. I was to deliver this letter to the cardinal during my first official encounter with him in June 1961 on the occasion of the completion of my university studies in preparation for the priesthood. The cardinal, to my surprise, immediately expressed his agreement with Fr. Houben's proposal. For some time now, he said, I have been feeling the need for a priest of the archdiocese to get thoroughly acquainted with the Christians and Muslims of the Middle East. For this the solid knowledge of Arabic was needed, and since Arabic was a difficult language, I should learn it as soon as possible. So, the cardinal sent me, exactly as Fr. Houben had proposed in his letter, to the Centre Religieux d'Études Arabes (CREA), the language school attached to the Université Saint Joseph, Beirut, situated at Bikfaya, then a small, relatively remote township about nineteen miles north-east of Beirut, about 2,600 feet above sea level on the western slopes of Mount Lebanon.

My motivation for going beyond the boundaries of normal Catholic theological studies was missionary. From the time of my first Holy Communion at the age of ten, on the Sunday after Easter 1947, I had felt a calling to serve God in a special way. This calling persisted somehow throughout the following years; it moved me, after completing my *Abitur*, to ask to be admitted as a seminarian, which in the Archdiocese of Cologne meant living in a college with other candidates for the priesthood as a student of the Faculty of Catholic Theology of Bonn University.

However, the Church worldwide, "the missions," had begun to interest me much earlier. My father was an internationally known geographer at Bonn University. We children, nine sisters and brothers, were regularly present when geographer colleagues, friends, and acquaintances of my parents, would share lunch or dinner with our family. The blessing and thanksgiving that my father recited at the beginning and end of each meal, was said equally in the presence of guests who obviously did not share our Christian faith. Over the years this made me think and ask questions.

The library at home spread over the corridors and along the staircases of the house. From the walls fascinating book titles as well as geographical maps carried my imagination to far-off continents. At the same time, almost daily, I served as an altar boy in the parish church and loved singing in the city's Bach Choir. One day, at the age of thirteen, I told my parents that

I would like to train as a missionary. Thus I came to spend several years in two grammar schools. In the first, which was run by the Missionaries of the Divine Word, I lived as a boarder; the other, run by the Redemptorists, I attended as a day boy. My ideal was to serve somewhere in the worldwide Church. In both schools the regular practice of liturgical and personal prayer as well as meditation on Holy Scripture played a central role and we had countless opportunities to learn about far-off countries. To this day I vividly remember occasions when missionaries on furlough from Asia and Africa, with the help of slides and other visual aids, talked to us with fascination about the people and country they had adopted.

Not yet decided upon the concrete path towards realizing my ideals, I began with the study of Catholic theology at Bonn University. From the beginning of these studies I frequented additional lecture courses and seminars offered by Protestant theologians and by historians of religion. Two years into my university studies, during my three semesters at Tübingen University (1959–60), I took the initiative of founding at the Catholic chaplaincy, a circle of students from overseas. They were studying in various faculties of the university. Many of them were Muslims, Hindus, or Buddhists. We met every week during semester-time in a private home. One of us would give a talk about a topic of interest usually related to her or his home country, culture or religion. These meetings and those I encountered made a lasting impression on me.

About that time I decided to commence the study of Arabic. Having gained access to the primary sources of Christianity and Judaism through Hebrew, Greek, and Latin, I wanted to get to know Arabic and the religion of Islam that meant so much to a number of my student friends from abroad. I joined a small group of first-semester students of Islamic studies. Prof. Rudi Paret, already then quite well-known as an outstanding scholar of Islam, initiated us personally into Arabic script and basic grammar. It was through him that I heard for the first time about such great scholars of Arabic and Islam as Theodor Nöldeke, Carl Brockelmann, and Gerhard Ritter, and also about such groups of Christian believers among Muslims as the Little Brothers of Jesus, founded in 1933 in the Sahara by René Voilleaume, based on the rule formulated by Charles de Foucauld (d. 1916), the Institut des Belles Lettres Arabes of the White Fathers at Tunis, and the Trappist Monastery of Thiberine in the Atlas mountains of Algeria.

Back in Bonn I happened to listen to a talk by the Benedictine scholar of religions and of Christian missions, Thomas Ohm of the University of Münster, about the need for a renewal of missionary practice and thought. In a booklet entitled *Muslims and Catholics* (München: Kösel, 1961) published at that time he argued the need for a "new spirit" in living and acting together with the Muslims.

> The spirit that the Christians need in the mission to Islam is not the spirit of enmity, of dominance, of arrogance, of antipathy, but rather the sprit of friendship, brotherliness, sympathy, understanding—the Holy Spirit of Agape. Who goes to the Muslims, should go as Peter may have gone on his mission, after he had denied his Lord three times, hence he should go conscious that the Christians in the past have made many mistakes. . . . In the end it will be crucial to omit or do nothing without the Love of God and neighbor . . . (1 Cor. 13:7f). (Ohm, 9 and 85)

Arabic in Lebanon, the Novitiate, Philosophy, and Vatican II

With regard to the "quest for the Muslims and their Islam" I consider the two years of intensive study of Arabic (through the medium of French) in Mount Lebanon (1961–63) the most formative period in my life. We formed a group of about fifteen biennium students. Most of them were Jesuit scholastics from the Netherlands and France. I was the only German. Looking back, I consider the two years in Mount Lebanon, separated from home, secluded from city life, and fully concentrated on the intricacies of Arabic grammar and style, the novitiate as it were of my life in the service of Christian–Muslim understanding. The discipline this biennium demanded and the effort to give the best of ourselves to the study of Arabic, about ten hours every day, were accompanied by weekly excursions up into the mountains or down to the seashore, by frequent visits to families in the nearby villages and to monastic communities in the vicinity of Bikfaya. We also began to understand, through reading the local press, the complexities of Near Eastern politics, all this in a Lebanon that, although politically already in a somewhat precarious situation, was still considered then "the Switzerland of the Near East."

The founder and spirit of the Centre Religieux d'Études Arabes was Père André d'Alverny, S.J. (d. 1965), professor of Arabic literature at the Institut Oriental de l'Université St Joseph. He was assisted by Père Louis Pouzet, S.J. (d. 2002), who later succeeded d'Alverny as professor of Arabic literature at the same university and who is the author of outstanding works on Yahya an-Nawawi's (d. 1277) *Al-Arba'in* and on the religious life of thirteenth-century Damascus. Our language tutors were specially trained Lebanese schoolteachers.

This intensive and demanding effort to enter into the world of Arabic, together with the first encounter with central foundational texts of Islam in the Arabic original, left a lasting impression on me and has shaped my later encounter with Muslims and their culture and faith. The daily celebration of the Eucharist in the Melkite or in the Maronite rite helped to give these two years a religious and ascetic quality.

In the summer of 1962, after my first year in Lebanon, while staying in a village of the Biqa plain to learn spoken Lebanese, I gained the certainty that I was to ask to be received into the Society of Jesus. But first I was told by the Jesuit provincial of the Near East that I should finish the course in Arabic for which the Archbishop of Cologne had sent me to Lebanon and complete it with the Diplôme de Langue Arabe of the Université St. Joseph, Beirut. When I returned from Lebanon to Germany, I entered the Jesuit novitiate in Westphalia and this was followed in Bavaria by two years of studying for the licentiate in philosophy.

The thirty days' Ignatian retreat during the novitiate acquainted me with the mechanism of discernment in spiritual matters. Ignatian discernment asks: What does God want of me in a concrete situation, in circumstances that are not clear and where reflection and conclusions do not result in a clear answer? The method of such discernment includes total openness (indifference) in the face of God and of all reality. It leads the person gradually into a real encounter with the Jesus of the Gospels who enables the seeker to assess the movements in his or her soul by the criterion of his life and spirit. I discovered in the course of time that the critical openness for God's spirit at work in a given movement and its teachings— when applied *mutatis mutandis* to the world of living religions—definitely can help in trying to discern in the attitudes or teachings of such a movement the presence of "good" or "evil" spirits. Viewed in the perspective of Ignatian spiritual pedagogies for instance, the *a priori*, clear-cut dividing of the world of lived religions into natural and supernatural or into clearly evil/erroneous and clearly good/true realms, looked at from this perspective, turned out to be too simplistic. Such a view of things does not take sufficient account of the fact that in the perspective of Christian faith all reality, not least that of lived religions and cultures, is marked by signs of the Holy Spirit as well as by signs of the absence or opposition to this Holy Spirit. In addition, the study of philosophy made me convinced of the need, in the effort to understand religious traditions—one's own as well as others—to define concepts clearly and avoid tearing statements out of their context.

Spiritually and theologically the process of the Second Vatican Council (1962–65) and its final documents turned out to be crucial for the whole of my later engagement with Muslims and Islam. At the time of the announcement of the council by Pope John XXIII, on January 25, 1959, I was still pursuing my theological studies at Bonn University. Hubert Jedin, the well-known historian of the Council of Trent and later a key advisor to Pope John XXIII in organizing Vatican II, was my main tutor at that time. Immediately after the announcement of the council, "prophetically" he impressed upon us students the extraordinary impact this council would make on the future life of the Church. Lecture courses and personal contact with two other *periti* of the council, Joseph Ratzinger at Bonn and Hans Küng at Tübingen, brought the inner-Catholic wrestling with fundamental questions of *aggiornamento* close to my attention. This made me ask analogous questions regarding the development of contemporary Islam.

The importance of the documents of the council for any Catholic working in the post–Vatican II period in the field of Christian–Muslim relations is obvious. Texts like paragraph 16 of the Dogmatic Constitution on the Church (*Lumen Gentium*); the Declaration on the Relationship of the Church to Non-Christian Religions (*Nostra Aetate*), especially its paragraph 3, and, last but not least, the Declaration on Religious Freedom (*Dignitatis Humanae*) became for me firm points of reference and a constant source of motivation. I personally, however, was especially impressed by Pope Paul VI's encyclical letter *Ecclesiam Suam* of August 6, 1964. The key elements emerging for me from Paul VI's and the council's teaching on interreligious dialogue were these: reciprocal communication, mutual friendship, and respect, as well as a joint effort for the sake of shared goals, all in the service of a common search for the fuller realization of the truth.

London and South Asia

During the first half of 1966, towards the end of my licentiate course in philosophy, I asked to be sent to work as a member of the Jesuit community in Lahore, Pakistan in order to engage in the study of Muslim culture and in interreligious dialogue in the spirit of Vatican II. In preparation, in the autumn of 1966, I went to the School of Oriental and African Studies in London and began with a BA (honors) course in Urdu Language and Literature. The honors course included the study of classical Persian and of medieval and modern Indian history. These years culminated in my

PhD thesis and subsequent book: *Sayyid Ahmad Khan (1817–98): A Reinterpretation of Muslim Theology* (New Delhi: Vikas, 1978; Karachi: OUP, 1979).

Early in 1976 I moved from London not to Lahore but to New Delhi. The Jesuit superior general wanted me to teach Islam and Christian–Muslim Relations at the Vidyajyoti Institute of Religious Studies, the Jesuit Faculty of Theology in Delhi. In this way I was to be of help to the Indian Church in the effort of entering into dialogical relations not only with the Hindus but also with the Muslims of India and their Islam.

The decade in London from 1966–76 was a period of intensive study and encounter with Muslims, most of them from South Asia. The first two years were dedicated almost entirely to acquiring basic language skills in Urdu and Persian. The Urdu course was designed to enable the student, practically from the beginning, to converse with Urdu speakers. I spent many weekends in Urdu-speaking homes practicing the language, talking about South Asian Muslim tradition, reading Urdu poetry or listening to its recitation, and watching Urdu videos and films. It was exciting thus to enter into the world of Indian and Pakistani Muslims. As far as Persian is concerned I remained on the level of reading texts of classical works of historiography and literature and of Sufism in the original. For four years my main tutor in Urdu was Ralph Russell, an outstanding teacher, together with Khaled Hasan Qadiri and Dr. Timur Gandjei. During those years I also had the opportunity of spending several extended summer holidays reading selected classical Sufi texts in Arabic and Persian under the personal guidance of the outstanding scholar of classical Sufism, Richard Gramlich, S.J.

Surely, there were times during this long period of preparatory immersion into the world of South-Asian Muslims in London and South Asia—at a relatively advanced student age—when I felt stretched and became impatient. But my curiosity and fascination with the languages of Urdu and Persian and with the whole South-Asian Muslim universe that these languages and literatures opened up to me, carried me on. The British academic system allowed me to spend a whole year of my course traveling on my own in Iran, Afghanistan, and South Asia, visiting Muslim scholars and institutions, and finally taking tutorials with Urdu scholars in Lahore, whom I had met at the University of London earlier. During my years of doctoral research under the intensive guidance of the historian of South Asia, Dr. Peter Hardy, again I was able to travel to Pakistan and India, meeting scholars knowledgeable in the field of my research and frequenting the relevant libraries in Aligarh, Rampur, and Patna.

Reflecting on this period now I notice that my priestly ordination in July 1971 did not alter my desire to spend all my energy in the study of Islam and in frequent personal encounters with Muslims. However, being sent to give myself to this task as an ordained priest of the Church not only strengthened my sense of commitment but also gave me the knowledge of doing this work in the name of the local and universal Church. The Church, by assigning me as an ordained priest to this work, had committed herself to the task of intensive Christian–Muslim dialogue. So, for example, studying a Muslim text possibly for weeks or spending whole weekends discussing with educated Muslims trends in contemporary Islamic thought, I considered to be an expression of my priestly apostolate. These activities— including, for example, the learning of a language like Turkish relatively late in life—constituted for me one and the same process of being drawn ever more deeply into a presence, an encounter to which I had been empowered and sent officially by my religious order and thus by the Church. I have never lost this sense over the years. Meeting Muslims and thus Islam at a deep level, I consider to be my way of participating as a priest in the larger and centuries-old encounter between Church and Mosque. In and from the regular encounter with the Lord in the daily celebration of the Eucharist, I receive the motivation and strength needed to follow on his way.

The greatest gift of the years that I spent teaching and researching in London and then in Delhi and many other parts of India, I consider to be the lasting friendships with a number of Muslims who represent to me some of the finest qualities of Indo-Muslim culture and religion. I can mention here only a few of them: Syed Vahiduddin (1909–98) who over the years conveyed to me a unique synthesis of Hindu and Muslim philosophy, modern Western thought, Sufi wisdom and contemporary Christian theology. Syed Vahiduddin made me understand and appreciate essential aspects of the Qur'anic idea of God and of the meanings of Islamic prayer. Then Khwaja Ahmad Faruqi, the accomplished scholar of English and Urdu literature, Muhammad Ishaq Khan, the outstanding scholar of Sufism, past and present, in the Kashmiri environment, Maulana Wahiduddin Khan, the remarkable leader of the Al-Risala movement, these and many others— among whom especially those who collaborated with me for the book series *Islam in India: Studies and Commentaries*—became dear and esteemed colleagues.

But of course in Delhi my main assignment was to introduce the Catholic students of theology to Islam, to Indian Muslim culture and to the encounter and dialogue of Muslims and Christians. Already at my priestly ordination in 1971, I had chosen the motto from the Second Letter to the Corinthians: "Servant of Reconciliation" (2 Cor. 5:18–19). Now in India I saw myself being called in some small way to help the Church in her task of promoting reconciliation between the worlds of Hinduism and of Islam.

Soon after arriving in India in 1976, I met Fr. Paul Jackson, S.J., in Patna/Bihar who, inspired by the late Fr. Vincent Courtois, S.J., of Calcutta, was engaged already in the study of Islam and the dialogue with Muslims. We began in 1977 to meet regularly and eventually formed JAMI, a group of Jesuits Among Muslims in India, which in 1983 became ISA, the Islamic Studies Association. During the same year we founded the quarterly publication *SALAAM*, which is now in its thirtieth year of publication. The small group of Indian Catholics organized in ISA, made it possible to maintain the vision, and to pursue the work, of initiating dialogue at various levels—contacts as neighbors in everyday life, teaching and publishing, discussing questions of common social, cultural and religious interest and so on—within an environment that was and remains largely uninterested, if not at times hostile to it, because reaching out deliberately to the Muslims was seen then (not only by Hindus and Sikhs but also by many Indian Christians) as weakening enculturation of Christian life in Hindu culture and religion.

On the international level, from 1975 onwards I participated in almost all the meetings of the *Journées Romaines*. These meetings, from 1956 onwards for nearly half a century, were held every two years in Rome (or, as often later, in its vicinity). They allowed hundreds of Christians to reflect on the theological, spiritual, sociological, and cultural dimensions of their dialogue with Muslim friends. It was a meeting of Catholics (and an increasing number of Christians from other traditions) who in different parts of the world practiced and promoted Christian–Muslim encounter in the spirit of Vatican II. Maurice Borrmans, who for decades has been one of the outstanding figures of Christian–Muslim dialogue, in a recent essay rightly describes the *Journées Romaines* as "a school of formation and a place of information" in this field.[1] At the *Journées Romaines* I developed personal contacts with such key figures in Christian–Muslim relations as Jacques Jomier, Georges Anawati, Robert Caspar, and Louis Gardet, and I was able to feel the pulse of Christian–Muslim dialogue worldwide.

---

1. Maurice Borrmans, "Les 'Journées Romaines' et le Dialogue Islamo-Chretien." *Islamochristiana* 30 (2004): 111–22, esp. Conclusion on p. 121.

Back in Europe

In 1988 the Centre for the Study of Islam and Christian-Muslim Relations
at the Selly Oak Colleges, Birmingham, officially invited me to join its
staff. David Kerr, the founder of the center, had left England to take up the
directorship of the Duncan Black Macdonald Center for the Study of Islam
and Christian-Muslim Relations at Hartford Seminary in Connecticut as
well as the editorship of the renowned quarterly *The Muslim World*. In the
study center at the Selly Oak Colleges, Muslims and Christians together
engaged in studying, teaching, and researching in the field of Islam and
Christian–Muslim Relations. Its academic courses and exams formed part
of the program of the Faculty of Theology of Birmingham University and
included undergraduate and postgraduate courses, up to the level of PhD.
At the same time the center offered in the Midlands and beyond training
courses and study sessions to Muslims and Christians who in their pastoral
and social activities were in need of knowledge about Islam and Christian–
Muslim relations. The center's activity and concern thus had both a worldwide and a local dimension.

In India, at Vidyajyoti Institute, as well as at various other faculties and
seminaries throughout the country, I had been teaching students of
Christian theology, introducing them to Islamic faith and practice, South
Asian Islam and Christian–Muslim relations past and present. For all of
these students the courses on Islam and on Christian–Muslim relations
were of relatively marginal importance. Regrettably they had neither the
time nor the languages, let alone a sufficiently strong motivation, to go
deeper into the study of Muslim culture and Islam. Now, at Selly Oak, I
was working as part of a team of Christian and Muslim colleagues, teaching
students graduate and postgraduate courses as well as directing PhD theses.
This new challenge attracted and motivated me considerably. At Selly Oak
I entered naturally into regular conversation with religiously educated
young Muslim women and men hailing from different parts of the world,
where Christians and Muslims together were trying to enter into meaningful dialogical relations with one another. Staff and students at Selly Oak
were united in the effort to deepen their own and one another's understanding of Islam and of Christian–Muslim relations, in the framework of
a common academic undertaking. So, for example, I was able to teach a
one-year course called "The development of Islamic religious thought
from the Qur'an to our time" in close collaboration with the eminent
Pakistani scholar Dr. Khalid Alawi (d. 2008). This turned out to be a refresh-
ing and satisfying experience for me in both human and academic terms.

Also, initiating together with my Muslim and Christian colleagues on the staff at Selly Oak a new international biannual journal (later to become quarterly), *Islam and Christian-Muslim Relations*, brought me into regular contact and intellectual exchange with Muslim and Christian scholars of Islam and Christian–Muslim relations the world over. And last but not least, in and from Birmingham, one of the important centers of Muslim immigration in Britain, I began to learn rapidly and in concrete ways about the problems Muslim immigration to Great Britain posed for local and national politics, for the Muslim communities themselves as well as for the Christian churches.

In 1993 I was asked by my superiors to take up a professorship at the Pontifical Oriental Institute in Rome, an academic institution mainly dedicated to teaching and research about the Oriental Churches. The main reason for asking me to move to Rome was to enable me to go regularly— in the name of the Pontifical Gregorian University Consortium—as exchange guest professor to the University of Ankara's Ilahiyat Fakültesi. A Turkish professor from the Ankara Faculty would teach on aspects of Islamic culture and faith at the Pontifical Gregorian University in Rome, and in return I would give lectures and seminars on Christian and Christian–Muslim themes at the Ankara faculty, and from there, as it turned out, sporadically in a number of other Muslim theological faculties. I taught at the Ankara faculty over a period of nine years, on each occasion for one to two months. After having been engaged in India and in England in explaining aspects of Islam and Christian–Muslim relations to Christians, especially students of Christian theology, I was asked now to do the opposite, namely to explain aspects of Christian faith and practice, such as the biblical scriptures and the history of the Christian Churches and of their relationship with Islam, to Muslims. Frequently I was also asked to discuss more recent Christian developments such as the Protestant Reformation and the Catholic Counter Reformation, the Christian responses to the Enlightenment and to modern, critical scholarship, the ecumenical movement and the First (1869–70) as well as the Second Vatican Councils.

Eagerly I took advantage of the opportunity to learn Turkish. At the well-known TÖMER Institute for Turkish Language at the University of Ankara I found myself learning Turkish from scratch, in the company of students—most of them some thirty-five or even forty years younger than myself—hailing mainly from Central Asia and from the Caucasus region. In these and countless other fascinating ways I was able to approach yet another great geographical and cultural region of the Islamic world, different from, and yet also in many ways related to, the world of Arab and of South Asian Islam that had hosted me earlier.

Also in 1993 I was appointed a member of the subcommission for Religious Relations of the Catholic Church with Islam of the Pontifical Council for Interreligious Dialogue in Rome. The annual working sessions of this body to which I was privileged to belong for twelve years, usually stretched over several days of extended exchanges and conversations. The ongoing shared study projects and dialogue initiatives of this group took me into many different parts of the Muslim–Christian world. It also gave me the immeasurable gift of getting to know personally, and interacting regularly with, a number of female and male fellow believers, committed like myself to living among Muslims, to Christian–Muslim encounter as well as to protracted study of Islam and Christian–Muslim relations. The same holds true, *mutatis mutandis*, of my membership in the subcommission for Interreligious Dialogue of the German Bishops' Conference, since 1999 and my regular collaboration with CIBEDO, the German Bishops' Institute at Sankt Georgen in Frankfurt (Main) for Christian–Muslim Encounter and Documentation.

Right from the beginning of my guest lecturing in Ankara for the Pontifical Gregorian University I had an idea at the back of my mind that one day, upon my eventual return to Germany, my acquaintance with Turkey and its language might be of significant help in mediating between the majority population and Turkish immigrants. This thought from 1993 onwards provided me with additional motivation to enter the world of Turkish language and culture. And in fact, in 1999 I did return to Germany, first to the Catholic Academy of Berlin, where I established the Forum for Christian–Muslim Dialogue. There I became acquainted with a city that not only was still reeling from the effects of the rather sudden event of reunification of East and West Germany but which also, at least in its western half, in the course of two or three decades, had turned into a major center of Turkish and Muslim immigration and permanent presence. However, after two-and-a-half years, in 2001, I left Berlin to become once more part of an academic setting, the Jesuit Faculty of Philosophy and Theology of Sankt Georgen, in Frankfurt. There I started a certificate course called Introduction to Islam and Christian–Muslim Relations for students and professionals and found the time and space to enable me to accompany Christian–Muslim developments in critical study and debate.

So after encountering Muslims and studying Islam in many settings and facets for more or less four decades, I find myself back in my home country. However, Germany's society—its social, political, and ideological preoccupations and debates—when compared with the mid-sixties, have changed beyond recognition. I feel privileged now to have the opportunity to try to understand my country and continent anew. I notice that the massive immigration into Germany not only poses problems but also, and above all, has brought about a vitality and plurality that turns out to be enriching as well as stimulating. Having lived over the past decades in countries with various majority-minority constellations, I look at the present-day German and European discussions about identity, integration, and assimilation with a sense of calm and confidence.

The electronic media, especially the Internet, enables me to answer questions about Christian faith and practice put to me regularly from Muslims and Christians from around the world in various languages (to date: English, German, French, Indonesian, Italian, Russian, Spanish and Turkish).[2] Also, now, finally, I hope to find the time for undertaking an extended study into aspects of a core area of Muslim faith and piety: How do Muslims in their great variety today portray Muhammad, whom most Muslims revere deeply as the person who was asked to convey to all human-kind, past and present, the Qur'an and who is believed to be for all times the first and the authoritative interpreter of its divine message.

To conclude let me state succinctly three elements that above all else have inspired and sustained me as a student of Islam in my lifelong engagement:

The daily celebration of the Eucharist;
The daily contact with Muslims, in immediate, personal encounter as well as through study of texts and other media;
The awareness that grows daily of global interdependence and of the responsibility this puts on Muslim and Christian believers everywhere.

---

2. See www.answers-to-muslims.com.

A Man of Dialogue

Christiaan van Nispen tot Sevenaer

Fr. Christiaan van Nispen tot Sevenaer was born on March 15, 1938, in the Netherlands, into a noble family traced back to the fourteenth century. After his secondary schooling he entered the novitiate of the Society of Jesus on September 7, 1955, at the age of seventeen.

The following text is made up of extracts from his book: Christians and Muslims: Brothers before God?[1] *He describes his experience of discovery and meeting with Muslims and Islam, to which he was to devote his whole life.*[2]

---

1. Christian van Nispen tot Sevenaer, *Chrétiens et Musulmans: frères devant Dieu?* (Paris: Les éditions de l'atelier, 2004).
2. Christiaan van Nispen tot Sevenaer expressed his desire and intention to contribute a reflection for this volume, but debility came upon him quickly and he was prevented from fulfilling his purpose. The editors did not want to have this work impoverished by the omission of a record of this remarkable man and wish to express their gratitude to those of his confrères who compiled this article and sought his agreement to include it.

Before Entering the Society of Jesus

I do not think I had ever met any Muslims before the sea voyage that took me, as a young Jesuit with three other Dutch confrères, from Venice to Beirut, in August 1960, on our way to help the Near East Province of the Society of Jesus. Islam was at that time a distant and rather exotic phenomenon, known only through books, which spoke of the lands of Africa and Asia. We did not even realize that there were Muslims in Eastern Europe (the Balkans and Russia).

It was in 1955 that I entered religious life, with the express wish to be sent on the missions. During my second year of the novitiate (spring 1957), a Dutch confrère, who was a professor of Arabic and Islamic studies at the Catholic University of Nijmegen, came to talk to us about our order's work in Muslim regions. I do not remember the details of what he told us, but it fired me with enthusiasm. It turned out later that the aim of his visit had been precisely to arouse the enthusiasm of certain novices, of whom I was one! That was the first time that Islam entered my life in a direct and explicit way.

There was no immediate practical follow-up, but in 1958 our superior general officially requested the Dutch Jesuits to help their confrères in the Near East, and thus it was that I put myself forward as being ready and willing for this mission.

In 1960, after obtaining my degree in philosophy, I was sent to the Near East, first to Lebanon to learn Arabic, together with the three confrères who were sent at the same time. We went first by train to Venice and from there by ship to Beirut, and it was on the ship that I had for the first time in my life the opportunity to meet a Muslim. At last Muslims could become real-live persons, not just a concept.

After our arrival in Lebanon, we were sent to the Centre Religieux d'Études Arabes (CREA), in Bikfaya in the Lebanese mountains, to devote ourselves full-time for two years to the study of the Arabic language. CREA was run by a French confrère, Fr. André d'Alverny, who made a deep impression on me with his approach to the study of the Arabic language and his approach to Islam and Muslims.

Having completed the two years of Arabic, I was sent to Egypt in 1962 to specialize in Arabic and Islamic philosophy, in the Department of Philosophy of the Faculty of Letters of Ayn Shams University, the second state university in Cairo. It was at the university that I then had my first in-depth contacts with Muslims. Some of the friendships formed at that time have lasted until today and have become an essential part of who I am.

My firmest friendship was with someone whose father was a *shaykh*, a Muslim "man of religion," trained at the famous Islamic university of Al-Azhar, and who, towards the end of his life, was director of the group of preuniversity Al-Azhar institutes. I was very soon adopted by my friend's family as one of their own, and the *shaykh* really looked on me as a son.

The Role of Specialization

In 1966 I left for France for my theological studies in Lyon, where at that time Prof. Roger Arnaldez was teaching Islamic thought. It was through him that I came to know an important modern commentary on the Qur'an, known as the Manar Commentary.

In 1968 I enrolled to work for a doctoral thesis on this commentary. At that time in my theological studies I was much preoccupied by the whole problematic of faith and so at first focused my research on faith in the Manar Commentary. This was helpful for me, but did not let me enter very far into the preoccupations of the commentary's authors themselves. I had imposed my own problematic on those authors, instead of listening first to them.

I then set myself to read the whole text of the commentary, and this presented an extraordinary immersion, not only into the Qur'an, but into the whole history of Islamic thought and into a good number of the issues taken up by this thought.

My work for this thesis was frequently interrupted, which is why I did not defend it until finally, in 1987, at the University of Paris III. This research really did represent for me a training in *intellectual sensitivity*.

This also helped me to learn (to try) to reflect *with* Muslims, to understand with empathy *and* friendly criticism. It is this also which was the basis for my teaching of Islamic studies in various Church institutions especially in Egypt. For I try to present Islam, as far as possible, as Muslims would wish to see it presented, with objectivity and affection, which in no way prevents a critical view and questioning. I consider it necessary to apply the Golden Rule of the Gospel to one's observation and understanding, then to try to look at the other and understand him as I would myself wish him to regard and understand me.

Another experience which influenced me, at the level of Muslim–Christian relations, was taking part in the (re-)birth of an Egyptian Muslim–Christian dialogue group, which took place in February 1975, after it had almost disappeared since 1953. After the Egyptian revolution of

July 23, 1952, the new regime was afraid of everything that could be seen as a clandestine group. Also in 1953, the Minister of the Interior demanded that regular meetings of the association should cease. In 1975 circumstances had changed considerably. So on February 14, 1975, Mlle Mary Kahil (1889–1979), a great friend of Louis Massignon and one who had devoted her entire life to bringing together Muslims and Christians, gathered in her house some fifteen persons, Muslims and Christians, most of whom had formerly been members of the association.

Very soon the question was raised of official recognition by the state, so as to avoid any ambiguity or suspicion. This recognition was obtained on April 6, 1978, and the group was registered with the Ministry of Social Affairs, under the name Association of Religious Brotherhood.

Beside my experience in this association, I was also given the opportunity to experience another, complementary, Muslim–Christian collaboration— also a source of true friendships—the Egyptian Commission of Justice and Peace.

Very soon the commission organized sessions on subjects of vital importance for the whole of society, the first of which was on the problem of the environment. For organizing these sessions we then sought the participation of Muslims as well as Christians. These Muslims have since become true friends of the members of the commission, and, in time, permanent collaborators (called *counselors* of the commission). The commission did not wish to be a group focused on Muslim–Christian dialogue, but one brought together by the common will to contribute jointly to the construction of a better society, a group that lived out cocitizenship in a practical way.

All these contacts, friendships, and collaboration between the members of the Egyptian Justice and Peace Commission led several of us to forge close links with the Al-Ahram Centre for Political and Strategic Studies, an important institute in Egypt for study, research, and publication on all aspects of socio-economic and political life in Egypt and the Arab world. Some of us were in particular involved with a significant initiative taken by this center several years before, which was to publish twice a "Report on the religious situation in Egypt" (the first appeared in 1997 and the second in 1998).

Since the end of the 1980s I have been increasingly involved in collaborating with the Dominicans at the Institut Dominicain d'Études Orientales (IDEO) in Cairo. The IDEO possesses a remarkable asset—its library, which can be considered one of the best for everything concerning Islam (religion and civilization) and the Arab world (countries, history, literature, and thought). This library, which already holds nearly 100,000 volumes, being no longer sufficient, has now been replaced by a new one, whose opening in October 2002 almost coincided with the arrival of several young Dominican brothers. For a dozen or so years, I have been a collaborator with IDEO, and more recently—with some other non-Dominicans—an official member, wholeheartedly associating myself with this process for meeting through intellectual work, a work of study, reflection, and publication.

Another setting in which I find the subject matter to be a place of encounter is that of philosophical meetings in Egypt (arising from the fact that I teach philosophy at the Coptic Catholic major seminary). On the one hand, at the Egyptian Philosophical Society, and on the other in certain university Philosophy Departments and in the Philosophy Commissions of the Higher Council of Culture and of the new Library of Alexandria. These meetings are for me opportunities to listen and understand, as also for myself to be heard, in a sphere of philosophical thinking which tries to find its specificity in Egypt, with a fidelity to the Arabic and Islamic heritage and an openness to the universal, which represents an equilibrium that is not easy to find.

It is clear that it is above all my life in Egypt—a country that has an outstanding position in the Muslim world and that at the same time holds the largest Christian population in the Middle East—which has marked my experience in Muslim–Christian relations and my grasp of the nature of Islam. However I had the opportunity to undertake several journeys—all too rapid—that have enabled me to enrich this experience a little through different contexts.

I was first able to discover Algeria during the summer of 1997, invited by Mgr. Henri Teissier for a visit of nearly three weeks, during which I was able to appreciate the diversity of Algerian society. After this summer visit to all these places, I was able to return there in November of the same year, invited by the Higher Institute of Islamic Studies in Oran to take part in a colloquium organized by this Institute. The encounter with Algeria gave me a lasting link with this country and its people, and at the same time helped me understand better the specific nature of Egypt, my second homeland for the past forty years.

In 1998, with my friend Nabil Abd al-Fattah (of the Al-Ahram Centre for Political and Strategic Studies, and the compiler of the two volumes of the *Report on the Religious Situation in Egypt*, mentioned above), I was invited to take part in a Muslim–Christian colloquium in Indonesia, the country that holds the largest population of Muslims anywhere in the world. The colloquium itself was a most enriching experience, where Indonesian

Muslims and Christians spoke with great openness of their experiences and their mutual apprehensions. I have wanted to share these experiences, since they represent, for me, a true gift and symbols of hope.

Discovering the Importance of the Spiritual Dimension in Encounter

In these last few years I have been able to discover the importance of the spiritual dimension in meetings between Muslims and Christians. Too often in speaking of "Islam" one thinks at once of politics—and the consequences of September 11, 2001, have not helped to improve matters!—and forgets that Islam is before all else a religion, based on faith in God, and that Muslims are thus in the first place believers. It is not a question of denying the importance of the political dimension or of the cultural and sociological. However, we have a false perspective if we reduce Islam to these dimensions leaving out the religious. I have come to feel this because I am aware to what extent many Muslims suffer greatly when it is reduced in this way, and how sensitive they are to the fact of striking the spiritual chord, the dimension of faith.

When I began to feel the importance of the spiritual dimension for many Muslims, I expressed all this in two texts, which I was led to write when preparing two lectures that I had to give to university students, both Muslims and Christians. To one I gave the title "Together before God, and thus together to defend humanity," and to the other "The spiritual life: meeting place between Muslims and Christians."

The Arab Team of Muslim–Christian Dialogue

Another experience of relationship and dialogue between Muslims and Christians, in which I have been able to take part in these past years, is the work carried out by a group which began in 1995 and with which I have been associated, The Arab Team of Muslim–Christian Dialogue (L'equipe arabe de dialogue islamo-chrétien). This comprises a group of Arab intellectuals, Muslims, and Christians, coming from Lebanon, Egypt, Jordan, Palestine, Syria, sometimes also from the Sudan and the United Arab Emirates (in these gatherings I am practically the only one not of Arab origin). These began to meet, thanks to an initiative of the Ecumenical Council of Middle Eastern Churches, in May 1995.

Some meetings are regularly given over to a focus on our shared life as Christians and Muslims in the different countries, and we talk on this subject very freely. Recently the team has managed to crystallize the result of these years of work, the basic convictions of the team, in a common document, on which we worked for a year and a half, and which was adopted at a meeting in Cairo on December 19, 2001, entitled "Dialogue and Common Life: Muslim-Christian Arab Charter" (Le dialogue et la vie commune: charte arabe islamo-chrétienne).

Personally, my whole path in relations between Muslims and Christians makes me all the more realize how much these many experiences of friendship that I have been privileged to experience are a blessing and a responsibility, where I believe—in the most fundamental sense of the term believe!—that God is present. It has been granted to us indeed to "be together before God, and thus together to defend humanity."

This chapter was originally written in French,
translated into English by Dr. Penelope Johnstone,
and second-read by Anna-Regula Sharp.

A Boy from God's Country

Andreas D'Souza

Kerala is often called "God's own country." Rightly so because of her natural beauty: backwater rivers, coconut and banana groves, emerald paddy fields, spice gardens, the undulating mountain regions and the plains often surrounded by wide expanses of blue water. In a similar fashion Mangalore, too, should be named "God's country" because it is very similar to Kerala in landscape, water sources, and vegetation. I was born in Negiguri, a small village in Mangalore, which literally means "paddy hole." It is a veritable hole (*guri*) surrounded by hills on all sides. A small river irrigates the fertile land. During the monsoon season rainwater from the surrounding hills gushes forth in frothing currents carrying rich red soil from the hills. During the summer people join together to build small stone and mud dams to store the water, so that farmers can irrigate their fields, vegetable gardens, coconut and areca nut groves. The neighboring village is called Halthot, "swinging garden," because of its tall areca nut palms and the cluster of villages together is called Pachchanadi, "the green land." Growing up in this veritable paradise I learned to accept and respect various faith, caste, and cultural communities. My Hindu neighbors respectfully addressed my male family members as *porbul* (lord) referring to our Brahmin caste.

The exact place from where my ancestors came is not certain. My family name D'Souza indicates Goan origin. It is probable that they had migrated to the coastal region of Mangalore during the Portuguese persecution of Christians. In the fifteenth and sixteenth centuries entire villages of higher castes (Brahmins and Kshatriyas) in Goa converted to the Catholic faith. These new converts retained many of their ancestral Hindu practices and customs. It was the time of the Inquisition in Europe and the Portuguese government enforced it in Goa. In its effort to do away with non-Christian practices and enforce a "pure Catholic" faith it enacted laws and enforced them on these converts. In order to escape persecution many of these converts migrated to the coastal region of Karnataka. The Nayaks of Keladi ruled this region and they welcomed the migrants warmly and allotted them land for cultivation and facilitated their commercial activities. It is possible that my ancestors were part of this migration.

My grandfather was a good farmer, so was my father but he had chosen to be a businessman and he owned a bar where he sold toddy, the tapped and fermented juice from palm trees, a favorite drink of the villagers. He was thus able to supplement the agricultural income to raise a family of nine children. However disaster struck the family when one year my father collected all the money he had and went to a bar auction to bid on an additional bar.[1] There was a long delay in auctioning and my father grew tired and fell asleep. When he woke up he found his wallet gone and returned home empty-handed and without the bar. That was a terrible loss for him; he became depressed and tried to drown his sorrow in alcohol.[2] My mother was very resourceful. She rented a two-room shop in Padangadi, a centrally located area, and opened a coffee shop where she sold tea, coffee, various snacks, and other items. My father helped her by making the purchases in the town market approximately 5 miles away, stone grinding the ingredients for *idlies* (rice cakes)[3] and generally being available for male clients in the outer room while my mother prepared tea or coffee and served women

1. As is still the practice in some parts of India, wine shops and bars need a special license from the Government and these licenses are often expensive.
2. Bootlegging is quite a widespread problem, not only in many of our villages, but also in many cities. In my village people produced alcohol from various ingredients like cashew fruit mixed with *jaggry*, palm juice, or from a mix of other fruits, like bananas. This problem is compounded in states where prohibition is enforced. In order to make quick money bootleggers add dangerous substances like used battery cells. There are stories of people dying by consuming this dangerous stuff.
3. This is a popular breakfast item in South India whose ingredients include rice and black gram lentils ground and left to ferment over several hours and

in the inner room. Most of her clients were women laborers from a nearby
cashew nut factory. Clients bought on credit and would settle their bills
each week when they received their pay. Her clients came from all backgrounds and castes: Hindus, Muslims, and Christians. For me this shop
became my first school of interfaith learning. I was the eldest of nine children. When my mother was confined for forty days after the birth of a
child, which happened every two years, I helped my father in running the
shop and I often accompanied him on his weekly trips to the market in
town for buying provisions for the shop as well as our home. There were
only four Catholic families in our village, the other five or six households
were Hindu. Each of these households had farmland and cultivated two
crops of rice and at least one crop of vegetables. I grew up with my immediate Hindu neighbor, who was of the same age, a *poojari*.[4] His caste or
creed had little impact on my life. He often came to my house and I to
his. On feast days like Christmas and Dassera we exchanged especially
prepared food and invited each other for the festive meal.

Even though I had no immediate Muslim neighbor, Muslims came to
our shop. Two incidents come to memory. One was a Muslim wedding to
which we were invited. The *barat* (wedding procession) came in boats down
the river. The whole river seemed lit up with lamps as the boats moved
slowly and it was beautiful to watch from the hilltop. As with all Muslim
weddings the signing of the *nikah* (marriage contract) was brief and around
midnight we had the wedding meal. A huge plate filled with biryani (rice
and mutton cooked with spices) was set before a group of four or five men
to eat together. Women were served in a different quarter. For me this was
a veritable communion meal, sharing food with people I hardly knew. The
other incident involved a Muslim on his way to the market with a basketful
of mangoes on his head. I was riding a bicycle at full speed on a sloping
road. By the time I realized what was happening, I had crashed into the
man sending the mangoes flying all over the road. He readily accepted my
profuse apologies and my help to pick up the scattered mangoes.

I did my elementary studies at the local convent school and the parish
school and then went to St. Anthony of Padua High School, which was run
by the diocese in the town. I soon became friends with four other boys
from four different backgrounds. Viraragava was a Brahmin, Ratnakar
Bhangera a Protestant (a convert from a lower caste), Bhujanga a Hindu,

---

then steamed. They are served with coconut chutney and *sambar*, a thin curry made
of yellow or red lentils and vegetables.

4. The word literally means one who worships.

Dawood a Muslim, and I was a Catholic. We were close friends competing in studies and sports. All five of us were once invited to a meal at our sports instructor's house; he was a Brahmin. We were served our meal outside and after the meal we had to clean the place with cow dung. This was the first time I became aware of the Brahmin sense of pollution. The headmaster, a diocesan priest, arranged a special retreat for the graduating Catholic boys and the year I was graduating the preacher was a Carmelite. He was look-ing for candidates for his order and had a special eye on me. After the retreat he came to my home to talk to my parents about my future. My parents offered him hospitality and respectfully listened to his suggestions about my future studies. After he left my father was furious and forbade me to see this priest again. I had no qualms about agreeing with him for I had already decided to join the Capuchin Order.

I owe my call to the Capuchin Order to my classmate and friend Felix who had joined my class in the eleventh grade. He had a brother in the Order and used to tell me many stories about his life. It was also at this time that I happened to read the life of St. Francis of Assisi, which left a deep impression on me. After I completed high school I declared my intentions to become a Capuchin monk. My father, grandfather, and one of my uncles were against my decision. They wanted me to continue secular studies. One evening just a week before I was to leave my village to join the Capuchin Order, I was returning from a farewell party organized in the church and heard angry voices emanating from my grandfather's house. My father, grandfather, and uncle had gathered together with some of our Hindu neighbors and had decided to break my legs and confine me to a room. There was a lot of commotion. I could hear the noise from the top of the hill. I took a different route to reach my house and hid in the attic until the commotion was over and the mob had dispersed. Neither the physical threat nor inducement from my grandfather could shake my resolve. I was the first to finish high school in the entire family and my grandfather and my father wanted me to study to become a medical doctor, lawyer, or engineer. But I remained steadfast in my resolve and in May 1957, I left home by train to Coimbatore, Tamilnadu, for three years of preparatory studies in Latin, Hindi, experimental psychology, sociology, and related subjects. One year of intense spiritual training in the novitiate in Farangipet, Mangalore, three years of Philosophy in Kerala (Quilon and Trichur), four years of theology and scriptural studies in Kotagiri in the Nilgiris brought me the long sought-after goal: priestly ordination in 1967. My father's first cousin, who was then bishop of Mangalore, ordained me in my parish church. It was a grand occasion, the church was completely packed and people had to stay outside. My parents had organized a festive meal for the invited guests.

During my theological studies, I obtained permission to study Hindustani classical music at the summer course at a beautiful town called Mussoori in the foothills of the Himalayas. On my way to the north I visited the Capuchin mission in Agra. Aligarh Muslim University is about 25 miles from Agra and one of the Capuchin priests was chaplain at the university. I went to visit him and he volunteered to show me around. The university was closed for almost three months due to Hindu–Muslim riots. I was wearing my brown Capuchin habit with a white cord around my waist attached to which was a heavy rosary. A young man approached us and pointing his finger at me said, "It is people like you who must work for reconciling the two communities." At the moment I did not realize how prophetic this voice would be. The seed for Islamic studies was planted in my heart at that moment. One year after my ordination as a priest, I spent five months in Paris studying French in preparation for three years of Arabic and Islamic studies at the Pontifical Institute of Arabic and Islamic Studies in Rome. My teachers were White Fathers bringing with them a profound knowledge of lived Islam in North Africa and imparting to their students a genuine love for Muslims. My sojourn in Tunis during two summer vacations, four months each year, helped not only in improving my mastery of the Arabic language but also deepened my understanding of Muslims.

As a next step in my preparation for this special ministry with Muslims, I enrolled in a PhD program at the University of Edinburgh. Prof. William Montgomery Watt was to be my guide and I selected the development of early Muslim thought as a topic for my doctoral dissertation. Unfortunately my mother became seriously ill and I had to come home to look after her. After three months, as she was recovering, I received an invitation to join the Henry Martyn Institute of Islamic Studies in Hyderabad as a lecturer and in charge of interfaith dialogue. The institute was started in 1930 as a school to train missionaries to evangelize Muslims. During its long years of sojourn in various parts of India it remained committed to this goal, even when the Church at large started talking about interfaith dialogue. The director and staff on the one hand took part in dialogue meetings but on the other encouraged the conversion of Muslims by producing literature and guidelines for missionaries. Most Muslims viewed the institute's call to dialogue with suspicion and evangelical Christians kept asking "how many Muslims have you converted?"

This ambiguous situation at the institute, where dialogue was understood as a tool for evangelization, threw up two practical challenges for a young man full of plans for bringing my learning from Rome. One was to convince Muslims that I had no hidden agenda. The other challenge was to help Christians understand Muslims, get rid of their deep-rooted preju-dices and become friends with Muslims. With this in mind I travelled throughout India giving lectures on Islam to seminary students, sisters in convents, schoolteachers and other groups. Fr. Albert Nambiarparambil, then secretary of the dialogue commission of the Catholic Bishops' Conference of India, traveled with me and spoke eloquently about the need for dialogue with people of other faiths. Even though it was a time of intense learning and building friendships with a large number of Muslims, not only in Hyderabad but all over the country, I felt frustrated because it was not easy to dismantle the deep-rooted agenda of the missionary church and remove the equally rooted suspicions of the wider Muslim community.

After three years working at the institute, I decided to make another attempt at doctoral studies. I had heard of Prof. Willelm Bijlefeld, the editor of the *Muslim World* and the director of the Duncan Black MacDonald Center at Hartford, Connecticut. I enjoyed reading his sympathetic inter-pretation of Islam and his personal engagement in dialogue with Muslims. In response to my enquiry, he invited me to join him at McGill University's Institute of Islamic Studies. The Hartford center had decided to run a joint program with the institute in Montreal that year. Would you call it destiny that the collaboration between McGill and Hartford lasted only for three years but I continued to study at the institute for ten years? The institute was unique. Wilfred Cantwell Smith had started it after his experience in India (before independence) with the stipulation that Muslim and Christian students and professors study Islam together in a spirit of dialogue. In my master's thesis under the supervision of Prof. Bijlefeld, I analyzed the works of Kenneth Cragg and William Montgomery Watt and concluded that Islam is what Muslims say it is. In order to know the true Islam it is not enough to read books but one must observe living Islam, and in order to know this living Islam one must go and live with Muslims and not confine oneself to libraries. In my desire to understand Islam as Muslims under-stand it, I elected to work on the writings of three Indian Muslims for my PhD dissertation. It was a time-consuming task since all three Muslim scholars—Sir Sayyid Ahmad Khan, Abdul Kalam Azad and Abul A'la Mawdudi—were prolific writers on various aspects of Muslim life. Prof. Charles Adams, then director of the institute was my thesis supervisor. Islam is what Muslims say it is, but the question remained; which Muslims? The analysis of the writings of these three giants of Islam made me realize that there are as many understandings of Islam as there are Muslims.

My commitment to the Christ of the Gospels, whom I saw through the Poverello, and the guidance of professors like Bijlefeld and Charles Adams, only confirmed my desire to dedicate my life to interfaith dialogue. The ten years at McGill were years of deepening my understanding of Islam. I was deeply moved by the mystical writings of Ibn Arabi and Ala al-Dawla Simnani under the able guidance of Prof. Herman Landolt, Islamic History taught by Prof. Don Little, Muslim Theology led by Prof. Wadi Haddad, and Qur'anic studies with Prof. Boullata. All of them were able teachers and helped me grasp the inner spirit of Islam; a trajectory amply aided by my Muslim companions coming from many Muslim countries.

Returning to the Henry Martyn Institute (HMI) in 1985, after ten years of absence, I found no change in the attitude of the staff regarding dialogue. I was invited to become associate director and eventually to take over as director when the incumbent retired in 1989. The year following my return, the director went on sabbatical leave. Even though one of my senior colleagues was appointed acting director, I was asked to run the institute with the understanding that eventually I would take over as director. Occupying the director's office, I discovered deep down among some files a document entitled "HMI: A Ministry of Reconciliation." Going through the document I was excited to see right there in the document were described the ideals, which I had wanted to reach. David Lindel, the acting director encouraged me to present this document at the next board meeting. The board took some serious decisions at its meeting, one of which was to call for an international consultation to take a closer look at the above-mentioned document. Of course the director upon his return from his sabbatical was not pleased to find a consultation already in its planning stage involving Indian church leaders and international partners. The consultation took place as planned with a strong exhortation to change the orientation of the work of the institute. Since the director and a majority of the staff were not in favor of changing the evangelistic orientation, nothing was done until the incumbent director retired and I was made associate director of programs and director-designate in 1989.

1990 was a year of great significance in the history of the institute. Nationwide it was one of the most turbulent years. On September 25, the BJP leader L. K. Advani started his *rathyatra*[5] from the Somnath Temple in Gujarat with a call to all Hindus to unite to destroy the *Babri Masjid* in

5. Literally chariot procession, annually observed by Hindus around a temple. Usually the deity is taken out in a colourfully decorated chariot drawn by devotees and taken around the whole village or district as the case might be.

Ayodhya and rebuild the Ram temple.[6] Clashes between Hindus and Muslims turned into pogroms in all the regions through which Advani traveled or had the intention to travel. Hyderabad has a long history of feuds between Hindus and Muslims. The happenings elsewhere in the country created tension between the two communities, which resulted in riots already in the beginning of November. Foreseeing greater trouble, I called a meeting of all religious leaders and some political leaders. The result was the formation of the "Aman Shanti Forum," a loosely organized popular movement dedicated to work for peace. We organized public meetings and peace rallies all over the city, at which representatives of different religions took part and gave a strong call to maintain peace. It was amidst this tension-filled context that I called for a consultation from November 23 to 26 to review and refocus the mission of the institute. This consultation was prophetic: the participants, among whom were the institute's international partners, board and council members, and the staff, after three days of discussion, unanimously decided to recommend that the institute move from its efforts to covert Muslims, give up the ambiguity between dialogue and evangelization and have a single focus, namely reconciliation. In order to do this they also recommended that the constitution of the institute should be amended appropriately to reflect this new focus. During these three days of reflection and prayer I heard anew the voice of the young student in the campus of Aligarh University: "It is people like you who must work for reconciliation between us."

In spite of all our efforts to maintain peace, violence broke out on the night of December 6, 1990, in the old city of Hyderabad, which lasted for three weeks; many Hindus and Muslims lost their lives, many houses and business places were looted and burned, many temples and mosques were desecrated. I worked with my friends of the Aman Shanti Forum day and night in the local general hospital and in the narrow streets of the old city of Hyderabad. That was a terrible experience. And that experience led me to develop a program for the institute and construct a theology to sustain the work. We rewrote the constitution with an emphasis on working for reconciliation and interfaith relations. We also changed the name of the

6. This claim was not new but Advani, for political reasons, opened and revived the long-standing controversy over this mosque/temple issue. Even though he did not reach Ayodhya, he was arrested in Bihar; he succeeded in galvanizing votes for his party, which succeeded in forming a coalition government a few years later.

institute to the Henry Martyn Institute: International Centre for Research, Interfaith Relations and Reconciliation.

When I took over as director in 1992, the institute was still a small organization with three teaching staff and three support staff. With the new name and new constitution, the work of the institute expanded rapidly. I started hiring new staff to become truly interfaith and soon we had around forty people, men and women from various faith backgrounds. We developed various methods to bring about reconciliation. We undertook development work in communally sensitive areas with the aim of bringing the two antagonistic communities together. We organized workshops in different parts of the country to train people in methods of transforming conflicts into peace. Our diploma and master's level courses included not only the study of Islam but also other religions with an emphasis on interfaith relations and reconciliation. For me personally this was quite a learning experience. I realized that when we have a good program, funding was not an issue. The institute became truly international. Students and others came from as far away as the Samoan islands and Venezuela.

To give an ideological base to this ever-extending praxis, I began developing a theology, which I called "A Theology of Relationships," based on a South American model of liberation theology but adapting it to the Indian context of multifaith, multicaste, and multirace. I argued that as long as we hold on to "absolute," "unique," and "only" claims we cannot engage in interfaith dialogue. All the differences and diversities surrounding us are God-given. If God had willed, he could have created one community, to borrow a phrase from the Qur'an. It is through our commitment to and involvement in the other as other that an authentic relationship can be built and sustained without becoming a threat to the other's identity. As dialogue partners, we not only respect the other's diversity but also sustain and nurture the diversity. Conversion is not the goal of this endeavor but mutual transformation.

This theology of relationships has emerged from my study of the Bible, Christian theology and particularly lives of saints like Francis of Assisi, Theresa of Avila and John of the Cross. In a similar fashion, I am deeply moved and challenged by my study of the Qur'an, Islamic theology and more powerfully by Islamic mysticism. In the book of Genesis, I see God hastening to build a relationship with Adam and Eve after their fall. Christ's words in Matthew's Gospel, "if you remember that your brother/sister has something against you, leave your gift at the altar and go and first be reconciled" are powerfully inspirational. St. Paul's reminder that we are

ambassadors of Christ to bring the message of reconciliation to the world
kept reminding me of the need for bringing people of all faiths together in
reconciliation. One of the most powerful verses in the Qur'an that keeps
adding to my Christian conviction is from *Sura Nur* (Q. 24:35):

> Allah is the Light of the heavens and the earth. The parable of His
> Light is as if there were a Niche and within it a Lamp enclosed in
> Glass: the glass as it were a brilliant star: lit from a blessed Tree of
> Olive, neither of the East, nor of the West, whose Oil is well-nigh
> Luminous, though fire scarce touched it: Light upon Light! Allah
> guides whom He will to His Light: Allah sets forth Parables for men
> and Allah knows all things.

The Light in the lamp is sustained by olive oil that is produced from a
tree, which belongs neither to the East nor to the West and Allah guides
whom he will. In God all differences exist, everything comes from him.
During my student days at McGill Sufism fascinated me. In Rabi'a al-
Adawiyya, I saw St. Francis of Assisi, the poverello who gave up everything
for the love of God. Rabi'a's words, "if I love you because of my desire for
Paradise, debar me from there; if I love you because of fear of hell cast me
in there; but if I love you for your own sake, do not hide your face from
me" resonated in me.

Reading Ibn Arabi, the great master of Sufi thought, whom I studied at
McGill, taught me the deep relational love that exists between God and his
creatures: *kuntu kanzan makhfiyyan, lam u'raf fa ahbabtu an u'rifa, fa khalaqtu
al-khalq*, which may be translated as, "I was a hidden treasure, not known,
so I desired to be known, so I created the world." This seems to imply that
God needs the bond of relationship with the cosmos. And it is this constant
reminder of God's presence that animates and enlivens the everyday life of
Muslims, for true Islam does not only mean external surrender to the will
of God but constantly living in the presence of God who is closer than the
jugular vein. As in one of the revelatory experiences of Muhammad, when
Angel Gabriel asks, "what is *ihsan?*" the Prophet says, "*ihsan* is to worship
God as if you could see him, for indeed even if you cannot see him, he sees
you."[7] Not only sufis who dedicate their entire lives to strive to live in the
aura of God's presence but also the everyday life of all Muslims is to some
extent pervaded by God's omnipresence. A Muslim will begin his or her
day with *bismillah* (In the name of God), if you question "how are you" he

7. Quoted by Jonathan A. C. Brown, in *Hadith: Muhammad's Legacy in the
Medieval and Modern World* (Oxford: Oneworld, 2009), 186.

or she will answer *al-hamdullilah* (All praise be to God), if someone dies in the family, the response will be *ma shah Allah* (Thanks be to God), you invite a Muslim to your home or for a meeting you will hear the words, "yes, *insha' allah*" (God willing). Many Muslim house doors or gates display in bold letters the words, "*min fadlillah*" (from God's generosity); this list could go on. It is not only the written Qur'an but also the day-to-day lived Qur'an that serves as a powerful inspiration not only for thinking theology but also to doing theology.

I will conclude this biographical essay by recalling the incident on the Aligarh Muslim University campus: "it is people like you who should work to bring reconciliation between us." This call is alive even today. We all are called to bring reconciliation between people no matter where we are.

Teaching the Religion of Others

Michel Lagarde

Many missionary lives, my own included,[1] start with a confrontational attitude, or rather, apostolic zeal, with all the impetuosity and unworthiness this can entail, as does anything indicative of conquest.[2] "Woe is me, if I do not proclaim the Gospel!" Yes, indeed, but after forty years of experience, my concept of evangelization has perceptibly changed. In a letter to a friend, Ernest Renan wrote: "where usefulness ends, beauty begins. God, the Infinite, and the pure air coming from there; that is life."[3] In a certain sense, this is in a small way the summing-up of my spiritual journey in the

1. The author teaches at the *Pontificio Istituto di Studi Arabi e d'Islamistica* (PISAI) in Rome, which provides intensive courses (thirty weeks a year, five days a week, five to seven hours a day) on Arabic language and Islamics. In the first year the students are in Cairo, and in Rome for the following two years. The *licence* is granted after three years of study and the doctorate after five years. The Institute publishes three journals: *Islamochristiana* (annual), *Etudes Arabes* (annual), and *Encounter* (monthly).

2. In the same sense, Charles Peguy and Simone Weil both remarked that victory is always impure because it implies violence.

3. *Souvenirs d'enfance et de jeunesse* (Paris: Calman-Levy, n.d.), 341–42.

Muslim–Christian encounter: at first I aimed for the useful, that is to say, to defend myself and to convince; then, gradually, the beauty of the disinterested encounter appeared to me more and more as an ideal.

I have been in the company of diverse Muslim communities, for nine years in Mali, and for a year in Jerusalem. For the rest of the time, my life has been divided between study, research, publication, and teaching, always concerning Islam. In doing all this, I have for many years resided at the Pontifical Institute for Arabic and Islamic Studies (PISAI) in Rome.

Stages of Immersion

I soon came to understand that with Muslims and Islam, the work of encounter required one to live a cultural and religious immersion, working at this with great patience. Having questioned the attitude of my initial commitment, I try to live this immersion in line with the following four forms. First comes the stage of understanding the internal coherence of the mental, intellectual, and religious universe of Islam, or in other words, the stock of its riches both apparent and hidden; this requires us constantly to reject any value judgment starting from a reference system foreign to it. The greatest virtue here should be rigorous intellectual honesty. Next comes the stage of respect and sympathy for the universe into which I have entered, where I gradually discover its organization, order, workings, balance and harmony. Here, the greatest virtue lies in an open mind, abandonment, and availability.

Then there is the stage of rediscovery of my mental, cultural, and religious identity which, through this overwhelming adventure, leads to greater consciousness of itself, more focused upon its own consistency, more appropriate to the vocation necessary for what I am. It is more positive because it is no longer borne by the previous perception of accidental, superficial and false opposites, but by the new realization of an essential difference that determines the way our destinies diverge. The great virtue here is to recognize the mutual right to be different.

Finally, comes the stage of witness, that of the person who, while always aiming for a competent and qualified knowledge of Islam's inner coherence, and sincerely respecting the ways in which it is manifested, while being completely aware of his own identity, is able to live out this dual dimension in a way so rich and happy as to arouse in certain Muslim colleagues the wish to follow, in relation to Christians and Christianity, the same path that he has taken with regard to Muslims and Islam. Here the most valuable assets are generosity and creativity.

Obviously this spiritual enterprise, even imperfect, cannot fail to have a determining influence on my way of perceiving the teaching that I deliver at the Institute, which constitutes my chief activity within the Church. Above all, as I have said, marked by the concern to respect the other as he is, and to live out in an intense way my own identity, I would wish that my teaching of the religion of the other would be an education for difference.

A Vision of Teaching

I often remind my students of Ferdinand de Saussure's words: "In language there are only differences."[4] In other words, the meaning lies in the differ-ence; it lies not in the words, but in the relationship they hold between one another. It is somewhat similar for cultures and religions: they lose their significance, if we consider them in isolation; they acquire depth and inter-est as soon as they are seen in the perspective of variety, otherness, and difference. In addition, constant contact with Arab–Muslim culture has convinced me that the relationship can be more successful in paying atten-tion to differences than in searching for what is similar or identical.

For this reason, I would like to give a brief overview of my three major concerns, as a Christian teacher of Muslim culture and religion. First, to point out the difference with respect to the awareness we have of ourselves; next, to emphasize the difference with respect to the stereotyped awareness we have of the other; and finally to stress the difference which constitutes the other's self-awareness.

POINTING OUT THE DIFFERENCE WITH RESPECT TO OUR SELF-AWARENESS

I would like to illustrate my first concern—to point out the difference with respect to our self-awareness—by the following example, thanks to which students gradually come to realize that their cultural-religious framework is structurally other than that of Arab–Muslims. It concerns a section of Sura 30, *The Byzantines*, which from verses 17 to 28 deals with the signs of creation (*al-ayat*), mentioned seven times. Their purpose is to show that

---

4. Ferdinand de Saussure, *Cours de linguistique generale* (Paris: Payot, 1972), 166.

God exists, that he is unique, all-powerful, omniscient, by appealing solely to the intellectual faculties, which are reflection (*al-dhikr*), knowledge (*al-'ilm*), listening (*al-sam'*), and reason (*al-'aql*). This passage represents perfectly one of the major themes of the Qur'an which is at the foundation of later theological development, to the extent that for Mu'tazilites and also a good number of Ash'arites, reason takes precedence over tradition: *al-'aql qabl al-naql*. The word *al-naql* refers to everything that is transmitted and thus includes revelation.[5] Thus the intellect becomes, in many cases, the final point of reference. For example, it is not possible to uphold the Qur'an as divine speech, simply because it contains such a statement: this would be an untenable vicious circle. It is, then, reason which must decide on the divine nature of the Book, according to criteria which it puts down *a priori* and which it applies in practice to the case of the Qur'an.

The great importance given to the intellectual faculties, already in the Qur'an and especially in the developments of later theology, makes it clear to us that Islam is a gnosis, in the etymological meaning of the word and not in the popular meaning of heretical teaching; in other words, an initiation into the knowledge of truth or reality (*al-haqq*). To clarify, by comparison and difference, we would say that Christianity, on the contrary, is a "mystery" of a soteriological nature, as are, for example, the mysteries of Eleusis, of Isis and Osiris, or Mithras. In other words, if Islam essentially seeks to make the truth known, Christianity's primary aim is salvation.

What is the foundation of such a difference, one that is of a structural nature? To put it briefly, we would say it is the divergent concept of Adam's sin. While for a Christian original sin has deeply wounded human nature, in the view of the Qur'an that was only a mild slip (*izlal*).[6] In Islam, the person is born possessing a completely sound human nature (*al-fitra al-salima*) which therefore has no need to be restored or redeemed; in Christianity, by contrast, humanity's redemption requires the incarnation, passion, death, and resurrection of the Son of God. This vital difference can be summed up: On the one hand, according to Islam, the human being is merely forgetful and distracted,[7] and thus has need only to be awakened and challenged by the revelation, to be initiated into the truth; on the other

---

5. On this, see Michel Lagarde, *Les secrets de l'invisible. Essai sur le Grand Commentaire de Fahr al-Din al-Razi* (Paris: al-Buraq, 2009), 213–14.

6. Q. 2:36.

7. This is part of explicit traditional teaching, for Muhammad is credited with saying: "I am only a mortal; I forget just as you forget; so when I forget, remind me" (al-Bukhari, *Kitab al-salat*, 31).

hand, according to Christianity, the human being is mortally wounded, and therefore has to be healed and saved. This is the difference between Islamic gnosis and Christian soteriology, and seeing this clearly students are enabled straightaway to take up a position in relation to the new religious culture which they gradually discover.

To Emphasize the Difference

My second concern in teaching is to emphasize the difference in respect of the stereotyped awareness we have of the other. It is a commonplace to say that the majority of Westerners have ready-made notions and *a priori* assumptions about Islam. And it is precisely on this point that I wish to bring my students to react. Let me take one example, the Qur'an. The general belief is that it is a fixed, untouchable, text, not to be relativized, never troubled by the idea of historical criticism. To make it understood that this is not the case, I do not quote modern attempts by Muslims of Western training, which would be too easy, but I use a great classic of exegesis, Fahr al-Din al-Razi (1149–1209). In the first place, there is for him not merely a single Qur'anic text, but a great number of recensions (*masahif*) to which he frequently refers: the recensions of Basra, al-Haramayn, Syria, Iraq, Kufa, Medina, Mecca, and, in more detail, those of Ubayy, Ibn Anas b. Malik, Hafsa, 'Abdallah b. Mas'ud and 'Uthman.[8] And the divergences between these recensions are sometimes significant.

Second, the different orthodox readings of the Qur'an, bearing on the vocalization and sometimes even the consonantal *ductus*, with the aid of diacritical points, are so numerous that a contemporary writer, 'Abd al-Latif al-Khatib, compiled the systematic and exhaustive catalogue of these, filling no fewer than eleven volumes.[9]

Third, the theory of abrogating and abrogated (*al-nasikh wa-l-mansukh*), which allows for one verse's effect to be cancelled in favor of another's, is a quite remarkable attempt at flexibility. In addition, there are theories of the general meaning and the particular meaning (*al-'amm wa-l-khass*), of the real meaning and the metaphorical meaning (*al-haqiqa wa-l-majaz*),

8. See the numerous references in Michel Lagarde, *Index du Grand Commentaire de Fahr al-Din al-Razi* (Leiden: Brill, 1996), 336–37.
9. Abd al-Latif al-Khatib, *Mu'jam al-qira'at*, 11 vols. (Cairo: Dar sa'd al-din, 1422/2002).

of the literal meaning and the meaning that can be interpreted (*al-zahir wa-l-ta'wil*), which give plenty of latitude in understanding of the text.

Fourth, we have the study of the occasions of revelation (*asbab al-nuzul*) which link the text specifically to a place, a time and the surrounding events. To all this must be added the multiplicity of divergent interpretations by the exegetes. Finally, al-Qurtubi, from Andalus (d. 1272), reported possible different orders of the Qur'anic text.[10] Taken as a whole then we have a wide, flexible, and well-nuanced vision of the text; which runs counter to the habitual and unconfirmed view of the Qur'an held by Westerners.

To Stress the Difference That Constitutes the Other's Self-awareness

Finally, my third concern in teaching is to stress the difference that constitutes the other's self-awareness. By that I mean that even if a Muslim, well-informed on his tradition, knows that internal divergence can damage the community and is thus severely condemned,[11] he knows equally well that the difference with regard to others is what constitutes the *umma*, as it constitutes the normality of every group. My aim is thus to bring the student to envisage the right to be different, or in other words, the significant and positive aspect of this right for the other.

It often happens, when I present the Islamic Studies program, that one of the first objections from many students is to say that Muslims had copied from the Jews and Christians and that the content of Islam is therefore only ill-digested plagiarism. To that my reply is to show that it is possible to use material from predecessors, to arrive at the construction of an edifice with a completely different purpose. As an example, I take the narrative of the Seven Sleepers of Ephesus which is found, prior to Islam, in the Syriac tradition reported by James of Saruj, Jacobite Bishop of Batnan (d.521) and in liturgical hymns of the Coptic tradition.[12] This same narrative is found in Sura 18, of the "People of the Cave."[13] Setting aside the

10. Al-Qurtubi, *al-Jami' li-ahkam al-Qur'an, al-Hay'a al-misriyya al-'amma li-l-kitab*, i (Cairo, 1987), 59–60.

11. For example, in Muslim, *Kitab al-'ilm*, 2: "Those who, before you, differed regarding the Book have been destroyed."

12. Numerous Christian texts relating to this legend can be found in Ignazio Guidi, *Raccolta di scritti* (Rome: Istituto per l'Oriente, 1945), 198ff.

13. Q. 18:9–26.

divergence of details, it is the purpose of the story that changes entirely: in Christian tradition, the aim is to refute the distant disciples of the Sadducees who do not believe in the resurrection of the dead; while in the Qur'an, the objective is to show that Muhammad's ignorance of certain specific points does not invalidate the authentic nature of his prophetic office. In this way a narrative more-or-less the same takes on a completely different significance, according to the context. Cultural difference is reckoned, in the Qur'an, as eminently positive, since it is a proof of the existence of the unique God: "Among his signs: the creation of the heavens and of the earth and the variations in your language and your colors; indeed in that are signs for those who reflect."[14] This very clearly means that cultural difference is theologically significant.

Finally, the Muslim knows that the divergences between groups, allowable up to a certain point, are a gift of God, with a view to arousing dynamism, emulation and renewal among people, according to the very words of a tradition of the Prophet which, although apocryphal, nonetheless reflects the vision of the first community: "*Inna fi khtilafi-kum rahmatan min rabbi-kum*—Indeed, your differences are a mercy coming from your Lord!"[15]

Perhaps I am mistaken in my initiative of education for difference, since Islam, it is said, is naught but an exaggerated proclamation of the divine oneness, unique and indivisible.[16] This is true; however, God is at one and the same time the First and the Last, the Visible and the Hidden, the Gentle and the Tyrant, and he "is known only in the conjunction of opposites; moreover, he is the essence of the opposites and not an essence which would unite the opposites," as expressed by 'Abd al-Qadir.[17] In other words, he is the very difference itself; such is the meaning of his transcendence.

This chapter was originally written in French,
translated into English by Dr. Penelope Johnstone,
and second-read by Anna-Regula Sharp.

---

14. Q. 30:22.

15. It is apocryphal, in fact, since it is not included in the compilation of A. J. Wensinck, *Concordance et indices de la tradition musulmane*, 2nd ed. (Leiden: Brill, 1992).

16. This is indeed the message of Q.112.

17. 'Abd al-Qadir al-Jaza'iri, *Le Livre des Haltes*, presented, translated, and annotated by Michel Lagarde, vol. 1 (Leiden: Brill, 2000), 45.

An Engagement with Islam

Christopher Lamb

I was born in 1939 and grew up in the city of Bristol, in the west of England. This should have given me a sense of the wider world, since Bristol was a significant port for centuries. "All ship-shape and Bristol fashion" is an expression still used with pride by Bristolians to mean something tidy and organized. But it was only at university that I met a Nigerian student for the first time and began to register the darker side of my home city's story. Bristol was instantly familiar to him from the slave trade, in a way that his city, Calabar in eastern Nigeria, was not to me. It was the first of many times when I was reminded of how little I really knew of the impact my country had had on the world, and how what was new to me was only too familiar to those who had experienced the British presence of the past. "Ah, Bristol," he said, and continued with great good humor, "your people loaded their ships with manufactured trinkets and things and came to my city and bought slaves from my people to sell them on in the West Indies and America." It was a disturbingly different view from the patriotic children's books I had grown up with, books like H. E. Marshall's *Our Island Story* (1905) and *Our Empire Story* (1908), and Rudyard Kipling's *Kim*, from the same era.

At the independent boarding school I went to were a handful of boys from the Indian subcontinent, some with names I now recognize as Muslim. At the time their origins were a matter of indifference to me as to the other boys. The only consideration was whether they were able to contribute to "our side" in the intensely competitive world of schoolboy games. There was a boarding house reserved for Jewish boys, an unusual innovation by the Victorian founding headmaster of the school, so I was alert to Jewish festivals and fasts, especially since the major ones came at the beginning of the school year. There was a small degree of casual prejudice towards the Jewish boys in the rest of the school, but the mid-1950s was a time before any widespread consciousness of the horrors of the Nazi Holocaust. I remember, all the same, being surprised to discover that people could be disliked simply for being Jewish. Whether their segregation into a separate boarding house was a good idea or not, I don't know. The intention was to allow them the same opportunity to worship and observe their faith that the rest of the school, assumed to be Christians, had in the school chapel under the guidance of the two school chaplains. Some years ago, after over one hundred years of existence, the Jewish house was closed. I believe it never had a future rabbi among all its boys. Perhaps it satisfied neither religious nor secular Jews.

At Oxford many things changed for me. I had first set foot in another country at the age of eighteen. Now at university I was in a wider world altogether, and it is interesting to reflect that it was the Church that played the largest part in alerting me to the world outside Britain. I had been baptized and later confirmed in the Church of England, but also attended a Baptist church, where I still remember a sermon dealing with world faiths in relation to Christian faith. At Oxford my faith matured into a personal commitment to God in Christ, and I was accepted for ordination training. The romanticism of empire seeded by childhood reading must have taken root in me because in my newly awakened faith I began to take an interest in the worldwide church, especially in India, through meetings of the student branch of the Church Missionary Society (CMS), now the Church Mission Society. CMS was founded in 1799 by Church of England evangelicals concerned for the spread of the Christian Gospel in Africa and the East. After ordination training and an initial five years of parish ministry in suburban north London, my wife Tina and I offered ourselves for service with CMS and arrived in Pakistan with our two children in September 1969.

Tina had grown up in the Congregational Church, now the United Reformed Church, where a minister of her local church had been

Dr. Norman Goodall, later an Associate General Secretary of the World Council of Churches, and an elder statesman of the missionary movement. Tina had spent what is now known as a gap year between school and university as an eighteen-year-old in Nazareth, helping to care for Arab orphan children, an exotic adventure for the 1950s, so her experience of the developing world was considerably greater than mine. Together we had concluded that if we had set ourselves to serve God in his world, we could not set limits on where that might be. Her parents were supportive, and so was my widowed mother, although I was her only child, and despite the fact that communication, without email or even telephone, was confined to a weekly letter and the uncertainties of the Pakistani and British postal services.

Pakistan

We were based in Lahore, the cultural capital of Pakistan, and lived in the house first used by Thomas Valpy French (1825–91), known as the "seven-tongued padre." French was the first Anglican bishop of Lahore (1877–87) and a pioneer educationist whose diocese covered the whole of northwest India. He built Lahore Cathedral, a huge undertaking which he justified on the grounds that Muslims had such fine buildings in Lahore that they would think little of a faith which did not attempt to match them. After returning to England because of ill health in 1887, he subsequently went to Muscat, where he died and is buried. Because of the restrictions on non-Muslim burials in the Arabian Peninsula his grave can only be reached by sea. Rowan Williams, the current Archbishop of Canterbury, has named him as a personal hero.

It was a daunting inheritance, therefore, and thoroughly in the spirit of a Christian version of the "romance of Empire." But it did later inspire me to re-found the Lahore Divinity School, which French had opened in 1870. Initially my task was to follow, with far poorer linguistic gifts, in the steps of a man who taught his students whilst translating the New Testament and patristic texts directly from the Greek into Urdu, Punjabi or Pashtu. I found Urdu hard work, and I never became proficient, but language learning illuminated many cultural puzzles, and alerted me to the way that Islam shaped the language and so the way of thinking of Pakistanis, whether they were Muslim or Christian. A brief spell observing the process of creating a new Urdu translation of the New Testament revealed that almost the entire religious vocabulary of Urdu, words meaning: Lord, faith, prayer, grace, or spirit, were Qur'anic words saturated with Islamic references. Pakistani Christians read their Bible through Muslim spectacles. How could they not? The point was vividly brought home by the experience of a convert to Christianity from what was then East Pakistan. Converted in Karachi, he initially read the Bible in English, but soon wanted to read it in his native Bengali. We secured a Bengali Bible for him, but he was deeply disappointed in it. "This is all Hinduism!" he said. Because most Bengali Christians come from a Hindu background, the Bengali Bible uses Hindu religious terminology. Eventually we managed to find an "Islamic" Bengali Bible for him. The opposite problem occurred among the Sindhi tribal people from a Hindu background when they were confronted with Punjabi Christian missionaries using their own Urdu Islamic terminology. "You sound as if you want us to be Muslims!" they said.

It was soon clear that the significance of all this was not just linguistic. Translation is an intricate art, but depends fundamentally on the possibility of shared meaning. If the Christian message is to find verbal form in a language and culture shaped by Islam there must at the outset be extensive common ground in shared meaning, or else the message cannot possibly be understood in that language. When we use a word for *God* there must be a basic common understanding about God. At the same time the receptor language will be "stretched" to accommodate the new meaning of God as known in Jesus Christ, or else it will seem to the Urdu speakers that they are hearing only what they have always known. Christian discourse has always had to negotiate the twin perils of not being understood at all, or of saying only what is already accepted and thought of as self-evident and obvious. In the same way, Islam has been understood by some Christians as entirely hostile to the Gospel, and by others as an acceptable alternative. Christian theology, it seems to me, refuses to be impaled on either horn of this dilemma.

I was not sure that either my missionary colleagues or my Pakistani friends saw things in this way. Pakistani Christians, being associated with the low status "sweeper" classes, generally suffered from both religious and social prejudice, and so were inclined to react by repeating unthinking stereotypes about Muslims. The views of missionaries about Islam ranged from those who advocated friendship with Muslims but hostility to Islam, to those who saw the missionary task as enabling Muslims to be better Muslims. To me the former seemed self-contradictory and the latter at best naive. How were we to judge what constituted a "better Muslim"? I began to read again the books of Kenneth Cragg, and found in his writing themes of embassy and hospitality that made sense of what I was experiencing in

Pakistan. To be an ambassador for Christ, he was saying, you have to be resident in the country to which you are sent, and fluent in its language, its ways, and its thinking. This means a glad acceptance of the hospitality offered to you by your hosts which alone can enable you to learn these things, and an answering hospitality of your own mind and heart to what you are experiencing. But you do not cease to be an ambassador with a message from the one who sent you, and this message needs to be expressed in terms that your hosts can understand and perhaps accept. You will never cease to be a foreigner but your very foreignness is of value and you should not attempt to jettison it, or in the old colonial language, "go native."

Towards the end of my brief six years in Pakistan I had the great privilege of arranging Kenneth Cragg's visit to Lahore during his visit to Pakistan. It was a revelation to go to the Department of Islam at the University of the Punjab and meet staff there to suggest they might invite him to lecture. Initial suspicion changed to open enthusiasm when I mentioned the name of Kenneth Cragg. It was like a series of doors opening all the way down a previously closed corridor.

Hospitality was a lesson constantly enforced in Pakistan. Economically impoverished people invited us to tea in their homes and brought in cakes and bottled drinks they could ill afford. When I joined the Sociology Department of the University of the Punjab my fellow students greeted me with genuine regret that they could not offer me anything because it was Ramadan. More than once complete strangers stopped unasked to help when our car broke down or my bicycle chain came loose. When our eldest daughter died two hundred miles from where I was in Lahore I was dimly conscious in my grief of the efforts being made to get me a seat on a heavily booked aircraft so that I could get to Rawalpindi in time for the funeral on the same day that she died. Afterwards Pakistanis came to express their condolences and cried or laughed with us as we felt moved, while a few of our expatriate friends could find no words for the occasion, and failed to mention her death at all. Were they trying to avoid distressing us, or themselves? No Pakistani friends made that mistake.

Birmingham

After six tumultuous years—with the birth of a third daughter, the death of our eldest, Pakistan's third war with India in 1971, and a foray into theological education with a hand-picked band of ordination candidates—I was asked to join the staff of the CMS training college at Crowther Hall in the

Selly Oak Colleges in Birmingham in 1975. This was a time when migration, especially from the Caribbean and the Indian subcontinent, was rapidly changing the face of big industrial cities in the British midlands and north, and above all in London. The churches were largely unprepared for this influx. Black Christians from the West Indies found themselves cold-shouldered by white worshippers, and where they were accepted felt the style of worship cold and unemotional. With Indians, Pakistanis, and Bangladeshis there were the additional barriers of language and faith. Some churches made serious efforts to help the newcomers establish their own worshipping communities, converting private houses into makeshift mosques and temples. Other churches hung back feeling inadequate to the task, or unconvinced that they should enable worship that was not directed to God in Christ.

It was a new missionary situation where the British churches needed sustained theological resources, so CMS and another Anglican missionary society, the Bible Churchmen's Missionary Society (BCMS, now Crosslinks) jointly appointed me to a new venture, the Other Faiths Theological Project, under the chairmanship of Bishop Stephen Neill, the veteran missionary scholar. Some members of CMS had split from the parent body to form BCMS in 1922 over the issue of the authority of the Bible. Mine was the first joint appointment by the two bodies, so there was always an anxiety on the part of BCMS that my contribution might be theologically unsound. Bishop Neill was seen as the guarantor of my orthodoxy.

In fact much of the work I did was simply urging church congregations to engage with their neighbors of other faiths and suggesting ways that this might be done. I recall a visit to a well-supported evangelical church in Manchester which was located almost opposite a mosque. A formal visit to the mosque had been arranged but when I arrived it was evident that the leaders of the church were anxious about their ability to articulate their faith to the Muslims they were about to meet, and to defend it from the criticism they anticipated. They need not have worried. The Muslims were mainly concerned to defend their building from vandalism and racist graffiti, and saw their Christian church neighbors as potential allies. They showed us the scorch marks inside the letterbox on the front door, where attempts had been made to set the mosque on fire. Too often Christians were so conscious of the theological profile of the newcomers that they neglected the simple duties of common humanity. "What do you say to a Muslim?" was the earnest question among evangelical Christians concerned for the Gospel. The obvious answer was "How about saying 'Hello, how are you?'" It was essential to see people threatened by British xenophobia as human beings first and Muslims second. How could those rejected as unwelcome strangers be expected to reconsider the faith that sustained them in an alien land?

Kenneth Cragg

The job gave me ample opportunity to study and I began a doctoral dissertation on the work of Kenneth Cragg under the supervision of Dr. David Kerr, Director of the Centre for the Study of Islam and Christian–Muslim Relations. The fascination of Cragg's writing for me was his love of poetry and literature, his playfulness with words, his alertness to contemporary issues, and his ability to ask the deeper questions which lie behind the contradictory claims of Christianity and Islam. Writing of the "harshness" of the Muslim response to Christian convictions he says, "The harshness has to be transcended, for much of it is well-intentioned. And in any event the story to be told is only safe in the custody of those for whom every antagonism is an opportunity. For that, precisely, is the heart of the story itself." The commending of the Christian faith has to be in accordance with its own character, with the inner coherence of word and deed in the person of Jesus the Christ. The heart of the Christian Gospel is reconciliation, and the restoration of unity between God and humanity and between human beings themselves. This approach offers a context for the study of Islam and for personal relationships with Muslims which is more than the mere acquisition of knowledge about another worldwide religious culture, and more than the self-aggrandizement of a Christian collective. It demands a recognition that Islam claims universal relevance. Of the title of his first and most famous book, *The Call of the Minaret*, Cragg writes, "Its title tells what it would constitute, as well as what it would describe." The call is not a call to Muslims alone. "Can we," he continues, "so become aware of Islam as to enter into all its implications for the Christian?"

At the heart of Cragg's theology is a sense of the reciprocal relationship between humanity and God. Men and women are made in the image of God, and are partners in the dialogue he opens with them. "Where are you?" asks God, walking in the garden in the cool of the day (Gen 3:9). But the Qur'an has no equivalent text to Genesis 1:26, 27 (". . . in the image of God he created them"), though the idea of humanity as *khalifa* or viceroy comes close to it. But is Cragg then simply using Islam as a way of exploring the distinctiveness of Christian faith by contrast with Islam? Is he really more interested in Christianity than in Islam? That would be an unwarranted judgment on someone who has written so extensively on the Qur'an and contemporary Muslim thinking. Inevitably the themes he selects are those made significant for him by his Christian experience, notably the Biblical literalism and doctrinal rigidity he rejected early in his adult life, and encountered again in some strands of Islam. Cragg has been accused both of undue sympathy with and undue hostility to Islam. How does anyone, standing outside the tradition being studied, come to an objective account of it, and is such a thing possible anyway? I found that studying Cragg's work closely brought me to the heart of the issues inherent in the encounter of peoples of faith.

Coventry and London

These questions continued to preoccupy me in my subsequent work, first in Coventry as advisor to the diocese on community relations, and then in London as advisor on interfaith relations to the Church of England and the national council of churches. The main task of these years, however, was to help create a local and national neighborhood in which the new communities of Muslims, Hindus, Sikhs, and others could feel at home. A democratic society that rejected discrimination on religious grounds had to make space for unfamiliar beliefs and customs. Much was said in these years about the Church of England being the "gatekeeper" for the entrance of other faith communities into full membership of the wider society. It is true that successive archbishops and bishops used their own privileged positions in English society as a kind of umbrella under which other religious communities could shelter rather than obliging them to fight outside for acceptance. Muslim and Jewish leaders were heard to welcome the official "establishment" of the Church of England provided it continued to operate in this way. Some Muslim communities even referred to "our bishop" where there were particularly positive relationships with the local Anglican leader.

Undoubtedly this was consonant with Government policy, and echoed a widespread impatience with religious dogma, and a general assumption that "all religions are the same, aren't they?" British pragmatism and obsession with sport was more interested in whether the newcomers supported England or their country of origin when they played India or Pakistan at cricket. It was also a continuation of colonial policies which had aimed at minimal disturbance of religious sentiment in the British Raj and in Africa. The danger was always that Christian church leaders in positions of influence were speaking on behalf of the leaders of other faiths rather than enabling them to speak for themselves. This was particularly evident in the early years when Christians were effectively determining which individuals would represent communities that had no mechanism of deciding that question for themselves.

It was the Muslim community that was the most multiethnic, and that, partly for that reason, began to bring specifically religious issues to the fore. Whereas many Hindus and Sikhs from the Indian subcontinent were content to describe themselves as "Asians" in the British context, Pakistani, Indian, and Bangladeshi Muslims rejected that term in favor of calling themselves simply "Muslims." "My family happens to originate from Pakistan, but what is important about me is that I am a Muslim," I was told. In this way Muslims raised the whole profile of religion in the United Kingdom, much to the frustration of secularists. Muslim implication in international terrorism has produced a backlash in recent years, and a vociferous demand that religion should have only a private and no public dimension, but the clamor belies the fact that that battle is lost. Secularists continue to use the fact of a religiously plural society in their attempts to deny public expression of Christian faith in such things as the celebration of Christmas, and in their criticism of faith schools, but members of other faiths know that their interests are not served by the downgrading of Christianity.

Muslims in Britain are not of course a single entity, but ethnically, culturally, and theologically very diverse, more so than any other religious community, with members from the Middle East, the Indian subcontinent, and Africa; converts from the indigenous British community; and refugees from almost everywhere. The current preoccupation with security issues and Islamic radicalism has tended to mask the issues raised by this new and permanent Muslim presence in Europe. It has, however, jolted memories and a renewed awareness of the older European engagement with Islam in Spain and the Balkans. Serious attempts have been made in popular television programs to explore the European debt to Arab pioneers in philosophy, medicine, and science. The more this common inheritance is known, the more chances there are of developing a mutually tolerant society.

In this process Islam itself will take on a European and a specifically British dimension. The late Zaki Badawi, frequently the national spokesman for Muslims in the United Kingdom, confided to some of us that he saw the future of Islam in the West rather than in, for example, his native Egypt. "Why?" we asked. "Because of the freedom of speech in the West," he responded. I was startled at a conference for some hundreds of Muslim students at Warwick University to hear the Pakistani speaker praise Britain as the best place for Muslims—a remark that drew the loudest applause of the evening. The contentment of young British Muslims with Western culture is of course only partial, and there is also a disaffected under-class of young British Muslims mired in drugs and crime, as well as the fringe of radicals drawn towards violent political action. Nevertheless the openness of new generations of British Muslims to what is best as well as to what is worst in our history and culture must bring with it an unprecedented Muslim openness to Christian thought and literature and Christian friends. This alone is enough to encourage me to continue in a reciprocal engagement with the thought and literature of Islam, and of course with Muslim friends.

Liminality: Living on Borders

Patrick Ryan

I turned seventy in August 2009, fifty-two years after I entered the Society of Jesus. I have spent half of my life as a Jesuit in Africa and half elsewhere, mainly in New York City. I have always felt that I lived on the borders of any country or community. In a sense, as the anthropologist Victor Turner maintained, religious men and women are called to liminality, living on borders.

Many who hear me speak wonder where I come from. My accent is not typical of New York City. I grew up Irish in New York, most of my relatives either living in Ireland or living in Irish enclaves in that metropolis. This is not the same thing as being Irish American, a description used by Americans of Irish descent, no matter how remote. My family lived in New York City, but we resolutely faced towards Ireland, which I have visited regularly since my ninth year.

My maternal grandmother, Maria Guilfoyle Kennedy—the only grand-parent I ever knew—had no formal education, even though free primary education was available in Ireland's National Schools when she was a little girl in the 1870s. She was what we would call today sight-impaired or legally blind, eventually wearing thick glasses that enabled her to see partially.

But she was never taught how to read. My mother revealed that fact to me the year I was ordained, just before I began my doctoral studies at Harvard. I have often thought it is the reason why I have many illiterate or only semiliterate friends in Africa.

My father hated school when he was a boy growing up in Ireland. Family tradition preserves the name of Mr. Fleming, the harsh schoolmaster in a remote corner of north Tipperary as the reason for my father's antipathy to school. My father never went on for more formal schooling after his primary school years. He later regretted this lack of more formal education when he became involved in the Irish struggle for independence from Britain (1919–22), the subsequent civil war (1922–23) and his own somewhat truncated political life as a Sinn Fein member of Dail Eireann who, along with the rest of Sinn Fein at that time, boycotted the Free State legislature. The Garda Siochana, the Irish police force, followed my father's movements with great interest throughout the 1920s until, at the age of thirty, he emigrated from Ireland to the United States in 1929.

My father found himself excommunicated along with the rest of Sinn Fein and the Irish Republican Army on October 10, 1922. On that date the Catholic Bishops of Ireland issued a pastoral letter in which they instructed faithful Catholics to accept the half-loaf of a Free State offered by the British in the Anglo-Irish Treaty. They also condemned those who were pursuing what the bishops considered an unjust war, declaring that they were to be denied communion. My father ceased to practice as a Catholic for the next decade. But he continued to live on the borders of the Church.

My mother, nine years younger than my father, grew up in New York in a family of very modest means headed by her father and mother, earlier immigrants from Tipperary. After Catholic primary schooling she went on to public secondary school for two years. When her father lost his job because he was trying to organize workers involved in the construction of the New York subways into a union, she quit secondary school and went to work. Later on she remembered the union meetings at which they sang the *Internationale*.

My mother met my father shortly after he arrived in New York. When they decided to marry in October 1932, my father, still alienated from the Church, refused to write to his parish priest back in Ireland and ask for a copy of his baptismal record, and so they were married civilly. Less than two months later my mother, conscience-stricken, told my father she would leave him if they did not marry sacramentally, which they did on December 31, 1932. My father's American-Irish cousin, a diocesan priest and Louvain-educated philosopher named James F. Coffey, managed to reconcile my father more fully with the Church over the next few years, although my father remained somewhat anticlerical to his dying day. I don't know what he would have made of his Jesuit son.

My father died in 1944 at the age of forty-five, only eleven years after marrying my mother; my sister, Mary, was ten and I was four at the time. Our family went through financial hard times around 1950, but a stroke of luck visited us in 1953 when I received admission into the Jesuits' fully endowed Regis High School in Manhattan. I had an excellent educational foundation at Regis, especially in Latin, Greek, and French. In my final year I participated in the Homeric Academy that studied the entire Iliad and even presented a public "defense" of our work before a panel of professors of Greek from Princeton, Fordham, and Columbia.

Immediately after finishing high school, I entered a novitiate of the Society of Jesus at Plattsburgh, New York, near the Canadian border. (The New York Province had two novitiates at the time, so great was the number of those entering.) I had wanted to be a priest since early childhood, fascinated by the liturgy, but I also wanted to teach, as I discovered under the tutelage of the Jesuits who taught me at Regis. When I entered the Jesuit novitiate, I thought I would like to return eventually to a school like Regis and teach what I had been taught, and especially classical Greek literature.

About two months after entering the novitiate, but before we began the thirty days of the Spiritual Exercises, a second-year novice said one day that he thought that the greatest Jesuits he had met were not teachers, like the ones we knew in high school, but missionaries, men whom we met in the novitiate from time to time when they were home on leave from Micronesia in the western Pacific, the Philippines, Japan, and (at least once) the Middle East. I didn't like what he was saying, since it seemed to suggest that my desire to teach classical Greek at Regis or elsewhere was being devalued.

But my conscience was stung by what he had said, and later that afternoon, during the course of a half-hour meditation we always had in addition to the hour in the morning, I reached the conclusion that I should become a missionary. Hard as it seemed, and especially in view of my mother's widowhood and the projected marriage of my sister, which would leave my mother alone, I decided I would volunteer at the earliest opportunity to work overseas.

Making such a sudden decision in a time of tumultuous feelings is not thought commendable in Jesuit tradition, but Saint Ignatius does list as the first time for making a sound and good election: a time "when God our

Lord moves and attracts the will in such a way that a devout person without doubting or being able to doubt, carries out what was proposed. This is what St Paul and St Matthew did when they followed Christ our Lord" (*Spiritual Exercises*, no.175). I often thought of this, much later, when I saw in Rome two paintings of Caravaggio: "The Call of Matthew" (in the Church of San Luigi dei Francesi) and "The Conversion of Paul" (in the Church of Santa Maria del Popolo).

Throughout my novitiate long retreat (October 1957) the call to missionary life loomed large in my imagination, even though the director of novices was trying to divert me from pursuing that theme so early in my Jesuit life. Annually, over the next seven years, I told the Provincials, face to face or in writing, that I wanted to go to the missions, but I hardly told anyone else, except for one Jesuit friend, a man a year ahead of me in philosophy. This Jesuit, suitably named Francis Xavier Hezel, a missionary and prolific scholar of the Western Pacific, has since the 1960s spent more than forty years in Micronesia.

In 1964, as I was finishing my licentiate in philosophy in our house of formation in Shrub Oak, New York, as well as a master's degree in English Language and Literature at Fordham University, I was assigned by the New York provincial to Nigeria. He was reluctant at first to send me, but another man he did assign decided a week later that he really wanted to leave the Society. I arrived in Nigeria the first time on the feast of Saint Augustine, August 28, 1964. I had just turned twenty-five. New York Jesuits had just begun work in Nigeria two years earlier. Four of us went to teach in a Catholic but non-Jesuit secondary school that year. It was a year of great internal political tension in Nigeria, with some polarization starting between northern Muslims and southern Christians. The civil war that broke out three years later proved to be the long-term result of that political tension, although the issue was not entirely Muslim–Christian at that time.

My first few months in Nigeria proved difficult for me. I seemed more prone than my Jesuit colleagues to tropical ailments, landing up in the hospital once a month with bacillary dysentery and eventually a combination of dysentery, malaria and bronchitis, all before Christmas. There wasn't much for a regent to do in Nigeria at the time, so I was sent back to the United States in 1965 to start theological studies in preparation for ordination. But, for all its brevity, that first year in Nigeria, 1964–65, began the African phase of my education. The town where we taught was Akure, in the eastern part of the then western region of Nigeria. Although the five hundred students in the school came from many ethnic communities, most of them were Yoruba, members of a large ethnic group or, more accurately, language family found in southwestern Nigeria and adjacent parts of what is now called the Republic of Bénin. Today the Yoruba number about thirty million.

I learned much more than I taught during that year, beginning to read the history of Nigeria and of the Yoruba people. I also began, rather informally, some study of the Yoruba language under the tutelage of my best student, Anthony Akingbade, now the medical doctor for most Jesuits in Nigeria and one of my closest friends. One thing that fascinated me was that the Yoruba were about half-Muslim and half-Christian. At that time, and still today with some exceptions, the Yoruba have cohered despite religious differences. Many northern Nigerian Muslims look down on Yoruba practice of Islam, describing the Muslim Yoruba as "mixers" (in Arabic, *mukhallitun*) of Traditional Religion and Islam, but I was intrigued by the Muslim Yoruba, as I also was by the many varieties of Christian Independency that the Yoruba have known over the past century. These are people who lived on the borders of at least three traditions of faith: Traditional, Muslim, and Christian.

After I returned to the United States to start studying theology, it occurred to me that I wanted to pursue studies after theology that would prepare me to understand Nigeria and Africa more generally. Even during my first cycle of theology at Woodstock College (then in rural Maryland), I took four graduate courses in anthropology at Catholic University and one each in political science and anthropology at Columbia University. The professor of theology who had the most influence on me at Woodstock was undoubtedly Avery Dulles, although I was also taught by a great scholar of the New Testament, Joseph Fitzmyer. John Courtney Murray was still alive during my first two years of theology, but he died suddenly in the summer of 1967, before I had a chance to take any course with him.

One of the greatest influences on my life, spiritual and intellectual, started during the summer of 1966, while I was taking courses at Columbia. An Irish professor of political science from Nigeria, James O'Connell, then a priest, was teaching a course on African politics that summer. On the eve of my twenty-seventh birthday he introduced me to friends of his, Austrian-born New Yorkers, Charlotte and John Lichtblau. Charlotte is a painter and John an economist specialized in petroleum industry issues. Charlotte's paintings, along with the carvings of the Washington-based sculptor Sy Gresser, arise from a profoundly imagined encounter with the Jewish and Christian traditions. As artists, Lichtblau and Gresser are quintessentially people who live on borders. I cannot estimate how much I am indebted as a person to them.

In the spring semester of 1967 a large and very professional seminar on the theology of mission was organized at Woodstock, during which I met Wilfred Cantwell Smith from Harvard for the first time. Other participants included Fr. (later Cardinal) Jean Daniélou, Isma'il al-Faruqi, Kenneth Cragg, and others. The results of that conference were published as *The Word in the Third World* (1968).

During the summer of 1967, between my second and third years of theology, I returned to Africa for the summer, but not to Nigeria. Under the auspices of Operation Crossroads Africa, a work-camp organization founded by the charismatic African-American Presbyterian minister, the Reverend Dr. James Robinson, I led a group of twelve American and Canadian university undergraduates in The Gambia, a small but largely Muslim country considerably north and west of Nigeria. My Canadian and American group was made up of eight Protestant and four Jewish students; the Reverend Dr. Robinson, with whom I became good friends until his death in 1972, had a sense of humor. So did my superiors at Woodstock, since it was only possible for me to attend mass on Sundays in rural parts of The Gambia that summer. The Gambian counterparts of my North American group were ten Muslims, one Methodist and one Catholic. We were together day and night for six weeks. Not all the Muslim young people were very devout, but my coleader was, and I became accustomed to the pattern of his daily worship, since we roomed together. More than forty years later I am still in contact with one of the Gambian participants in that group, Ebrima Ousman Camara; he eventually worked for the United Nations High Commission for Refugees and is now retired in South Africa, the place of his last posting. Nominally Muslim, he is in fact nonpracticing, although his children do practice, to their father's bemused dismay.

During that summer of 1967—and in the aftermath of my first encounter a few months earlier with scholars like Wilfred Cantwell Smith, Isma'il al-Faruqi, and Kenneth Cragg—I began to think more about Islam, and especially about Islam in West Africa. That same summer of 1967 I had met, quite fortuitously, a New Zealand–born historian at London's School of Oriental and African Studies, Dr. Humphrey Fisher. Fisher was completing a sabbatical year in Sierra Leone, but was spending some time in The Gambia tracing the historical memories of a Muslim reformer who had passed through that area in the nineteenth century. Fisher, a man of deep faith and surpassing gentility, gave a brief scholarly presentation to my band of students one evening, and I kept in contact with him ever after.

I was ordained on the feast of Corpus Christi, June 13, 1968, in the Fordham University Church. On July 1 that year I began the study of

Arabic at Harvard, having been accepted into a doctoral program in the Comparative History of Religion with Islamic studies as my concentration. That particular program at Harvard was jointly administered by the Graduate School of Arts and Sciences and the Divinity School. It engaged students in the study of at least two major religious traditions, but with a synoptic introduction in translation to other world traditions. Each doctoral candidate had to prove himself or herself adept in the scriptural languages of two religious traditions. My background in Greek and the study of the Hebrew Bible and the New Testament exempted me from any further courses in those areas.

Although no one at Harvard at that time was particularly specialized in the study of Islam in Africa, I did have the opportunity to study with some excellent scholars of the Islamic tradition: Wilfred Cantwell Smith, George Makdisi, Muhsin Mahdi, Ilse Lichtenstadter, and the *shaykhah* who finally guided my doctoral dissertation, Annemarie Schimmel. Schimmel's expertise not only in Sufism but also in folk varieties of Islam in South Asia proved surprisingly useful to guide me as I did my field work in Nigeria (1972–73) and wrote my dissertation on the "clerical piety" of professional Muslim holy men in Yorubaland. During my time at Harvard I also met for the first time John Alden Williams, an Islamicist (on a sabbatical year at Harvard) who has been an immense support for me, especially when I am far from good libraries, willing to read and criticize, where necessary, writings of mine on Islam.

The lack of any African Islamicist at Harvard persuaded me to renew my acquaintance with Humphrey Fisher in London. Not only had he tutored me privately in West African Islamic history in the summer of 1969, steadfastly resisting any offer of a stipend, but he also undertook to read each chapter of my dissertation as I completed it in 1973–74. I have since met many other former students of Humphrey's (including Rex O'Fahey of the University of Bergen and the late Nehemia Levtzion of the Hebrew University) who were unanimous in their praise of Humphrey's gentle, even pastoral care for his students. It was no surprise when he was ordained an Anglican priest shortly before his retirement from SOAS. I realize now in retrospect what a grace I had in the direction of both Annemarie Schimmel and Humphrey Fisher.

My dissertation work was anthropological and historical in its methodology, prompting me to learn enough Yoruba to be able to understand the religious language of the Muslim Yoruba. The main sources of this were vernacular prayer and even hymns in Yoruba, exhortation (*wa'z*) before Friday worship and ordinary conversation with Muslim informants on

Islamic subjects. Very hospitable Muslim Yoruba men of middling education proved my best informants, and they were always enthusiastic about
the fact that I was interested in what they had to say. With the help of a
Yoruba youth who was a recent secondary school graduate and the cousin
of a former student from my regency, I not only recorded but also tran-
scribed, translated word by word, and translated more colloquially many
conversations, interviews, homilies, and vernacular prayers. At the end of
ten months (October 1972–August 1973) I had accumulated twelve thick
foolscap-sized notebooks of these transcriptions. Sometimes they were
repetitious, but they served to demonstrate how the Muslim Yoruba
thought about their faith as Muslims.

Most of the Arabic recited by the Yoruba was memorized and not really
comprehended, except by a few scholars. Although all the Muslim Yoruba
denied that they practiced divination like their Traditionalist (so-called
pagan) fellow Yoruba as well as many of the Christian Yoruba, they did
indeed indulge from time to time in folk practices known elsewhere in the
Islamic world and the Ancient Near East, such as sand-cutting (*khatt al-
raml*), a pre-Islamic practice of geomancy that corresponds rather interestingly with Yoruba traditional geomantic divination (*ifá*). It was also obvious
that they thought of the life to come as a place, *ile-alukiamo*, "the land of
al-qiyama [the resurrection]." Intercession with God was sought not only
through the Prophet Muhammad, but also through certain Suras from the
Qur'an. The creation of amulets as protective devices against evil influences, real and imagined, was a growth business for certain Muslim "cler-
ics" (*alfa* or, more dialectically, *aafa*). A Salafi Indian Muslim scholar then
teaching in Nigeria, Abdurrahman Isma'il Doi, urged me to entitle my
thesis "Syncretistic Islam among the Yoruba," an idea I rejected. Taking my
cue from certain themes in the writings of Wilfred Cantwell Smith, I entitled it *Imale: Yoruba Participation in the Muslim Tradition*. (*Imale* is a word in
Yoruba, used more commonly in earlier times than today, to characterize
Islam in Yorubaland; it probably means "the Mali religion"). I sympathized
with the Muslim Yoruba as people who lived on the borders of two religious communities, with one foot in both. My thesis was eventually published by Scholars Press for the Harvard Dissertations in Religion series
for the *Harvard Theological Review* in 1978.

I returned to Harvard in September 1973, living as I had for the two
years before I left for my fieldwork, in an undergraduate hall of residence
called Eliot House, named after a long-time president of Harvard (1869–
1909), Charles William Eliot. President Eliot, an educational innovator as
well as a notoriously anti-Catholic and anti-Jesuit bigot, is still remembered

in Catholic Boston for the way he made mockery of then fledgling Boston College. Prof. Kevin Starr, a well-known scholar of California history, then the senior tutor in Eliot House, invited me in 1970 to move in, and the master of Eliot House, Prof. Alan Heimert, a specialist in American religious history, confirmed this appointment. At the time it was considered quite unusual to have a Jesuit living in such a secular environment. I made friends at that time with students ten to fourteen years younger than I, who have remained good friends ever since.

With my dissertation coming close to conclusion, I received permission from the New York Provincial at the time to accept the offer of a lectureship at the University of Ghana, Legon, on the outskirts of Accra, Ghana's capital. Some of the New York Province Jesuits then working in Nigeria were annoyed that the Provincial had allowed me to take a position in a university outside Nigeria, where I had no clear offer. A little less than three years later, on May 4, 1977, Father General Pedro Arrupe received my final vows in the Catholic Chapel in Mensah-Sarbah Hall of the University of Ghana. I explained the final vows nine years after ordination to the students the previous Sunday by an analogy with the often delayed sacramental marriages of West African Catholics: "At long last the Society of Jesus is marrying me in Church." One thing that added to my consolation that evening was the presence of my mother, who came to Ghana for the occasion. When I met Fr. Arrupe in Rome two years later, the first thing he asked was, "How is your mother?" My mother was five weeks older than Fr. Arrupe and she died five weeks before he did in 1991.

In Ghana I continued research on the history of Islam in that predominantly Christian country, but I was also fascinated by the culture of the Akan peoples in Ghana (Asante, Fante, and so on) who make up nearly half the national population. Basically matrilineal, the Akans have generally resisted Islamization, although there are more or less indigenous Muslims among the Akan, what are called in Asante Twi (the language of the Ashanti kingdoms) *Asante Nkramo*, best translated as "those who perform Muslim worship of/among the Ashanti," not quite the same thing as "Ashanti Muslims." Everything else of importance in the Ashanti areas is inherited matrilineally; Islam tends to persist in certain patrilineages. Patrilineages do not inherit chieftaincies. The one Asantehene (paramount chief of the Ashanti, guardian of the Golden Stool) who seems to have contemplated conversion to Islam around the year 1800, Osei Kwame, was "de-stooled" and driven to suicide.

The students at the University of Ghana, Muslim and Christian, never ceased to be puzzled, and at times amused, by the fact that I was both a priest and an Islamicist. For part of the time I taught at Legon I had as my colleagues Lamin and Sandra Sanneh, who have remained close friends ever since. Lamin, a Muslim Gambian by birth who converted to Methodist Christianity before I ever met him, was received into full communion with the Catholic Church in 1999. From his position at Yale University Sanneh has revolutionized the way scholars think about mission history today, laying greater emphasis on the reception of Christianity by the evangelized than on the propagation of the Gospel by the evangelizers.

Fascinated as I was by Ghana, after nine years there I decided, in consultation with the then New York Provincial, to return to New York and take a position offered at Fordham in a small program in Middle East studies. Whatever expertise I had built up as an Africanist was of no interest to Fordham, so my first few years at Fordham were spent playing what Americans call "catch-up ball" with the history and politics of the Middle East, North Africa, and South Asia. But many of the classes I had taught in Ghana on the Qur'an, early Islamic history and Islamic theology proved valuable preparation for introducing undergraduate students to the development of the Islamic political culture of the Middle East.

The New York Provincial who urged me to return to Fordham in 1983 left office in 1984 and his successor asked me why I was back in New York. In 1986, just as I felt I was settling into Fordham, he sent me back to Nigeria, but not to an academic setting. I spent the next three years in Lagos as the *Socius* (administrative assistant) of the regional superior of Nigeria and Ghana. Apart from the work of vocations director, which introduced me to many welcoming Nigerian homes, the other two things that sustained me during those three dry years were part-time work as a hospital chaplain and a commitment that lasted six years to write a column on the Sunday liturgical readings in the US Jesuit weekly journal of opinion, *America*. Some of those columns were eventually published in a book on the Advent-Christmas-Epiphany Cycles called *The Coming of Our God* (Paulist, 1999) and another on Lent called *When I Survey the Wondrous Cross* (Paulist, 2004). I wanted to do one on Easter, too, and have completed half of it, but Paulist Press told me that people don't buy Easter books!

What little time I could devote to continued study of Islam during those three years was made possible by Fr. Thomas Michel, then adviser to the Jesuit superior general on Islamic affairs, who invited me in January 1987 and again in October 1988, to larger and smaller gatherings of Jesuits in Islamic studies, respectively in Cairo and Toulouse. I found those meetings intellectually very stimulating, oases in an otherwise dry time.

I returned to New York in the autumn of 1989, hoping to divide my future teaching career between Fordham (in the first semester) and Hekima College, the Jesuit theologate in Nairobi (in the second semester). That was never to happen. On November 12, 1989, the local superior of the Jesuits in Ghana, Fr. Raymond Adams, a good friend over many years and an anthropologist specialized in the cultural complexity of Lebanon, was murdered by a young man who had become a beneficiary of Jesuit community charity in Ghana. The young man who committed the murder, a self-described political exile from the Republic of Bénin, was more likely a fugitive drug-runner. My sister asked, later on the day we heard the dreadful news of Ray's murder in New York, "They're not going to ask you to go back to Ghana, are they?" I assured her that my future, to be split between Nairobi and New York, was carved in stone. Four days later, a message was conveyed to me by the New York Provincial that my high school classmate Fr. Peter Schineller, by then the regional superior in Nigeria-Ghana, was asking whether I would be willing to replace Ray as local superior in Ghana. Somehow, it was an easy choice to make, and I assented on the spot. Once again, I thought of "what St. Paul and St. Matthew did when they followed Christ our Lord." As soon as the semester ended at Fordham, I returned to West Africa. Eventually, in order to assure a residence permit in Ghana, I managed to get another teaching appointment in that country, this time at the University of Cape Coast, where I taught for the next six years when the staff was not on strike.

I handed over the job of local superior in Ghana to another Jesuit in 1996, eventually resigning as well from the University of Cape Coast. I then spent two years as a visiting professor (in the Loyola Chair in the Humanities) in Middle East Studies at Fordham. I left Fordham for Rome, where I was fitted into the Faculty of Missiology at the Gregorian University. I loved Italian and managed to teach in a semblance of that language by my second semester. But the new regional superior in Nigeria, Fr. Ramon Salomone, at the end of a letter of thanks for the twenty years I had spent in Nigeria and Ghana, appended a request asking me to return to Nigeria to become president (a hard-to-define role) of our new boarding secondary school in Abuja, Nigeria. The administration at the Gregorian University was none too happy about this recall, but I told them that I had long since determined that I could not say "no" to any request from the part of Africa where, I felt, I had grown up. I left Rome reluctantly; the wide variety of international students I taught from Africa and Asia fascinated me. In my one year there, 1998–99, I taught three courses: Islam and Politics, History of Islam in Africa, History of Christianity in Africa.

During the following six years (1999–2005) as president and Jesuit superior at Loyola Jesuit College, I did some writing about Islam—especially in the aftermath of the events of September 11, 2001—but much more of my life was caught up in the endless details of administration. The friendship of the parents, especially those who were Muslim, helped to sustain me throughout those years. I always wished there were more Muslim students in the school, but many Nigerian Muslims were reluctant to send their children to schools where boys and girls studied together or to schools under Christian supervision. The archbishop of Abuja also opposed the offering of Islamic Religious Knowledge as a subject in the school, which I thought a pity. The Muslim students were exempt from Christian Religious Knowledge classes, although some of the parents insisted that they take them; one, in particular, always topped the class.

In 2003—at the invitation of a former colleague from the University of Ghana then established at Northwestern University, Prof. John Hunwick—I participated in an academic conference there on the theme of Muslim–Christian Encounters in Africa. My presentation at that conference, a comparative study of the implantation of Catholicism in the Igbo area of Nigeria and the original implantation of Islam in the Hausa-speaking area of Nigeria, was published in a 2006 volume edited by Benjamin Soares for Brill.

In 2005, after six years in Abuja, I was asked to return to Fordham once again, this time as the vice president for University Mission and Ministry, another hard-to-define post. I presided over the university chaplaincy (Campus Ministry), a program of short-term immersions for students in situations of impacted poverty, national and international (Global Outreach), and the Community Service Program. I also gave invocations of various sorts at most university public events. Following the death of Avery Cardinal Dulles, S.J., who had occupied the Laurence J. McGinley Chair in Religion and Society with great distinction for twenty years, that university professorship was offered to me in April 2009. For four years before this I had been pressing for the establishment at Fordham of a university public seminar on what I call the *trialogue* of Judaism, Christianity, and Islam. Under the auspices of that chair I hope to start towards that goal.

As I write this, my first public lecture as the McGinley Professor, "Faith and the Possibility of Jewish-Christian-Muslim Trialogue," is to be delivered twice, on November 18 and 19, 2009. A friend from graduate student days at Harvard, Rabbi Daniel Polish, is to give a Jewish response, and Prof. Amir Hussain, a Pakistani-born Muslim Canadian, who lectures at Loyola-Marymount University in Los Angeles, will give the Muslim response. Both also formerly studied with Wilfred Cantwell Smith. I hope to continue with this pattern in subsequent McGinley public lectures twice a year. I also continue to teach an undergraduate course in Islamic political thought and one graduate course a year in various parts of the university, since the holder of a university chair is not tied down to a particular department. In the spring semester of 2010, I will teach a course at Fordham's Graduate School of Religion and Religious Education entitled "Culture, Dialogue and Proclamation."

One lesson has been particularly significant in my understanding of all kinds of monotheistic faith. The Yoruba like to paint proverbs on their trucks, buses and taxis. One that always delighted me was *Oba bi Olorun ko si*. Literally, that translates as "There is no king like God." To catch the irony of that proverb, one has to realize that the sixteen traditional kings of the Yoruba peoples, their *oba*, were considered *ikeji orisa*, second only to the *orisa*, the lowercase g "gods." About half of the Yoruba are Muslim and half Christian; they get along fairly well, perhaps precisely because they are Yoruba, people with shrewd balance and healthy compromise built into their culture. Some of their cultural neighbors, more bellicose peoples, mock the Yoruba for this. But at certain times in the past the traditional kings of the Yoruba—and some modern political and military rulers as well—have forgotten that only God with a capital G is God. "There is no king like God." Those are revolutionary words, if you think them through.

The Muslim Yoruba often use that proverb to translate the first article of the *shahada: La ilaha ill' Allah*: "no god but God." The sin of the Umayyad caliphs of the seventh and eighth centuries CE was to forget that lesson, laying the blame for all their moral deficiencies on God's predestination. Many other Islamic styles of government—and not a few Christian and secularist ones as well—have made the same mistake. Our God challenges all such human tyranny. In the very late medieval imagery of Saint Ignatius, "the three Divine Persons, seated, so to speak, on the royal canopied throne of their Divine Majesty . . . are gazing on the whole face and circuit of the earth; and they see all the peoples in such great blindness, and how they are dying and going down to hell" (*Spiritual Exercises*, no. 106).

The absolute oneness of God proclaimed in the Islamic tradition (*tawhid*) strikes me less as a critique of the Trinity than as a condemnation of the sin of Adam and Eve, human self-divinization, and especially the political self-divinization of every political tyranny. I am grateful that I learned that lesson of what I have called the *onliness* of God, not only at my mother's knee, but also from my friends who are Muslims in West Africa.

Every night, waking or sleeping, my mind drifts back to West Africa. "If I forget you, O Jerusalem, let my right hand wither; let my tongue stick to my palate, if I cease to think of you" (Psalm 137:5). I thank God for all the friends I made on those West African borders of Islam, Christianity, and Traditional Faith. We lived out our liminality together. William Butler Yeats put it well:

> Think where man's glory most begins and ends,
> And say my glory was I had such friends.

Growing in Love and Truth with Muslims

Thomas Michel

Until I was 28 I had never met a Muslim. The world in which I was raised was pretty much circumscribed by our Catholic parish in St. Louis County in the Midwest of the United States. The people we prayed with on Sundays and feasts, and at novenas and Perpetual Help devotions, were the same people whose children I went to parochial school with, that my brothers and sisters dated, that my parents played cards with, and at whose house they square-danced (the fad in the 1950s) on Saturday evenings. The parish provided not only our place of worship, but also school, apostolic and social clubs, gym, and ball fields, and thus fulfilled our spiritual, educational, recreational, and social needs.

In our mainly Irish neighborhood, the few German and Italian Catholic families were acceptable, if "different," but Protestants were shadowy characters who went to the public schools and impinged but marginally on our consciousness. The elderly widower next door went to the Lutheran Church, which we thought was exotic but definitely heretical. I don't think I knew personally any other Protestants. Jews lived in another part of St. Louis, but I never even met a Jew until I was almost through high school.

All this goes to say just how far off our radar screens were Muslims in St. Louis in the 1940s and 1950s. What was very much on our radar screens, however, were the priests of our parish. We had very good priests and they brought Christ into our lives by presiding at the Eucharist and other acts of worship, but perhaps even more, they represented Christ in our neighborhood and families. They rejoiced with us on the happy occasions of births, baptisms, first communions, graduations, parish picnics, weddings, and anniversaries, and they brought solace and hope in times of crisis, sickness, and death.

Like many of my classmates, I felt this was a good way to serve God and God's people, and after completing high school I entered the seminary to study for the priesthood. In the seminary, Muslims were just as absent as they had been in our neighborhood. Very few of us could have said what Muslims believed or practiced; if pressed, we might have said that Mohammedans worshiped Mohammed. I can't remember the religion of Islam having been mentioned in any of our courses or the question of relations with Muslims ever arising either in casual or theological discussions. In any case, there was no mosque, prayer room, or Islamic Center in St. Louis and whatever scattered handful of Muslims who might have lived in the city kept a very low profile. (Today, sixty years later, there is a thriving Bosnian community.)

Twin Earthquakes

For me, the years 1964–65 were pivotal. I was twenty-three and two things were happening in the world that drew me out of the comfortable Catholic Irish-American nest in which I had been reared. The first of these "conceptual earthquakes" was the Second Vatican Council. In August 1964, when I was in second-year (of a total of four years) theology, Pope Paul VI's encyclical *Ecclesiam Suam* was published, in which he referred to Jews and Muslims as worthy of respect. In the encyclical he spoke of,

> Those who worship the one supreme God, whom we also worship. We mean the Jewish people, worthy of our affectionate respect, who are faithful to the religion that we call the Old Testament, and those worshipers of God according to monotheistic religion, especially Muslims. We do well to admire these people for all that is good and true in their worship of God. (*ES* §107)

Respect Jews and Muslims! Admire them!? Why? Is there really something good and true in their worship of God? These were new ideas to grapple with and integrate into my thinking. Actually, it was less difficult to make a shift in my attitude towards Jews and Muslims, whom I had spent little time considering previously, than it was to appreciate Protestants, under whose majority domination in the United States we felt as Catholics to have suffered. Toward Jews and Muslims, I didn't have deep-rooted prejudices to overcome because neither of those faith communities had ever seriously been a part of my life or thinking. When *Ecclesiam Suam* appeared, I was not greatly challenged; I wanted to be a good Catholic and Christian, and if the pope said we should respect and admire Jews and Muslims, I saw no reason not to.

If *Ecclesiam Suam* opened the door for me, the Second Vatican Council kept pushing it wider. Three months after Paul VI's encyclical, in November 1964, appeared *Lumen Gentium*, the council's Dogmatic Constitution on the Church. Here again, the question of Muslims arose, and the document went further than *Ecclesiam Suam*. It asserted:

> But [God's] plan of salvation also includes those who acknowledge the Creator. In the first place amongst these there are the Muslims, who, professing to hold the faith of Abraham, along with us adore the one and merciful God, who on the last day will judge mankind. (*LG* §16)

Here it was not a matter of attitudes to be changed, as in *Ecclesiam Suam*'s call to respect and admire, but of new doctrinal material to be absorbed. Muslims are included in God's plan of salvation; they profess the faith of Abraham; they adore *with us* the One God and await God's final judgment! This statement, enunciated by no less than the dogmatic constitution of an ecumenical council, really set me on a new path in my attitude toward Muslims. The implications, when I began to think about them, were sweeping. Christians and Muslims were worshiping the same God. Muslims had a place in God's plan of salvation. Muslims continue to profess the faith of Abraham.

Even though Church teachings were instrumental in changing my views toward Muslims, my new attitudes remained at the theoretical level, as I still had not met a Muslim. However, when the Second Vatican Council's document on the relation of the Church to non-Christian religions, *Nostra Aetate*, appeared the following year, in October 1965, for me it was almost anticlimactic. The document merely confirmed the direction in which my understanding on how we should regard Muslims (and Jews and others) had already been moving.

Moreover, the world in which I lived was changing radically and I was changing with it. The second "earthquake"—the social motor that impelled me and countless other Americans into a new, wider world—was the human rights movement. In March 1965, it was almost ten years since Rosa Parks had been arrested for refusing to give her seat to a white woman and move to the back of the bus. In the ensuing decade in America, the civil rights movement did what a comfortable reading of the Gospel was unable to do; it set "father against son and son against father, mother against daughter and daughter against mother, mother-in-law against daughter-in-law and daughter-in-law against mother-in-law" (Luke 12:53).

At the same time that the civil rights movement divided families, parishes, neighborhoods, and religious groups, it also brought together people from different backgrounds, created new alliances, forged new friendships, and produced—at least for me—the first glimmers of a new vision of what it meant to be religious and Christian. Many of the leaders of the civil rights movement were Jews, whom we came to know as colleagues and coworkers. Many of the meetings and rallies were held in the historic "black" churches and were for some of us Catholics the first occasion we had to take part in ecumenical prayer and worship in Protestant churches. We were, for the first time, serving on the same committees, folding flyers and invitations side by side, traveling on rickety school buses, and sleeping over at the homes and churches of Protestant pastors and seminarians, Jewish rabbinical students, and nonreligious people of all types.

The march from Selma to Montgomery, Alabama, in March 1965, led by Martin Luther King, became in America the symbolic litmus test of the kind of country a person wanted. The march in Alabama took place three months after the publication of *Lumen Gentium* and six months before that of *Nostra Aetate*. 1964–65 was also the year in which the Free Speech Movement at the University of California in Berkeley gradually metamorphosed into the student protests against the Vietnam War that spread throughout the country.

It was impossible that the seminary where my friends and I were studying theology would not reflect the tumultuous changes going on around us. We began to understand theology as an expression of God's "defense pact" with the poor, the suffering, and the victims of discrimination. The old controversies about Chalcedonian formulations seemed as distant from our lives as did the Perpetual Help devotions and church socials of our home neighborhoods.

A short time later, in 1967, I was ordained a priest in my home diocese of St. Louis. At ordination, I presumed that I would serve as a parish priest in that city the rest of my life, but that was not to be. My bishop, at the last session of the Vatican Council, met a bishop from Indonesia, who asked him for the loan of a priest to teach English at a teachers' college and seminary in that country. I left St. Louis and went to Cornell University in Ithaca, New York, to study Indonesian language, and for the first time in my life personally encountered Muslims. Cornell still specializes in Southeast Asian language programs and in the study of the histories and cultures of the peoples of that region. As a consequence, there were Muslim students from Indonesia, Malaysia, Philippines, and Myanmar (called Burma in those days). I was even asked to officiate at a Muslim–Christian wedding, since the local imam was not yet recognized by New York State as an official witness to marriages.

Indonesia: Students and Prisoners

Indonesia, as is well known, is the country with the largest Muslim population in the world, with a total of 220 million Muslims at the time of writing (2009). At the teachers' college in Yogyakarta, where I began to teach English, the students were of religiously mixed background. About half were Christian; most of the others were Muslim, with some Buddhists of Chinese background and a few Hindus from Bali. The village in which the teachers' college was located, Mrican, was populated mainly by nonpracticing or nominal Muslims, the people that Clifford Geertz referred to in his sociological studies of Central Java as *abangan*.

Aside from teaching English, my main assignment during these first years was to visit the political prisoners. Since 1969 was only four years after the anticommunist coup (or counter-coup, according to how one interprets the events of that period) that brought Suharto to power, there were over 100,000 political prisoners in the country. In Yogyakarta, four makeshift prisons were designated for *tapol* (short for *tahanan politik*, that is, "political detainees").

I visited each prison weekly at the prisoners' request. None were Christian and most—as communists, sympathizers, or members of the procommunist teachers' and postal workers' unions—were not practicing any of the officially recognized religions of Indonesia. The prisoners' religiosity mainly was expressed in *kebatinan*, a uniquely Javanese spirituality that brings together Sufi traditions and Hindu meditative techniques and aims at leading someone to an awareness of that person's harmony with the universe and within the human family.

What was I doing in the prison? I was not there to proselytize or try to make converts. That was strictly forbidden both by the prison authorities and by my diocesan and Jesuit superiors. I was in the prisons for an entirely different reason. The policy of the Suharto government at that time was that the prisoners should be completely isolated from the population. They were allowed no visitors and no contact by mail with family or friends. Telephones, newspapers, and televisions were not permitted in the prisons. The prisoners were moved around frequently from one prison to another, often in the middle of the night, so that they would not form bonds of friendship or conspire with other prisoners. In this situation, the prisoners, who had never been charged with any crime, had little hope that they would in the foreseeable future be tried, exonerated and released. They also had no information on how their families were doing. They heard rumors that the wives of "communists" were forcibly taken in marriage or concubinage by military officers or that their homes and rice fields were confiscated by army personnel.

My colleagues and I visited the prisons, first of all to make the statement that these prisoners (in three men's prisons and a fourth for women) were human beings and possessed human rights that could not be taken away. Secondly, we tried to serve the prisoners' needs within the strictures of the military rule that governed prison life. The prisoners' concerns were mainly focused on their families, from whom they had usually heard nothing since their arrest. When I visited the prison, a *tapol* would often ask me to go to his village, find his wife or parents, and bring back information on the family's health, his children's education, and the like.

I went by motorcycle and, in those days—given the state of the roads and in the rainy season the impossibility of crossing the rivers after a downpour—I was often forced to spend the night in the villages I visited, and I stayed either in the homes of prisoners' families or in the village mosques. Here was another point of entry for me into the world of Islam. The Javanese village mosques were materially very poor, but rich in hospitality. No one was ever refused permission to enter, and one could always count on being able to spend the night sleeping on the straw mats on the mosque floor. Some of the villages I visited were so poor that the only food they had to eat was bananas, but they never failed to share what they had with me. Some of my earliest encounters with Muslims took place sitting with the local imam and a small group of village men, drinking tea or hot water and conversing in the mosque until late at night by the light of a small oil lamp.

Sleeping on the floor of the mosque, one becomes aware of just how early Muslims arrive to worship God before dawn. In my case, I would hear the first *adhan*, or call to prayer, get up, say some brief Christian prayers and, as the first Muslim worshipers began to enter the mosque, I would head back to Yogyakarta on my motorcycle. In the course of the past forty years, I've known some Christians who feel threatened or angry when they hear the *adhan*, as though it were an invasion of their privacy or an expression of religious intolerance. But for me, these early experiences instilled in me a conviction that it is *my* God, *our* one and only God, worshipped jointly by Muslims and Christians, who is being praised in the *adhan*. How misplaced are any feelings of threat; I should be happy and grateful that so many of my fellow humans are starting the day by responding to the call to prayer and worshipping our God.

Studying Islam

I loved Indonesia and wanted to spend the rest of my life there. I loved the people, the culture, the beauty of the island of Java, and the Indonesian way of life, and I wanted to make some small contribution to the good of the nation. I didn't know in what way I could contribute; in the mornings I taught English in the teachers' college and in the afternoons I visited the political prisoners. I was ready to keep on doing something like that the rest of my life. My bishop, back in St. Louis, felt that if I wanted to remain in Indonesia, it would be better if I join a religious order. That way, he felt, I would belong to a supportive community and fit into an ongoing embodiment of Christian life.

The men who ran the teachers' college in Yogyakarta were Jesuits, and I was impressed by their dedication and their willingness to serve others without expecting any reward. The Jesuits were also known for their flexibility. They were not tied to any one type of apostolic work. Some were teachers, others worked in parishes, others in various social sectors. I joined the Jesuits and completed my novitiate in Indonesia, and I remain until today a member of the Indonesian Province of the Society of Jesus. As the months went on and the weeks drew near for me to take vows as a Jesuit, my provincial encouraged me to talk to knowledgeable people in the region to see what I would be doing on a long-term basis once I took vows.

Since I was already an ordained priest, it meant that I would not have to spend the many years in the long Jesuit course of philosophy and theology. At thirty, I was still young by Jesuit standards, and I had a block of time that could be used to pursue some field of specialization. I began asking people of various backgrounds how a foreigner like me could make a good contribution to Indonesian society. I also told my language students that I hoped to go on for further studies. The response of some of my Muslim students surprised me; they said, "Why don't you study Islam? That way, you can help Christians to understand Islam better, and you can help Muslims learn more about Christianity." We discussed this idea in class, and the Christian students joined in and also encouraged me in this direction.

After class, I went back to my room and thought and prayed about our discussion. Was the voice of God speaking to me through these Indonesian students? I took my copy of Vatican II documents and opened to the first sentence of the *Nostra Aetate* passage: "The Church regards with esteem also the Muslims" (paragraph 3). At that moment, I knew what course my future would take. I must learn from Muslims the reasons for the esteem in which we Christians should hold them, and I must learn how to communicate that esteem to my fellow Christians.

It seemed to me that in the late 1960s Christians in Indonesia were well placed to be agents of reconciliation. As a small community, they were not directly involved in the social upheavals that were going on in the country. People on the left felt that they could talk with the Christians, whose social justice concerns were similar to their own. On the other hand, Muslims, who often scorned and dismissed left-leaning activists as "atheists," felt that at least with Christians, who had a religious sense, they could hold an honest discussion about God and nation. In later years, as the social dynamics of the country evolved, tensions between Muslims and Christians grew and on occasion even erupted into violent conflict. At other times, as in the ferment in the 1990s that eventually toppled the Suharto dictatorship, members of the two communities, especially the university and high school students, were allies in working for justice, democracy, and civil rights and were actively sharing their views on the shape and direction the nation ought to take.

After my Jesuit provincial approved my plan to study Islam, I left Indonesia in 1971 for Lebanon where I entered an Arabic language school run by the British Foreign Office. After continuing my Arabic studies in Cairo, I entered the University of Chicago in order to study with the late Fazlur Rahman. He was the man, more than anyone else, who guided my study of Islam and taught me, by personal witness, the Islamic virtues. He was not only a wide-ranging and insightful scholar, but also a true gentleman. After a class in which several of the students were asking questions about Islam in a rude and defiant manner, I asked him whether it bothered him to hear his religion challenged in this way. He gave me an answer that helped me greatly in my own teaching later on. He said, "Since I believe that Islam is true, I can feel comfortable discussing any aspect of my religion." Often when I'm giving a lecture on Christian faith and a Muslim listener raises a question in an offensive way, or when a Christian student begins to rant about what he sees as the failures of Islam, I remember the words of Fazlur Rahman and try to emulate my teacher's forbearance.

Fazlur Rahman greatly admired the scholarship of the fourteenth-century Hanbali scholar Ibn Taymiyya, although no two personalities in the history of Islamic thought could have been more different than the fiery, inflexible Ibn Taymiyya and the gentle, indulgent Fazlur Rahman. When I was searching for a dissertation topic, my professor suggested that I could not do better than to examine Ibn Taymiyya's long (1,400 pages) and incisive critique of Christianity, *Al-Jawab al-Sahih* ("The Correct Answer to those Who Changed the Religion of Christ"). Rather than being an onerous duty to fulfill a degree requirement, my dissertation was an opportunity to confront one of the Islamic tradition's most learned scholars and grapple with his mainly negative evaluation of my Christian faith. I emerged from my doctoral research both with a real respect for Ibn Taymiyya's intellectual brilliance and his unshakeable Islamic convictions, as well as with a hard-fought appreciation of the validity of my own faith in God's saving work in Jesus Christ.

From Rome to Turkey

After a brief stint teaching Islamic philosophy at Columbia University in New York, while I waited for my new Indonesian visa to come through, I returned to Yogyakarta in 1978. My provincial gave me a new assignment: half-time teaching in the Theology Faculty of Sanata Dharma University, half-time "making contact with Muslims." Newly armed with my doctorate in Islamic thought, I found the Muslims I encountered ambivalent about my studies. Some were cautious and skeptical about the motives of a non-Muslim "orientalist" in their midst, but most were happy to avail themselves of my academic studies. I had two strong credentials in my favor: Ibn Taymiyya's unassailable position of orthodoxy in the history of Islamic thought and Fazlur Rahman's stellar reputation among Indonesian Muslims. Some of Indonesia's leading scholars—Amien Rais, Nurcholis Madjid, Syafii Maarif—had, like me, gone to the University of Chicago precisely to study under Fazlur Rahman. I had many opportunities to lecture and contribute to Indonesian scholarly works on Islam.

When I returned to Indonesia, I presumed that I would be spending the rest of my life there. On visits to the Jesuit novitiate in Giri Sonta, I used to visit the cemetery of deceased Jesuits and think, "Someday I will be here also." However, only three years after I returned to Indonesia, my life took another turn. Archbishop Jean Jadot, the president of the Secretariat for Non-Christians (later renamed the Pontifical Council for Interreligious Dialogue) asked the Jesuit General for an English-speaker trained in Islamic studies for the post of head of the office for Islam at his Vatican department. Since the dominant tradition in Islamic studies among Jesuits had been in French, there were not many Anglophones to choose from, and I was sent from Indonesia to work in the Vatican.

In Rome, where I served for thirteen years, I was involved in a new aspect of dialogue, the "official" encounters of the Catholic Church with Muslim scholars and religious leaders. Dialogue at the level of scholars has a limited but significant role to play in the effort to build esteem between Christians and Muslims. In the years I spent at the Vatican, we met with seventy to eighty groups of Muslims and discussed almost every aspect of relations between the two communities. The pope at the time was John Paul II, who was probably more responsible than any other individual for showing Muslims that the Catholic Church truly respected them and wanted to live in peace and work together with Muslims for the good of all.

In 1986, when I had been at the Vatican for four years, the pope received a letter that would eventually have strong repercussions on my life. The rector of Ankara University asked the pope to send a Christian theologian to teach an introduction to Christian theology at Ankara's theology faculty. As head of the Office for Islam, the task fell to me to find someone for Turkey, but I was not successful. Everyone we asked declined for one reason or another. Either they felt they were not prepared, or had family commitments they could not leave for a year, or tenure commitments they could not get out of. Some expressed a fear that maybe some Muslim students or teachers would be violently opposed to a Christian in the faculty.

We had a small meeting in the Vatican. The general feeling was one of frustration, in that we keep talking about dialogue, but when an influential Muslim takes an initiative in favor of dialogue, we can't find anyone to accept the invitation. Rather than tell the Turks that we had no one to send to Ankara, it was decided that I would go. This was for me the beginning of a new stage of involvement with Muslims. Since that first time in Ankara, I have taught many courses in ten Turkish theology faculties.

In most of the places where I taught in Turkey, there have been no Catholic churches or religious communities, so I've lived in ordinary apartments and university guesthouses. This has actually served to facilitate dialogue outside the university. Many Muslim neighbors, friends, colleagues, and students have felt free to drop by evenings and, over a steady consumption of tea and pistachio nuts, we discussed everything: life in Turkey, life in America, life in Indonesia, sports, movies, food, the economy (always disastrous), and politics (usually a mess).

At some time in the course of the evening, my Muslim friends find themselves explaining what it means to be a Muslim, the glories of the Qur'an, and what they must do to live according to the teachings of their faith. Similarly, I explain my faith in what I believe that God has accomplished for all humankind through the life, death, and resurrection of Jesus. I have never felt uncomfortable when Muslims bear witness to me about their faith, nor have I ever found them offended when I share with them what it means for me to be a Christian.

What I've learned from these many evenings spent with Turkish Muslims is that the dialogue to which the Church calls us finds its true context in a life shared in common. When there is respect and trust, Muslims and Christians can share at all levels, from the superficial (for example, sports and movies) to the most profound (for example, how God is at work in our lives). Of my forty-two years as a Catholic priest, forty have been spent mainly with Muslims. I believe that through these many encounters with Muslims, God has made me a better Christian and a better person. This knowledge gives me a strong basis for hope that my presence in the lives of my Muslim friends will also be an occasion of God's grace for them, to lead them in ways that only God knows. If through our mutual encounters we become Muslims and Christians who are more loving and more devoted to the truth, and more eager to do God's will in all things, I will praise the God whom we jointly worship for bringing this about.

An Interfaith Experience of Dialogue as Love in Action, Silence, and Harmony

Sebastiano D'Ambra

Dreams often have guided me beyond the "normal way." The first dream that touched my life was the fruit of the prayers of my parents when, in 1950, at the foot of the grotto of Lourdes in France, they asked God, through the intercession of the Virgin Mary, for the grace of a priestly vocation for me. My parents told me about their dream and prayer when I was already in the diocesan seminary. The same dream inspired me to leave the diocesan seminary when a missionary visited us one day and his words remained in my heart: "We have only one life in this world and we have to spend it the best way we can. What is the best way for you to spend your life?" In my search for the best way to spend my life, I left the diocesan seminary to become a missionary. I must admit that during my years in theological studies, I was guided by a romantic concept of the missions and by negative perceptions of people of other religions. These came from my cultural and historical background.

A "superiority complex" in relation to other cultures and religions was still very strong in Italy at that time. The Second Vatican Council (1963–65) was a great spiritual awakening and renewal that changed my perception towards people of other cultures and religions, to a point that I became interested in experiencing interreligious dialogue in my mission. I asked my superiors to send me to a mission country where this would be possible. Convinced by my deep desire to experience a dialogical approach with people of other religions, the superiors assigned me to Thailand with two other companions. We were to start a special mission of dialogue with the Buddhists. I was thirty-five years old. Being older than my two companions I became the leader of the group. We dreamt and shared the same desire to live "a new way" of mission.

God's "style" manifested itself. We were not able to get our visa for Thailand. Our superior decided to send us to the Philippines instead. I took this as a sign from God so I prepared myself to go to a country and people strange to me. I went to England to study English. In February 1977, I arrived in the Philippines with Fr. Salvatore Carzedda. There was political turmoil. The country was under martial law and the dictatorship of President Ferdinand Marcos. The Pontificio Istituto Missioni Estere (PIME) community was in big trouble. Three of our companions had been deported and one was in hiding in Manila. The military accused them of rebellion because of their life and ministry among the poor in Tondo. Church people working with the poor suffered the same fate. Fr. Salvatore and I met the PIME community and we were given an orientation of the situation in the country, especially the plight of the poor and human rights violations. We were not discouraged. We were challenged and inspired by their stories about the life and aspirations of the people; the stand of the Church, and we wanted to help those who suffered most.

The Mission in Siocon

For a while we forgot our initial desire for a dialogue experience among people of other religions and we volunteered to be assigned in Tondo, a poor area of Manila. But God had a way of guiding us back to our "first love." Our local superior, unaware of our initial dream, accompanied us to our new mission in Siocon, Zamboanga del Norte. We landed in Zamboanga City and realized that we were confronted with another social reality. In the evening of our arrival in Zamboanga we took a small motorboat from Zamboanga City to Siocon. I was awake the whole night. The people travelling with us were curious and asked questions about us. Who were these two young foreign priests? We were encountering another culture, another people, and we were excited. It was our "baptism" to the Philippine mission.

Siocon is a town near the sea, isolated from the rest of the Zamboanga Peninsula. At that time there were no roads and the nearby mountains were controlled by rebels: the Moro National Liberation Front (MNLF) and the New Peoples' Army (NPA). The two groups had a "strategic agreement to avoid conflict between them" but each one fought for a different cause. The majority of MNLF members were Muslims and they resisted the Marcos dictatorial regime. They fought for independence or genuine autonomy for Mindanao. The NPA were mostly Christians and their fight was for basic social issues, like land reform and social justice. The joint MNLF and NPA operation in Siocon invited heavy military presence in the area. Unfortunately, Muslims often identify the military with the Christians because most of the soldiers in the Philippines are Christians.

The land area of Siocon is big, with a population at that time of about twenty-five thousand: about 60 percent of them were Christians, 30 percent Muslims, and 10 percent Subanons, an indigenous community most of whom practiced their native religion. Inspired by my dream and desire to bring peace to the area, I studied first the Cebuano language spoken by the Christians and later the Tausog language spoken by the majority of Muslims in the area. Our presence was not new to the people of Siocon. The PIME missionaries started their mission in 1969. They had always been close to the people, especially during the critical times of heavy militarization and continuous fighting between the Philippine Army and MNLF. The period 1973–76 was the most critical. Adding to the conflict was the presence of the Ilaga, a group organized by some politicians and the military to kill Muslims. As a reaction, a Muslim group called the Barracudas was also organized to retaliate against the Ilagas. When I arrived in 1977, I heard many stories of violence and killings: Christians against Muslims and Muslims against Christians.

My Life with Muslims

One day I told my four PIME companions assigned with me in Siocon that I wanted to experience immersion with the Muslims in the Bucana area of Siocon. It was not easy to convince them but they finally agreed on the condition that I continue to do some pastoral work among the Christian communities.

This was the beginning of a journey of no return, a spiritual journey that gradually unfolded before me. The only point of reference was the example of Fr. Santo and other missionary priests who lived among and dialogued with the Muslims before me. Now I was alone in Bucana with my dream and my God.

One day I was introduced to Habib Mujella, a Tausog from Jolo and a Muslim leader of Bucana. He was respected by the Muslims in the area because he belonged to a royal family in the *Salsilah* (genealogical tree). We became friends after the first meeting. This friendship opened the way to friendships with many other Muslims. Each day offered new discoveries and new challenges. In the silence of my heart my daily prayer was "O Lord, what am I to do? Why am I here? What is my next step?" I started to live in the house of one of the relatives of my Muslim friend, shared their simple life, listened to their stories and aspirations, and offered help in any way I could. I was happy, but still felt I was a stranger in the place. The presence of many children inspired me to build a little *nipa* hut near the river and the sea where I could gather them. I named the hut "Muslim-Christian Brotherhood." The Muslim community of Bucana offered the property to me. This was my first initiative in the Muslim community. The location was so accessible that people passing by could stop and talk with me. The "Muslim–Christian Brotherhood" center soon became a meeting place for all.

On December 28, 1979, the MNLF rebels attacked a *lancha* (boat) whose passengers were going to Zamboanga. We had just celebrated Christmas. That was a terrible experience for all of us in Siocon. The rebels forced the operator of the boat to proceed to an isolated seashore near Siocon where many were killed and about twenty persons, mostly girls and business people, were kidnapped and brought to the mountains. I experienced an internal struggle but I put aside my "whys." I hurriedly went to the Christian families of the victims, imploring them to avoid any form of retaliation. I met with the Muslim leaders of Bucana to find solutions and to ask help for the release of the hostages.

The old prejudices between Christians and Muslims were reawakened and became very palpable in Siocon. After this violence caused by MNLF rebels, which had many victims, we could feel the tension on the road and in the market place. I started to question my own involvement and was tempted to abandon my dream of being a bridge. In addition, the Christian community started questioning my presence among the Muslims, telling me, "You have been sent to Siocon for the Christians and not for the Muslims!" Others said, "It is useless to continue your dialogue with them."

A part of me refused to surrender in the face of difficulties. I was convinced this was the will of God and the right thing to do. I processed the events in silence and prayer. As in the past, difficulties and obstacles have a way of challenging me to find new ways and means. I went to see Habib Mujella, my first Muslim friend, to share my pains and difficulties. He told me, "Father, you can live with my relatives on the other side of the river. That is my land, we will protect you, you are already part of our community. We know and respect you. We know that you are not here to convert us, but to be our friend." Yes! I was waiting to hear those words of encouragement.

One day I crossed the river with my little bag and went to live in the house of Habib's married daughter. The husband was a good man, who was always ready to help me. With him I met the community of about a hundred families. I began to be one with them. The place was beautiful, near the sea, and the houses were built under the coconut trees. But the area had no potable water and the people were very poor.

It didn't take long for me to notice the presence of some men in the area. Most of them were MNLF rebels, living there with their relatives and families. I was not disturbed by this strange setup in the village. For me they were all friends. They would invite me to their homes to drink coffee with them. I truly became a part of the community. I joined and shared their joy in celebrations of weddings and other events. I also suffered with them during painful events like the death of their loved ones, often children.

Towards the Silsilah Vision

It was there among the simple and poor Muslims that I heard the voice telling me the deeper reason why a Christian has to be in dialogue with Muslims and with all other people and groups of different cultures and religions.

"Dialogue starts from God and brings people back to God." These were the words that rang in my ears. This message gave me the courage and conviction to continue my mission of peace. This spiritual experience in Bucana became the foundation of my mission and has become a great source of joy and inspiration for me to go on and share my mission of dialogue with others. This profound understanding brought me to the source and fountain of dialogue and gave me the deep motivation to pursue living a life-in-dialogue with my Muslim brothers and sisters. It is only when we discover the ordinary in the deeper part of our being that it becomes great and extraordinary. It then generates power to change our lives and we nurture this new orientation by allowing it to be integrated in our way of life— new and transformed. People of all religious persuasions are called to rediscover the God of dialogue.

When we enter the field of interreligious dialogue we discover beautiful things, but we remain in a posture of awe and reverence for each one's belief. Interreligious dialogue is not just a sharing of commonalities and differences. It becomes an experience of faith that is rooted in our spiritual traditions.

My spiritual experience has led me to many insights that continue to nurture my mission of dialogue. We cannot hold the fullness of God, but God can hold us. People and institutions have offered their own "recipe" to achieve peace. My immersion experience with the Muslims helped me understand that any effort toward peace can only be sustained by a deeper dialogue that starts from God and brings people, in a mysterious way, back to God. Thus, dialogue is essentially a spirituality, an integration of faith and life.

Journeying with the Rebels

This initial experience of dialogue with my Muslim friends had such a deep impact on me that even now, as I talk about the essential attitudes for genuine dialogue, I would say that these are sincerity, sensitivity and solidarity. This orientation was put to the test when after almost a year of experience in the Muslim village, I was challenged to apply these values in a concrete situation. I decided to move to Santa Maria, a mixed community of Muslims and Christians not far from my Muslim village. It is near a beautiful bay where the MNLF started the revolution in the early seventies and it eventually became a battlefield. Christians fled, the church was burned, and many civilians, both Christians and Muslims, were killed in the crossfire during the encounters between the MNLF and the military. It was in Santa Maria that I was requested by the Moro National Liberation Front to become their negotiator.

One of my peak experiences came when I was in the final stage of negotiating the surrender of Commander Magellan's group. Through coordination with SouthCom in Zamboanga City, the military promised to send helicopters to Siocon to conclude the negotiations with the MNLF. I prepared for my secret trip to meet the MNLF group in a place along the seashore between Siocon and Sirawai.

I was aware that all my moves were being monitored by the military and some of them would have preferred to kill all the rebels than negotiate for their surrender. Together with my Muslim friend who became my special security and companion, I waited for two days to meet with the MNLF group. My companion, with facility and skill, had built a tent-like shelter made of coconut leaves and bamboo where we could spend the night. It was a good in-service training on forest survival for me. Part of the group arrived after two days, about sixty women, children and old people, and about forty young men who were armed. For a week I stayed with them, waiting for another group who were also part of the negotiations. We had plenty of time for sharing.

While waiting, they spent the days looking for food and training in communication and strategies in case of an attack from the government troops. Commander Magellan expressed his suspicion that there might be trouble with the military. He was right.

On the last day of our agreed schedule with the military, we spotted a group of soldiers near our area attempting to surround us. Commander Magellan gave instructions to the group to start moving. He came to me and said, "Father, it is better for you to escape to the village nearby and for us to escape into the forest." How could I leave them alone in that critical moment? So without hesitation I answered, "No, I have been with you this far, I will continue to be with you. God will help us!" I saw the look on Magellan's face. He was deeply touched. He told the group, "We have to protect Father." And turning to me he continued, "Father, in case of an attack, we will protect you, we will give our lives for you. You will be the last to die." It was my turn to be deeply moved. Magellan's words reminded me of Jesus' words, "The real friend is the one who is ready to give his life for the other." This experience made me more convinced that in every human heart, even amidst dangerous and threatening situations, compassion, love, and kindness dwell. Until we are ready to risk and reach this level, our attempts at dialogue will not be effective.

My First Exile

While in Siocon, I was informed that a professional killer of the military arrived in town. Friends, both Muslims and Christians, were afraid for my life. They warned me to avoid any encounter with that man whom I saw on some occasions. I prayed for protection for myself and for the others. One evening, while I was in the parish house with Fr. Salvatore Carzedda and other priests we heard shouting outside. I was quiet, trying to understand the commotion. Fr. Salvatore interrupted my thoughts and told me, "Sebastiano, we have to see what is happening in the town." He was confident that because of my successful negotiations, it would be safe. But I did not like to move. An inner voice told me to stay where I was. I have escaped harm or even death on many occasions because I listened to this inner voice. But this time I accepted the challenge and answered, "Okay, let's go!" I drove my motorcycle with Fr. Salvatore riding on the back. An eerie silence met us but we were determined to find out what was happening.

We were met in front of the public market by a couple who were friends and by Boy de Guzman, my leader and companion in the Subanon program. He went outside because he heard the sound of our motorcycle. After a few moments of conversation, we heard a shot coming from the canal at the edge of the road near us.

The bullet passed near me and instinctively I fell to the ground and remained motionless, pretending I was hit. I remembered my friends' advice to avoid the professional killer and they were right. I motioned to Fr. Salvatore who was standing in panic, to fall down. I signaled him to run inside the nearby house for refuge. When we were inside the house, Boy de Guzman fell beside me saying, "I'm hit, I'm dying!" Trusting in God's protection, I rushed outside to ask for help. I met the killer with some soldiers who came and pretended to help us. They said they heard the shouting and they came to see what happened. I saw the surprise in their faces when they saw I was alive. We brought Boy to the hospital. Meanwhile, two priests arrived at the hospital because they were informed that I was dying. It seems that after the shooting, thinking I was hit, some soldiers went to the parish house to inform the priests that I was shot. Boy died after two hours, holding my hand and my rosary. Because of all these new events in my life, my superior asked me to go back to Italy. This was my first exile to my own country.

Discovering Silsilah

My exile in Italy proved to be providential and vital to the future of my mission. I was allowed to study at the Pontifical Institute for Arabic and Islamic Studies (PISAI) in Rome from 1981 to 1983. I had quality time to reflect and synthesize my past experiences and to pursue further studies in Islam and Arabic. I looked at this as preparation for my going back to the Philippines. I was convinced that this exile was not the end of my dream. I prayed continuously that someday I would be allowed to go back to the Philippines, continue to share my experiences of dialogue among Muslims and Christians and hopefully, start a group.

During my studies, I grew in knowledge and appreciation of Islam. I was especially touched by the experience of the Sufis. The Sufi experience began during the first centuries of Islam. They are more concerned with the spiritual dimension of the Islamic faith. For them, one priority is the *silsilah* (chain) that links them to God.

This concept of *silsilah* is applicable to the universal experience of faith of Muslims, Christians, and peoples of other faith traditions. Entering into the dynamics of the concept, it can be applied to each one's religion: to the *umma*, to the Church, as well as to other communities who have experience of the Divine. *Silsilah* is the root word of *salsilah* or *tarsilah* which means genealogical tree. I shared the concept with some Muslim and Christian friends; that we belong to the same genealogical tree and that we are members of the human family because God is the creator of all.

Back to the Philippines

After two years of studies in Rome, I wondered about my future. The answer came through a call from the Philippines. During the PIME regional assembly of 1983, the community in the Philippines elected me *in absentia* as regional superior. They informed me of the results and invited me to accept the will of the assembly. For me, it was a clear sign that my "exile" had ended. I accepted the mandate. I answered "yes" to God's will and in two months, I was on my way back to the Philippines.

The next sign for me was meeting Bishop Bienvenido Tudtud of Marawi. We became friends. He was a man of dialogue and faith. I shared with him my vision and my plan to start a group in Zamboanga City following the concept of *silsilah* as a spiritual foundation for interreligious dialogue, focusing on Muslim–Christian relations in the context of the Mindanao conflict. Bishop Tudtud listened intently and at the end he told me, "Sebastiano, go on! But remember, this vision of Silsilah is a project of a hundred years!" Initially, I was a bit disheartened by his prediction of a hundred years. I was eager to see results. Now after almost twenty-five years of Silsilah experience, the good bishop has been proven right! Bishop Tudtud continues to be a source of great inspiration for me. He was a man of vision and was able to inspire people. Unfortunately in 1987, he died in an airplane crash on his way to Baguio City. I lost a friend but his words continue to inspire me, "Sebastiano, go on!"

Silsilah Spirit of Padayon

Padayon for us in Silsilah is not only a Cebuano word which means *to move on* or *to go on*, but also a message, a commitment, a memory, a greeting, and a mission of hope in spite of difficulties. In the end these have helped us become stronger and to continue on in the spirit of *padayon*. To illustrate, I share these concrete incidents.

Kidnapping Attempt

In March 1992, I was approached by an MNLF commander who was my friend and whom I had helped during my Siocon mission. It was a joy for me to see him after a long time and I started asking about our other friends.

Shortly after our conversation, he told me, "Father, there is a new group who asked me, as commander of Zamboanga del Norte, to kidnap you." We had been together many times in the forest while I was doing the negotiation role. I was close to his family and would extend help to their relatives on many occasions and I know that he was a trusted friend. His confession about his mission caught me by surprise and was something new to me, so I asked him, "What do you plan to do now?" "You are my father!" he answered immediately and added, "You have helped my family, my people; I cannot do anything to harm you. These people who ordered me to kidnap you do not know that we are friends and I plan to bring you to them in Zamboanga right now to tell them not to touch you." I smiled at him to express my gratitude. I remembered other incidents when I was saved by Muslim friends. He added, "Are you afraid to come with me?" "No, I trust you," I answered. Together we visited three different areas where we met some leaders of the new group.

A Blood Pact of *Padayon*

I have mentioned that in 1977, I was sent to the Philippines with Fr. Salvatore Carzedda. When in 1981, I was forced to leave the Philippine mission for my "first exile" he continued his mission in Siocon, trying also to take care of some activities that I started with the Subanons and the Muslims.

In 1990 Fr. Salvatore joined me in Silsilah and in 1992 during the Summer Course gave a presentation on "Mission, Dialogue and Liberation: a Christian Perspective" with such enthusiasm. As usual we shared ideas about the activities of the day and then he prepared to go home to the PIME house, which was about four kilometers from the summer course venue. I normally went home every night, but that evening I decided to stay with the summer course. Fr. Salvatore drove his car, which was similar to mine. That was the last time I would see him alive. According to investigation reports, he was followed by two motorcyclists and was ambushed, riddled with bullets and died on the spot. As soon as I got the news, I went to the place where a lot of people were already gathered. He was dead. "Who killed him? Why? Was he the target or was it me?" These are still unanswered questions. What is clear is that he was killed by people who were against our dialogue and peace efforts. The death of Salvatore changed many things in my life. In 1992 I received a letter from my superior general asking me to go back to Italy considering that I was in danger and in some way my presence could be also a problem for other PIME fathers.

Sharing Pain and Building Hope

My second exile in Italy was not easy. I was emotionally affected by the death of Fr. Salvatore and I was disturbed by the recent events in Italy and Europe. Many were preoccupied by an influx of migrants from different countries, especially the increasing number of Muslims who were bringing with them cultural and religious issues that were causing social instability. People were not ready to live in a pluralist society.

In 1995, after three years of activity in Italy, my superior in Rome received the request from the bishop who heads the Episcopal Commission for Interreligious Dialogue of the Philippines to allow me to take up the position as executive secretary of the commission which I held in 1990 when the commission was formed. Once again the Lord made it clear that my future is in the Philippines.

Before the end of 1995, I was already back in the Philippines and started my work in the Catholic Bishops' Conference of the Philippines' (CBCP) commission whose office is in Manila. With new enthusiasm, I moved around the country to meet different groups, organized the office, and made plans. This was also the time when I felt called to deeper "silence." This was not the first time, but I was not yet ready to share this call openly since the task at hand was to consolidate the mission of Silsilah and serve as executive secretary of the CBCP Commission for Interreligious Dialogue.

While in the process of reflection, evaluation, and exploration of possibilities to start an experience of "silence," the Lord once again gave me a clear sign. One day while attending a big gathering of Christians, Muslims, and indigenous people in Davao City, I was rushed to the hospital after a major heart attack. Up to this point, I had never been sick in my life. I tried to read the new sign of God. I experienced the love of those who assisted and saved my life, the internal peace during that critical time and the closeness of Fr. Salvatore. After a week I was out of the critical condition and the doctor told me: "I do not know how you survived in your condition . . . it was a miracle!" I felt Fr. Salvatore's prayers and intercessions.

This event of my life remains the most powerful spiritual experience for me. I understood what it means to start a stage of my life in deeper silence. While recovering from my heart attack I finalized a plan to start a new experience of "silence" by building an *ashram* open to people of different religions near Manila. This was a response to my new call without leaving completely my commitments to Silsilah and to the CBCP Commission for Interreligious Dialogue.

Silsilah After Twenty-five Years

On May 9, 2009, Silsilah celebrated the twenty-fifth anniversary of its foundation. I know that I am identified with Silsilah as the founder who formed a movement of dialogue in the conflict situation of Mindanao, and that this is a sign of hope.

It is true, my contribution has been vital for Silsilah. But I'd like also to say that the Lord has sent me people and resources that allowed me to meet my expectations. I see how God is guiding the movement always. In time of difficulties and pain God has always provided a solution.

Today Silsilah is involved in many programs of solidarity, education, and formation but the priority remains the sharing of the spirituality of life-in-dialogue as an experience of life that we in Silsilah live and promote with all Muslims, Christians, and people of other faiths. It is a holistic spirituality of dialogue with God, with the self, with others, and with creation. In this context we have formed thousands of Muslims and Christians. A lay-consecrated community among Catholic women called *Emmaus* has been formed. A similar effort, in the context of Islamic teaching and tradition, has been carried out, forming a group of Muslim women called *Muslimah* (Muslim Women for Dialogue and Peace). Today the movement has spread to many areas of the Philippines through the Silsilah Forum and the spirit of Silsilah has been spread in many countries, promoting a spiritual "chain" of prayer for peace called the "Harmony Chain Initiative." What will the future bring to Silsilah? We do not know, but my experience tells me that along the way the path will be shown to us. For this reason our mission remains a mission of hope, living and promoting the culture of dialogue that is inviting people to change paradigms and consider dialogue as an expression of love.

Spiritual Paths as Ways of Dialogue

Giuseppe Scattolin

When in July 1969, a year after my priestly ordination, I disembarked at Beirut harbor, I had a very vague idea about the purpose of my trip. I went there to learn Arabic. Then, according to my superiors' plan, I was to proceed to the Sudan to be installed in one of our schools to teach there until the end of my days. This had been the way of many others before me, and this was supposed to be my way of life too. My congregation, the Comboni Missionaries, has been engaged in the work of evangelization for more than a hundred years, starting from the Sudan and expanding into many African countries. The "Islamic question" was never really tackled by our people, and the dominant attitude towards it was quite negative. Islam was seen as a dark world, full of fanatics beyond conversion, and worse of all it was considered the archenemy of the Church, a very strong opponent to any form of evangelization. Missionaries working in Islamic environments were seen to lead quite sterile and frustrating lives, full of dissatisfaction, except for some rare surreptitious converts, plucked from the grips of the Islamic community, with a lot of risk. Moreover, deep tensions had broken out in the Sudan between the Muslim north and the Christian–Traditionalist south. These tensions had erupted into two terrible civil wars full of casualties and all sorts of brutalities, perpetrated especially by Northerners against Southerners. All this had worsened the picture of Muslims in the eyes of most missionaries. Therefore, the option of going to work in Islamic contexts was at its least attractive. Thus, when I asked to go precisely there, to work amongst Muslims, my superiors must have felt a sense of relief and there I was sent without delay.

In spite of such negative premises, something new had started among our generation of priests, that of the 1960s, something that was to bring about many changes in the life of the Church and also of its missionaries. I did my theological formation in Rome, in the years of the Second Vatican Council. It is difficult to convey the tremendous impact such an experience had on us young theologians. The council represented a deep renewal of Church theology and praxis from its very foundations. No question was avoided in our discussions. Nothing could be accepted but on sound investigation, discussion, and proofs. In particular, the relationship of Christianity with other religions, a point never challenged up to that time, was now put into question from all points of view, and the traditional exclusivist position was brought under critical examination. The council document *Nostra Aetate* (1965) opened the way for a new look at world religions. Also our traditional stance on Islam was called into question. New experiences lived out by some pioneers, like Charles de Foucauld (d. 1916), were great stimuli that led us to challenge the closed attitude of our people. The book *Priest of non-Christians*, written by a famous Dominican, Fr. Serge de Beaurecueil (who in 1987 would be on the examination panel of my PhD thesis at PISAI), and others in the same vein, were great inspirations for us. De Beaurecueil showed how he, a Catholic priest, was able to live in deep human and spiritual companionship with Muslims to the point of becoming a "spiritual animator," an example of true religious life for many of them. Some of my young companions, who had preceded me to our missions, reported that they were finding new possibilities, and that new relationships with Muslims could be built beyond the traditional negative attitude in which most of our people had immured themselves.

So when I disembarked at Beirut harbor in July 1969, I had a lot of questions in my mind, and nothing was clear to me. I had first of all to become familiar with the Islamic environment and the Muslim mind, starting with the Arabic language, an enterprise that had put the character of many people before me to the test. As many of us had done before, I joined the Arabic course for beginners organized by the Jesuits, namely by Fr. Henri D'Alverny. The Centre Religieux d'Études Arabes (CREA) was affiliated with the Université de Saint Joseph of Beirut, and was situated in Bikfaya, a small town about 20 miles northeast of Beirut, at about 2,600 feet above sea level, on the western flanks of Mount Lebanon. From there one has a splendid vision of the Mediterranean. By the end of the two-year course, I had a clearer vision of my future. I intended to delve further into the Islamic world, starting with the Arabic language, the true key to it.

First Steps

Once in the Sudan, my first destination was the Comboni College of El-Obeid, a town about 220 miles west of Khartoum. This school was founded to prepare young people to work in business. My job was to teach English and at the same time to do some pastoral work in the local Christian communities. However, my aim was now becoming clearer. I had to get deeper into the Islamic world. At the first opportunity, I asked my superiors for permission to enter the Department of Arabic Language and Literature at Cairo University (Khartoum Branch), taken over some years ago by the Sudanese government of Omar al-Bashir. It had the advantage of offering evening courses, so I could carry out some work during the day and study in the evenings. This was an important step in achieving full immersion in Islamic culture. Of course, I was the only Christian there, and the other students were curious about my presence, as a Catholic priest. Many questions were put to me and I had to clarify my position. I always stressed that precisely because I am a priest I am interested in all values found in all religions. So my studying Islam had nothing to do with proselytizing or religious propaganda, or with the idea of a "plot against Islam," an oft-repeated conjecture. In this way, I was able to get acquainted with what normal Muslim students know about their culture and language, and this from their point of view. This experience surely helped me a great deal in reaching a deeper understanding of Muslim mentality and feeling. I could compare the two worlds: the Christian on one side, the Muslim on the other. Both appeared to me quite self-centered, umbilical, one could say. Each one from its own "fortress" peered out at the other through an emotional fog of apologetics and fear. Despite the presence of our schools, where the majority of students and teachers were Muslims, there was almost no real exchange between the two worlds. Living as a student on the university campus left me convinced that there was a tremendous need for communication. While these reflections were crystallizing in my mind, I obtained in 1978 my *licence* (bachelor's degree) in Arabic Language and

Literature from Cairo University. This was another important step on the road to dialogue.

The next step was to go on for a PhD in Sufism. Sufism, the spiritual dimension of Islam, has always appealed to me as a basic field of meeting at the level which I consider the core of any religion, and so of Christianity and Islam. This is the level of the living encounter with God. In 1979 I went to Egypt in the hope of continuing my studies at Cairo University. For a number of reasons, I wasn't able to finish my studies there, so I joined PISAI (the Pontifical Institute for Arabic and Islamic Studies) in Rome, where under the supervision of Fr. Robert Caspar, a well-known scholar in Islamic theology and Sufism, I did my research. Under his guidance, I could develop better research methods. Finally, in 1987, I presented my PhD thesis on a quite famous but also difficult Sufi poet, 'Umar Ibn al-Farid (d. 632/1235). This poet, known as the "Prince of Lovers" for his beautiful verses on divine love, is very popular among Sufis, and my study, a semantic analysis of the text of his famous ode, the *Great Ta'iyya*, has been much appreciated also by Muslims, even though I criticized many aspects of the traditional Islamic understanding of his poetry. The following year (1988), Fr. Caspar fell ill and could no longer teach, therefore, I had to take over his courses in PISAI, and I have continued teaching Sufism there ever since.

Traveling with Sufism

In this way, Sufism, or the mystical dimensions of Islam, has become the major interest of my life in an Islamic context. It represents in my view the deepest core of Islamic religious experience. I believe that it is particularly at the level of mystical experience that a true meeting between religions should take place. In fact, religious interchanges that do not reach down to the depths of spiritual experience are unsatisfying, missing the main point of religion, which is and must be a living experience of God. "Where is your God?" we read in Psalm 42:4. Such a question must be answered by every religion, not necessarily alone but possibly in dialogue with others. The challenge of spiritual experience is in my view the basic challenge for all religions in our postmodern world. On this basis, I have always found a profound link between my Christian experience and the Sufi one, and in the end with that of all the great religions of humanity. Interspiritual dialogue is necessary at this level because we all are facing the same basic human problems and, increasingly, the challenges of the globalized world in which we all live. Humankind in fact, in spite of all its technical progress, is now in ever-greater danger of losing its deep human identity, transforming the human being into a type of "highly developed robot." This is surely a critical issue, to be studied in all its dimensions.

Since 1988 my time has been divided between Cairo and Rome. On the one hand, I wanted to continue living in Cairo, so as to be in touch with the actual life of Muslims and the concrete problems they face, in my case in the Egyptian society. I did not want to be just a scholar of Islam in some comfortable western university. On the other hand, I was happy to pass part of my time in Rome, teaching at PISAI, keeping in touch with the life of the Church and the cultural trends of the western world. I can say that I was lucky, or better yet, that God disposed that I live such a shuttle-style of life for some purpose I did not know. A further step in my research on Sufism was a two-year postdoctoral fellowship (1990–92) at Yale University, under the supervision of another great scholar of Sufism, Dr. Gerhard Böwering. There I studied an important commentary, written by Sa'id al-Din al-Farghani (d. 699/1300), on the same Sufi poem of Ibn al-Farid, the *Great Ta'iyya*, on which I had done my research. During this time, my methodology of studying improved a great deal. Later on, after some years of teaching, I went for a one-year course (2000) at Heythrop College (University of London), where I obtained a master's degree in Christian spirituality. In this way, I further polished my academic tools for a better understanding of spiritual experiences in Islam and Christianity.

Cairo remained my principal residence and there I found many people who had long been working in the field of interreligious dialogue. I must mention first of all the late Fr. George Anawati (d. 1994), the famous Dominican scholar, a true pioneer in this field. The library he founded in Cairo with other Dominican confrères has become a central point of meeting for many people involved in the field of Islamic and Arabic studies and in Christian–Muslim dialogue. I had the good fortune of enjoying a long and deep friendship with him until the end of his life. With him, I took part in many meetings, lectures and events in Cairo, making the acquaintance of a great number of people. Another important person with decades of experience in this field has been a great help to me in Cairo, the Dutch Jesuit priest, Fr. Christian van Nispen. He was renowned for his great gift of establishing contacts and friendships with all kinds of people and through him my circle of contacts continued to expand. So I must say that, even if many people around me were not much open to the dialogical dimension, I still found many opportunities to delve in the Islamic environment.

On the other side, Egypt is famous as the center of Arabic and Islamic culture. Being in Egypt, one finds oneself in contact with the living source of Arabic and Islamic thought. All the problems Islam is facing in confronting modernity as well as in dealing with radical Islamic movements are found here in Egypt, represented in living persons. Here one can be in touch with the most open as well with the most conservative Muslim thinkers. Cairo is full of all sorts of cultural centers where one can meet a host of interesting people with whom a living dialogue can be developed. Among them one can mention: the Egyptian Philosophical Society, founded and directed up to now by the famous scholar Hassan Hanfi, the French research centers Centre d'Études et de Documentation Economiques et Juridiques (CEDEJ), Institut Français d'Archéologie Orientale (IFAO), and the Dominican Institut Dominicain d'Études Orientales (IDEO).

When I look back on that period of my life, I see that I was still in search of a breakthrough in order to enter in my own personal way into the Islamic world. I saw that other people were already well introduced in it, being accepted and recognized as true partners. The old dream of incarnating myself, so to say, in a culture, being accepted as part of its living people, carrying on a dialogue from within, as it were, and not from outside and afar, has always been somewhere in my mind, but such a dream had not yet become a concrete reality in my life. Moreover I was living inside the Catholic community in which there was, and still is, a great distance between our ecclesiastical life and that of Muslims around us. We were, and unfortunately continue to be, a world living in parallel to our Islamic milieu without any true and deep meeting with it. Moreover, most of the time there is a quite hostile attitude towards it. Such an attitude was, and still is, a handicap for a true communication between the two worlds.

A Breakthrough

A true breakthrough came for me almost by chance. In 1994 I decided to change my usual shuttle route: Cairo-Rome-Cairo, and to go to visit the shrine of Jalal al-Din Rumi (d. 672/1273), a most celebrated Sufi poet. So that year I traveled via Istanbul, and from there to Konya where the shrine of this great Sufi poet is found. There I happened to come across, by chance one might say, the oldest manuscript of the *Diwan* of my beloved Sufi poet, 'Umar Ibn al-Farid. This manuscript was not listed in the official catalogues and was still unpublished. Such a find left me facing a difficult choice: should I engage in the painful work of editing it or should I leave such a job for other people? In the end, I concluded that it was my duty now, in spite of all the difficulties to be faced, to edit this manuscript in the best way. Actually I compared the Konya manuscript with seven others among the oldest unpublished manuscripts of the *Diwan*, as well as with the thirteen most important modern editions of it. The work took some years to complete, but in the end it resulted in an edition of an Arabic text that has almost no match in all Arabic literature. The subtitle, *Reading of its Text Throughout History*, indicates the rationale of my work: what we have in our hands is not the Text (with capital "T") of the *Diwan*, but the text as transmitted throughout history by human means, in which a lot of variants and mistakes are to be found. My basic idea was to stress the historical dimensions of any literary text, even the religious ones. Such a critical-historical approach to an important Arabic text coupled with the semantic analysis of it (the method I employed in my doctoral research), became an innovative contribution to Sufi studies. The result was that a number of Egyptian and Arabic scholars became interested in my work, and I was invited to present it in many cultural events. All this helped greatly in my being accepted ever more as a working partner in the Arabic cultural milieu, i.e. as part of a common work of research, study and exchange. At least at the intellectual level, I think, a real dialogue has been started.

On this basis, many other breakthroughs occurred. In 2007 I was invited by Munoufiyya University (in the Nile delta) to become the supervisor of a master's student in Sufism. The student, Ahmed Hasan, was a recent acquaintance of mine and asked to carry out his research with my help. The professor supervisor agreed, though practically I performed the bulk of the work. This was an unusual situation. I, a Catholic priest, was supervisor of research in Islamic Sufism for a Muslim student in an Egyptian university, in a completely Islamic context. I think that in Rome the opposite (i.e., a Muslim scholar supervising research on Christian mysticism for a Christian student) would hardly be possible. I must say that I was most cordially welcomed there, and with this event my presence at the university level increased. A great deal of cooperation in the field of research has grown out of it, such as writing on Sufism, cooperation in research, meetings, and more, and I hope to continue working in this line in the future. I believe that the Islamic, as well as the Arab world, is in need of a more scientific approach to its cultural tradition, freeing itself from the traditional dogmatic mind-set and opening itself to a more critical view. A true critical work can be better done, in my view, from inside the Islamic culture, as a partner of it, not from outside, as an imposition on it. This is, in my view, a matter of great moment for the Arabic-Islamic world to make it overcome the dominant mentality, still quite self-centered and self-referent. Such an uncritical mentality is, as is well-known, fertile ground for many fundamentalist and fanatical movements that are spreading in the Islamic world, causing a lot of conflicts, wars, and destruction.

In an article about interreligious dialogue, which I presented, amongst others, to the professors of al-Azhar University of Cairo, I have outlined what should be, to my mind, the basic features of the "religion of the future." Such a religion should first revisit its sources, going back to its first, original message, purifying it from many historical developments that have encroached upon it. The word *reform*, in fact, has always been a key issue for all religions in all ages. Secondly, it should confront modernity, acquiring a critical mind and approach to its tradition. Such a critical mind is not just a Western idiosyncrasy, as many Muslim thinkers still believe. A critical mind is a basic need of all human cultures in order to overcome all fundamentalist temptations. Thirdly, it should enter into dialogue with other religions, going beyond the umbilical attitude of self-centeredness and self-reference. True identity is not to be found in isolation and exclusivity, and even less so in conflict with the other, but in interrelatedness and dialogue. Fourthly, it should commit itself to justice in the world, confronting the globalization process that with its marketing mentality dominates our world with the risk of destroying all human values. Here collaboration among all religious traditions is required in a particular way to create a new "global humanism," based on the true human values of justice and fraternity, through which human living together can be possible. Such topics have become part of my meetings with Muslims, and I am looking for solid foundations for them, to be found also in the Islamic tradition, especially the mystical. Only in this way can a true exchange purify our relationships and foster mutual cooperation.

In 2009 I published with my Muslim student Ahmed Hasan an anthology of Sufi texts covering the first seven centuries of Islamic history, under the title *Al-tajalliyat al-ruhiyya fi l-islam* (*Spiritual Manifestations in Islam*). I wrote in it the introduction to Sufism as well as the introductions to the periods and lives of the Sufi authors mentioned there. In this way, I could present to Muslims my view of Sufism and its issues. The scope was to make the discourse on Sufism more popular, countering the many attacks launched against it by fundamentalist Islamic groups, foremost among them the Muslim Brotherhood. We wanted this book—based on solid scientific studies on Sufism, taken also from many Orientalists—to counter also the prejudiced anti-Western mental attitude, common in many Arabic and Islamic intellectual milieus. Dr. Ahmed al-Tayyeb, the rector of al-Azhar University (now Sheikh al-Azhar, the highest authority in Sunni Islam), wrote a positive foreword to the book. The book had a tremendous success in Egypt, as well as in the Arab world at large. The first two thousand copies were sold out in a few months and it is becoming a reference point for studies, meetings, and discussions. This too is an important breakthrough in interreligious dialogue, the dialogue of spiritual experience. Now an increasing collaboration in the field of scientific research at academic level is developing with positive results. In 2009 the University of Kafr al-Sheikh (in the Nile delta) decided to give me the annual Award for Humanities. This will help greatly to make me part of Egyptian culture and to enter into collaboration with Muslim researchers on their own cultural ground.

Now more than ever, I have the definite feeling of having become part of Arabic Islamic culture, and so of being in tune with the basic issues that are facing the Islamic world and millions of Muslims in our postmodern times. More than ever, I see that Muslims around me feel that I am a brother for them, with a deep concern for their religion, culture, and moral values, and that I am sincerely working for the betterment of their life, both material and spiritual, and that my faith is not an obstacle but the inner force that moves me in my work. I feel deeply accepted by them as I am, and nobody now tries to provoke me with the invitation of changing my religion. My Muslim friends know very well that I am deeply attached to my faith and, at the same time, deeply interested in all the human and spiritual values that I find in Islam, and that I am working to help them grow in a similar attitude. Of course, I wish to be able to present my faith in terms that are acceptable to the Muslim mind, overcoming a lot of past verbal disputes and quarrels based on abstract dogmatic formulations. I think it is possible to open the Muslim mind to a new approach to the mystery of Jesus. At that point, I insist, everyone is free to choose his or her own faith, not in front of people, but in front of his or her conscience and God. Dialogue is not a trick to convert people, but a way to know the whole truth, my truth and that of the other, and so to come to a fuller and more mature act of faith. Nevertheless, one must always stress, faith is not just the result of human capacity but a gift of God and as such must be accepted.

Looking back on my past experience, I can see now that there was a sort of plan carrying me on and preparing events I could never foresee. I can also bear witness to the fact that a deep desire for something, when kept alive, will always find a way to fulfillment, though fullness and perfection cannot be expected here, in our present time. However, I must also avow that a more positive attitude towards Islam on the part of our ecclesial and missionary milieus, and a deeper attention to the examples of people involved in a positive dialogue with Muslims could have helped a lot in my long and, at times, difficult journey on the road to dialogue with the Islamic world. A lot of futile disputes could have been avoided and useful work could have been developed in common in a more positive attitude. It is my hope now that my work will contribute in fostering an ever more open mentality from inside the Church towards Islam, and also from Islam towards Christianity. A serious, committed dialogue between the two faiths is all the more necessary in our time.

Setting Sail on the Sea of Interreligious Dialogue

In the new age that human history is now entering, dialogue at all levels has become a most vital dimension of humankind to answer the tremendous challenges it has to face. History has not become easier and simpler in our time, as many dreamers from the age of the Enlightenment fancied, with the idea of infinite, positive human progress. On the contrary, history has become more complicated and threatening in our present "global village." Only religions and cultures working in true dialogue will be able to offer a positive contribution to the situation of our contemporary humankind, threatened, as it seems, by a dreadful robotic future.

An unrestricted reciprocal opening amongst religions seems to be the only alternative to the resurgence of tribal conflicts of all kinds—ethnic, cultural, and religious—that since time immemorial have plagued human-kind, plunging it into an endless chain of conflicts, wars, and catastrophes. Dialogue at all levels seems to be now the only true and realistic answer to the challenges of our time. But dialogue implies a deep and profound change of mentality, a historical turning point and conversion. All religions are called, now in particular, to be positive partners in such a historical predicament. The motto of Hans Küng, repeated many times and by many people—"There cannot be peace among peoples, if there is not first peace among religions"—is pointing to a basic issue of our time. In this sense, dialogue has become our present, most urgent and vital challenge and task.

Christ, calling his disciples to follow him, ordered them to cast their nets into the sea to catch fish, and as the Gospel records, they caught a great quantity of all types of fish. A similar call is now addressed to us in our present situation. Now we are invited to cast the net of dialogue into the sea of human history trusting that, in spite of all obstacles and difficulties, our little net will be part of the great net of the Kingdom of God, which as the Gospel says, will gather at the end of time fish of all kinds. It is not up to us to judge and to separate the catch now. Such a task must be left to God alone, in times and ways he alone knows and fixes. Our task now, in our time, is only to cast the net, thus bringing about "truth in love" (Eph. 4:15), so as to make the seed of the Kingdom of God penetrate and grow in all peoples, religions and cultures.

This seed will surely work in human history and in the depth of the conscience of every human being. This seed will lead us all, even the whole universe, towards our final growth and destination—the Kingdom in its fullness, when God at the end of time will be "All in All" (1 Cor. 15:28).

A Dominican Friar in a Land of Immigration and in a Land of Islam

Emilio Platti

My father, Giuseppe, being an Italian immigrant, would talk to me in the dialect of Bergamo. From my mother and grandparents, being Flemish, I would hear the gentle tones of Dutch in Flemish pronunciation. But to preserve harmony between everyone, we spoke French at home. I was certainly immersed in a multilingual environment, but nothing to signal my later study of Arabic. In this Catholic milieu, in a Catholic Flemish region, nevertheless an implicit theology of welcome and openness prevailed. A terrible tragedy occurred to our neighbors, who were the only Protestants in the street. Their small daughter was burnt to death. I remember the extent to which my mother embraced this grieving family, how, with other parishioners, she shared in their grief in going to the little Protestant church of the town to pray with them. That is something I have never forgotten.

On leaving high school, in 1961, I entered the Dominicans of the province of St. Rose in Flanders. There, too, nothing could have signaled my encounter with Muslims. Besides, where were they? Certainly not in Belgium! Immigrants were mainly Italians, like my father, or Polish or Portuguese.

So why was it, at the Dominican novitiate of the province of St. Rose in Flanders, that one day I traced in Arabic the *Fatiha* of the Qur'an, the first chapter? I have no idea. Our missions were to the Congo, and if any brothers had gone to Palestine, it was to study the Bible. No one around me had any interest whatever in Islam.

Why then, two years later, would I have asked the provincial superior for permission to read the Qur'an, which was still on the Index [of Forbidden Books]? And why, still later, would I have listened to a Jesuit father, Frank De Graeve, who told me that to study the theology of religions with him at the Catholic University of Leuven (Louvain), it was necessary to study one in-depth, and why not Islam? My fellow Dominicans in Cairo specialized in Islamic studies, with Fr. Anawati at their head; he was often in Louvain and its Higher Institute of Philosophy, and he had received an honorary doctorate from Louvain.

Why did I find myself involved in 1969 with Fr. Pol Steels, a Redemptorist, who appealed for volunteers for his newly founded Young People's Foyer in the northern quarter of Brussels, situated in two bars previously given over to prostitution, dilapidated, and condemned for demolition, in a notorious quarter, in the street of a long-ago vanished theatre? This meeting place was open especially for young Muslim Moroccans and I had myself entered a religious order as a Catholic: some "1968-vintage" Dominican brothers became very strange monks indeed!

Meanwhile, I had met Fr. Charles Deckers, who welcomed me at the El-Kalima Centre, a center for dialogue with Muslims, located in Brussels. Later I became more involved in this center, when Fr. Deckers returned to Algeria, where he would be one of the first victims of the civil war. He was assassinated on December 27, 1994, at Tizi-Ouzou.

Why did I later keep on asking my provincial superior to let me become more committed to the Cairo Dominican community and the Institut Dominicain d'Études Orientales (IDEO), while he saw me rather as fitted for editing the Flemish review of spiritual life? My mother, who had long outlived my father, who died in 1958, had to ask herself frequently where the Lord would lead me! Not to speak of my superiors, who, nonetheless, gave me the freedom to involve myself in these different ways.

I am often asked how I came to commit myself to this path and in response I can only describe these various stages. Certainly, at the Young People's Foyer, I had the vague awareness that I was also the son of an immigrant, who had arrived in Belgium with hardly any resources. There was that social characteristic, which predominated over the religious side, and of which I have never lost sight. Certainly, we were in 1968 filled with new and fresh ideas, with the theologies of Rahner, Schillebeeckx, and Chenu, but also of Ebeling, Bultmann, and Tillich, of philosophies which were still somewhat Thomist, but which faced up to Heidegger and to many others; and, for my part, there were also in-depth readings on Marxism and dialectical communism! Did someone not tell me one day that this initiative of a Foyer for young people in such an area must be of communist inspiration!

The Dominicans, the University of Leuven and what was to become the Centre for the Study of Religions, the Young People's Foyer, the El-Kalima Centre, and IDEO in Cairo: five enduring anchor points for me and from which I could no longer detach myself. They must have corresponded to something deep within me, which is not entirely subject to reasoning: "the heart has its reasons" (as Blaise Pascal wrote).

It was at the Foyer that I met Muslims for the first time; initially these were youngsters, from five to seventeen years old, coming straight from the Rif Mountains. Sometimes their parents joined them there; when, for example, the great 'Id was celebrated by sacrificing a huge sheep, which afterwards the Muslim families would eat with Belgian *frites*.

It did not enter our heads to think that one day this Islam could pose a problem. Mainly we were concerned with the social aspect—to welcome the children of migrant workers was the main preoccupation. Did not the state official who visited the Foyer tell us that we had entered there "the fourth world"? I would never forget the social dimension, which goes hand in hand with the cultural and religious, in what one now calls the migration movements. Nor indeed that it was the Belgian state which invited Moroccans and Turks to *live and work in Belgium*, as a brochure from the Belgian Ministry of Employment and Work told them in the 1960s. After 1969, I found myself involved as a volunteer monitor in the Young People's Foyer. I saw it move premises twice, from *la rue du Théâtre*, in the northern quarter of Brussels, ending up at Molenbeek, near the canal, in *la rue des Ateliers*. At first simply a welcome center for young people, in 2009 it celebrated forty years of its existence. But meanwhile it had developed vastly, in particular since 1981, under the impetus of another Dominican, Johan Leman, and of the director, Loredana Marchi. Besides welcoming the young, other activities had been developed: social and juridical services for immigrants, the El-Amal Centre for women immigrants, and bicultural projects organized by the Foyer in schools. I am no longer attached to the Foyer as a volunteer but as a member of the administrative council. Nevertheless I still consider this grassroots work as being that which is most needed in our society. It is there that we see the working-out or the failure of the grand ideas that we develop in our academic colloquia on the subject of integration and citizenship.

Starting in 1972, taking advantage of scholarships in Belgian-Egyptian cultural relations, for several months each year I joined the group of Dominicans at IDEO in Cairo to prepare a doctorate there. I already had a degree in Oriental studies, and as the University of Louvain had a strong tradition of studies of the Christian Orient, Fr. Anawati and Fr. Mistrih, of the Franciscan center of Mouski, directed me towards an Arab Christian author, Yahya ibn Adi (d. 974). Fr. Mistrih had discovered two unknown manuscripts of works by Yahya at the Coptic patriarchal library.

It was over a weekend at the Foyer, on an old typewriter, that I prepared the few pages of introduction for the defense of my doctoral thesis on Yahya ibn Adi. I defended my thesis in 1980 at the Faculty of Letters of the Catholic University of Leuven. Yahya ibn Adi was a great translator of Aristotle into Arabic, a transmitter of Greek thought, and the leader of a school of thought in Baghdad; as such, he was the very pattern of an animator of a circle of disciples from various Christian and Muslim traditions. In a certain way, this was a "dialogue" before its time. Some claim that there is no mutual understanding possible between Christians and Muslims, the former having integrated the ancient Greek thought, while Muslims, through the Islam they profess, are resistant to this whole stream of thought. The intellectual interaction between Arabic-speaking Christians, Jews, and Muslims between 850 and 1050 in Baghdad is undoubtedly proof to the contrary.

Though the Foyer and the El-Kalima Centre in Brussels were close to my heart, and I continued to go there during my periods of residence in Belgium, in my spirit and my affections it was the Cairo house which gradually assumed the greater importance. Up until now, I have never failed to spend several months there every year. From the beginning, I found an amazing ambience, of which in Belgium I never had the faintest idea. In an old photo from 1974, I am shown behind Cardinal Pignedoli, who, in the spirit of the Second Vatican Council, had given a lecture at al-Azhar. In the photograph, he is surrounded by Frs. Jomier, Anawati, Fiey, Monnot, Cortabarria, and Morelon; so many Dominicans committed to the study of Middle Eastern cultures, whose writings enriched Islamic studies, but who, above all, were committed heart and soul, and at various levels, to a dialogue with Muslims. They represented for me the great movement of involvement in the dialogue of cultures and religions to which the Second Vatican Council had given so great a stimulus, and of which I had caught sight in my studies at Louvain. But I was far from having sufficient knowledge fully to appreciate what they gave me.

Anawati introduced me to mediaeval Arabic texts and read with me some manuscripts of Ibn Adi. He enabled me to meet Madame Tāha Husayn, who gave me a glimpse into what was then a still recent past. Jomier's manual of Egyptian Arabic let me understand this endearing Egyptian people and he spoke to me of congresses at al-Azhar whose proceedings he studied. He enabled me to meet Mary Kahil and thus opened my mind to the period which was coming to an end and which had been dominated by that inescapable figure, Louis Massignon. Fiey remained only a short time in Cairo and then returned to Beirut, where he was to live for the whole period of the civil war, but it was he who brought me to know the Christian milieu under the Abbasids, helping me to locate such manuscripts of Sharfeh, Aleppo, and Mardin, that were accessible to me. Monnot wrote his articles for the annual *Melanges* of IDEO and prepared works on the religions described by mediaeval Muslim scholars.

Among the residents at the Dominican house in Cairo, I could not forget two other persons: Dr. Ernst Bannerth (d. 1976), whom I willingly accompanied to the *mawlid*s and *dhikr*s of the Sufi brotherhoods. He took me to the sanctuaries of Sayyida Zaynab, Sayyida Ruqayya, Sayyida Nafisa, and others. He opened up for me a Muslim devotional world of which I had no idea. Serge de Beaurecueil had already left for Kabul, and the Sufism which he studied through his beloved Sufi master, Abdullah Ansari, remained strange to me for a long time: I have the impression that I did not dare to touch it. There was, however, the somewhat mysterious figure of Dr. Uthman Yahya, who lived with us in the Dominican house. He showed me the many index cards of the *Futuhat al-Makkiyya* of Ibn Arabi which he was editing from the autograph manuscript, volume after volume, and one day suggested that I could perhaps join him in his work. I was far from being suitably competent, and from 1976 onwards, had to divide my time between Leuven and Cairo. My Dominican superiors did not look favorably on my attachment to Cairo turning into a continuous residence.

After 1980 and the defense of my thesis in History and Oriental Philology at Leuven, I was appointed to teach there, first for Arabic language at the Institute of Living Languages and later for various other Islamic courses in the Departments of Letters and Theology. Fortunately my appointment was never full-time, which allowed me to spend long periods of time at IDEO and to continue to teach elsewhere: at El-Kalima, at the Catholic Institute in Paris, and even the UST in Manila. In fact, I am very thankful to God never to have been appointed full time! I was left free to breathe the atmosphere of Cairo, to immerse myself in the rich IDEO library, which I helped Frs. Anawati and Morelon to reorganize, to recover

there the spirit of dialogue with Muslims in flesh and blood. From then on
I took part in that search for what is at the very heart of the Muslim faith,
and which had to such an extent inspired this *kairos*, this unique period of
grace, that was the years 1955 to 1975, when every hope of dialogue and
mutual understanding was permitted. So it was not without reason that in
courses and in numerous sessions and lectures, I tried to reply to the inevitable question dealing with Islam's strangeness, by going beyond appear-
ances, to the heart of the act of Islam, the act of faith. Had not the Second
Vatican Council, in *Nostra Aetate* (paragraph 3), explicitly referred to "the
Islamic faith"? And was not Pope John Paul II himself fully committed to
a similar path?

For my part, I remained committed to this approach long after 1981 and
the assassination of President Sadat; one could say, right up to the death of
Fr. Georges Chehata Anawati, on the feast of St. Thomas, January 28,
1994. Yet in 1981, something of this spirit and this hope of calm coexistence was shattered. Fr. Anawati quickly became aware of it, and I sensed a
kind of shared intuition between him and Jean-Pierre Peroncel-Hugoz, of
Le Monde newspaper, whom I saw so often come to talk with him. This
renowned journalist certainly had a prophetic vision of the terrible tragedy
which was to fall upon the Muslims and the tearing apart of their community from within, when he wrote *Le Radeau de Mahomet* (1983). Anawati
himself analyzed clearly the reasons for a *neo-kharijite* extremism that, with
the assassination of Sadat on October 6, 1981, gave rise to a long period of
terrorism that was to extend well beyond Egypt (*Mideo* 16, 1983).

Terrorism within Egypt culminated in the senseless massacre of tourists
at the Temple of Hatshepsut, November 17, 1997. It was then that the
authorities stepped in to put an end to it. From my readings on the subject
of Islamist militancy, I thought not only of the Muslim Brothers, the
Iranian revolution or the Algerian FIS, with Ali Belhadj and his diary written in prison, which I was able to read briefly, but a name which recurred
everywhere in writings concerning these milieux was that of Abu l-A'la
Mawdudi who died in 1979, but whose writings have spread worldwide.
Travels to Pakistan and Great Britain enabled me to acquire his works in
English. I soon became aware that I had in my hand the key to understanding the actual foundations of a militant ideology based on identity, more
significant than Sayyid Qutb or Hasan al-Banna, which was wreaking havoc
worldwide by spreading his writings in English throughout the Muslim
community. Reading his commentary on the Qur'an and also by getting
hold of a collection of articles by Mawdudi, *West versus Islam* (New Dehli,
1991), I understood how much this thought could incite polarization

between Muslims and the West; a polarization that was later aggravated to the point of ending in warfare. In 1994, after Fr. Michel Hayek had retired, I suggested as the subject for a course at the Catholic Institute of Paris "The sources of Islamic militancy," a subject which I taught until 2008.

Questions put to me by listeners went beyond Mawdudi. Is this polarization not natural to Islam in relation to the other cultures that it encounters? Surely the conviction of being "the best community" amongst humankind, joined to an attempt at limitless expansion, can make Islam "naturally" violent? "Is Islam naturally an enemy," whether of the Christian or of the modern West? Having already been long familiar with the polemical literature of Arab Christians, I wished to go beyond the single question of Islam's strangeness, to look in depth into the relations of Muslims with others and the image held in the past by those who were in contact with them; that is to say in the first place the Arab Christians. Somewhat by chance, on reading an article by a colleague in Leuven, I realized that a text by an Arab Christian exactly suited us: the (so-called) *Apology* of al-Kindi, a polemic work *par excellence*, written at the beginning of the ninth century. It tackled virtually all the questions that are "painful" for a Muslim: the status of the Qur'an, its editing, and especially the status of the prophet of Islam. The *Apology* is a text of great importance, for it had been translated into Latin, and this translation had an influence even on Thomas Aquinas and many others later. I was aware that the negative image which Westerners gradually had adopted was just as bad as that of the Latins of the Middle Ages. But did it correspond to the lived reality of Muslims? It was necessary to acknowledge the fact that there existed in Muslim history a temptation to hegemony, which in recent centuries had turned into resentment, because of an unparalleled regression of civilization. The hope for a dialogue of civilizations and for citizens to share a common life, however, seemed to me to be intact, since the values of the existential dimension of the Muslim faith takes priority over any other lived dimension of Islam.

From 2000 onwards, I felt that Mawdudi was now out of date; and that in two completely opposite directions. On the one hand, there was extremist Islamism going to the limits, symbolized by the vague entity which is al-Qaeda, which goes from violent confrontations to multiple suicide attacks, in defiance of everything represented by the West. On the other hand, still in a minority but growing, there is that diversity of Muslims who are deeply committed to rethinking Islam, ranging from a reformism which is still "right-thinking," to a liberalism which is close to postmodern thought; tendencies that are described by Jasser Auda in his book *Maqasid al-Shariah as Philosophy of Islamic Law* (2008).

There are new ways of thought, especially when expressed in English, which foresee a totally different future for Muslims from the one described by Mawdudi and his followers. We met some of these "liberal" thinkers at Leuven in the postdoctoral seminars in which I took part and which were organized by Prof. Marie-Claire Foblets. Yet again there is a quite different tendency, which I would call rather neo-Sufi, which I encounter at El-Kalima and even on Mindanao in the Philippines: It is the movement animated by Fethullah Gülen, whose thinking in a certain way agrees with that of the Indian Maulana Wahiduddin Khan.

During the last course on contemporary Islam at the University of Leuven in 2008, I said to my students that they should be ready to note other evolutions in the Muslim community apart from those about which the media tell us daily, and that it would soon be necessary to add several chapters to my course. They were aware also that, in all the bewildering diversity of present-day Islam, the scholars in Islamic studies can hardly make sense of what's going on!

In an environment radically different from that which I had known during the years 1965–75, the various anchor points of the time of my youth have nonetheless been confirmed. They allow me to consider that the interreligious dialogue of civilizations is more than ever necessary and that it is undoubtedly always potent, but above all, that it is the only possible solution to the profound current crisis of the Muslim community in its relationships with a globalized world, influenced by the West, deeply imperfect, but with which numerous people around the world quickly catch up.

This chapter was originally written in French,
translated into English by Dr. Penelope Johnstone,
and second-read by Anna-Regula Sharp.

How Did You End Up in Islamic Studies?

Jane McAuliffe

If I had a dollar for every time I have been asked that question, I would be a wealthy woman. Of course, it is a perfectly reasonable inquiry. The number of American Catholic women of my generation who became scholars of Islam and the Qur'an could probably be counted in single digits. It was not a common career path when I was a child nor can I recall any role models at all. Like many of us, however, I find that life's surprising journey does make sense—when glimpsed through a rearview mirror. With a backward glance, I can see the childhood interests and inclinations that eventually prompted my choice of academic focus: a curiosity about other cultures, a love of language learning, and an immersive experience of religious belonging. Religion was important in my family and our local parish was the hub of both our spiritual and our social lives. In my parochial elementary school, the self-sacrificing sisters who struggled with huge classes of students taught a Tridentine theology of *extra Ecclesiam nulla salus*[1] but

---

1. "There is only one universal Church of the faithful, outside which none will be saved," originally a declaration of the Fourth Lateran Council (1215) against the Albigensian heresy; see Denzinger, para. 802

did so with a compassionate nod to "baptism of desire," a desire they were willing to attribute to most of the human race.

The world of mid-twentieth-century American Catholicism, so well captured by the contemporary sociologist of religion Robert Orsi, bustled with rituals and routines that could fill the weekly calendar. Family rosaries, "First Friday" devotions, May processions in honor of Our Lady, novenas to St. Jude, Sodality, and Legion of Mary meetings, parish missions—all of it reinforced a strong sense of Catholic solidarity and Catholic superiority. Within that cocooned Catholicism of the American fifties and early sixties, encounters with Protestants and Jews occasionally occurred but Buddhists, Hindus, and Muslims were largely absent from the religious world of my childhood.

I feel deeply fortunate, however, to have entered young adulthood in the decade that produced two extraordinary engines of change: the Second Vatican Council and the US Immigration and Nationality Act of 1965. When Pope John XXIII launched the Second Vatican Council on October 11, 1962, I was just beginning my studies at Trinity College, a Catholic women's college in Washington, DC. The discussions and declarations of the council reverberated through my undergraduate years and through my family life. Theology classes became sites of lively and engaged debate. Priests and nuns, whom my childhood eyes had viewed as immutable beings, suddenly began to speak differently, to live differently, and to dress differently. (The shock of finally seeing Sister Hiltrude's hair remains an indelible memory!) My parents were sometimes puzzled and sometimes exhilarated by the near-constant novelty—liturgy in English, optional fish on Fridays, ecumenical outreach—and I learned an early lesson about the interaction of religion and culture.

The consequences of change in US immigration policy were less immediately evident but over the next several decades they transformed the religious landscape of North America. Since 1965, the most significant population increases have occurred in the religions that predominate in West, South, and East Asia. Immigration from these areas has rapidly increased the proportion of Hindus, Buddhists, and Muslims in the US population. With both Buddhism and Islam, this increase has been augmented by native-born converts. Within the last decade, the Pew Forum on Religion and Public Life has emerged as an important source of information on America's evolving religious demography. A ground-breaking 2007 study entitled "Muslim Americans: Middle Class, and Mostly Mainstream," presented the results of the first nationwide, random sample survey of

US Muslims.[2] Subsequent worldwide surveys have situated the expanding American Muslim population within global demographic growth and shifts.[3]

Both the transformations wrought by the Second Vatican Council and those consequent upon the revamping of US immigration laws have shaped the context of my adult professional life. Shortly after completing an undergraduate degree in philosophy and classics, I married my husband Dennis and the first of our four children quickly followed. The second arrived soon after, so hopes for advanced study were put on hold, at least temporarily. When I did eventually begin to take one graduate course at a time, my interest as a new mother was drawn to the field of religious education. I wanted to understand my own faith better and I wanted to know how best to educate my children in that faith. I started with some courses at Fordham University, New York, which has an excellent program in Catholic religious education. At Fordham, I was lucky to fall under the charismatic tutelage of Ewart Cousins, whose broadly ecumenical interests and sensitivities were well ahead of his time. Recognizing my growing interest in philosophical theology and comparative religion, Prof. Cousins urged me to continue my studies at Union Theological Seminary where I might eventually be able to enter the joint PhD program between Union and Columbia University.

Union Theological Seminary was a revelation and another step beyond the tight circle of Catholic schools and colleges that had circumscribed my education. Union's classrooms offered me my first sustained experience of ecumenical immersion. Both faculty and students were drawn from the major Christian denominations and the seminary fielded an all-star lineup: Paul Tillich for systematic theology, Raymond Brown for New Testament, Beverly Harrison for feminist ethics, and James Cone for black liberation theology. Switching the adjective for all fields of the curriculum—theology, ethics, biblical studies—from Catholic to Christian was an important personal prelude to my eventual move into the world of interfaith study and engagement.

---

2. "Muslim Americans: Middle Class and Mostly Mainstream," May 22, 2007, http://tinyurl.com/muslim-americans-middle-class.

3. See "Mapping the Global Muslim Population," October 7, 2009, http://tinyurl.com/mapping-global, and "The Future of the Global Muslim Population: Projections for 2010–2030," January 27, 2011, http://tinyurl.com/future-muslim.

True to Ewart Cousin's advice and prediction, I planned to enter the joint Union/Columbia PhD program but fate intervened in the form of a job offer that my husband, who was then completing his PhD in Medieval and Renaissance Italian literature, received to teach at the University of Toronto. By great good fortune, however, the University of Toronto was just launching its own PhD program in religious studies in that same year and I was happy to accept admission to the inaugural cohort of students. Building on some introductory work in comparative religion which I had begun at Columbia, I quickly signed up for courses at the University of Toronto in Jewish philosophy (with Emil Fackenheim), Buddhist ethics (with Sulak Sivaraksa) and Islamic political philosophy (with Michael Marmura). While all three were fascinating, the last-mentioned was a revelation, opening for me the previously unknown world of medieval Islamic thought and setting the future direction of my intellectual and professional life.

From that first exposure to Islam, a fairly straightforward academic story unfolds. I plunged into the study of Arabic and Persian, took all the relevant courses offered by both permanent and visiting faculty, passed my qualifying examinations and settled on a thesis topic. The centrality of the Qur'an to all Islamic religious discourse, combined with a growing interest in textual hermeneutics and exegetical methodologies made *tafsir*, the literature of Qur'anic commentary, an obvious choice. But the echoes of that earlier focus on comparative religion refined the topic to a study of those verses in the Qur'an that speak about Christians. Guidance and mentoring by two superb scholars, G. Michael Wickens and Roger Savory, brought me safely through the rigors of dissertation research and writing.[4]

In reflecting upon this brief sketch of my graduate education, I recognize how very different my entry into the world of Islamic studies was from that of many of my Catholic colleagues, especially those who had entered religious life before beginning their formal studies in this field. My first years of exposure were linguistic and textual, exploring the primary sources from which, and with which, the edifice of Islamic thought is constructed. I concentrated on the classical and medieval periods, paying less attention to the world of contemporary Islam. Other than a few fellow students in my graduate program, I had rather limited contact with Muslims. Aside from a short stay in Istanbul, I never visited a Muslim-majority country until after I had completed my PhD. This was primarily a consequence of personal circumstances. As the mother of a young and growing family,

---

4. Jane Dammen McAuliffe, *Qur'ānic Christians: An Analysis of Classical and Modern Exegesis* (New York: Cambridge University Press, 1991).

I could neither leave home for extended periods nor did we have the funds to support such travel.

Fortunately, the situation would be different for most graduate students today, even those with families. Not only is travel comparatively cheaper but the ubiquity of web-based media has brought the many worlds of Islamic life and ritual as close as the nearest computer screen. I marvel at what finds its way onto YouTube and other video collectives. A teacher need not rely on descriptive accounts of the pilgrimage or the ritual prayer. Visual examples are easily accessible.

Opportunities to spend extended periods in Muslim countries did eventually enter my life and, not surprisingly, they transformed my understanding and appreciation of the subject that had become my central intellectual inquiry. Book knowledge was brought to life. A summer in Egypt was the first of these experiences and to this day, I can vividly recall standing for hours outside the funeral tents frequently erected in downtown Cairo and listening to the professional Qur'an recitation that was often a feature of these gatherings.[5]

Like other Christians who have spent prolonged periods in the Muslim world, I soon found myself engaged in impromptu interreligious dialogues with many of the people whom I met. These were inevitably challenging conversations, exchanges that usually began in a tentative fashion but quickly grew more animated and unrestrained. For my Muslim dialogue partners, I was a puzzling phenomenon. How could someone who knew a great deal about Islam not become a Muslim? My status as a knowledgeable nonbeliever constitutes a theological conundrum for Muslims and while that status usually prompts curiosity, it has sometimes occasioned hostility and even anger. Knowledge of Islam is expected to be compellingly persuasive.

In 1986 I moved to Atlanta, Georgia, to join the faculty of the Candler School of Theology at Emory University. Once again, I found myself among an ecumenically minded group of Christian scholars who were dedicated to educating and training the next generation of ecclesiastical and academic leadership. As an Islamicist, I brought a new subject to the seminary curriculum and expanded the intellectual horizon from intrafaith to interfaith. This was a bold experiment for Candler and I know that the then dean, James Waits, did not escape criticism for allocating scarce

5. For a short, evocative description, see Kristina Nelson, *The Art of Reciting the Qur'an* (Cairo: American University of Cairo, 2001, repr. of Austin: University of Texas Press, 1985), xiii.

resources to non-Christian instruction. Some students from rural and mountain regions of the state were uneasy with Catholics, to say nothing of a Catholic who had studied a "foreign" religion. But they were smart and curious and interested. Teaching Islam and other non-Christian religions in this academic context was interreligious dialogue "on the ground" and gave me a more informed appreciation of the difficulties and complexities of sustained interfaith engagement.

As one of the only scholars of Islam in the state, I was frequently asked to lecture at local churches and community centers. Simultaneously, I was becoming involved during those Atlanta years in efforts taken by the US Conference of Catholic Bishops to develop regular dialogue meetings with American Muslim organizations. This was not my first entrance into formal interfaith work. Even as an advanced graduate student, I had been invited to join some of the Toronto-based forums, such as Islam-West and the Christian-Muslim National Liaison Committee, which represented the earliest, sustained efforts at national interreligious dialogue in Canada.

In 1992 I returned to the University of Toronto as the Chair of the newly formed Department and Centre for the Study of Religion and found a city undergoing ever more rapid transformation. In 1988 Canada had embraced a national policy of multiculturalism as an appropriate response to the changing immigration patterns of the preceding decades. Nowhere were the effects of this policy more apparent than in Toronto, one of the most ethnically and culturally diverse cities on the globe. In contrast to the prevailing American metaphor of the "melting pot," of ethnic and cultural assimilation, Canada chose to celebrate and encourage diversity. Pluralism was a plus and government funding supported programs and practices that promoted intercultural understanding. Interreligious dialogue initiatives could flourish in such a public policy environment and they expanded.

But perhaps the most exciting discoveries and dialogues took place in the classroom. By the mid-nineties, the ethnic and cultural composition of the student body at the University of Toronto had been transformed. The children of those families who had come to Canada as a result of the changes in immigration legislation three decades earlier were now entering university classrooms. More than half of these undergraduates were from homes with a foreign-born parent or where English was not the first language. Unlike those at Emory, most of my students at the University of Toronto were Muslim. When I taught courses on Islam or the Qur'an, I might be the only non-Muslim in the room. Yet many of these students had little or no formal education in their own religious tradition. University classes were often their first exposure to the systematic study of Islam.

I also found myself engaged in another, and somewhat unexpected, form of interreligious dialogue, as students from different Muslim backgrounds encountered each other in the safe space of the secular classroom. Pakistani Isma'ilis, Egyptian Sunnis, and Iranian Shi'is learned from each other and, sometimes, confronted each other. Unqualified assertions that "Islam says this" or "Islam says that" were quickly challenged by classmates whose faith was equally sincere but differently comprehended and expressed.

During the 90s, I persevered in these dual pursuits of scholar-teacher and interfaith activist. I began to work on a large publishing project, the production of the first multivolume encyclopedia of the Qur'an in a Western language. The planning and coordination of this endeavor involved academics from around the world and took ten years to complete.[6] The opportunity to work with both Muslim and non-Muslim authors and to include multiple scholarly perspectives on the study of the Qur'an was an important part of this work. At the same time, I was becoming more deeply involved in Roman Catholic interfaith work, both nationally and internationally. In 1997 I was appointed to the Vatican's Commission for Religious Relations with Muslims as its only North American member. For the next decade, I attended the commission's annual meetings in Rome, submitting reports on interfaith work in both the United States and Canada and contributing draft chapters to the documents that the commission published during that period. The commission forms part of the Pontifical Council for Interreligious Dialogue, which was created as a direct consequence of the Second Vatican Council, particularly its promulgation of *Nostra Aetate* (Declaration on Non-Christian Religions).[7]

Moving to Washington, DC, in 1999 to become Dean of Arts and Sciences at Georgetown University opened other opportunities for both scholarly enterprise and interfaith activism. Georgetown has long been a leader in Arabic and Middle Eastern studies and in Catholic–Muslim interaction. During my near-decade as dean, I was particularly pleased to foster three programmatic additions to this legacy. These were: the creation of a PhD program in religious pluralism, a PhD program in Islamic studies, and the early stages of the Berkley Center for Religion, Peace, and

6. Jane Dammen McAuliffe, general ed., *The Encyclopaedia of the Qur'an*, Volumes I–VI (Leiden: Brill, 2001–6). Also published in web-based and CD-ROM versions.

7. "The Pontifical Council for Interreligious Dialogue," http://tinyurl.com/PC-Interreligious.

World Affairs.[8] Taken together, these represent an extraordinary resource for Catholic engagement with Islam and the Muslim world.

Two years into my tenure as dean, the tragedy of September 11 occurred. Georgetown University sits on a hilltop overlooking the Potomac River just north of the Pentagon, and students and faculty standing on the university's rooftops could see the flames and could watch the smoke billowing up the river. That was a watershed moment for the university, the American public, and the field of Islamic studies. Suddenly, anyone with expertise in Islam and the Muslim world was in high demand. People were hungry for knowledge and countless invitations for lectures and interviews were the consequence. Students both at Georgetown and elsewhere began enrolling in Arabic classes and courses on Islam. Christian–Muslim dialogue initiatives proliferated at local, national, and international levels. Two of the most important of these are the Building Bridges Seminar series, which has been hosted annually by the archbishop of Canterbury since January 2002, and the Common Word document that has now garnered more than three hundred signatures from Muslim leaders and scholars around the world. Both of these became a prominent focus of my own interfaith efforts and each offers an interesting model for Muslim–Christian engagement.

The Building Bridges Seminar, which is led—and quite actively guided—by Rowan Williams, the archbishop of Canterbury, places scripture at the center. Each year a group of Muslim and Christian scholars gather for intensive study sessions on selected passages from the Bible and the Qur'an. These are preceded by several public lectures on the theme for the year that pair speakers from each tradition on specific aspects of the topic. The scriptural study, however, is conducted in closed session so that the conversations can be as frank and free-flowing as possible. A key ingredient to their success is the trust that continuity can foster. Although the participant list changes from year to year, a core group of scholars has attended annually, assuring a consistency of planning and approach. But the seminar has the added benefit of moving from place to place, ordinarily alternating between Muslim-majority and Christian-majority countries. The latter venues include London, Rome, and Washington, DC, where Georgetown University, which cosponsors the Seminar, has been a regular host. The other meeting

8. "Ph.D. in Theological and Religious Studies with a focus on religious pluralism," http://theology.georgetown.edu/programs/graduate/; "Graduate Programs," http://arabic.georgetown.edu/programs/grad/; and, the Berkley Center website, http://berkleycenter.georgetown.edu/, respectively.

places, in chronological order, have been: Doha, Sarajevo, Singapore, and Istanbul.

A particular benefit of the Seminar is the ecumenical character of both groups of scholars. Christian participants are drawn from several different denominations and Muslim participants reflect a range of Islamic groups and cultural backgrounds. Occasionally, the intrafaith dialogue during meetings of the seminar overtakes the interfaith exchange. This phenomenon signals an area of interreligious engagement that remains insufficiently developed. Speaking only from the Christian perspective, there is an urgent need for Christians of different denominations and affiliations to converse about their attitudes and approaches to Islam and the Muslim world.

The Common Word initiative, which began as a twenty-eight-page appeal to Pope Benedict XVI and twenty-five other Christian leaders, was released on October 11, 2007, at press conferences in Washington, DC, London, and Dubai. It expanded an earlier appeal that a smaller group of scholars made to the pope in the aftermath of his controversial lecture at the University of Regensburg. The significance of the Common Word document lies in both its genesis and its continuing virtual presence. As an act of Islamic ecumenism, it is virtually unprecedented and although the rate with which it attracts additional signatories has slowed, it has not ceased. Several responsive conferences and seminars, including one at the Vatican in November 2008, have been followed by persistent press attention and media references. The document itself, now translated into many languages, offers a juxtaposition of Qur'anic and Biblical passages about love of God and love of neighbor that has formed the basis for countless interreligious events and conversations.

The practice and pursuit of interfaith dialogue, in both academic and nonacademic venues, has certainly been a central concern of my life. But another, and equally strong preoccupation, has been the roles that women play—or cannot play—in their religious communities. Returning to the frequently asked question with which I began this reflection, I will add another that I often receive: "Why are women treated so badly in Islam"? While the question undoubtedly reveals an ignorance of Islam's historical complexity and of the huge variety of its cultural contexts, it does point to a heartfelt concern. People today worry about a religion that demeans or undervalues women and, as a woman, I hear the distress in this question. As a Catholic woman, there is also a way in which I share this distress. The constraints—ecclesial, liturgical, or theological—that afflict Catholic women within their own faith community have troubled me since childhood.

I have watched many in my generation leave the Church, finally despairing that any real change will occur in their lifetimes. I have seen even more women of the younger generation dismiss the Church as hopelessly anachronistic and even antithetical to a woman's full spiritual development. As the president of a women's college whose distinguished alumnae have made extraordinary contributions in every professional field, I find it doubly difficult to deal with the continuing gender inequity in the Church.

In this decade, the drama of Islamic feminism is capturing attention across the Islamic world. Courageous Muslim women of all ages and from many different societies are seeking to reclaim an authentic understanding of their faith and to counter repressive misinterpretations. Those with the benefit of an advanced education are reading the Qur'an and Hadith, as well as their centuries-long exegetical traditions, and schooling themselves in the intricacies of Muslim jurisprudence. Recognizing that they must speak to authority as authorities, they are creating an intellectual discourse of religious recovery and renewal. Key verses in the Qur'an serve as touchstones for this exercise and orient Muslim feminists toward a positive reappropriation of those religious texts that can sustain their continuing religious growth. The patience and contextual sensitivity that so many Muslim feminists manifest in the face of obstinate intransigence inspires me. It also challenges me to adopt the same attitudes when I am feeling particularly frustrated by the slow pace of change in my own faith tradition.

A Call to Muslim–Christian Dialogue

Francesco Zannini

My deep desire to implement Muslim–Christian dialogue through my life experiences and serious Islamic studies is rooted in a call that has connected all of the events in my life—even in the changing of places and personal situations.

The First Call: From Theological to Arabic Studies

I was brought up in a family that was open to dialogue and promoted respect for others, with a strong sense of values. My father was a strenuous freedom fighter against Nazi fascism, a real Christian, strong in his faith and faithful to the Church. His life and personality instilled in my heart a deep faithfulness to the truth and at the same time a great respect for the rights and opinions of others. These values, together with a profound spirit of tolerance and love for all creatures are the characteristics of my mother who chose to name me after the "poor man of Assisi," St. Francis. Sharing in the namesake of the saint, who deeply loved the God of the poor and who chose the way of dialogue with Muslims during the Crusades, was probably a sort of foretelling of my future life.

At the root of my spiritual formation is the Bible, the teachings of the Second Vatican Council, and the example of two great popes: Pope John XXIII, with his great spirit of tolerance and his affectionate love for human-kind and Pope Paul VI, with his deep interest for dialogue based on the solid ground of truth. The first paragraph of the Second Vatican Council's Constitution *Gaudium et Spes* has always been a mission statement for my life:

> The joys and the hopes, the griefs and the anxieties of the men of this age, especially those who are poor or in any way afflicted, these are the joys and hopes, the griefs and anxieties of the followers of Christ. Indeed, nothing genuinely human fails to raise an echo in their hearts. (*Gaudium et Spes*, para. 1)

In 1969, when I joined the Theological Institute of the Xaverian Fathers in Parma, I went deep into biblical studies and at the same time I tried to share as much as possible with the poor, the abandoned, and the drug addicts in the town as part of my theological experience.

One day, however, something new happened in my life: a professor from Turin University, Fr. Federico Peirone, came to our Institute to give a lec-ture on Islam. I was fascinated by the music of the Arabic language in his chanting of the Qur'an and I was taken by the discovery of a new religious world that I had never taken into consideration before that day. I felt that day a spiritual call coming from God to go to Muslim countries, to study in a scholarly way their religion and spend my life working for dialogue and reconciliation.

At the end of my theological studies I was appointed as a promoter of missionary activities in the area of Milan. Because of the distance from the main Italian centers for oriental studies and the pressure of the new job, I could not enter immediately into specialized Islamic studies. This, how-ever, did not prevent me from carrying on my research on Islam at the Faculty of Modern Foreign Languages of the Sacred Heart Catholic University, where I studied Arabic language and culture. I worked hard to set up with the faculty a plan of study that could serve my purposes, and in order to deepen my study of the Arabic language I also joined the Institute for Middle and Far East Studies (IMEO) where, in 1978, I got my first diploma in the Arabic language. I had to work hard but all the effort was rewarding.

During my university studies, I tried to refine my linguistic knowledge with internships with the Arabic language course at the University of Cairo

(1976), courses in the Arabic language at the American University of Cairo (1977), and the Bourguiba School in Tunis. Here I had the chance to visit the Institute de Belles Lettres Arabes, which was run by the White Fathers, where Muslims cooperate with Christian scholars. Long dialogues with Fr. Robert Caspar, a scholar in Muslim theology, opened my mind to the world of the Muslim theological debates. My vision of Islam and Muslim–Christian dialogue was enriched by conversations with Fr. André Demeerseman, who used to mix scholarly talks with his experience of living among the Bedouins. My frequent visits to the Little Sisters of Charles de Foucauld allowed me to experience the life of prayer and bearing witness to Christ among Muslims, which was preached and lived out by Charles de Foucauld. The sisters lived among the poor in a completely Arab Muslim environment.

It was during these years that I had my first encounter with PISAI which was enriched by long conversations with Fr. Maurice Borrmans. He became, from that time onwards, a kind of tutor and spiritual guide in the field of Muslim–Christian dialogue.

At the end of my university studies, in order to deepen my knowledge of the Qur'an, I chose to translate into Italian *The commentary of the Qur'an of the two Jalal* for my doctoral thesis, which, at that time, happened to be the first translation into a European Language. I did this not because I considered the *Jalalayn*, to be the best of all the commentaries on the Qur'an, but because it was the commentary which was studied the most by young Muslims from many *madrasas* all over the world. It also would help me become more acquainted with an important text used in the basic formation of many Muslim *ulama* and *mullah*s.

A Renewed Call to Dialogue with Muslims in Egypt

To accomplish my doctoral research, I decided to go to Egypt where, with the help of a local Muslim teacher, I spent hours and hours trying to understand the meaning of the *Tafsir al-Jalalayn*. I felt tired and frustrated at times but that inner call I once received allowed me to carry on in my research.

In Egypt, I had the opportunity to visit the IDEO and particularly enjoyed becoming friends with great scholars like Fr. Jacques Jomier and Fr. George Anawati. The latter helped me in my research and shared with me his long experience of Muslim–Christian dialogue and also his immense knowledge in Islamic studies.

After I had successfully defended my doctoral dissertation in 1983 in Milan, I went back to Egypt several times to brush up on my Arabic and to continue my Islamic studies. The time I spent in Egypt was also enriched by my joining the *Ikha' al-Din*, an association of Muslims and Christians founded by Louis Massignon. Here I had the fortune of becoming friends with some Al-Azhar professors, namely Shaykh Taj al-Din, a specialist in Sufism, who introduced me to the knowledge of several *turuq*. I also attended the prayer meetings of the *Badaliyya*, which is another association founded by Massignon where Christians offer their lives to God along with the Muslims, making them part of a unique spiritual sharing in Jesus Christ.

A new opportunity arose to compare my Western approach to Islamic studies with the Muslims' during my postdoctoral studies at the American University in Cairo (1986–87). I had Muslims as classmates who came from all over the world and they had a completely different formation in Islamic studies than the one I had received. In Egypt, I also managed to get some tutorials on *tafsir* at the Al-Azhar University under the direction of Masmu' Abu Talib, a specialist in Qur'anic exegesis. I used to go to that university regularly and, during the breaks, I had the good fortune of meeting Muslim students. I shared with them my experience of being a Christian who remained solid in his faith while being seriously interested in studying Islam.

Encounters with Islam in Bangladesh

In 1979 I left Egypt for Bangladesh and I was happy to share my life with the poorest of the world in a Muslim environment. I tried my best to learn the Bengali language (Bangla) and I started eagerly reading Bengali literature. I eventually discovered that it was rooted in a culture that contributed to that of Buddhists, Hindus, and Muslims, as well as Christians.

Before my arrival in Bangladesh, Muslim–Christian dialogue had already started with a "Muslim–Christian Brotherhood." This was founded by the contribution of Mgr. Pietro Rossano, who was the Secretary for the Roman Secretariat for Non-Christians, and also by Mawlana Abul Khair, with whom I was able to entertain a friendly relationship through my entire time in Bangladesh.

In 1980 I was appointed to be the secretary for Islam on the Commission for Interreligious Dialogue of the Catholic Bishops' Conference of Bangladesh. I was asked to lecture on Islam and the history of Muslim–Christian

Dialogue at the National Catechetical Training Centre of Jessore (1980–94). It was a real surprise for me to see a great response from the Catholic catechists who found a new opportunity to discover a vital element of Bengali culture. They had not had the chance of knowing its history and its theology and it helped them deepen their knowledge of Islam. In 1982, I wrote for them, in Bangla, a booklet *Muslim Khristan shanglap (Muslim–Christian Dialogue)* which helped also Muslims understand Christianity a bit more clearly.

In this period, I had the opportunity to meet Fr. Christian Troll at his institute in Delhi. He is a German scholar in Islamic studies who lived and studied in India, and with whom I was able to start a deep and lasting friendship as well as a solid scholarly exchange. He asked me to write a chapter on "The birth of Islam (Muhammad and the Qur'an)," in the book *The Muslims of India* which would be a textbook for most of the theological institutes in India. In order to write this chapter and make it suitable for Muslim readers, I had many long and interesting discussions with local Muslim scholars on the person of Muhammad, who is at the core of Islam. I also spent some time in Patna, where the editor of the book helped me in correcting the text. Fr. Paul Jackson is a Jesuit scholar who dedicated his entire life to studying the writings of the Sufi Sharafuddin Maneri. He took me for visits to the Muslim shrines there and introduced me to the Khuda Bakhsh Library where he gave a lecture. I did some research there and I discovered so many valuable manuscripts and other Muslim literature.

My friendship with Pir Abdur Razzaq Chishti, a Sufi from Jessore, gave me a new impulse for interreligious dialogue. We spent long hours discussing our points of view on each other's religious experience and I also went with him and some of his *murid*s on a pilgrimage to the tomb of Mu'iuddin Chishti in Ajmeer Sharif. On the long journey through the north of India, I had the opportunity to discover the deep thoughts of these Sufis, witness their *dhikr* and visit not only some holy shrines but also some interesting libraries where there are some hidden treasures of Islamic literature.

As professor of Islamic studies at the National Major Seminary in Dhaka (1983–94), I was happy to share my knowledge of Islam and my experience of interreligious dialogue with new generations of priests. I wrote two articles in Bangla for the seminary journal *Prodipon*: "Akhristan dharmashomuer bishoe Mandalir shikkha" ("Teaching of the Church on Non-Christian Religions") and "Khristio o Muslim drishtibhongite manush: tulonamulok nritotter chorcha" ("Man from Muslim and Christian Perspective: A Comparative Anthropological Study"). Both of these were written for the seminarians and the local church to help them go deeper in the study of these fields. During this period, I published another article on "The History of Muslim-Christian Relationships" in *Encounter* (1986). It was a wonderful occasion to go through the history of Muslim–Christian dialogue with the discovery of so much Christian literature on the matter. I was able to accomplish the work thanks to the help of Fr. Jean-Marie Gaudeul, who, at that time, was a doctoral student and teacher at PISAI, and was preparing his doctoral dissertation on a similar matter.

It was again in Dhaka that I received a call to dialogue: this time from the Muslim side. Prof. Deewan Muhammad Ashraf and Prof. Kazi Nurul Islam had started an association of professors at Dhaka University who belonged to different religions. It had the purpose of spreading religious tolerance and mutual understanding among people from different cultural and religious traditions. This allowed me to share my views with them in long encounters where literature, philosophy and theology mixed together in an atmosphere where scholarly research became part of a common spiritual experience. However, it was always clear, as Deewan Muhammad Ashraf used to say, that some doctrinal limits belonging to the core of the two religions could never be overcome but this did not hamper our friendship and love. When the Italian Embassy asked me to teach Italian at the Institute of Modern Languages at Dhaka University, I was able to enter the world of the university students there, with their strong debates between traditional and modern Muslims and fundamentalist groups. The encounter with some of these groups was another aspect of my life in Dhaka where I was able to study Asian Muslim fundamentalism directly. In fact, thanks to my friend Mawlana Abul Khair, I was allowed to attend *Jamat-i-Islami* meetings where the reading of *Tafhim al-Qur'an* of Abu al-Ala Mawdudi was the basis for sharing life experience in a way very similar to the meetings of the basic Christian communities in Latin America.

Because of my knowledge of the Muslims in Asia, I was called in 1991 to be a member of the standing committee of the Journées Romaines. I remained there until 1995 and I shared my studies on Islam and Muslim–Christian dialogue in the article: "Muslim–Christian Dialogue in Bangladesh," which was published in *Islamochristiana* (1991). In order to prepare for it, I spent several days in Calcutta, where I met important Muslim scholars. In Delhi, I worked day and night in the library of Vidiyajoti where I found interesting documents not only on the Muslims of India, but also on the early Christian communities of Bengal and their relationship with Muslim rulers. It was on that occasion that Fr. Christian Troll introduced me to some scholars from Jamia Millia University and Hamdard Nagar who became beneficial to my studies on Islam.

In the last year I spent in Bangladesh, I took on the burden of organizing something similar to the Journées Romaines. I did this for two reasons: to encourage the exchange of experiences and thoughts among Christians who were working with Muslims in Asia, and to reach a serious analysis of the problems and achievements in the field of Muslim–Christian relationships. It was difficult to prepare for it but finally my efforts were successful and the meeting called Asian Days (later changed to Asian Journeys) was held in Jessore (January 11–17, 1993). It was an open forum where all the concerns, anxieties, problems, and difficulties that Christians had living in a Muslim world emerged.

Call to Islamic Studies in the United States

With the help of a scholarship from Missio, I was led to Yale University to continue in my Islamic studies as a postdoctoral fellow under the guidance of a Jesuit scholar, Fr. Gerhard Böwering, and also with the help of many other great scholars like Franz Rosenthal. Before that, I spent some time in Germany in order to learn German, which I thought was fundamental for Islamic studies. There I had the opportunity to visit the Orientalische Seminar in Tübingen, where a lot of scholarly work on Islam is done and I got to know the world of the Turkish immigrants in Europe. I also got some opinions from some German friends; especially about their views on Islam and Muslims.

The years I spent at Yale University (1987–89 and 1993–94) represented for me a hard but wonderful experience. I could be a full-time researcher by reading more than once the *Tafsir Muqatil Ibn Sulayman* while sitting in one of the best libraries in the world from early morning until late at night. I read studies on Muqatil's *tafsir* and on his personality. I went through all the main books written by both Western and Muslim scholars on *tafsir*, *kalam*, Hadith and so on. I also read through a wealth of Arabic and non-Arabic literature on history, geography, *tabaqat* and other literature on the subject. This reading was fuelled by a strong desire to enter into the Muslim world of thought. In order to expand my approach to Islam, I took a two-year course in the Persian language and an entire new world opened up in front of me. The lyrics of Hafez, Sadi and other mystical poets introduced me to a mysticism in which Islam is rooted in the local cultural and religious background. My great joy was to be able to read the original text of the *Mathnawi* of Jalaluddin Rumi. I discovered then how the knowledge of this kind of Islam was of radical importance in understanding Muslims in Asia where Islamic teachings are mostly expressed in this language.

Another relevant experience for me was being a scholar-in-residence at the Catholic Theological Union in Chicago. Besides teaching introductory courses on Islam, I had to give a series of seminars on Muslim–Christian dialogue at the master's level. I had the opportunity to interact with young theologians eager to confront their knowledge with the contribution of the classical apologists; both from the Muslim and the Christian side. They were also eager to rethink their theological and dogmatic data in order to make it more suitable for their Muslim partners. During this time, I was also a visiting scholar at the Center for Middle Eastern Studies at the University of Chicago. I gave some lectures, continued my research on Muqatil's *tafsir* and I had the chance to meet highly qualified modern Muslim scholars in the new atmosphere which was created by the teaching of Fazlur Rahman, who invited me to work with him but unfortunately died before I arrived there.

Back to Europe: A New Call to Dialogue

After my marriage, I went back to Italy in 1994. I found a completely new world from the one that I saw in my childhood and adolescence. Several waves of immigration had brought to Italy many Muslims from different countries and my call to Muslim–Christian dialogue was renewed there. I started to contact some Muslims who were present in my hometown and share with local Christians the fruit of my Islamic studies and my life of Muslim–Christian dialogue.

My first work in Italy was to translate into Italian the book by Jacques Jomier, *Pour connaitre l'Islam* which I thought would be a useful introduction to Islam and would prepare readers better to welcome new Muslim immigrants. I also worked to establish an Institute for Oriental Studies at my university which lasted from 1996 to 2001, when the activities had to end, because of a lack of financial and political support.

I gave several courses on Islam in teacher training programs in order to share my knowledge of Islam with local people and particularly with the teachers of elementary and high schools. I also wrote a book called *Ahmed il mio vicino di casa, guida alla conoscenza dell'Islam* (*Ahmed My Neighbor: A Guide to the Knowledge of Islam*), which I prepared while consulting some scholars at the Islamic Cultural Centre in Rome. In a joint effort, we sat together to analyze the text and to discuss it line by line.

Another work that I got involved with was the preparation of an international conference on Leopardi and the East (Recanati in 1998). As a member of the preparatory committee and as coordinator of research on the "Marche and Islam," I discovered the roots of the long-lasting relationship between our region and the Muslims. It was the long and difficult work of researching manuscripts and historical texts in several libraries which led me to two publications: *Le Marche e l'Islam dalla prime incursioni arabe ai tempi di Leopardi* (*The Marche and Islam from the First Arab Incursions to the Time of Leopardi*) and *Leopardi e Voltaire: due letture della figura di Maometto* (Leopardi and Voltaire: Two Perspectives on the Interpretation of the Personality of Muhammad). I also had the chance to encounter Muslims from Eastern Europe in Bosnia where the Italian Foreign Office sent me in 1997 as OSCE supervisor at the parliamentary election of the Serbska Republic. As an interpreter and cultural attaché for a mission of an Italian labor union to Pakistan in 1998, I also had the possibility of renewing my contacts with Muslims in Asia.

Teaching Islamic Law at the State University of Macerata, Italy (1997–99) was also a rewarding experience for me. I saw how future lawyers, notaries, judges, and advocates were eager to discover a completely new legal field at a time when the Muslim community was growing in Italy.

In 2000 I was invited to join the staff of PISAI in Rome, where I was later appointed to the chair of Contemporary Islam. I was very happy and enthusiastic to continue helping Christian priests, nuns and lay people to go deeper into Islamic studies and to share with them my lifelong experience in the field of Muslim–Christian dialogue. Besides that, the marvelous library of PISAI and the surrounding scholarly environment helped me to continue my studies and research which eventually allowed me to publish a series of articles and contributions in the field of Islamic studies; particularly in the form of a book.

In 2007 I was also appointed as the editor of the PISAI journal *Encounter*. This is hard but very rewarding work which allowed me to reestablish the international network of contacts that I had partially lost in coming back to Italy. During this period, I finally had the opportunity to publish part of my work on Muqatil as a contribution in the books *Im Dienst der Versöhnung*, entitled "A controversial exegete: Muqatil b. Sulayman revisited," and *L'Islam nel cuore dell'Asia: Dal Caucaso alla Thailandia* (*Islam in the Heart of Asia: From Caucasus to Thailand*). This allowed me to revisit all my experiences with Muslims in Asia and to discover various documents with the help of specialists in new fields. I also had direct contact with the Muslim authorities and scholars of Malaysia and Thailand.

My position at PISAI allowed me to increase the contact I had with the main Muslim representatives in Italy. This relationship developed through the courses I taught on Arabic and Arab culture in other universities and my sharing in the Commission for Muslim–Christian Dialogue of the Italian Bishops' Conference. Eventually, the minister of home affairs asked me to be a member on the expert committee, which was entrusted with writing the "Charter of Values for Integration and Citizenship." This was accepted by all the representatives of the religions that were present in Italy in 2007. It was a fruit, not of political negotiation, but of a common sharing and understanding of the fundamental principles that regulate the collective life in Italy with particular attention given to immigrants. The preparation of that charter involved a lot of scholarly research but it was also a good experience to make friends with many Muslims.

I now continue my studies on Islam and carry out Muslim–Christian dialogue in obedience to the call that came into my heart long ago. It is still present and alive in my heart as the call of someone who paves the way for Christ's Kingdom of peace, justice, and understanding. My journey in Muslim–Christian dialogue has been an Abrahamic experience, where God has led me through many different countries and life situations, reminding me always that "my thoughts are not your thoughts, neither are your ways my ways, declares the Lord" (Isaiah 55:8). The continuous and repeated call to Muslim–Christian dialogue and the desire to deepen my knowledge of Islam would never have endured without the support of daily prayers and sitting at the Eucharistic table where I meet the Word of God and the mystery of Christ's death and resurrection.

Grace Builds on Nature

C. T. R. Hewer

The maxim "grace builds on nature" applies. For the Christian who would go the solitary path of the study of Islam and actively promoting Christian–Muslim relations, it helps to have been born into an English recusant family, which retained its traditional allegiance during the times of the Penal Laws in England. Such breeding brings forth a nature that is independent, self-affirming, and dogged in regards to matters of faith, combined with the natural English yeoman character.

After an education that promoted independent thinking, specializing in the natural sciences, I commenced the study philosophy and theology in the spirit of the "wind of change" after the Second Vatican Council and the growth in the United Kingdom of the ecumenical movement. This was a time when the English-speaking student of theology devoured the output of mainland European writers, transatlantic offerings, and the broad British tradition without seeking the origins or ecclesiastical affiliation of the writer. As I look now along the rows of books on my shelves from that period many turn out to be Baptist, Calvinist, or Lutheran in provenance, to augment the Anglican, Catholic, Methodist, Pentecostal, and Orthodox teachers under whom I studied. Such a breadth of exposure to Christian thought is valuable when one tries to help Muslims to understand the wide variety of Christian theological positions on most questions. There is always the temptation in Christian–Muslim relations to identify my position as the position of our faith community. A comprehensive theological education building into an intellectual foundation upon which one can draw and build in later life, which covers a wide range of theological disciplines, must be regarded as an essential prerequisite for this work that cannot be replaced by an eclectic mixture of courses chosen on the basis of personal interest.

A philosophical education that ranged from the Greeks to the Existentialists enabled the student to gain a sense of the development of ideas and an awareness that "one size does not fit all" when it comes to matters of intellection. I was encouraged to begin immediately postgraduate courses in theology in a secular British university to broaden my education and develop a sense of independence of thought. The product of such a theological education can be judged from my first thesis on "Conciliators of the Reformation," which explored the work in humanism and theology of those who tried to hold the Western Church together in the sixteenth century at a time when other forces were driving it apart.

When it came to discerning an overarching charism, it was clear that mine was in teaching, whether face-to-face or in writing. This led me into freelance writing and editing and my first forays into adult popular education. To study and develop the art of teaching, both for personal competence and professional standing, the next step was to enroll in an Anglican college of higher education working in partnership with its Catholic neighbor. This led to an appointment to the religious education department of a particularly nonreligious state secondary school where I learnt how to make learning about and learning from the religious traditions of Judaism, Christianity, and Islam relevant to students with no familial background in understanding what it is to lead a life based on faith.

In my later twenties I went through an experience that brought with it a profound sense of being claimed by Christ and being totally dependent on God as the ground of my being. This experience brought with it the affirming strength exemplified by the Prophet Muhammad after his rejection at Ta'if: "If things are alright between you and me, God, I ask none other." It was at this time that I was given the gift of solitary contemplation, which enables me to immerse myself directly in the prayer of the presence of God, which has been the bedrock of my spiritual life, whether on the floor of a mosque or Gurdwara, during a church service or in the secret world of my own "cell."

This was the formation of the person who was called by Providence with no clear sense of ultimate direction as a master's student at the Centre for the Study of Islam and Christian–Muslim Relations at Selly Oak in Birmingham. The nature of the center was a spiritual experience in itself as one studied with Christian and Muslim teachers alongside students from both traditions in an atmosphere of "faith seeking understanding." The intuitive pole here is of great importance, as it had been in intra-Christian ecumenical study; by weighing the work of the Spirit of God in the hearts and lives of the center's members, one was brought to an inner assurance that the God who was the object of our explorations was undeniably at work in both traditions. The center pioneered a new way forward that left behind the traditions of polemic and apologetic for an open and honest exploration seeking to understand the sources, spirit, and practice of Islam as lived by Muslim fellow travelers.[1]

Several foundation stones are worthy of note. My introduction to the exegesis of the Qur'an was at the feet of the late Prof. Khalid Alavi, who combined a traditional Muslim education with a doctorate under Prof. William Montgomery Watt, and thus was able to expound the richness and range of Islamic scholarship of the Qur'an in a way that made it assessable and comestible for a Christian student of theology. Special studies of the *Risala al-Tawhid* of Muhammad Abduh showed the commonplace of scholastic philosophy and of the *Tarjuman al-Qur'an* of Abul Kalam Azad showed the breadth of the Indian humanist tradition. Of particular importance was the course on the historical development of Islamic religious thought, which I followed three times in all, first with the late David Kerr and then with Christian Troll. This rooted the student in the profoundly rich and varied intellectual heritage of Islamic scholarship, much of which was unknown to the Muslim people with whom I was later to work.[2] Two pedagogical devices are also noteworthy: the weekly Centre Seminar in which all members, staff, and students, habitually took part, in which a range of topics were explored to the mutual benefit of all; and the annual residential summer school, which attracted people from various countries to embark on ten days of mutual sharing and enlightenment with internationally established scholars such as Anton Wessels and Mahmoud Ayoub.

---

1. See C. T. R. Hewer, "An Enduring Vision: The Study Centre at Selly Oak" in *World Christianity in Muslim Encounter: Essays in Memory of David A. Kerr*, vol 2, ed. Stephen R. Goodwin (London: Continuum, 2009).

2. See C. T. R. Hewer, "Troll in Selly Oak. Teaching by example" in *Im Dienst der Versöhnung*, ed. Peter Hünseler (Regensburg: Verlag Friedrich Pustet, 2008).

My experience of the academic life of the center culminated in my choice of doctoral dissertation—to work on the writings of the late Fazlur Rahman of Karachi and Chicago, who was at home in both Arabic and Greek philosophy and yet found the need to attempt a reinterpretation of the Islamic intellectual tradition in the twentieth century with a huge breadth of subject matter, thus making the study of his *corpus* as wide as possible for a generalist Christian student of Islam.

Two practical projects during my time at the center were especially formative. First, three years of discussing, negotiating, and studying practical issues of Muslim education in Britain, which resulted in setting up the first teacher training program for primary school teachers in Britain with a major in Islamic studies. This brought me into regular contact with Muslim leaders with whom I shared this work. Second, setting up and running the center's Muslims in Britain Documentation Project, which brought me into daily contact with a wide range of Muslim affairs. These were the basis from which I began the essential experience of working alongside Muslims practically involved in developing their community life in Britain. This led to enduring personal friendships and discussions. This might be typified by a phone call late one night after *tarawih* prayers on *Laylat al-Qadr* to ask where I was and why wasn't I sitting in the mosque with them, which resulted in five hours through the night until *fajr* sitting on the floor of the mosque engaged in profound discussion disposed to be found awake by the angels sent to roam the earth looking for those so engaged. This "talking with Muslims" rather than just "talking about them" was a profound part of my spiritual and intellectual development.

My experience at the center prepared me for six years of practical engagement as adviser on inter-faith relations in Birmingham charged with building better practical relations between the faith communities of that city of many faiths. Of particular importance in the present context from those years was the opportunity to teach regular courses in a Shi'a seminary, both on Islamic topics and on Christian-Muslim relations, which helped me to build enduring friendships with young Muslim students and so begin to sense the necessary dimensions of the paradigm shift that is required in guiding Muslim students in their exploration of Christianity; a task that is still in its embryonic stage but with the benefit of several course-length attempts.

There is an old adage that "the best way to learn is to teach" and that certainly rings true from my experience of developing and delivering a basic twenty-hour adult popular education course titled Understanding Islam. The impact of delivering this course now more than one hundred times has been a profound learning experience. The nature of such a course is to be an immense challenge in the breadth of material covered in presentations and in response to questions. Always there is the demand on the part of teacher and students to make the leap of imagination to see things through a Muslim paradigm with fidelity and to live with the inherent challenge to one's own faith and the uncomfortable nature of Islam as "a corrective to the excesses of Christianity." In preparing and writing the course book to accompany the program, the whole thing was subjected to intense scrutiny by a range of Muslim scholars to ensure that justice was done to the correct Islamic voice that is presented.[3] Having one's work thus scrutinized, challenged, and corrected by Muslim scholars of much greater knowledge and experience is both humbling and hugely educative. The culmination of this work was to act as the coordinating draughtsman of an internet-based distance-learning project.[4] The body of Muslim scholars that reviewed the material came from across the range of Sunni and Shi'ite schools. Such a work requires fine balance between the various positions both in their particularity and commonality, thus requiring the skills of finesse in writing and diplomacy to deal with resolving variant positions. Indeed "to teach is the best way to learn."

What kind of a disposition does such work require on the part of the Christian student of Islam? Perhaps the first element is one of humility, "being subject to all human beings for God's sake" as Francis of Assisi wrote in his Early Rule of 1221. This was the product of Francis's formative sojourn amongst the Muslims of the Middle East at the time of the Fifth Crusade after his meeting with the Sultan outside Damietta in 1219. He returned with several enduring experiences of Muslim life, hospitality, and the sense of a life lived constantly in the presence of God. He counseled his Brothers who went to live amongst the Muslims that they should under no circumstances ridicule those things that Muslims hold holy but should seek to live a life of such exemplary goodness that their lives provoked questions, which should in turn be answered guided by the Christian virtues of charity, gentleness of speech and wisdom. As a follower of the one who humbled himself ultimately to assume our humanity unto death, this remains the profound challenge of engagement. Ultimately such a vocation requires such enduring humility and goodness that one is asked to

---

3. C. T. R. Hewer, *Understanding Islam: The First Ten Steps* (London: SCM, 2006).

4. "Understanding Islam," http://www.understandingfaiths.net.

give an account of one's Christian faith based on others' perception of one's actions.

Such a spirit of humility runs to an acceptance that God alone is God and I am not. Muslims and Christians adore the one merciful God and seek to live a life of prayer and charity, as the documents of the Second Vatican Council made clear. I do not understand fully the wisdom of God in speaking through Muhammad and the Qur'an subsequent to the unique revelation in Christ but God knows best her purposes. As I ask Muslims to allow me to explain my faith as Christians understand and live it, and not to work within a Muslim paradigm that "Christianity is Islam gone astray," so how can I present Islam as any other than the faith as believed and lived by Muslims? If I do that faithfully, then I have to live with the challenges that this brings to my own faith in the spirit of openness that maybe God is seeking to speak to me through the Islamic tradition and thus to bring me to question my own tradition, perhaps to modify it and perhaps to clarify and defend the truth as I have received it in the revelation in the Incarnate Lord. There is a natural fear here, if one takes God and the Day of Judgment seriously, but there is also the fearless assurance of one claimed by Christ, "here I stand and I can do none other."

Any Christian who seeks to engage with Islam must be prepared for the invitation to convert and embrace the faith. This invitation has come to me countless times from Africa and Pakistan to Birmingham and London. This invitation must be accepted with honesty as a request to take God seriously; maybe God is calling me to embrace Islam. To reject the invitation out of hand is perhaps to refuse to hear the "still small voice of God." Other Christians have heard the call and made their *shahada*; why not me? How then does one respond after mature reflection? One way is to stack up arguments to defend one's decision to remain a Christian. Another way is exemplified thus: I recall one such invitation, which came unexpectedly in an African village where I had gone to negotiate the gift of some sheets of tin for the roof of a *madrasa*. I was seated with a colleague in the middle of a compound in the growing twilight with a couple of hundred staff and students from the school looking on. By God's grace, I was gifted with the line of answering beginning with profound thanks that they had such a concern for my eternal well-being and then proceeding to answer "in spirit and in truth" according to what was in my heart, in the knowledge that I was to face God like them on that awesome Day. By taking the discussion out of the realm of amassing arguments to the realm of the spirit before God, the discussion moved through a mutual rejection of hypocrisy to an acceptance that "on that Day God will make clear all those things about which you disagree" and thus the encounter ended in mutual blessings and not cursings.

The question of course requires a more intellectual account in other circumstances. It comes often from Christian questioners, too, along the lines that "you speak with such warmth and affection about Islam, why are you not a Muslim?" This is an opportunity to explore some of the particularity of the Christian tradition based on the humanness of an incarnate revelation with all that that says about the human condition and the life of the Christian "in Christ"; supplemented by the profundity of the *kenosis* of God in Christ, "who was obedient unto death" and thus the power of the resurrection in whose life we now live; and thus our entry as *alter Christi* into the embrace of the eternal relationship with the triune God in the communion of the Godhead. This opens up an essential discussion of the specificity of the Christian message and can prove an interesting line of response to those Christians who doubt the genuine Christian faith of those who would seek to enter into filial relationships with Muslims. My parting response both to such Christians and to Muslims who wish to persevere in their invitation to me respectively to become "a real Christian" or to embrace Islam is to ask them to keep up their prayers; genuine prayer never hurt anyone!

In both our traditions we have wonderful ideals and sordid realities. If only Christians lived up to their high ideals then the world would be a different place and people might indeed believe that the messianic age is upon us; ditto Muslims, of course. I ask Muslims, whom I try to teach about Christianity, to look at the beauty of the ideals and not sink into the mire of sordid realities. Following a Master who calls me to take the initiative and positively "do unto others as I would have them do unto me" reminds me that I should do the same. No one can seek to accept or justify some of the sordid realities on both sides, even if sometimes we need to seek to understand how they come about. But what of the ideals of Islam that do not fit within the paradigm built on the revelation of God in Christ? Here one can only graciously but firmly beg to differ and leave it up to God. This is how I deal with those disparities of fact that exist between us, such as the death and resurrection to eternal life of Jesus or Jesus being taken up to God before the sacrilege of a public execution. There is, however, another dimension for the Christian student of Islam: Is Islam as taught and lived by Muslims truly in keeping with the "one true merciful God that we both adore"? This is a necessary "reality check" to prevent an over-romanticizing of the message of Islam. The response to which I return over and again is to look at the lives of Muslim friends and colleagues, and see therein the Spirit of God at work in a way that is undeniable. For me this is the acid test and reinforces the absolute necessity of Christians who go on this path having regular and intimate contact with Muslim fellow believers.

As with any true vocation, the journey alongside Islam and Muslims is not of our choosing. It is a calling to which we respond in faith and in which we persevere because "we can do none other." It is this twin sense of call and destiny that makes possible dealing with the rejection that one experiences both within one's own community and from Muslims who fail to see God at work in the Christian student of Islam. Such a life is peppered with missed opportunities, failed projects, seedbeds well-watered and sprouting only to be neglected by others who do not share the vision and suchlike. Like the whole Christian experience of a journey in faith, in John Henry Newman's words: "I do not ask to see the distance scene, one step enough for me." And to God is our return.

A Lenten Journey

Daniel Madigan

Lent was just beginning as I started out on this journey that has taken me to places, both geographical and theological, of which I would never have dreamed. It was in Delhi, the day before Ash Wednesday 1984, that I first met Christian Troll, who would introduce me to this new world. Looking back now, I see that the themes of Lent have marked these last twenty-five years and can help give some shape to these reflections.

Yet the journey did not exactly begin there. What really launched me on it was the question put to me by one of the people with leprosy for whom I had spent a summer working in India. "When will you be back?" he asked me during a small farewell tea. When would I be back? Probably never, I thought; though perhaps it might be possible to call in on the way from Australia to Europe, where I presumed I would be going for further studies in theology. However, his question stayed with me and disrupted the future of which I had long dreamed. If that summer had taught me anything, it was that India—even its poorest backwaters like this little colony of people marginalized because of their leprosy—was not "another world," as we are wont to say. There is only one world. On returning to Australia I found it difficult to settle back into the idea of a long-planned academic life. I feared

I would probably end up treating most of the world as something that unfortunately as an Australian you have to fly over to get to the other parts of "our world" in Europe and the United States.

At the time we Australian Jesuits were being asked to take responsibility for the Society of Jesus's small venture in Pakistan. Jesuits had been working in Lahore since the 1960s in the field of Muslim–Christian relations at the invitation of the Capuchins. The first time Islam entered into my consciousness must have been when I was assigned to that mission, and it was preparation for Lahore that brought me first to Delhi to finish my theological studies in a context a little closer to that in which I would eventually work.

One thing stands out for me about that time: the obvious respect and even love for Muslims which energized Christian Troll's apostolate, and I would find the same thing among other Jesuits in the years to come—notably the courtly Swiss Robert Bütler in Lahore, the earnest Dutchman Christian van Nispen in Cairo, the unsinkable Italian Paolo Dall'Oglio in Syria, and the affable American Tom Michel in Indonesia, in Rome and now in Turkey. I name only these few because they have been so important to me personally, yet there are others, too many to name, from other congregations and churches who have also inspired me by the way they spend themselves in love for Muslims.

In those days in India—and perhaps it is still true today—there was no great enthusiasm, at times not even much sympathy, for the apostolate of Muslim–Christian dialogue. Those who worked in it were regarded as somewhat marginal to the main thrust of dialogue and inculturation, which looked towards Hinduism as the prime interlocutor. Our commitment to this work was puzzling even to most of our fellow Jesuits, who found it difficult to imagine what fruit could possibly come of such an engagement. Many seemed to have imbibed the disdain for Muslims that pervaded the country. This was an experience that would be repeated with ever increasing intensity over the years in several countries.

These days, of course, people tend to see more reason to study Islam. Yet at the same time, given the increasing polarization and politicization of recent years, they see even less reason to do it with sympathy and openness. As Jesuits, those of us who do approach our Muslim sisters and brothers with open hearts and minds do so in the spirit of the Exercises of St. Ignatius, who laid down as the presupposition of all our interactions that we should seek the best possible interpretation of what our partner says rather than find fault with it. It is distressing how many Christians consider themselves absolved of any obligation actually to be Christian in their dealings with Muslims and in the opinions they express about Islam. I remain immensely grateful for the example of those Jesuit brothers who daily demonstrated by the commitment of their lives that dialogue is fundamentally an act of love. Like any genuine act of love, it is not for the faint of heart, because it demands sacrifice.

This is the first sense in which the journey has been a Lenten one. Devoting yourself seriously and sympathetically to the study of a religious tradition not your own requires continual sacrifice. It means dedicating years, even decades, listening attentively and with loving openness, doing one's best to understand an unfamiliar take on humanity and its relationship to the Absolute, and a very different reading of God's dealings with us. I sometimes envied fellow Jesuits who were able to expend the not inconsiderable energies required by doctoral studies on going deeper into an aspect of our own tradition. There, it seemed to me, would be rich nourishment for one's own faith, rather than what seemed the thin, Lenten fare that was my daily academic bread. Certainly it helped that this field of study was not one that I had chosen for myself, but which I had been asked to undertake by the superior general. I had got into it in what an American Jesuit once said to me was "the old-fashioned way."

For those of us who study the Muslim tradition there is, of course, at least a familiarity one does not find in the study of, for example, Hinduism or Buddhism. At the same time, however, we are immersing ourselves in a tradition that understands itself to be God's definitive reform of the Jewish and Christian traditions, a tradition that offers a substantially different understanding of the history of God's engagement with humanity from the creation of Adam and Eve, through Noah, Abraham, Isaac, Ishmael, David, Solomon, right up to Jesus and beyond—a history we both see as our own, and which for the most part we share with the Jews. Above all, the tradition we are giving our lives to studying proposes a very different assessment of what God was doing in Jesus Christ, and presumes that the Christian reading of that event is at best mistaken, and at worst impious. It requires humility and discipline to avoid simply becoming defensive or dismissive, and to take seriously the Muslim critique of our faith and the ways in which we express it.

Lengthening and Broadening

However, such discipline and preparedness to make sacrifices represent only one side of Lent. The English word Lenten comes from the Old

English word to *lengthen*. At least in the northern hemisphere, where it all began, the Lenten fast is a spring-time event. The short, bleak winter days are lengthening towards the equinox and brilliant summer. So it is a time of gradual expansiveness and fuller life. This is an aspect of our repentance to which we pay too little attention. Human sinfulness lies not in our being too expansively alive, but rather in our having closed down the life God has given us. It consists in resisting the creative love of God that would open us to God's universe, and in preferring the narrow confines of the world we create for ourselves. Thus, our repentance is not a closing down of our living but rather an expansion of it. It is a lengthening of the vision that has become foreshortened; it is a broadening of the focus that has narrowed itself to our own concerns.

This second aspect of Lent has been very evident to me in the journey of this quarter-century: My engagement with Muslims and their Islam has broadened my world enormously. We are, after all, speaking about having some sense of familiarity and solidarity with about one-fifth of the human race. I have the repeated experience of feeling at home with Muslims, at a time when much of the world views them as irreducibly different, to be feared and suspected. This has meant feeling at home with immigrants and asylum seekers, with students and academic colleagues in various parts of the world, and not least with taxi drivers in almost any city you care to mention. Particularly given our current world situation, to count Muslims among your close friends and to have studied the Islamic tradition with care and attention is to live in a much more expansive world than that to which many in the West now feel themselves fearfully confined. I count that a great blessing.

This sense of being at home with Muslims is, of course, only partly due to my efforts to learn their languages and study their religious tradition; it is also due to their welcome, and their appreciation of being taken seriously as believers. By *believers* I mean not so much people who are sure they have already heard all God has to say, but people who are constantly listening for God's Word. Here, I have learned, lies the key to our relationship: recognizing in the other that same attentiveness to what God is trying to show us, not only by means of our scriptures and traditions, but also through creation and the events of human history. This is what the Qur'an would call "the signs of God." Even though my Muslim friends would disagree with me about where God has spoken his Word most completely, I cannot fail to see the evidence that they have heard in some way—through and within their tradition, not in spite of it—the same Word of love that as a Christian I have heard spoken, I believe most expressively, in Jesus Christ.

I know they have heard it because they are re-expressing that love in their own living.

Theological Dialogue

It is in this lived experience that we discover we are not such strangers to one another, and moreover we begin to see that our theological dialogue is an internal dialogue. It is not so much the guarded and inquiring encounter of foreign systems of thought, or the negotiation of a generic, lowest common denominator religion, but rather the exploration together of a shared but contested history.

Christians rarely take seriously enough the fact that we have not yet found a convincing way to express our faith in Christ to more than a billion people who already believe in the God of Abraham. The perplexity that greets our affirmations of faith cannot simply be dismissed as ill will or ignorance. It is a challenge and an opportunity for us to develop an ever clearer expression of our faith. Most Jews have come to accept gracefully the idea that Christianity, with its radically alternative reading of the biblical tradition and of the figure of Jesus of Nazareth, is not going to disappear. So, too, we Christians will have to accommodate ourselves to the idea not only that Islam as a religion is not going to fade away, but also that it will continue to be a lively challenger of our reading of the Jesus event.

Taking seriously the Muslim critique of our faith, rather than simply becoming defensive or rejecting it out of hand, has in my experience been extremely fruitful theologically. It has been one of those expansive Lenten experiences, taking me beyond the rather narrow focus and the closed internal vocabulary that can characterize much Christian theological discourse. It has opened me to questions posed by a far wider public, as I have discovered that Muslims' questions are echoed not only by others who view Christian affirmations with some skepticism but also, even if more tentatively, by Christians themselves. It seems to me, therefore, that the effort required to develop a theology appropriate to our dialogue and truly responsive to Muslims has a benefit for the Christian community itself.

Muslims' questions may seem surprising at first to those who are used to particular ways of thought and expression. However, we discover that those questions are not extraneous and barren, but that they are natural and can be fruitful.

Being willing to hear out the Muslim critique of Christian faith is both a trial and an opportunity. There is, on the one hand, a constant pressure

to re-conceive the Jesus event and reduce it to fit within the Qur'anic paradigm of prophets, scriptures and laws. The Qur'an has God say, addressing
Muhammad:

> Surely We have communicated (*awhayna*) to you just as We
> communicated to Noah and the Prophets after him, and as We
> communicated to Abraham and Ishmael and Isaac and Jacob and the
> tribes, and to Jesus and Job and Jonah and Aaron and Solomon, and as
> We gave to David the *zabur*. (Q. 4:163)

This view of things fits with a certain trend in contemporary Christian
theology that finds congenial a "low" Christology that would see Jesus as a
prophetic figure, filled—perhaps to an exceptional degree—with the Spirit
of God. Such a Christology is seen as more appropriate to interfaith
encounter generally, not only with Muslims, since it makes more modest
claims for Jesus and so opens the way to a generous acknowledgment of
other spirit-filled figures as revealers and saviors.

These low-ascending Christologies, however, have a tendency to con-
firm Muslims in their belief that what Christians are up to is the elevation
of a merely human messenger to the divine plane where he has no place.
They tend to lock us into a fruitless, centuries-long argument about prophets and scriptures. However, the encounter with the faith of Muslims poses
a question more fundamental than "who is the definitive prophet and which
the most reliable scripture?" It challenges the believer to ask "where is
God's Word most clearly and faithfully expressed in our world?"

The Word

If we Christians are careful in our answer to that question, we will say that
it is in Jesus, the Word-made-flesh, and only in a derivative way in the
scriptures, which are, after all, words selected and canonized because we
believe that they put us in touch with the Word-made-flesh. Interestingly,
the Islamic theological tradition in its reflection on the Qur'an as God's
Word had to grapple with a number of issues quite parallel to those that
emerged in the Christological controversies of the early centuries of the
Christian tradition, as we worked through the implications of a Word-
made-flesh. These issues arose for the Muslim community because it professed that what many thought of as merely a human text—it seemed like
poetry, stories of the ancients, or a soothsayer's mantic utterances—was
actually a divine revelation; and furthermore that this revelation had—to

use a Qur'anic as well as Johannine turn of phrase—"come down from heaven," sent by God. Questions about the relationship of God's Word to God's self, about the relationship between the obviously human and historically conditioned elements of the word and its divinity, about the eternity or otherwise of this word—all these exercised the theologians of both our traditions.

For this reason, the relationship between our traditions can be more fruitfully conceived if we begin not from a competition about prophets and books but from our shared faith in an eternally expressive God, who communicates with us, who expresses himself in ways we can understand, and to which we can respond. This concept of the Word has formed the basis of the theological synthesis that has gradually developed for me in conversation with Muslim friends and students.

Though my theology has developed principally in conversation with Muslims, Christian readers will recognize the centrality of the concept of Word or *logos* to our theological tradition, even if more recently it has come in for some criticism as being a Greek intrusion into an originally more Semitic theology, an unwelcome philosophical turn in an otherwise more concrete and down-to-earth Christology. Yet John's *logos* Christology is anything but abstract. The divine Word is the energy vibrating within everything that has ever been created (John 1:3). And the language God has chosen in order to speak the Word most fully is the "language" of our own flesh (John 1:14)—"body language" we might say. I have found that the importance for the Islamic tradition of God's eternal speech (*kalam Allah*), which is an essential attribute of God, uncreated and nothing other than divine, makes the *logos* Christology of John's Gospel a particularly rich point of theological contact.

Our theological dialogue is often thought to be a comparison and competition between settled doctrinal positions; yet we discover that for neither of us are these positions as stable and straightforward as they might appear. In this conversation Christians recognize once again that many of our core professions of faith emerged from a long history of sometimes violent disagreement, and only after repeated unsuccessful attempts to express in words the mystery of God and of God's action in the world. Muslim participants too come to recognize that, while some of their own theological positions may appear settled, this is so not because they have reached a point of equilibrium, but rather because the exploration of them was cut short due to a growing sense of the futility of speculative theology and its methods. If Christians can share with Muslims our own theological perplexities—both those that led us eventually to the authoritative

definitions, and those that still keep us probing and interrogating those
definitions centuries later—they sometimes come to see that we are all "in
the same boat" theologically. That is, we are both in a position of having to
respond to the series of questions and paradoxes that arise from our shared
basic affirmation that the eternal and transcendent God has spoken a
word—God's own Word—in and to our world.

Any of the languages in which God might choose to communicate with
humanity is necessarily a human language; otherwise it would not be communication. This is so not only because language requires organs of speech
and hearing, or their analogical equivalents in the case of the deaf. Speech
exists in a cultural matrix that gives a consensual meaning to the sounds
and structures. In this sense, it might be considered no more scandalous
that God should speak in body language than the Hebrew or Arabic language. If God is capable of communicating through one or other of those
human mediums, God is no less capable of expressing himself through a
human life.

Muslims, of course, find it difficult to understand how Christians can
think of Jesus as in any sense divine. Yet in many respects what Christians
are doing is not much different from what Muslims are doing. We are both
recognizing the presence and expression of the eternal, universal, divine
Word in something which, to someone who does not believe, is merely
human; in the case of Christians, in a first-century carpenter from Nazareth;
in the case of Muslims, in a seventh-century Arabic text. The only appropriate response when confronted with what seems to us to be God's Word
is what we might call the submission of faith. Neither Christian nor Muslim
feels entitled to dispute or reduce the status of the Word-come-among-us.
While we both recognize that God has necessarily chosen a human language in order to communicate with us, we do not for that reason reject the
divine nature of the Word addressed to us.

The Word of the Cross

Of course, the crucial difference between us is not just a question of the
language in which we believe God has revealed himself to us. It is in the
content of that revelation, most particularly in the centrality of the cross.
John, who in his prologue declares that the Word became flesh and dwelt
among us (John 1:14), has that Word-become-flesh saying in the final
moment of his life, "It is accomplished" (John 19:30). The Word who came
to his own in order to re-establish the primordial relationship between

God and humanity (John 1:12) has in the vulnerability of the cross become most completely flesh, has entered most fully into the human condition, and therefore has united the human and the divine.

This sense that the self-emptying love shown on the cross is the fullest revelation of who God is and how things stand between God and humanity is not some late Johannine invention, but is expressed in a very early form in the hymn in Philippians Ch. 2. To the one who showed that divinity is not something to be exploited for oneself, but who poured himself out and humbled himself even to the point of accepting, without defense, without retaliation and without recourse to power, the unjust sentence of a shameful death, God gave "the name which is above all other names," that is, God's own sacred name: YHWH, or as we usually express it, the Lord. In the resurrection God is not so much overturning and reversing the death of Jesus as affirming it as the expression of the truth about divinity. God in effect declares, "This is how I am; this is who I am."

In the resurrection of Jesus, God is affirming the truth not only about divinity but also about humanity: That union of the human and divine in Jesus is opened to all of us. Self-sacrificing love, though it seems to be death-dealing, is revealed as ultimately the way to true life. In living out the same sacrificial love as Jesus did, we, too, share in his rising to life.

This is a further sense in which these years of study and engagement have been a Lenten experience: A theology more and more based on the Word, and hence on the Incarnation, has led me, as Lent does, into a deeper exploration of the mystery of the cross—an event whose significance the Qur'an seems to deny, not only as a uniquely revealing moment in the life of God but by most accounts even as a historical event. This has not been because of a defensive reaction to the Muslim position but because taking that position seriously has led me to see more clearly the particularity of the Christian proclamation. The cross is what clearly marks Christianity off from the kind of generic religion understood as a collection of rituals to be carried out and taboos to be avoided in order to remain in a right relationship with the divine.

A Muslim student in Ankara, after having heard my explanation of Christian faith in God's Word expressed in the "language" of a human life and death, asked whether it didn't make more sense for God to have expressed himself in a straightforward text rather than in the rather ambiguous language of the flesh which left itself open to such diverse interpretations. The question was understandable, even if she may have been somewhat naïve about the supposed straightforwardness of texts. As so often happens in these situations, the unexpected question catalyzed a new insight. If the message to be communicated is one of guidance and command, I said to her, then a text is surely desirable. But if, as Christians believe, the message is one of self-sacrificing love and unconditional forgiveness, then "body language" is surely more expressive. We know this from our own experience. Talk is cheap, especially when it comes to declarations of love and reconciliation. The engagement of the body demands more, puts us at risk and can cost us dearly. God chooses frail flesh to express to humans that vulnerable love God has for us—a flesh we could, and did, wound; a flesh that can continue to bear those wounds and yet raise the wounded hand in blessing rather than retaliation.

No Other Boast

The season of Lent is also a time for coming to a realistic understanding of oneself, one's failures, and one's need for repentance. It is a time for learning humility and recognizing that we have no merits of which to boast. The one thing we can glory in, says St. Paul, is the cross of Christ. Yet we don't boast of it as though it somehow makes us better than others. I have found myself in the strangest conversations in recent years with Christians who consider themselves so much better than Muslims because Christ's self-sacrificing love is so much better than anything they see in Muhammad. The cross of Christ does not belong to us. It cannot puff us up; it should humble us.

One of the great frustrations of Muslim–Christian relations, perhaps more so now than ever, is finding ourselves locked into a situation where each is comparing his own community's ideals with the much less edifying realities of the other's behavior. Even if we might not express it openly in our formal dialogues, there is all too often an underlying assumption that, whatever my dialogue partner may say about his ideals—justice, love, peace, equality, and so on—in reality he and his religious community have signally failed to live up to them. We even go so far as to question whether the other community really holds those values at all or are just being disingenuous. And, of course, it is true; as any honest observer can see, and as critics of religion are only too quick to remind us, we have both failed to live up to our ideals. At best we admit some of our failings but then excuse ourselves with the claim that the other's faults are much worse.

The only way out of this fruitless mutual recrimination is a Lenten movement towards repentance. Repentance makes us vulnerable: We run the risk that the other will not be as honest as we have been, and that we might find ourselves humbled before someone who arrogantly refuses to acknowledge his own faults. That is a risk we must run if we want to bear the name Christian. We cannot glory in the cross and at the same time cling to our self-righteousness.

So these years have been a Lenten journey in many senses of that word. They have been years that have called for discipline and sacrifice; but they have also been enormously rich and expansive. The journey has taken me much more deeply than I would have expected into the mystery of the Cross, and it is teaching me as I go that we can glory in nothing but the self-emptying love of God expressed there. On that way I have encountered others who know and live the truth of self-emptying love, even if they haven't recognized it in the Cross of Christ. I trust that, as St. John tells us, all of us who are living in love are living, and will live forever, in God.

Journeying toward God

Joseph Ellul

Before referring to my own experiences in the field of Christian–Muslim dialogue I believe that, for the benefit of the reader, a brief historical-cultural overview of Maltese society would help to situate my reflections within their proper context.

Some Preliminary Considerations

The Maltese Islands are strategically situated right in the middle of the Mediterranean Sea at the crossroads between two continents (Europe and Africa), as well as between two different worlds and two different cultures. In the past the country was considered a bastion of Christianity against the marauding Barbary corsairs and the encroaching military and naval might of the Ottoman Empire. Today it is viewed rather as a bridge between Southern Europe and Northern Africa.

The Muslim presence in Malta dates back to roughly the end of the ninth century, when the Aghlabid dynasty (800–909), which dominated what is present-day Tunisia and Algeria, occupied southern Italy and Sicily and, of course, Malta. A century later their rule was supplanted by another dynasty, that of the Fatimids (969–1171). The most lasting legacy of Arab–Muslim rule in Malta is, of course, the Maltese language, although traces of Christian–Arab presence can also be detected through theological terms that have remained with us to this day. Their rule ended with the conquest of the same territories by the Normans at the end of the eleventh century. This by no means meant the end of the Muslim presence in Malta. Muslims remained here for at least another two centuries before they were expelled by Emperor Fredrick II after an apparent plot to retake the islands was uncovered.

The ceding of the Maltese Islands on the part of the Holy Roman Emperor Charles V to the Sovereign Military Hospitaller Order of St. John of Jerusalem of Rhodes and of Malta as a fief in 1530, and the Hospitallers' presence during the following 268 years, was marked by a history of mutual hostility between the Knights and the then expanding Ottoman Empire. Much has been written about the Great Siege of Malta of 1565 and the Battle of Lepanto of 1571. What can be stated for certain is that the Knights succeeded in tarnishing the aura of invincibility surrounding the Ottomans with the first, and contributed towards turning the tide against them through the second. The Order's rule in Malta also helped secure the Catholic faith in the islands and enhance the contribution of the Catholic Church in the fields of culture, the arts, education, and philanthropy. But it also set the tone for a persisting attitude among the Maltese as regards Islam, both as a religion and as a civilization. Right up until the French occupation of the islands in 1798, almost the only Muslims present here were slaves captured during naval skirmishes.

Muslim presence began to take on added significance in the early 1970s as a result of the foreign and domestic policies of the Labor government. Its program spearheaded by the then prime minister Dom Mintoff (1971–84) aimed at securing and consolidating ties with the Arab world, especially with Libya. During this period Malta began to witness the first Muslim–Catholic marriages, a phenomenon that has been a constant feature of Maltese society ever since.

There are no indications that the Muslim community in Malta is in conflict with mainstream Maltese society. There have been individual claims by a few Maltese converts to Islam that Muslims in Malta should be governed by Shari'a; however, the overwhelming majority are well integrated into Maltese society and the Muslim school operating in Malta (Maryam al-Batool School) and run by the Malta branch of the World Islamic Call Society abides fully by the norms set out in the National

Minimum Curriculum, with the obvious inclusion of subjects such as Arabic and the Muslim religion. It is also an example of collaboration between Muslims and Christians, who work together in the formation of the future generation of Muslims in Malta and their eventual contribution to society.

The Muslim presence in Malta has lately increased through the arrival of illegal immigrants, a phenomenon that is affecting all southern European countries. Among them one may also find a significant number of Christians hailing from, among other countries, the Sudan, Ethiopia, and Eritrea.

It is quite obvious that all of these facts would not only have consequences for shifts in demography, but they also imply that the religious-pastoral situation of the Maltese islands has undergone significant developments. Among the Maltese, the attitude towards this continuously developing scenario oscillates from one of ignorance and prejudice, to one of accommodation and naiveté. One still encounters people who consider the Muslim presence in Malta to be incompatible with Maltese society and its Catholic roots. In their view such a presence is aimed at achieving what the Ottomans had failed to accomplish by way of the Great Siege. Then there are those who downplay or totally ignore differences in belief and practice between Christians and Muslims, basing their attitudes on the fact that both believe in the same God. This attitude betrays a deep-seated ignorance of both Christianity and Islam.

In this context it is all too obvious that Christian–Muslim dialogue in my country is no simple task. Malta remains a deeply divided country on the ideological as well as on the political level. Political agendas are ever present. Such a situation requires that enthusiasm be tempered with prudence and discernment. Every word and every gesture of goodwill counts, but they might also be misunderstood or taken out of their proper contexts.

Having set out the general framework, I can now begin to map out the story of my personal engagement with Islam and the questions and challenges that it poses concerning my journey in the Christian faith.

My Own Journey

I was born in a family that had decades-long ties with the Arab world. My paternal grandmother, Rosanna, was born in Tripoli (Libya). Her birth certificate attests that she was born in Tripoli di Berberia. My father, Victor, who was employed with the NAAFI, the suppliers of the British forces, worked for three years in Libya (1948–51). Among my mother's cousins there are quite a few who were born either in Tripoli or Benghazi and who resided there for many years. The same applies to their children.

During my early childhood, I used to enjoy listening to them speak of their experiences in living in a country and a culture that were as yet totally alien to me, their extolling of the noble sentiments of its inhabitants, and their recounting of the hardships they endured during colonial times. At that point in my life I was not yet acquainted with Islam as a culture, still less as a religion; all I knew was something about this North African country, but the foundations for such an understanding appeared to have already been laid.

My favorite subject at secondary school was history and I harbored a special interest in the mediaeval period in Europe. But the textbooks for our studies were very selective in their treatment of historical movements and there was no mention of the influence of Islamic thought on European culture (my secondary education took place during the seventies when Islam was not center stage, whether for right or wrong reasons). However, my interest in the monastic movements as well as in the contribution of the Order of Preachers (Dominicans) and the Order of Friars Minor (Franciscans) to mediaeval thought and culture were to serve me well years later, when I began to do research work in the area of Muslim–Christian encounters during that particular period and the synthesis that was achieved between Christian theological thought and Islamic philosophical discourse spearheaded among others by Albert the Great and Thomas Aquinas.

My first encounter with Islam took place around the year 1980, four years into my priestly formation as a Dominican. I chanced upon a small book in the library of our study house titled *The Bible and the Qur'an* written by the late renowned Dominican scholar Jacques Jomier. Its chapters were short and written in a style that was easy to follow. I took it for my bedtime reading! It was then that I decided to do some research (albeit very elementary, since I had no knowledge whatsoever of the Arabic language) into some themes found in the Qur'an and draw a comparison with the way they were dealt with in the Bible. During that same year, a Maltese Franciscan, Edmund Teuma, a graduate from PISAI, wrote an introduction to Islam in Maltese. I got in touch with him and he very generously and patiently offered to read whatever I came up with. It was the beginning of an enduring friendship that has gone beyond the merely academic. He was the first to undertake the task of rendering the Qur'an into the Maltese language, a project that lasted twenty-two years. Both of us are very much involved in dialogue with the Muslim community in Malta. I also obtained the address of Fr. Jomier in Toulouse (he had just settled there after spending some forty years in Cairo) and wrote to him about my intention to pursue Islamic studies. He wrote back giving me some much needed encouragement and advice.

The following year, the Institut Dominicain d'Études Orientales (IDEO) invited me to spend a month with their community in Cairo. I stayed with them from late July till late August. This sojourn proved in many ways to be a culture shock, since I had never ventured into a culture that was so different from the European one. It was also a time of extreme tension in Egypt. President Sadat was assassinated in early October 1981, barely one month after my return to Malta. On the other hand, I had the golden opportunity to meet the then Director of IDEO, the renowned scholar, the late Fr. Georges Anawati as well as Fr. Emilio Platti.

In 1983 I left for Rome in order to pursue further studies at the Pontifical Institute for Arabic and Islamic Studies (PISAI). There I benefited from the expertise of its professors, who are among the finest minds in Islamic scholarship, and a few of whom are contributors to this volume, including Maurice Borrmans (Marriage and Family Law), Robert Caspar and Gérard Demeerseman (Theology), Michel Lagarde (Exegesis), Giuseppe Scattolin (Mysticism), Jan Slomp (Protestant-Muslim dialogue), as well as Samir Khalil Samir (Christian-Arab Apologetics). All have left a lasting impression on my mind and on my work. I developed an increasing interest in the history of Islam and the exegesis of the Qur'an, as well as in Christian–Arab apologetics.

I obtained my license in Arabic and Islamic studies in 1986, having written a dissertation entitled: *Some meanings of the root "ḥlf" according to Zamakhshari, Razi and Baidawi* under the direction of Gérard Demeerseman. I then went on to read Ecumenical Theology at the Pontifical University of St Thomas Aquinas (Angelicum), where I obtained my license in 1987 and ten years later, my doctorate with a dissertation on Roman Catholic-Orthodox dialogue. Both degrees have served me well. My specialization in Arabic and Islamic studies has provided me with the necessary tools for understanding Islam and its religious and cultural heritage. My studies in Ecumenical Theology coupled with my studies at PISAI on Christian–Arab apologetics under Fr. Samir Khalil Samir have introduced me to the fascinating world of Eastern and Oriental Christianity and to the way Christian communities in the Middle and Near East engaged Muslims in dialogue, thereby acculturating their theological language within the context of Islamic civilization within which they lived and worked. During these years of specialization, I gradually became more acquainted with the leaders of the Muslim community in Malta, especially with the imam of the local mosque Mr. Muhammad El-Sadi, with whom I have maintained a warm personal and working relationship.

My subsequent lecturing responsibilities in the field of Muslim–Christian encounters and Islamic culture at the Angelicum and at PISAI, as well as at the University of Malta, together with my participation in various Muslim–Christian *fora* as representative of the Archdiocese of Malta for interreligious dialogue, have turned out to be an ongoing endeavor to increase my knowledge and appreciation of Muslim faith and practice. My membership in the Committee for Relations with Muslims of the Council of European Bishops' Conferences during the years 2005–9, as well as my present appointment as consulter to the Pontifical Council for Interreligious Dialogue, have proven to be a continuous learning and enriching experience in the field of Muslim–Christian dialogue as well as providing contact, by way of colloquia and conferences, with our human situations across the religious divide. Meeting Muslims face-to-face in the lecture hall as well as across the conference table has turned out to be a voyage of discovery, of self and of the "other."

The Necessity for Dialogue

One of the first lessons to be learnt from Christian–Muslim dialogue is that, if one wishes to play an active role in this area with a view to reaping success, then one had better look elsewhere for such a reward. Of itself interreligious dialogue is a challenge for the Christian. Muslim–Christian dialogue is even more so. The reason is that the Qur'an is full of references to biblical concepts, events, and characters. Many times these are presented in a different light to their biblical context. The Qur'an itself appears to deny the two basic pillars on which the faith of the Christian rests, namely the Trinity and the Incarnation. The faith and practice of my Muslim friend is a challenge to deepen my own faith, to ask searching questions as to what is my raison d'être as a believer in the Triune God and in Jesus Christ as the very Word of God made flesh. Every encounter with a Muslim is a call for me to deepen my awareness of my own faith and of my Dominican vocation. My engagement in Christian–Muslim dialogue is by no means alien to my Dominican vocation; it is an integral part of the history and the tradition of the Order of Preachers.

This latter element helps bring to mind the various projects undertaken by the Order to which I belong almost immediately after its founding, such

264

Joseph Ellul

as the schools of Arabic in Spain and Tunisia and the establishment of the Province of the Holy Land. It also brings to mind the engagement by Albert the Great (c. 1206–80) and Thomas Aquinas (1225–74) in dialogue with Islamic thought on a philosophical as well as on a theological level. It was the former who took as his personal maxim: *in dulcedine societatis quaerere veritatem* (to seek the truth in the delightfulness of companionship). Aquinas, on the other hand, integrated many of the ideas of Avicenna and Averroës into the framework of Mediaeval Christian thought. I look at the great missionary endeavors of Ramon Marti (c. 1220–84), William of Tripoli (c. 1220–c. 91), and of Ricoldo da Montecroce (1243–1320) and their efforts at direct involvement in dialogue with Muslims in Lebanon, Syria, and Iraq. I call to mind their enthusiasm and preparedness, as well as their profound faith in times of weariness, distress, and helplessness in the face of war and persecution. These moments are a painful reminder of our own human weakness and the need to place our human efforts in the hands of God.

Christian–Muslim dialogue is not an exercise in being chummy and patting each other on the back. It means ultimately getting to grips with what is essential to our respective faiths. Its role is not that of suppressing differences, but at looking at them as a means for creating mutual understanding, respect, and enrichment. It implies maintaining one's religious identity while respecting that of the other; it demands listening as well as speaking. It is an ongoing challenge to deepen one's own faith while appreciating that of the other. It also demands recognition of one's past and present failings and the honesty to admit them. All religious communities are undoubtedly marked by wounds, both old and new, which may lead them to justify having a "victim" mentality. Here I would like to make a personal appeal: It is about time that Muslims end their persistent demands on Christians— and Roman Catholics in particular—to beat their breasts continuously and cry out *"mea culpa"* in a paroxysm of self-loathing and abasement. Roman Catholicism has confronted its past and demonstrated repentance for the faults its members have committed. Islam has yet to undergo the same process whereby it would come out all the more purified and stronger for having done so. Muslims have every right to level criticism against others; they must also learn how to take it. This is also dialogue.

At the Heart of Christian–Muslim Dialogue

At this juncture it is important to recall the teachings of the Catholic Church in the light of the Second Vatican Council and of pontifical documents, which have constantly promoted dialogue on all levels between Christians and Muslims. One such instance is Pope Benedict XVI's speech during a meeting with representatives of some Muslim communities in Cologne which has, in my opinion, set out the guiding principles for fruitful Muslim–Christian dialogue in a globalized, multiethnic, multireligious world:

> The believer—and all of us, as Christians and Muslims, are believers— knows that, despite his weakness, he can count on the spiritual power of prayer. Dear friends, I am profoundly convinced that we must not yield to the negative pressures in our midst, but must affirm the values of respect, solidarity and peace. The life of every human being is sacred, both for Christians and for Muslims. There is plenty of scope for us to act together in the service of fundamental moral values. The dignity of the person and the defense of the rights which that dignity confers must represent the goal of every social endeavor and of every effort to bring it to fruition. This message is conveyed to us unmistakably by the quiet but clear voice of conscience. It is a message which must be heeded and communicated to others: should it ever cease to find an echo in peoples' hearts, the world would be exposed to the darkness of a new barbarism. Only through recognition of the centrality of the person can a common basis for understanding be found, one which enables us to move beyond cultural conflicts and which neutralizes the disruptive power of ideologies.[1]

For this reason I believe that we need to talk more about dialogue concerning God, lest our respective religions run the risk of becoming no more than parallel ideologies to secularism.[2] Above all, we, as Christians

---

1. Address of His Holiness Pope Benedict XVI during his meeting with representatives of some Muslim communities, Cologne, August 20, 2005, http://tinyurl.com/PBXVI.
2. On May 9, 2005, the Commission of the Bishops' Conference of the European Community (COMECE) published a document entitled *The Evolution of the European Union and the Responsibility of Catholics*. On this point COMECE has made the position of the Catholic Church very clear in paragraph 35:

> At the very heart of our faith experience, we find an invitation to dialogue with others. This dialogue is not external to our commitment to faith. It is an intrinsic part of faith, because we discover that we are all part of the same humanity created by God and saved by the irrevocable gift of the return of the Son. For our Christian conscience, there cannot be any contradiction a priori between our faith-based commitment, our will to live in a fraternal dialogue with those who do not share our religious convictions and our concern to contribute to the good of all humanity.

and Muslims in dialogue, have a significant opportunity to become ambassadors of reconciliation. This role is becoming ever more central when one
learns of the plight of Christians in some Muslim countries and the humil-
iations and deprivations that they have to suffer because of their faith.

Reconciliation means moving from a position of mere tolerance—which
reflects my reasoned conclusion that I have to put up with you—to one of
acceptance, leading to my recognizing you as a fellow human being who, in
the eyes of God as Creator of all, has rights and duties equal to my own.

Being a dynamic activity, Muslim–Christian dialogue is primarily an
encounter of believers who belong to diverse religious beliefs, civilizations,
and cultures and who share a common ideal: the advancement and well-
being of humankind and the belief that humanity is called to a higher destiny. This implies the acknowledgment and promotion of human dignity
and the securing of the inviolable rights of individuals and groups to freedom of thought, conscience, and religion.[3] From this point of view diversity should not and in fact does not become synonymous with divisiveness
but rather with mutual enrichment.

Christian–Muslim dialogue may not necessarily lead to agreement,
whether full or partial, on crucial issues, but it could—and in fact it should—
lead to mutual understanding. Dialogue does not lead to the reduction of
the other to oneself, but rather it creates self-disclosure to the other. Each
dialogue partner speaks out of his or her own convictions to the other, who
has different convictions of his or her own and who is genuinely interested
in them. The partners make a sincere effort to listen and learn; to seek
for meaning and to try to understand the mind and heart of the other in
openness and mutual trust.[4]

In order to be fruitful Muslim–Christian dialogue requires a certain
predisposition on the part of those who participate: respect, listening, sincerity, openness as well as being receptive and willing to work together in
an atmosphere of hope and patience. We all know from experience that
facing the truth is never an easy task. Truth is many times uncomfortable
and unpalatable. But we as Christian and Muslim communities are above
all *religious* communities; we look towards God. In a letter to one of his

3. See John Paul II, Address to the Ambassador of Pakistan, Rome, January 11,
1997, Published in *Osservatore Romano* (English language edition), January 20, 1997.
4. See S. Wesley Ariarajah, "The Understanding and Practice of Dialogue: Its
Nature, Purpose and Variations," in *Faith in the Midst of Faiths: Reflections on
Dialogue in Community*, ed. S. J. Samartha (Geneva: World Council of Churches,
1977), 54–58.

disciples the great Moroccan Sufi mystic Ibn Abbad of Ronda quoted another Sufi master as having said: "Journey towards God, though you are lame and broken." It is therefore incumbent upon us both, Christians *and* Muslims, to discern God's action in the world and to bear witness to it in our daily struggles with the harsh realities of everyday life and of our all too human frailty. It is a struggle that we must face together as believers.

"From the brook by the path"

Formation and Transformation in Meeting Muslims

Felix Körner

Reviews, especially those on one's own life, are rather hypothetical in their attempts to point out reasons, threads, and meaning. Why and how did I come to be a Jesuit in dialogue with Muslims and a theologian of witness? What influenced me, what drove me, what helped me? These are good questions. My answers, however, are an attempt only to discover consistency.

Offenbach

"How can a church possibly claim to be the only saving community?" Questions like this were usual topics around our family table in Offenbach, Germany. Our home was shaped by the encounter of our father's legal culture and our mother's poetic imagination. Father was a Lutheran. On his deathbed, in 2007, I read some verses to him by the seventeenth-century poet Paul Gerhardt, another Lutheran. At one point my father said, "Gut," which came to be his last word. I am quite sure that he did not only want to say, "These are good words," and "This was a good life," but also, "That will do; you might as well stop reading this pious text now."

Taking religious matters seriously but never slavishly was part of our family tradition; faith was food for dispute. After all, quite a few of our ancestors were pastors and lawyers.

My mother and her background, in turn, brought in a love of Jewish friends and thought. She was an intelligent Catholic, identified with the Church, interested in reflection, inspired by the Second Vatican Council; and she was never content with definitions or demarcations. Mother devoured classical and contemporary literature, and she kept questioning. When I gave her a book *Let's Learn to Pray* she said: "Do you think one can learn it?" (I only later discovered this to be a wise remark. Prayer is no technique, it is risking oneself.) My friends, and those of my brother and sister, loved visiting our home for an inspiring discussion; they even came after we had moved out.

I should therefore not be overly surprised about my interest in what is beyond traditional doctrines. Our high school, the Leibnizgymnasium, was similar in this respect. As opposed to most of my peers, I enjoyed going there. I remember our teacher of Greek, Dr. Günter Heil, whom I only later discovered to be the editor of a mysterious Church Father, Pseudo-Dionysius. Dr. Heil kept challenging our convictions with fundamental attacks. "What is it really, our Leibnizgymnasium?" he would ask, pointing out that it could neither be the building, nor the teachers, nor the pupils. Apart from textbooks and teachers, there was an even more enjoyable source of questions and attempted syntheses in school—my classmate Biagio Morabito from Messina, Sicily. An Arab name, an Italian background, an impressively deeper understanding of German thought than his indigenous peers. Biagio and I started off designing castles for our future kingdoms, then we visited last year's teachers at their homes to see them in other contexts; later we shot black and white pictures of ourselves reinventing clothing fashions. For me, Biagio represented the cultural integrity of Europe as the reflective readiness to rethink our identity by integrating the new.

Between 1979 and 1984, the questioning plurality of my cultured middle-class youth received several impressions that shaped the decision to become a Jesuit and scholar of Islam. I record three such experiences.

King's Canyon

My life received an unexpected spin when I was sixteen. Upon visiting relatives in California, I came to know a Presbyterian youth group. Their first questions were whether I was reborn and regularly read the Bible. On a backpacking tour through King's Canyon with the Presbyterians, I realized that I did not want Christianity to be one element of my life, like the cello I play; I wanted faith to become the form of my life. The hope to help others discover the source of the joy I feel, has been alive in me always since that day.

Katharina

At the age of nineteen, when I graduated from high school, I was unsure what to do next. So I was quite happy to be summoned for compulsory military service. I served as a medical soldier for two months and then worked for handicapped people as a nonmilitary community worker (*Zivildienstleistender*). One day, the director of the care center asked me to spend an afternoon with two women in wheelchairs. They had managed to escape legally from communist East Germany for three weeks. They asked me to drive them to, of all things, a sex film. I arranged it in downtown Frankfurt but waited for them in a nearby church, the Lutheran Katharinenkirche. What I experienced there is hard to describe. I was kneeling in a church that was lacking the focal point of the reserved Blessed Sacrament. My presence to God and God's presence to me appeared to be correlated. I left the place with a deep respect. The experience has ever since maintained its intriguing inexpressible quality. This may be the reason why I have always sensed the insufficiency of theist conceptual systems that put Creator and creation vis-à-vis each other.

Calligraphy

A third formative moment, after the Californian conviction and the German correlation, was Israel in 1984. In search for my personal call, I attended a Jesuit-run Bible School in Nazareth with twenty other searchers. Witnessing to Christ in a rather evangelical manner was part of the program's pedagogy, that is, telling others how the Gospel dynamics occurred in your own life.

It was in this context that I visited my first mosque: Jerusalem's al-Aqsa. With three fellow Bible students, I took off my shoes and entered. There I experienced attraction and repulsion. Why attraction? It was the time when my faith was more philosophical than historical. That is to say, with all my interest in Jesus and first-century Judaism growing during our studies in the Holy Land, I could not make sense of Christ's unicity. Calling Jesus God was, for us participants in the Bible School, "the language of love." We explained it as the crazy way lovers sometimes speak, but one need not and cannot make sense of it in the face of rational questions, we thought. So, in our Holy Land liturgies, we would praise Jesus as God with the whole Church; but in our reflections we declared it as enchanted exaggeration. We were unable to see the rationality of Trinitarian theology. We did not risk thoughts like: 'God does not impose himself, and therefore puts his divinity in the hands of his counterpart.' On the other hand, the Bible School was designed to make us discover and respect forms of religious life that were both familiar and strange: namely Judaism and Islam. Entering al-Aqsa with this mindset was bound to create a striking impression; and I was struck with the clarity of the architecture and of the theology that comes thus to expression. Shaped space and written quotations as the only means of artistic articulation appealed to me. I did not want representations to come in the way between God and myself. What also fascinated me, wandering on the carpets of al-Aqsa, was the immediate readiness of even young Muslims to practice their ritual obligations in public. It corresponded to an intuition of mine: believers should inspire their societies through the beauty of their liturgies. Besides attraction however, my first visit to a mosque was also a moment of repulsion. Moved with the new piety we encountered, it was natural for us to express recollection and respect by keeping our hands together in front of us as we walked about in silence. A bearded official came up to us shouting in Arabic and making gestures, both of which we did not understand. He therefore increased the intensity of his shouting and gesticulating, until we realized that he wanted us to keep our hands apart. The folding of hands was too Christian for him. So what I felt in my first encounter with Islam was an attracting and repelling authority.

Semitic Semantics

Would I be able to become a Jesuit, authentically? What had helped me overcome my fears was the example of Jesuits whom I found to follow Christ as liberated personalities. All through our basic formation, Judaism and Islam accompanied my theological explorations. I was eager to attend synagogues and mosques. I was looking forward greatly to learning Hebrew and, once I was able to start during my first year of philosophy, I discovered that I also wanted to learn Arabic as soon as possible. I found two great teachers to guide my first linguistic steps in Semitic languages. They were my fellow Jesuit, Michel van Esbroeck (d. 2003), an astonishing polyglot Belgian scholar in the Bollandist tradition, and a Protestant woman, Dr. Ruthild Geiger, who taught at the Jesuit philosophical faculty in Munich. Both invested precious time in Arabic tutorials with me. I wonder why I was so obsessed with Hebrew and Arabic, with Judaism and Islam. I was observing Christian theology from a distance. I thought that Christians had complicated Jesus's obvious message, the call to acknowledge the reality of God. In my studies of first-century Judaism, of the Hebrew Bible and of the Qur'an, I hoped to be closer to Jesus himself. I read the Qur'an in Arabic. My first Arabic copy was a Saudi Arabian gift by a German convert wearing a headscarf in Munich University's Arabic classes. I also started studying books on Islam: my first was William Montgomery Watt's in the Kohlhammer series *Die Religionen der Menschheit*. Funnily the Jesuit superior who gave me the book for Christmas 1989, following my request, used the same words my uncle Peter had said upon giving me Rudi Paret's Qur'an translation and commentary the year before: "Hopefully, you won't become a Muslim!" I thought to myself that somehow I was one already. On the other hand, I felt much of what I read to be unnecessarily brutal.

London

Reading theology at the Jesuit Heythrop College, London, was perfect for me at that time, because my linguistic, philosophical, and interreligious interests were lead on by experts. There were four encounters within the College that shaped my future, and five outside.

The first formative meeting was with the philosopher Peter Vardy. He helped me with a problem that I had acquired at the end of my undergraduate studies in Munich, where analytical philosophy was becoming fashionable. I had come to doubt that God could be a reality beyond our own concepts. Vardy pointed out to me that I should at least be consistent enough to accept that if God is not real, petitionary prayer and eternal life are pointless.

The other philosopher was Gerard Hughes, S.J., whose course not only attracted Christian students but also Bilal from Pakistan, my first Muslim peer. The course on Aquinas's doctrine of God was brilliantly clear but never questioned language that seemed to make an object of God; we despised as muddled thinking, ideas like the one that God might be a community in which we are taking part.

The great New Testament scholar Tom Deidun of the Rosminian Fathers introduced me, through specialized Greek classes, to Paul's dealing with his own experience: the experience of weakness and of Christ's work.

It was under the direction of Ann Jeffers, a Swiss Calvinist, that I wrote my essay on the Fourth Gospel. She generously accepted my proposal not to follow the set task to reconstruct John's presumed community. I rather wanted to understand the message of the gospel text. Perhaps it was, after all, more than the exaggerated language of the lover? I found the Johannine message to be the challenge to believe in Christ. In my reflection on faith, this was an important step away from an unreal God; but the point I had reached was merely that believing seemed now to depend on my own decision. Dr. Jeffers's interests were not in fundamental theology. As a scholar of Early Judaism, her research corresponded, however, to my fascination with Hebrew and intertestamental studies. I was at the point of becoming a researcher in Philo, Josephus, and Qumran. I found, however, that too many minds were already working in the field and I was angry because I didn't get the highest mark for my exam essay on Josephus, which I myself found insightful. In those months, my decision to go for Islamic studies matured. One fellow student, now a Benedictine monk, asked me about the turn from Qumran to Qur'an. He wanted to know what Islam meant to me and challenged me to use a metaphor. I said, "Islam is the castle I want to enter. I'm not sure whether I want to conquer or inhabit it."

During my London days I started a Zen formation with *kō'an* training. I kept it up from 1992 until 2003. The *kō'an* is an apt occasion to understand everything anew in one moment's formulation. Zen challenges the individual to get beyond categories of "I versus Thou." Zen, however, does not offer a constructive language to express where one is going upon leaving that dualism. Zen rather offers provocative paradoxes.

Five encounters outside Heythrop College became waymarks during this time of reorientation.

Christian Troll was the first Jesuit Islamicist I was able to meet. He was at that time teaching at Selly Oak, Birmingham, and proved to be a wise advisor. Probably the most important counsel I received in these years was from him. He told me, "If you want to make a valid contribution to interreligious dialogue, you need to be a good Christian theologian."

It was Fr. Troll who encouraged me to contact an Anglican theologian and priest of my own age, a doctoral student of his, David Marshall. He opened up the doors to his growing family but also to the workshop of his developing thought on the Qur'an. A decidedly biblical theologian, he was trying to do justice to Muslims' lives and Islam's texts. His attitude of respectful and serious thinking has always been exemplary for me.

Fr. Marshall also made it possible for me to be present at liturgies celebrated by Bishop Kenneth Cragg and at a seminar he held on the first *sura* of the Qur'an. Cragg's way of doing theology, his ever-new discoveries when closely studying the Qur'an, keeps shaping my own endeavors.

Our Jesuit provincial superior at the time was Bernd Franke. He brought the good news to London that the Society of Jesus wanted to see me ordained a priest; and he asked what I could see myself doing after ordination and pastoral work. I did not dare to say outright "Islamic studies." Would he not consider such a wish to be an attempt to escape from the urgent need for professors in Christian theology? So I responded, "I'd like to do biblical studies, with a perspective towards the Qur'an." Surprisingly he said, "I was expecting you to say Islam and that is exactly what we need!" He wisely added, "I do not know where you should pursue your studies. Get informed, and then present me your suggestions."

The Jesuit Islamicists that I asked all advised me according to the same principle. They all recommended as my place to study, those places where they had studied or taught. I found those answers rather frustrating and got in contact with the great scholar of classical Islamic theology, Josef van Ess of Tübingen. He was at the end of his academic career and in the middle of the production of his *magnum opus*. He would hardly have time for my question; but one day he appeared in the United Kingdom and spent an exhausting nine hours with me, talking and walking through London. At the end, his recommendation was clear: neither the United States nor the United Kingdom but Germany; not Tübingen, however, but rather Bamberg; a South German town I had never visited.

Bamberg

The young department of Islamic studies, with good scholars of Arabic, Iranian, and Turkish Muslim thought, and a focus on contemporary reflection, proved to be the right place for me. My supervisor was Rotraud Wielandt. Her thinking is characterized by the highest linguistic demands of Arabic and Turkish, and highest philosophical precision in thought and expression, but at the same time deep theological empathy. I had to attend introductory seminars once again and was able to produce my Master's thesis on Muhammad Shahrur's hermeneutics in 2001. How Muslims interpret the Qur'an today became my guiding question, but Bamberg offered many other inputs that shaped my understanding and theology of Islam. The lecturer in Arabic was an Egyptian Muslim, an Azharite; it was touching to see him entrust his own spiritual struggles to me, the young Catholic priest. He seemed to look on me as a man of God, rather than of the Church.

Many of my fellow students were Muslims. Discussions with them and my Christian or nonreligious peers were our daily bread but the greatest insights of my Bamberg years (1997–2002) I owe to three other sources. Surprising moments of theological discoveries were the Sunday excursions with Rotraud Wielandt. We used them for faith explorations that became more and more influenced by the other two sources. First, I was obliged to preach regularly, and I enjoyed it because the congregations of Bamberg challenged me to reflect and express our faith freshly; and secondly, when I started full-time encounters with Muslim thinking, I felt that I needed a Christian theologian to help me shape that new thinking apparently developing in me. I tried a regular reading of von Balthasar but gave up on him after two hundred pages of *Herrlichkeit*. I had the impression that he was speaking as an insider to insiders and did not want to make himself understood to someone asking the critical questions Muslims ask. It was Berthild Sachs, a Lutheran, then in her last years of formation for ministry, who recommended me to try her own theological teacher, Wolfhart Pannenberg. This suggestion proved to reshape my whole way of thinking and believing. I started reading his *Systematische Theologie* and decided to get hold of all of his texts. I kept a regular Pannenberg *lectio* up until I had read everything published by him. I wanted to know his thought as a whole and I also felt an urge to come to know the man himself, with whom I spent so many hours through reading. He and his wife received me generously. What is so important in Pannenberg's theology? It was when reading him that I was able to see Christian faith not as depending on my decision but on Jesus's life, death and resurrection, and thus on an anticipation of the completion of history, into which we can enter.

In 1999 I met another prominent Jesuit Islamicist, Fr. Tom Michel, who had called all young Jesuits in Islamic studies to Istanbul for a meeting. Fr. Michel asked me whether I could see myself as a partner in academic encounters in Ankara, where the Society of Jesus was about to found a community. I hesitated knowing that the German Jesuits expected me to work in Germany with its growing Muslim presence. But I liked the idea, and half a year later it was an open secret that the Jesuits wanted me in Turkey. So I quickly moved to finish my Bamberg studies with a doctorate on contemporary Turkish Qur'an exegesis. Initially Prof. Wielandt was reticent when she heard about the proposal put forward by Christian Troll. But one day she returned from a research tour in Turkey enthusiastically saying that she had found surprising movements of Muslim intellectual life there, especially at Ankara's theological faculty. She became a demanding director and solid supporter of my thesis, which I was able to write already in contact with some Ankara Qur'anic exegetes. I think I was as demanding in criticizing my Muslim counterparts as the director of my thesis was towards me but I still think that any dialogue requires one to say what one sees to be wrong with the other.

Ankara

I spent almost six years in Ankara. I had many friendly relations with Muslim theologians, but also in the workshops of our neighborhood. A young sociologist, Hasan Karaca, now working for the Religious Affairs Directorate, became my teacher; he had grown up in Berlin but returned to Turkey to start a family in the country of his parents. The most exciting thing I did in Ankara was teaching Philosophical Anthropology at the Middle East Technical University. I found interested students and interesting colleagues there, but the former dean, desperate to rebel against the rural Kurdish Islam of his youth, was suspicious of the religious man in the philosophy department. So they discontinued my contract after one term, claiming that I had been reading the Bible instead of philosophy. The claim is grotesquely false, but in one class I had actually read with the students a passage from the book of Ezekiel, explaining the concept of history. The lectures were creative presentations of basic concepts of European reflection. Once they were cancelled, I had time to fulfill a rather surprising new academic task. The Frankfurt Jesuit faculty had invited me to teach a regular course on Islam. I asked also to be accepted as a supervisor of academic theses. That, I learned, was impossible with only a theological degree from Heythrop and a doctorate in Islam. What I needed was an ecclesiastical doctorate. I was disappointed, but once again the shocking message proved to be the key to a greater future. From Ankara, and out of my work there, I wrote a second doctorate, for the University of Fribourg, Switzerland. The director I found (through the internet) was Prof. Barbara Hallensleben. When I googled her, she had just been elected the first woman in the pope's International Theological Commission. I was looking for solid dogmatic theology to guide my theology on Islam, so I proposed the project to her.

I did not know at that time that she is one of the leading theologians of Ignatian Spirituality, the ferment of my own life as a Jesuit! After a theological licentiate, I was able to produce under Hallensleben's supervision a new approach to dialogue between religions. It was, of course, strongly influence by my experience in Ankara, from where I wrote the book.

I should mention three backgrounds to my interreligious theology. The first is the product of my Muslim contacts: I found that the Muslim questions put to Christianity are valid and fundamental challenges. The second background was my companionship with traditional Middle Eastern Christians: Syrian youth groups, Egyptian high school students and Lebanese Jesuits. They all sense that their presence is meaningful although they often cannot name what is the point of Christianity. Finally I was able to accompany a small group of Turks from Muslim families on their spiritual and theological journeys towards baptism; it was not me who had converted them, but I was able to help them shape their understanding of the Good News. The train of thought I developed was this. In the encounter with believers of other religions, I am challenged to witness. What is witnessing? Christian witness is the integration of a historical event in which you are taking part, of my own experience of imperfection that leads to transformation, and the incapacity to make others into convinced Christians by rational arguments: defeat in dispute is no loss for the growth of God's Kingdom but a decisive moment in which God's capacity to act in surprisingly different ways becomes visible.

My systematic theology was shaped by biblical studies; witnessing to God, who is electing his people, became formative for me in presenting and representing Christ. This is perhaps why I am rather allergic to equalizing attempts of natural law thinking or the claim of different revelations. The challenge of Jesus's call is that divine communion depends on our decision for him. This decision, however, is reasoned. Its basis is history opened up for participation in the anticipation of the fullness, in Christ's resurrection.

I am grateful for the initial conditions my family provided but I think I haven't lived only on the provisions they gave me. They rather taught me to find sustenance and redirection from the unexpected interruptions along the road: as Psalm 110 has it, "from the brook by the path."

Intelligence, Humility and Confidence

An Agenda for Christian Engagement with Islam

David Marshall

I first studied Islam as an undergraduate reading theology at Oxford University in the mid-1980s. From where we are now it is striking to recall how marginal the study of Islam (or any other non-Christian religion) was in the Oxford theology faculty at that time. The syllabus was almost entirely focused on the Bible and the development of Christian doctrine, a grounding for which I am very grateful. There was, however, one Finals paper that presented a wider range of options. I originally intended to choose further Old Testament studies but was prompted by a television program on Muslims in Britain to think that learning something about Islam might be wise, particularly if I were to find myself a few years later serving in an Anglican parish with a significant Muslim population. So I chose the course on Islam. Teaching was not by lectures but by one-to-one tutorials so, in the absence of a suitably qualified tutor in the Oxford faculty, I was "farmed out" to Peter Clarke, who taught at King's College, London, but happened to live in Oxford, and I produced a sequence of essays for him.

This term of study was my first serious engagement with Islam. Although my experience has naturally widened since then—through personal contact with Muslims, working with Islamic institutions and some time spent in Muslim majority societies—the academic dimension of the encounter has remained of central importance. The impact of those initial studies was two-fold. First, they provided a way into a fascinating world of which I had previously known very little. I was introduced to Muhammad, the Qur'an, key aspects of the Islamic tradition, and something of the history of Islam. Within it all I was perhaps most struck by Islam's foundational religious vision, at once familiar but also different, bracing but also attractively simple.

Together with this intellectually stimulating experience, however, something else was going on at a different level. It was clear to me from the start that Islam addresses a very direct challenge to Christians, in effect telling them that it presents the final truth about Jesus and about God, truth that Christians may know in part but that they have also seriously distorted with their doctrines (*inter alia*) of the Incarnation, the Trinity, and Atonement. I also knew of those who had converted to Islam; for example, I heard Yusuf Islam (formerly Cat Stevens) address the university's Islamic Society. It therefore seemed obvious that if, after encountering Islam, I was to remain a Christian, I needed to be able to say why. So I needed to think particularly about those aspects of the Christian faith that Islam critiques most forcefully.

Paradoxically enough, that initial course on Islam therefore began a process that drove me deeper into reflection on—and appreciation of—the heart of the Christian faith than any of the courses on Christian theology which I was studying. This is not intended as criticism of those other courses, all of which served me well. Rather, I simply acknowledge my experience that where Christian theology is taught in an entirely or mainly enclosed context, an intra-Christian context with little or no reckoning with alternative understandings of reality, it can be difficult to grasp the shocking distinctiveness of the core Christian convictions about God-in-Christ. It is fundamentally natural for Christian faith to function in cross-reference,[1] interpreting and commending itself beyond its borders to those who think otherwise. Quite apart from the fact that this is simply to obey Christ's commandment to "proclaim the Gospel to the whole creation," it is also a sure way for Christian theology to stay in touch with its own identity and to be animated by the life that flows from its own depths.

This kind of fruitful theological and missiological engagement with "otherness" can happen in an infinite range of interfaces between Christianity and the wider world. This point applies not just to the world's

1. This echoes the suggestive title of Kenneth Cragg's work, *The Christ and the Faiths: Theology in Cross-Reference* (London: SPCK, 1986).

other religions but to all the ideologies and traditions—cultural, social and political—that give shape and meaning to human life. However, I have been especially influenced by the work of three theologians whose immersion in and study of a different religious tradition seems to have imparted a particular profundity to their writing on the Christian faith. John V. Taylor's formative encounter was with African Traditional Religion; Lesslie Newbigin's was with Hinduism in South India; Kenneth Cragg's was with Islam in the Middle East.

Like many others concerned with Christian response to Islam, I have been deeply influenced by Bishop Kenneth Cragg. I first sought him out shortly after my undergraduate studies. The meeting ended, as many have since, with the gift of one of his books, on this occasion *The Call of the Minaret*, inscribed with the Qur'anic text *allahu ghalib 'ala amrihi* ("God prevails in His purpose," Q. 12:21)—which was intriguing but at that stage incomprehensible, as I had yet to learn any Arabic. His writing has addressed a very wide range of themes, extending well beyond Islam, but what I have in the end most valued has been his articulation of core Christian doctrines against the backdrop of how they are seen from an Islamic perspective. Although this is a major concern running through much of his work, I find that I regularly return (particularly in teaching) to his systematic approach to this task of patient exposition in *The Call of the Minaret*.

After my initial study of Islam as an undergraduate, I was keen to go further and in due course became a student at the Centre for the Study of Islam and Christian–Muslim Relations at Selly Oak, Birmingham, first at master's and then at doctoral level. I was fortunate to experience the opportunities provided by the center to study alongside Christian and Muslim students from many parts of the world and a diversity of traditions. It was also good to be taught by distinguished Muslim scholars such as Khalid Alavi. It has since then been axiomatic for me that Christians wanting to study Islam must open themselves to Islamic accounts of Islam and not depend simply on Christian and other non-Islamic sources (as they are all too often inclined to do). I emphasize this point at the beginning of courses I teach at seminaries and churches, encouraging students to supplement what they hear from me, a Christian, with exposure to what Muslims have to say about their own faith, whether through personal contact or through Islamic books, websites, and so forth. I do, however, at the same time question the policy, which some Christian seminaries favor, of handing over the teaching of other faiths entirely to adherents of those faiths. In the context of formation for Christian ministry it seems to me essential that study of other faiths should happen within the context of Christian theological reflection and that students should be led to address theological and practical issues of Christian response, a process that a non-Christian teacher (however sympathetic) cannot be expected to facilitate.

I was fortunate to arrive at Selly Oak just in time to catch David Kerr's last term there and so was able to attend his outstanding course of lectures surveying the history of Christian–Muslim relations. David emphasized the relevance to the encounter between Christians and Muslims of the biblical commandment not to bear false witness against one's neighbor. The long history of casual stereotyping of the other faith and failure to understand it accurately shows how easily this commandment is broken and how much those in teaching roles must strive to avoid doing this.

David suggested as a theme for my Master's thesis the approach to Christianity of the Palestinian Muslim scholar Isma'il al-Faruqi. Al-Faruqi read widely in Christian theology and developed a sharp critique of its central doctrines so I found it a stimulating challenge to digest and analyze his writings. His style was robust and his tone could be withering, as in his account of what he saw as the two fundamental ways in which Christianity (or "Christianism," in his words) had distorted the original message of Jesus through its teachings of humanity's sinful condition ("peccatism") and need of redemption ("saviorism"). So it was a challenging intellectual encounter, but one that introduced me to the value of studying the range of Muslim approaches to Christianity. I see it as a significant part of my role as a teacher within the Church to help Christians grasp something of these "outsider" perspectives on our own faith and practice and also to reflect on what we can and indeed should learn from them. As Robert Burns suggests in his poem, there is in fact a divine gift within the sometimes unsettling experience of learning "to see ourselves as others see us."[2]

At Selly Oak I began to study Arabic and acquired enough to be able to read the Qur'an and make some use of the traditional commentaries. I regret very much that I have not developed my Arabic much beyond that; as a result my access to wider Islamic literature has in effect been limited to what is available in translation. Newcomers to the field would do well to heed Kenneth Cragg's eloquent account in *The Call of the Minaret* of the importance of studying Arabic and the rewards it brings.[3]

2. I explore this theme in a short publication *Learning from How Muslims See Christianity* (Cambridge: Grove Books, 2006).
3. *The Call of the Minaret*, 2nd ed. (Maryknoll: Orbis, 1985), 182–84.

When I began my doctoral research, directed by Christian Troll, I had
as one guiding principle that whatever else I covered I should engage thoroughly with the text of the Qur'an itself, and not simply refer to studies of
it. This reflected both my own enjoyment of detailed textual work but also
a sense that it would be odd to emerge from doctoral studies without a
good working knowledge of the Qur'an, in view of its centrality within
Islam. I soon discovered, however, that many scholars took a different view.
One senior Christian scholar told me that the sensitivities of dialogue made
it much wiser to study *tafsir*, Muslim commentary on the Qur'an, rather
than the scripture itself. On a quite different ideological basis, influenced
by postmodernist literary theory, other scholars expressed the same prefer-
ence for the study of *tafsir* over the Qur'an itself. I nevertheless persevered
with my original plan and my thesis was a study of a particular group of
Qur'anic narratives, which I argued shed interesting light on the evolving
relationship between Muhammad and his opponents.[4] I am grateful to
have had this period of sustained reading of the text at the very heart of
Islam, but must also recognize that whereas my study has generally been
reviewed fairly positively, there has been very little serious response to it by
Muslim scholars. The one notable exception was the external examiner of
the thesis, Mustansir Mir, who commented that although I had dealt with
a sensitive subject I had done so in a way that should not offend religious
sensibilities and that the study should "engage both Muslim and non-Muslim
readers in what is likely to become a highly useful dialogue." My impression,
however, is that Muslims have generally tended either to ignore it or to treat
it with considerable suspicion, with the result that it has made little if any
direct contribution to dialogue. This may simply be a reflection on my own
approach and does not necessarily apply to Christian studies of the Qur'an
more generally. It certainly is the case, however, that when Christians study
the Qur'an itself, rather than some other subject within Islamic studies, they
need to be aware of the particular dynamics that come into play.

Since completing my studies I have worked in various contexts and
capacities. Especially in the wake of 9/11, I was heavily involved for some
years in helping to facilitate and direct a number of initiatives taken by
the archbishop of Canterbury in Christian–Muslim relations, such as the
dialogue between al-Azhar al-Sharif and the Anglican Communion and the
creation of the Christian–Muslim Forum for England. It is clearly very
desirable that good structures for dialogue and cooperation between the

---

4. A slightly revised version was published as *God, Muhammad and the Unbelievers*
(Richmond: Curzon, 1999).

faiths should be put in place and it was satisfying to have some part in such work and to see initiatives develop and bear some fruit.

However, anyone who has worked on dialogue processes such as these, particularly when they include venerable religious institutions, will also know something of the frustrations involved. Sometimes difficult negotiations have to happen before certain kinds of dialogue can even begin. I recall protracted disagreements over the wording of communiqués taking up the greater part of dialogue meetings. One major disappointment occurred when, at the last minute, the delegation from al-Azhar pulled out of its annual meeting with the Anglican Communion delegation; this had been due to happen in New York at the invitation of the local Episcopalian bishop but al-Azhar decided that the recent election of an openly homosexual bishop to another diocese of the Episcopal Church of the USA made its participation impossible. At such moments it is important to remember that, in view of all the historical conflict and current tensions in Christian–Muslim relations, such setbacks are fairly minor and perhaps almost inevitable. If one keeps going, derailed processes will often come back on track; this was indeed true with the dialogue involving al-Azhar, which was soon functioning again and is still running some years on.

Much of the work in which I was involved on behalf of the archbishop of Canterbury did not draw particularly on my earlier studies. The notable exception was the Building Bridges Seminar for Christian and Muslim scholars, held annually since 2002. After leaving the archbishop's staff I have continued to facilitate Building Bridges and currently serve as its academic director. In contrast to the other dialogues mentioned above, this process specifically aims to draw scholars together in detailed discussion of theological themes in the interface between the two faiths. A particular emphasis has been the study of texts, usually but not exclusively scriptural texts. (Here then, at least, years of study of both the Bible and the Qur'an have proved an asset in the work of facilitating Christian–Muslim dialogue.) Over eight seminars, a wide range of themes has been tackled—including scripture, prophecy, law and rights, hermeneutics, and the relationship between science and religion. The Building Bridges process has become a major priority of Archbishop Rowan Williams and has flourished partly due to the enthusiastic support of Georgetown University. It has also become very important to a number of scholars, who find in it a comparatively unusual opportunity for dialogue focused unapologetically on theological questions.

A lesson that I have learnt through involvement in varied approaches to Christian–Muslim dialogue, such as those mentioned above, is precisely that a variety of approaches is needed to do justice to the multifaceted reality of Christian–Muslim encounter. Each approach has its own contribution to make and should not try to do everything. The Christian–Muslim Forum, for example, was formed after extensive grassroots-level consultations and has a primarily practical focus on issues such as conversions between the faiths and the development of interfaith work with teenagers. Building Bridges, in contrast, has a quite different, much more academic agenda and its goal is essentially the promotion of intelligent conversation between Christian and Muslim scholars. Whereas the work of the Christian–Muslim Forum is focused in England, Building Bridges has brought together scholars from many countries and has taken place in a variety of contexts around the world. There may, of course, be overlap at some points between the different processes but their methods are quite different. My involvement in Christian–Muslim dialogue is now almost entirely focused on Building Bridges. This makes good use of my academic training and I find it fascinating, satisfying, and challenging work. Like all approaches to dialogue, it has its limitations and to some observers it may appear too academic, but I believe that it makes a valuable contribution and that it should maintain its distinctive focus.

I am glad to have had these opportunities to facilitate Muslim–Christian dialogue and cooperation and I especially value my continuing role in the Building Bridges process. Alongside such work, however, I have always felt that an important aspect of my vocation is as a teacher within the Church. So in more recent years, I have made myself available to teach courses on Islam and Christian–Muslim relations in a variety of contexts such as seminaries, clergy conferences, and local churches. The underlying rationale is that the great majority of Western Christians need some help both to understand the basic beliefs and practices of Islam and also to reflect on Christian responses to Islam. One concern, which I share particularly with my mentor and friend Christian Troll, is that whereas Muslims tend to approach encounters and discussions with Christians with considerable confidence, basically because they are taught a clear view of Christianity as they are brought up in their faith, Christians are generally uninformed and unconfident, especially in dealing with the critical questions posed by Muslims about Christianity.[5] Thankfully, however, many Christians are now recognizing this and in a variety of contexts, across the ecclesial

5. I have translated from German two works of Christian Troll that seek to help Christians engage intelligently and confidently in dialogue with Muslims: *Muslims Ask, Christians Answer* (Anand: Gujarat Sahitya Prakash, 2007), also available online

traditions, I have found people highly motivated to learn about Islam and to reflect on the implications of what they learn for their own faith and practice as Christians.

It has seemed to me a particular priority to provide such teaching in the context of ministerial training, thus helping to equip those who will be leading and teaching congregations for decades to come. This has been stimulating and rewarding work, but within the Church of England it has only really been possible to do it by accepting the necessity of a largely freelance role, interacting with a number of theological institutions but on the margins of them all. This situation reflects some specific features of the Church of England, in which theological training takes place in a multitude of often very small institutions with correspondingly small faculties, within nearly all of which there is naturally no scope for posts in Islamic studies or even world religions. Broadly speaking it seems that other specialists in Islamic studies in the Church of England have either gone into university posts or are working in the wider field of interfaith relations, often as diocesan advisors. In both these roles it is of course possible to varying degrees to make a contribution to teaching within the Church but that can by definition hardly be the primary purpose of either. Thus even though there is much recognition in the Church of England of the need for an informed understanding of Islam, its present structures are not particularly well geared to encouraging and nurturing academic specialists in this field or to providing clear outlets for the use of such academic expertise within its own theological institutions. Although in other Christian denominations and in other countries the opportunities may be rather different, it is probably as well to accept that a vocation to study and teach about a different religious tradition may well lead to some degree of marginality in relation to church institutions. Depending on one's feelings about church institutions, and the availability or otherwise of alternative sources of income, such marginality may or may not seem an attractive proposition.

It is sometimes said by those engaged in interfaith dialogue that whatever its challenges might be these can be dwarfed by those of the accompanying *intra*-faith dialogue, the debates and controversies that can develop among Christians as they consider their responses to another faith such as Islam. A wide spectrum of questions has to be addressed, touching on (among other matters) doctrine, liturgy, mission, and the place of religion in public life. Christians display very different underlying instincts in

at www.answers-to-muslims.com, and *Dialogue and Difference: Clarity in Christian–Muslim Dialogue* (Maryknoll: Orbis, 2009).

dealing with such questions and their differences can lead to vitriolic exchanges. The stakes can seem very high on either side, with tensions exacerbated by a sense that those with whom one disagrees are either obscurantists blocking the way to the more harmonious coexistence of faiths which the world so urgently needs or, conversely, politically correct liberals betraying the Gospel entrusted to the Church. Although I have my own views on what are authentic Christian responses to Islam, in my teaching I try as far as I can to help students to understand the approaches of other Christians and to recognize what they can learn from them.

Through my work in this field I have also come to experience Christian diversity in a much more positive sense. Engagement with Islam has probably been the main route through which I have been led to an enlarged sense of the Body of Christ. This enlargement has been both in geographical terms and in terms of different Christian traditions. Through learning about Christian–Muslim relations and through visits to different parts of the Muslim world, I have been enriched by my experience of various churches. I think, for example, of encounters with the Coptic Orthodox tradition, including vibrant youth meetings in Cairo and the stillness of the monasteries of Wadi Natrun. In my work I have naturally learnt a great deal from Christian scholars of Islam from other traditions, especially Roman Catholics, and am very grateful for opportunities to work together across denominational boundaries.

I was once asked to summarize what I felt were the most pressing needs in the development of Christian responses to Islam. The answer I gave is one to which I often return as a rationale and an agenda for my work. Christian responses to Islam should be characterized by intelligence, humility, and confidence: the intelligence that seeks an accurate and sympathetic understanding of Islam; the humility that is open to what God may have to teach us through our encounters with Muslims; the confidence that is willing and able to give an account of the Gospel of Jesus Christ, to Muslims as to all other people. In each category I am conscious of how much progress is needed, both in myself and in the wider Church.

So What Have We Learned?

Christian W. Troll and C. T. R. Hewer

When the disciples of John saw Jesus, they asked him "Teacher, where do you live?" and he replied "Come and see" (John 1:38–30). The importance of place, institution and teacher as the *loci* for engagement in the study by Christians of Islam shines out from these articles. If one were to trace the circles of influence of men like Georges Anawati, Maurice Borrmans, Robert Caspar, Kenneth Cragg, Jacques Jomier, David Kerr, and Christian Troll as they run through the lives of the authors, then one would see that so many lives have been influenced by "sitting at the feet of the master." Four from this list have died and the youngest of the others is in his seventies; "surely this is a sign for the people who reflect" as the Qur'an would remind us (Q. 10:24).

From ancient times, scholars have grouped themselves into centers where their study can influence their colleagues and where they can receive students. The centrality of centers like IDEO in Cairo, the Arabic language centre (CREA) at Bikfaya, Lebanon, PISAI in Rome, and the centers at Hartford and Selly Oak radiate their importance as places where people study and teach, where visiting scholars pass through and where libraries are collected. Some of them have already closed and others are shadows of their former glories; without such centers, where do we send the next generation of students?

Glimpsing the Vision

There was a profound sense of the Spirit moving in the 1960s at the Second Vatican Council, the influence of which has been noted often. The key documents of *Lumen Gentium, Gaudium et Spes, Dignitatis Humanae*, and *Nostra Aetate* come to mind; these were bracketed by the pioneering work of Popes Paul VI and John Paul II. This was compounded by the Christian ecumenical movement that swept to life in the latter part of the twentieth century. Many of the contributors to this book had studied and taught in centers founded outside their own Christian tradition and the influence of ecumenical activities was often the first broadening of a vision that went beyond the visible Christian family to embrace the greater ecumenism of the whole of humanity under God and thus to include Islam. This broadening encompassed challenging ways of speaking about God, prompted by the study of Islamic theology, breaking new ground on the dignity and integrity of the human person, indeed to a new theological world view. Seminal theologians of this period opened up new vistas beyond what the authors could have imagined once their work passed into the hands of Christian students of Islam. The short book by Karl Rahner in the *Quaestiones Disputatae* series titled *Visions and Prophecies (Visionen und Prophezeiungen)*, for example, prompted thoughts about the status of Muhammad within the biblical model of prophecy. International experiences and undertakings and the meeting of Christians and Muslims on the institutional level prompted local Christian–Muslim initiatives to flourish.

A strong sense comes through these pages of being open to the promptings of the Holy Spirit to engage in this work. Sometimes this is manifested through family, youth or student activities, sometimes it is a response "in obedience" to a superior, which is only understood much later, sometimes as a vicarious atonement for the injustices of the colonial period, sometimes in a desire to see the arrival of Muslim communities in Europe as an opportunity for a fresh start in Christian–Muslim relations, and sometimes the workings of Providence remain a mystery to this day. A strong emphasis is given to living by Gospel values and thus displaying the living gospel written on our hearts. This work requires the dedication of sacrifice, for extended study or travels, and service to the community far from home. Such a life, characterized by self-sacrificing love, in which the "second mile" is always to be expected, becomes a norm of life for many. Witnessing the sacrificial love of one's teachers and confrères prompts humility and an openness to embrace a similar gesture oneself.

Many of the Catholic contributors are members of religious orders in which the charism of the founder or the inherited apostolate is central to this engagement. The counsel of St. Ignatius to seek the best possible interpretation of what our partner says and does rather than to rush to find fault with it can serve as an inspiration for a far wider circle than the Jesuits alone. The pioneering commitment of an earlier generation, like Louis Massignon and Georges Anawati, can provide a vision that can sustain one for decades. Part of the anxiety at the decline in the number of Christian students of Islam in Europe is mirrored in the decline in men and women entering the religious orders that not only provided an inspiration and a supportive community but also funded the years of study required. The customary spiritual training in these religious orders also provided the basis for developing spiritual gifts, like the discipline of contemplative study or the gift of discernment, which are so necessary for the Christian to discern the Spirit of God at work in Islam and Muslims. The centrality of Bible study and *lectio divina* have been noted. More reflection is needed to map out various ways in which the spiritual infrastructure can be developed and strengthened to provide the necessary inner strength to sustain the journey of study and relationship building.

Because I am a priest, says one writer, I am interested in all matters religious, all values and spiritual insights. How is this work then a priestly vocation? The presence of a minister of the Church engaged in study and practical work with Muslims is a powerful sign in two directions. It is a sign that the Church itself is interested and committed to this work and it is a channel through which local engagement can be telegraphed higher into the councils of Church leaders. But is it a priestly ministry? The priestly office has about it the character of being a channel through which the transforming divine love is poured out in this world. The priest, in a particular way, represents the Christian presence within society, through which Christians are called to be a sacrament of encounter with God. As a "man of God" as one writer puts it, the Christian priest amongst Muslims bears witness, through life, intellect, spirit, and service, that the redemptive presence of Christ is active in such work in a special way.

There is naturally another side to being a Christian minister engaged in such work that requires no less endurance and spiritual strength and that is learning to live with misunderstandings, suspicions, indifference, and outright objections from Muslims, fellow Christians, members of one's family or religious community, and indeed from the Church authorities themselves. It requires a special sort of spiritual discipline to live with such negative appraisals of one's lifework and still to persevere to the end. Christian–Muslim study and encounter is no place for spiritual softies!

Setting Off on the Journey

The very nature of this set of collected articles demonstrates that the Christian study of Islam is a long-term commitment that brooks no short-cuts. For almost all of the contributors, the first step on the journey is through language acquisition. Many were fortunate enough to go through the kind of schooling system that saw people leave school with one or two ancient languages, which were normally augmented during initial theological education, and a couple of modern languages, which provide the basic tools to reach the starting point. Such a humanist education is often less prevalent in the modern period than it was fifty-plus years ago. Acquiring the languages of Islamic scholarship, the keys to understanding the literary, cultural, and civilizational heritage of Muslims is a task that can take many years. Many writers have gained proficiency in up to four such languages during their careers. Such language learning was normally accompanied by traveling in the Muslim world for study, immersion, and seeking the company of Muslim fellow students.

Once the languages have been mastered, they become the tools for an in-depth study of the corpus of Islamic scholarship; the ideal being to achieve such mastery that one wins the respect and admiration of Muslims. With this goes the study of those periods in history and intellectual meeting places where Muslims and Christians were engaged in joint philosophical and theological struggles, striving to expound common themes to the extent that cross-fertilization can take place. There is an experience of learning the lessons of history so that the negative ones are not repeated and positively allowing one's expectations to be raised by the achievements of past generations. It is here that one encounters the interactions of our two principal faiths with Judaism, Hinduism, and Buddhism, the fruits of which can contribute both in terms of methodology and insight into the Christian–Muslim crucible today.

All our contributors have at some stage made the transition from student to teacher; here the challenges of teaching become a fecund spur to further and integrated study. An oft-recurring concern is to keep the focus on the religious, spiritual and theological encounter, one of faith seeking understanding, rather than becoming consumed in the socio-political dimensions of Christian–Muslim relations. Taking the faith of the other seriously leads to a desire to know Islam through the texts that are important to Muslims, above all through an in-depth study of the Qur'an, Hadith, and Muslim exegetical tradition, where academic study transforms into a psycho-spiritual understanding of the part that these source texts play in the living faith of Muslims.

Such academic textual study has in several cases been enhanced and deepened by a study of the Sufi writings, thus entering into the very soul of Islamic spirituality. Such a study cannot be academic alone and many contributors record the transformative effect of both study and experience of the Sufi tradition along with Muslim adepts and practitioners. The living out of the fruits of such experience in Muslims' daily lives gives another dimension to the immersion in Muslim communities where faith transforms practice. So many reinforcements of the centrality of hospitality: to be a guest, both physically and spiritually, in the embrace of living Islam. In this regard, the importance of pilgrimage has been noted, both in the travelling and on arriving in centers of Muslim pilgrimage (for example, at the shrine of a Muslim saint) where members of both faiths can truly stand in the presence of God in a particular way.

A feature both of some of the centers established for study and in the individual experience of traveling for the benefit of one's education is that a particularly rich conjunction is created when Muslims and Christians work together at joint ventures. Such teamwork can range from the social to the academic; it may be small-scale or involve the great intellectual institutions of both traditions. It promotes an intellectual sensitivity through working with Muslims and not just studying about them. Such "being together before God" gives rise to the imperative to struggle together to defend human dignity and cooperate for the benefit of all humanity; thus joint spiritual and intellectual endeavor transforms into joint outreach to humankind.

Such an engagement with Islam raises for Christian students the necessary question of how to handle the ongoing and fundamental challenges to Christian faith and theology that are posed by Islam. Such theological challenges need to be taken seriously; they have been around for a long time and will not go away. By paying attention to what Muslims are saying about Christianity, the student is brought to consider what God might be saying to Christians through these very theological challenges, which brings with it the invitation to revisit and refine our understanding and exposition of Christian doctrines. Engaging with the Muslim intellectual tradition can indeed be the seedbed for fresh Christian theological thinking and invites all to humility in sharing openly the provisional nature of both faiths' attempts to speak about the ineffable God. Several contributors have noted the imbalance between Christian scholars' knowledge of Islam and Muslim scholars' knowledge of Christianity which is a source of frequent frustration. Both Christians and Muslims engaged in this way have to address the desire of both communities that the other should "know Christ" or "see the truth of Islam" and thus convert; is it possible to distinguish between this desire and the explicit invitation to convert, and at the same time leave open the possibility that God may call a believer to leave one tradition and embrace the other? However this issue is resolved by the individual, there is an affirmation that dialogue is a journey of faith that begins with God and brings people back to God.

As one contributor notes, Muslims want to hear from their Christian dialogue partners a clear and comprehensible account of what Christians believe and of the Christian theological tradition. This requires not only a solid theological training on the part of the Christian student but also the ability to communicate such knowledge in a way that is comestible for Muslims; it requires knowledge, communication skills and confidence. Similarly the Christian student is often called back to reflect on the various branches of Christian theology with the benefit of the perspective gained from an encounter with Islam. How are we to build this into our theological education, especially in contexts in which Christians and Muslims are sharing common territory and citizenship?

Muslim Fellow Travelers

The task of the Christian student engaged with Islam is in part to build long-term friendships whereby one learns through the living reality of Muslim faith in addition to the texts already mentioned. The long-term dimension is important, as this promotes a spirit of honest human exploration in which "the talk" must be transformed into "the walk" alongside Muslims. Many of the contributors to this book have done this by living with Muslims, alongside Muslim communities, working with Muslim fellow teachers, traveling with Muslims and learning from their students while teaching and from their fellow students while studying. Such living side by side needs to be done in a deliberate and conscious way, notes one writer; the mere fact of running a mission school, for example, does not of itself bring one into the spirit of encounter. Like any relationship, this is a journey in faith and there are pitfalls on the way; the key is "to listen for the call of God at every step."

Friendship leads to study, as I seek to know more about my friend, but it also promotes an interaction between intuitive and intellective knowledge; what do I know of my friend in my heart and how can I make sense of that knowledge intellectually? Such relationships might not always be on the individual level alone, as those contributors with many years of experience in living in grassroots Muslim communities note, one can draw from the natural piety of the people amongst whom one lives and works. As with all relationships, the key is genuine love and not affectation, so that the heart can speak to the heart of the other in the Spirit of God in sighs too deep for words. The spirit that is noted is one of being a fellow pilgrim on the spiritual path, like fellow guests in the Tent of Abraham. There comes to many contributors the profound knowledge of the heart, of the indwelling virtues of love, compassion, and kindness that can only arise in the lover of God.

Language plays its own part in spiritual development. When Christians and Muslims share a common language—Arabic, Urdu, Swahili, other African languages, Turkish, Indonesian, English, or French—it operates on deeper levels and necessarily promotes a spiritual sharing. In such a situation, there is an openness to the sudden in-breaking of the Spirit of God. Christians, individually or collectively become the presence of the Living Christ in the midst of a Muslim community. Only this kind of experience can equip the Christian teacher to initiate other Christian students into this work. It requires a certain "lingering with intent" and is likely to be fostered by a steaming teapot or the gurgle of coffee rather than by hastening towards an end. Based on these, there develops the capacity for the pastoral support of those who engage in this dialogue, whether through work, study, or marriage, just as the Christian student of Islam is supported by a wife or husband, a religious community, or friends.

Safeguarding and Deepening One's Christian Faith

The work of Christian–Muslim study and dialogue is necessarily "living on the margins"; how then does one develop and preserve one's Christian faith? The universal starting point for all contributors is a solid Christian theological education of a kind that is still commonplace in some parts of the Western Church but has been eroded in others for the sake of making up the shortfall in numbers entering active ministry. This is not the ministry for theological lightweights. There is the need for combining fidelity to the Christian heritage and core faith with the ability to think theologically in new ways. The commandment "not to bear false witness" must operate in both directions. Such a deep grounding allows the student to develop reconciliation to the divine will and fidelity even in the face of the apparently unfathomable workings of God.

The structured discipline of a daily routine of prayer, in-depth Bible study and the ruminative reflection on the sacred texts of the Christian tradition (indeed some contributors would add the meditative reading of the Qur'an and other Muslim spiritual texts) becomes the bedrock. For many contributors, this is centered around the frequent or daily celebration of the Eucharist as the place of ultimate transformative encounter. Breaking the Word and breaking the bread sustain what one author describes as a spirituality based on "an experiential relationship with the person of Christ." For most of our contributors, this is sustained through a fellowship with those who tread the same path and thus meeting places, like the former Journées Romaines, become an important factor. Such fellowship can be a critical part in maintaining an enthusiasm that can sustain faith in times of weariness, aloneness, helplessness, and indeed distress.

An emphasis on contemplation comes up frequently in these accounts; the prayer of the heart in deep communion with the One, the Supreme Being, the unique source, flow, and quality of life and love that we term God. Such a contemplation expands the heart to engage with the divine mystery, especially in God's dealings with "the nations." Through contemplation, the student is taken deeper into fathoming the mysteries that lie at the core of particular Christian faith: the fellowship of the Trinity, the paradigm shift of the Incarnation, and the ramifications of the redemption wrought in the life, death, and resurrection of Christ. It is through contemplation that the person undergoes the spiritual "purification of the heart," with all the overtones of the Sufi system and tradition, that enables words and actions to flow in a translucent way from the cultivated heart in which the Spirit of God has made her dwelling.

The priest, as instrument of sacramental transformation and as "official representative" of the Body of Christ, has a special part to play in this work, not only as the bearer of the Church's mandate but also as the locus of intercession "for all manner of people" through which the Christian shares in the redemptive work of Christ reconciling the world to God.

The Wider Outworking of This Special Ministry

The most obvious outworking of this ministry of Christians amongst Muslims is that of teaching in all its forms, so that the specialist knowledge accumulated can be transferred to humanity at large. One particular contribution of almost all of our authors has been through the apostolate of writing and publishing to disseminate knowledge and strengthen those already in the field. Appropriate structures are needed to carry on this work: personnel, institutions, and support from the churches. We need to consider this especially in the changing faith composition of Europe and North America, on the one hand, and in realization that the numerical concentration in both communities is moving rapidly towards Africa and Asia, on the other. How are we to include in the training of ministers and teachers a study of Islam and Muslims—both in a discrete way, as befits the integrity of another faith community, but also integrated into the theological curriculum—so that the critical voice of Islam might be heard and considered?

This educative process goes both ways as one outworking of this ministry is to make the fruits of contemporary academic methods accessible to Muslims in their effort to deepen their knowledge of their own Islamic tradition with a view to the promotion of a critical and self-critical mind among believers.

There is an impact on ecumenism through this work. First, to contribute to intra-Christian ecumenism by scholarly working together to heal the wounds of Christian division, which are perceived as scandalous by many Muslims. Second, to take seriously the reality of the Word of God speaking in the lives of all human beings and that Christ fundamentally changes the human condition for all women and men, so that the Body of Christ is seen to be expanded to embrace not just the visible Church but also the whole of humanity, thus provoking an emphasis on a Kingdom-orientated mission rather than one limited to the visible Church. This will have its impact on working with Muslims and all humanity to build the Kingdom through local and global justice, peace, and harmony. In this way, this work is part of the universal mission of Christ reconciling the world to God.

Sebastiano D'Ambra (b. 1942) was born in Italy and ordained priest in 1966. He is a member of the Pontificio Istituto Missioni Estere (PIME) and was assigned to the mission in the Philippines in 1977. He studied Islam at PISAI, Rome, and then pursued a doctoral degree in the Philippines on education, peace, and development. He was appointed regional superior of the PIME in the Philippines in 1983, and in 1984 he founded the Silsilah Dialogue Movement in Zamboanga City, Mindanao. From 1979–81 he acted as negotiator for the Moro National Liberation Front (MNLF) to achieve peace in Mindanao.

Maurice Borrmans (b. 1925) studied in Lille, Tunisia, and Paris. He is a member of the Missionaries of Africa and has taught in Tunisia, Algeria, and from 1964–2004 at PISAI, Rome, where he specialized in Arabic language, Islamic law, mysticism, and the history of Christian–Muslim relations. He has been a long-serving counselor for the Pontifical Council for Interreligious Dialogue and is the author of numerous books and articles. Since 2005 he has resided in France where he continues to study and publish.

David Burrell, C.S.C. (b. 1933), Theodore Hesburgh Professor emeritus in Philosophy and Theology at the University of Notre Dame, Indiana, is now serving his Holy Cross community in East Africa. Efforts since 1982 in comparative issues in philosophical theology in Judaism, Christianity, and Islam are evidenced in comparative studies and two translations: *Al-Ghazali on the Ninety-Nine Beautiful Names of God* (1993) and *Al-Ghazali on Faith in Divine Unity and Trust in Divine* Providence (2001).

Kenneth Cragg (b. 1913) has served as both scholar and bishop in the lands of the Middle East and has also held academic posts in the United Kingdom, Lebanon, Nigeria, and the United States. His numerous and wide-ranging publications include *The Call of the Minaret*, *The Event of the Qur'an*, and *Muhammad and the Christian*. The archbishop of Canterbury has written of his "uniquely rich contribution to the life and mission of the Anglican Communion." A former Bye-Fellow of Gonville and Caius College, Cambridge, he now lives in Oxford, where he is an Honorary Fellow of Jesus College.

Joseph Ellul (b. 1960) joined the Order of Preachers (Dominicans) in 1976. He was ordained priest in 1985. He is currently Professor of Ecumenical Theology and Islamic Studies at the Pontificia Studiorum Universitas a S. Thoma Aquinate in Urbe (The Angelicum), Rome, and visiting professor of Islamic Philosophy at PISAI. He also lectures in Islamic studies at the University of Malta and is the president of the Commission for Interreligious Dialogue for the Archdiocese of Malta. He serves as a consulter to the Pontifical Council for Interreligious Dialogue.

Michael L. Fitzgerald (b. 1937) is a member of the Society of Missionaries of Africa (White Fathers). He studied in Rome and London and taught in Uganda and at the Pontifical Institute of Arabic and Islamic Studies, Rome. After a period on the General Council of the Missionaries of Africa 1980–86, he was appointed as secretary of the Pontifical Council for Interreligious Dialogue (ordained bishop 1992) and in 2002 he became its president and an archbishop. Since February 2006, he is the Apostolic Nuncio in Egypt and delegate to the League of Arab States.

Jean-Marie Gaudeul (b. 1937) is a Catholic priest in the Society of Missionaries of Africa (White Fathers) and worked for several years as a parish priest in Tanzania. He taught at PISAI, Rome (1975–82) and at the Catholic University, Paris (1985–2000). His doctoral dissertation dealt with the history of Christian–Muslim encounters and controversies. From 2000 to 2006, he was head of the French Bishops' Service for Catholic–Muslim relations. He has lectured in a number of African and Asian countries. He now lives in Paris and publishes *Se Comprendre*, a bulletin for Christian–Muslim understanding.

C. T. R. Hewer (b. 1952) studied Christian theology, education and Islamic studies mainly in Birmingham, Liverpool, and Manchester. He was a member of the Centre for the Study of Islam and Christian–Muslim Relations, Selly Oak, from 1986, and was adviser on Inter-Faith Relations to the Bishop of Birmingham (1999–2005). From 2006–10 he was St. Ethelburga Fellow in Christian–Muslim Relations in London.

Paul Jackson (b. 1937) was born in Brisbane, Australia. He joined the Society of Jesus in 1956 and came to India in 1961. After the normal period of Jesuit training, followed by working as a priest with tribal people, he continued his studies in Medieval Indian History, Urdu, and Persian. He completed doctoral research into the life and teaching of Sharafuddin Maneri in 1980. Since then he has been translating Maneri's writings, meeting Muslims, conducting courses on Islam, and playing an active role in the Islamic Studies Association.

FELIX KÖRNER (b. 1963) joined the Jesuits in 1985. He received his PhD in 2003 and STD in 2007. After a six-year assignment in Ankara, he is now directing the Interdisciplinary Institute of the Gregorian University, Rome, where Christians and non-Christians are trained for interreligious encounter. He teaches theology of religions and sacraments.

MICHEL LAGARDE (b. 1939) is professor of Arabic and Qur'anic Exegesis at PISAI, Rome. He is a Member of the Missionaries of Africa and, in that capacity, spent ten years in Mali. His principal publications are: *Index du Grand Commentaire de F.D. al-Râzî* (Brill, 1996), the complete translation into French of *Le Livre des Haltes of 'Abd al-Qâdir al-Jazâ'irî* (Brill, 2000, 2001, 2002), and *Les Secrets e l'Invisible: Essai sur le Grand Commentaire de F.D. al-Râzî* (Albouraq, 2009). He was awarded the Sharjah Prize for Arabic Culture from UNESCO in 2005 and the Book of the Year Prize from the Iranian Ministry of Culture in 2011.

CHRISTOPHER LAMB (b. 1939) is an Anglican priest. After Oxford University, he worked in a north London parish, and then as a CMS missionary in Pakistan. Returning to the United Kingdom in 1975 he worked in interfaith relations in Birmingham and Coventry, becoming a Canon Theologian of Coventry Cathedral and the staff member for Interfaith Relations in both the Anglican Board of Mission and Churches Together in Britain and Ireland. His final ministerial post was as incumbent of four village churches in south Warwickshire. In retirement he writes and chairs the local interfaith forum.

DANIEL MADIGAN (b. 1954) is an Australian Jesuit who has also studied and taught in India, Pakistan, Egypt, Turkey, Italy, and the United States. From 2000 to 2007 he was the founding director of the Institute for the Study of Religions and Cultures at the Pontifical Gregorian University, Rome. He currently directs a PhD program in Religious Pluralism at Georgetown University in Washington, DC. He also is a Senior Fellow in the Al-Waleed Center for Muslim-Christian Understanding and in the Woodstock Theological Center, where he directs a program on Christian Theologies Responsive to Islam.

DAVID MARSHALL (b. 1963), a priest in the Church of England, studied theology at Oxford and Islamic studies at Birmingham. He has worked in Christian–Muslim relations in various contexts, including a period with responsibility for the interfaith work of the archbishop of Canterbury. He has taught on Islam and Christian–Muslim relations in many seminaries and universities. He currently works in partnership with Georgetown University, Washington, DC, as academic director of the archbishop of Canterbury's Building Bridges Seminar, a dialogue process bringing together Christian and Muslim scholars. He lives with his wife and two sons in Cumbria, in the north of England.

JANE MCAULIFFE (b. 1944) is president of Bryn Mawr College and formerly dean of the College at Georgetown University. Her research focuses on the Qur'an, early Islamic history, and the interactions of Islam and Christianity. She has recently published the six-volume *Encyclopaedia of the Qur'an* (Brill, 2001–6) and is the author or editor of the *Cambridge Companion to the Qur'an* (Cambridge, 2006), *With Reverence for the Word* (Oxford, 2002), *Abbasid Authority Affirmed* (SUNY, 1995) and *Qur'anic Christians* (Cambridge, 1991). President McAuliffe is the recipient of fellowships from the National Endowment for the Humanities, the Mellon Foundation, the Rockefeller Foundation, and the Guggenheim Foundation. She is an elected member of the American Philosophical Society and the Council on Foreign Relations.

THOMAS MICHEL (b. 1941) is a Jesuit priest of the Indonesian province. After receiving a PhD in Islamic theology at the University of Chicago, he taught in Indonesia, then served as head of the Office for Islam in the Vatican, ecumenical and interreligious secretary for the Federation of Asian Bishops' Conferences, and secretary for Dialogue for the Society of Jesus. In addition to Indonesia and Turkey, he has also taught in the Philippines, Malaysia, Thailand, Albania, Italy, and the United States. He is now a parish priest and teaches theology in Ankara, Turkey.

CHRISTIAAN VAN NISPEN TOT SEVENAER (b. 1938) was born in the Netherlands and entered the Society of Jesus in 1955. He studied in the Netherlands, Lebanon, Cairo, Lyons, and Paris. For more than forty years, Cairo has been the center of his engagement with Islam, teaching in the Coptic Catholic seminary there and engaging in many philosophical and theological encounters. He is the author of several books and numerous articles.

EMILIO PLATTI (b. 1943) was born in Belgium and professed in the Dominican Order in 1962. He studied both Theology and Arabic Language at the Catholic University of Leuven, from where he holds a doctorate in Oriental studies. He taught at Leuven (1980–2008) and at the Facultés Universitaires de Namur (1990–2008); simultaneously he was a member of IDEO, Cairo, from 1972 until the present. He is visiting professor at UST, Manila, and editor of *MIDEO* (*Mélanges de l'Institut Dominicain d'Études Orientales du Caire*).

Lucie Pruvost (b. 1932) was born in Bouïra, Algeria. After school in Algeria, she entered the Missionary Sisters of Africa (MSOLA) in 1958. She studied personal, civil, and criminal law in Tunisia (1968–72), and received her doctorate from Paris in 1977. She taught in Tunis (1972–76), at the Institute of Canon Law of Paris (1978–80), in Algeria (Centre d'Etudes Diocésain, 1981–2004), and at PISAI, Rome, from 1982–2002. Since 2005 she is a member of the secretariat of her order in Rome.

Etienne Renaud (b. 1936), a member of the Society of Missionaries of Africa, studied in Paris, Damascus, and Rome, and has worked in Tunisia, the Yemen, Zanzibar, and Sudan. He twice served on the staff at PISAI, Rome, and was superior general of his order (1986–92) during which appointment he traveled extensively throughout Africa. He now works in a largely Muslim quarter of Marseille.

Arij Roest Crollius (b. 1933) was born in Tilburg, The Netherlands, and joined the Society of Jesus in 1952. He received his academic formation at the universities in Nijmegen, Beirut, Cairo, Rome, Bombay, Jerusalem, and Kyoto. Between 1974 and 2005, the center of his activities was the Gregorian University in Rome. Since 2005 he has been teaching theology and the history of religions at the Jesuit Institute of Theology in Abidjan, Côte d'Ivoire.

Patrick Ryan (b. 1939), a member of the Society of Jesus, became the McGinley Professor of Religion and Society at Fordham University in New York in 2009. He earned a doctorate at Harvard University in the comparative history of religion, specializing in Arabic and Islamic studies. In 1964 he began a long career as a teacher and academic administrator in West Africa, where he spent twenty-six years. He is the author of three books and numerous articles, scholarly and popular. As McGinley Professor, Fr. Ryan hopes to establish a "trialogue" of Judaism, Christianity, and Islam at Fordham.

Giuseppe Scattolin (b. 1942) was born in Italy. He is a member of the congregation of Comboni missionaries, and has studied and worked in the

Arabic-speaking world since 1969. He studied in Milan, Lebanon, Cairo, Rome, Yale, and London. His particular field of specialization is Islamic mysticism. He is professor of Sufism at PISAI, Rome, and at Dar Comboni in Cairo. He taught also comparative religion at the Theological Institute, Sakakini, Cairo. He has written several books and articles on Sufism.

SIGVARD VON SICARD (b. 1930) was born in Southern Rhodesia (now Zimbabwe). Growing up in a totally African setting infused him with a love for Africa and the Africans. Theological studies in South Africa and Uppsala (1949–54), Islamic studies in Hartford (with Kenneth Cragg 1954–55) and Cairo (with E. E. Calverley 1955–56). Posted to Tanganyika (now Tanzania), he was involved in education and schools in the Dar es Salaam Region (1956–65), before teaching at Makumira Theological College (1965–68). In 1970 he moved to the Selly Oak Colleges, where he was a founder-member of the Centre for the Study of Islam and Christian–Muslim Relations. Since 1996 Honorary Senior Research Fellow, University of Birmingham. His specialist area is Islam and Christian–Muslim relations in Africa, on which subject he has and continues to publish extensively.

JAN SLOMP (b. 1932) studied theology and Islam at: Free University in Amsterdam, 1951–60 and Graduate School of Ecumenical Studies, World Council of Churches, 1958–59. He was ordained in Zijldijk in 1962. Other appointments include: district missionary, Sahiwal, Pakistan 1964–68; Christian Study Centre, Rawalpindi, 1968–77; Islam Desk Reformed Churches in the Netherlands 1977–94; Islam in Europe Committee, Conference of European Churches and Council of Roman Catholic Episcopal Conferences, 1978–97). Publications, until 1994 listed in G.M. Speelman, ed., *Muslims and Christians in Europe. Breaking New Ground: Essays in honour of Jan Slomp* (1993). Slomp is married with Iny Mobach and has two sons, two daughters, and seven grandchildren. In 1994 appointed an Officer of Orange-Nassau for services to society in the Netherlands.

ANDREAS D'SOUZA (b. 1939), originally from Mangalore, India, presently lives in Toronto, Canada. Until his retirement in 2008, he worked for thirty-six years at the Henry Martyn Institute, Hyderabad (since 1992 as director). With a lifelong interest in interfaith relations and reconciliation D'Souza received a diploma in Islam and Arabic from PISAI, Rome, a diploma in Arabic literature from the University of Tunis, an MA in Islam and Interfaith relations, and a PhD in modern Indian Islamic thought both from McGill University. As director of HMI, he changed the mission of the institute to focus on conflict transformation and building relationships across faith boundaries.

CHRISTIAN W. TROLL (b. 1937), a Jesuit priest, has engaged in studies of Islam and of Christian–Muslim Relations since 1961. After studying in Bonn, Tübingen, Beirut, and Munich, he graduated and received his doctorate from the School of Oriental and African Studies, London University. He is the author of several books and numerous articles and has taught in India, Rome, the United Kingdom, and Germany.

FRANCESCO ZANNINI (b. 1948) was born in Falconara, Italy. He holds the Chair of Contemporary Islam and is professor of Arabic and Islamic Studies at PISAI, Rome. He has researched and lectured in Arab and Asian countries, as well as in the United States, where he was a post-doctoral fellow at Yale University. He spent several years in Bangladesh working in the field of Muslim–Christian dialogue and teaching Islamic Studies at the National Major Seminary. He was a member of the Scientific Council of the Italian Ministry of Home Affairs for the formulation and implementation of the "Charter of Values of Citizenship and Integration."